CAPITAL MARKETS, DERIVATIVES AND THE LAW

CAPITAL MARKETS, DERIVATIVES AND THE LAW

ALAN N. RECHTSCHAFFEN

Oxford University Press, Inc., publishes works that further Oxford University's objective
of excellence in research, scholarship, and education.

Oxford   New York
Auckland   Cape Town   Dar es Salaam   Hong Kong   Karachi   Kuala Lumpur   Madrid   Melbourne
Mexico City   Nairobi   New Delhi   Shanghai   Taipei   Toronto

With offices in
Argentina   Austria   Brazil   Chile   Czech Republic   France   Greece   Guatemala   Hungary   Italy
Japan   Poland   Portugal   Singapore   South Korea   Switzerland   Thailand   Turkey   Ukraine
Vietnam

Library of Congress Cataloging-in-Publication Data
Rechtschaffen, Alan N.
  Capital markets, derivatives and the law / Alan N. Rechtschaffen.
    p. cm.
  Includes bibliographical references and index.
  ISBN 978-0-19-533908-6 ((hardback) : alk. paper)
  1. Financial instruments—Law and legislation—United States.
  2. Securities—United States. 3. Capital market—Law and legislation—United States.
  4. Securities industry—State supervision—United States. 5. Securities industry—
Deregulation—United States. 6. Stock exchanges—Law and legislation—United States. I. Title.
  KF1070.R42 2009
  346.73'096—dc22   2009013421

1 2 3 4 5 6 7 8 9
Printed in the United States of America on acid-free paper

Note to Readers
This publication is designed to provide accurate and authoritative information in regard to the subject
matter covered. It is based upon sources believed to be accurate and reliable and is intended to be current
as of the time it was written. It is sold with the understanding that the publisher is not engaged in rendering
legal, accounting, or other professional services. If legal advice or other expert assistance is required, the
services of a competent professional person should be sought. Also, to confirm that the information has
not been affected or changed by recent developments, traditional legal research techniques should be used,
including checking primary sources where appropriate.

*(Based on the Declaration of Principles jointly adopted by a Committee of the
American Bar Association and a Committee of Publishers and Associations.)*

To the Source of all that I have to be thankful,
and to my beautiful wife Miera who is my light;
to my daughters Ronit Florence and Eve who make me so happy,
and to my parents who have given me so much.
Thank all of you.
I love you very very much.

CONTENTS

CHAPTER 12 FIDUCIARY OBLIGATION TO MANAGE RISK 221

FOREWORD

SUSAN M. PHILLIPS

Alan Rechtschaffen and I met in 1997 when I was a Member of the Board of Governors of the Federal Reserve System. Alan was chairing the International Symposium on Derivatives and Risk; he invited me to speak at Fordham University School of Law where he helped to create one of the first courses of study in the law governing derivatives transactions. I commented at that time that financial engineering had profoundly changed the structure of many leading banks and that these processes continue to reverberate throughout the industry.

Twelve years later, banks continue to engineer products to shift business risks to others that had been borne routinely in the past. The reverse side of the coin is that derivatives allow market participants to assume risks through alternatives to traditional lending and investing. However, it is clear that a lot has changed since 1997.

The events beginning in 2008 demonstrate the effects of unfettered innovation, perhaps even careless contract design without adequate imbedded credit safeguards much less awareness of the interconnectivity of capital market participants. The interconnection of counterparties to one another is the backbone of over-the-counter derivatives market trading activities and at the same time sows the seeds of risks to the system.

Our financial system is built on the ability of participants to meet their obligations. Those accessing capital and using derivatives and other financial instruments to manage risk or to enhance yield trust the fidelity of their counterparties or obligors. Businesses strive to gain market confidence. The breakdown of counterparty reliability, a lack of diligent risk analysis or poor contract design, and incomplete risk management contributed to recent markets events.

The past two years demonstrate that regulators need to continually review and revise their standards to encourage best practices throughout the banking industry and the financial markets. As a former chairman of the Commodity Futures Trading Commission, I encouraged efficient and well informed market practices in the futures markets, including exchange trading and use of centralized credit clearinghouses. As Dean of the George Washington School of Business, I encourage our students to understand and take responsibility for the decisions they will make in business and throughout their careers.

Dr. Phillips is Dean and Professor of Finance at the George Washington University School of Business. She was a member of the Board of Governors of the Federal Reserve System and a former Chairman of the Commodity Futures Trading Commission.

Market participants strive to be well informed about the risks they take and the financial instruments that they use. Alan Rechtschaffen has incorporated basic descriptions of how financial instruments and the capital markets work in order to bring the reader into the world of capital markets trading activities. His case studies demonstrate the consequences of proper and improper use of derivatives and the other tools of capital exchange.

Sharing the insights gleaned from years of working in the capital markets as a participant and as a sounding board for domestic and international regulators, educator Alan Rechtscahffen demonstrates a common sense and practical approach to understanding the capital markets and derivatives—what works and what does not work.

The incorporation of the insights of his students provides a fresh approach to understanding the law. This book is useful to everybody who works in, thinks about, or has financial exposure to the capital markets. Such an understanding will help market participants and regulators alike make adjustments to trading systems and regulations to minimize the chances of repeating the mistakes of the past.

PREFACE

On June 17, 2009, President Barack Obama made the following observations about innovation in the capital markets:

> In recent years, financial innovators, seeking an edge in the marketplace, produced a huge variety of new and complex financial instruments. And these products, such as asset-based securities, were designed to spread risk, but unfortunately ended up concentrating risk. Loans were sold to banks, banks packaged these loans into securities, investors bought these securities often with little insight into the risks to which they were exposed. And it was easy money—while it lasted. But these schemes were built on a pile of sand.[1]

The "schemes" the President describes are structures and transactions designed to package, negotiate, and shift risk. Understanding risk is the key to capital market participation. With an appreciation of risk, comes the ability to capitalize on opportunity; awareness of risk and the tools used to manage it facilitates the disposition of unwanted exposure.

Complex financial instruments, like derivatives, are tools designed to shift risk; they also make possible the assumption of risk where an investor is looking to enhance yield. President Obama identifies the repercussions of misunderstood risk shifting and its results on the broader economy. Key to appreciating how derivatives and other financial instruments contributed and arguably caused the financial crisis is looking at how they shift and concentrate risk; understanding their operation requires grasping how they are created, structured, and utilized

The President describes the far-reaching effects of the misuse of derivatives and other financial instruments. He argues that a lack of understanding coupled with malign intent has affected the health of the broader economy; as market participants have become limited in their ability to access capital, the economy contracted:

> Now, we all know the result . . . the failure of several of the world's largest financial institutions; the sudden decline in available credit; the deterioration of the economy; the unprecedented intervention of the federal government to stabilize the financial markets and prevent a wider collapse; and most importantly, the terrible pain in the lives of ordinary Americans. And there are retirees who've lost much of their life savings, families devastated by job losses, small businesses forced to shut their doors.[2]

---

1. *Remarks by the President, 21st Century Financial Regulatory Reform*, June 17, 2009, East Room, The White House, available at http://www.whitehouse.gov/the_press_office/Remarks-of-the-President-on-Regulatory-Reform.

2. *Id.*

The capital markets provide market participants the opportunity to access funding and make investments; financial instruments are the tools of that marketplace. As market participants failed over the last two years, the repercussions were felt throughout the economy. President Obama identifies financial instrument abuse and misuse as stimuli for government intervention and regulatory reform. The President declares a need for " . . . sweeping overhaul of the financial regulatory system, a transformation on a scale not seen since the reforms that followed the Great Depression."[3]

It is clear that the events of the financial crisis have made people feel defenseless. Desire to stop the bleeding in the economy has given way to Executive steps to reconstruct regulation. Indeed, the U.S. Treasury Department, in its white paper *Financial Regulatory Reform: A New Foundation*,[4] describes Americans' suffering as the motivation for regulatory reconstruction:

> Over the past two years we have faced the most severe financial crisis since the Great Depression. Americans across the nation are struggling with unemployment, failing businesses, falling home prices, and declining savings.[5]

Whatever the origins of the momentum, one thing is clear: new regulation is coming.

President Obama's administration is not the first to encourage revision of the current regulatory structure. Indeed, even when the broader economy was relatively healthy, Hank Paulson, the Secretary of the Treasury under President George W. Bush, advanced the notion that " . . . our complex and fragmented regulatory system complicates an already difficult situation. . . . This patchwork structure should be streamlined and modernized."[6] Secretary Paulson further describes the target for future regulatory initiatives: "Our goal is to improve oversight and allow our financial services industry to better adapt and compete in the global marketplace." In recognizing that the need for new regulation predates recent events, President Obama's Treasury puts the current economic crisis into broader historical context:

> The roots of this crisis go back decades. Years without a serious economic recession bred complacency among financial intermediaries and investors. Financial challenges such as the near-failure of Long-Term Capital Management and the Asian Financial Crisis had minimal impact on economic growth in the U.S., which bred exaggerated expectations about the resilience of our

---

3. *Id.*

4. *Financial Regulatory Reform: A New Foundation*, U.S. Treasury, June 17, 2009, available at http://www.financialstability.gov/docs/regs/FinalReport_web.pdf.

5. *Id.* at page 2

6. Remarks by Secretary Henry M. Paulson, Jr. on Current Housing and Mortgage Market Developments, October 16, 2007, Georgetown University Law Center, available at http://www.treas.gov/press/releases/hp612.htm.

financial markets and firms. Rising asset prices, particularly in housing, hid weak credit underwriting standards and masked the growing leverage throughout the system.[7]

Like his predecessor, Secretary Timothy Geithner describes the current regulatory framework as "A patchwork of supervisory responsibility; loopholes that allowed some institutions to shop for the weakest regulator; and the rise of new financial institutions and instruments that were almost entirely outside the government's supervisory framework left regulators largely blind to emerging dangers. . . . regulators were ill-equipped to spot system-wide threats because each was assigned to protect the safety and soundness of the individual institutions under their watch. None was assigned to look out for the system as a whole."[8] Because of the current and fragmented regulatory regime, the Obama administration proposes establishing oversight to bring together the major federal financial regulatory agencies and removing from the Federal Reserve and other regulators, oversight responsibility for consumers.

Consumer protection would be handled under a new Consumer Financial Protection Agency and "will serve as the primary federal agency looking out for the interests of consumers of credit, savings, payment, and other financial products."[9] The Obama proposals meet five key policy objectives:

(1) Promoting robust supervision and regulation of financial firms.
(2) Establishing comprehensive supervision of financial markets.
(3) Protecting consumers and investors from financial abuse.
(4) Providing the government with the tools it needs to manage financial crises.
(5) Raising international regulatory standards and improve international cooperation.

The challenge for a new regulatory regime is discouraging abuse while encouraging financial innovation; balancing efficiency and stability. The recent crisis strengthens the argument for new regulation. The administration thinks " . . . that the best way to keep the system safe for innovation is to have stronger protections against risk with stronger capital buffers, greater disclosure so investors and consumers can make more informed financial decisions, and a system that is better able to evolve as innovation advances and the structure of the financial system changes."[10]

---

7. *See* note 5.

8. Treasury Secretary Tim Geithner's Opening Statement before the U.S. Senate Banking Committee, Financial Regulatory Reform Opening Statement—As Prepared for Delivery, June 18, 2009.

9. *Id.*

10. *Id.*

The first step to understanding new regulation is appreciating how the capital markets function and how financial instruments and derivatives work. Making informed economic, regulatory, and legal decisions requires facts about the products involved. *Capital Markets, Derivatives and the Law* provides the knowledge necessary for making informed, well-reasoned decisions about capital market participation, derivative utilization, and adherence to regulation present and future.

Alan N. Rechtschaffen

July 2009

ACKNOWLEDGMENTS

Capital Markets, Derivatives and the Law is designed to convey complex financial and legal information in a way that is easy to grasp. My approach in writing this book is based, in no small part, on the speeches of Ben Bernanke which are included and summarized throughout. I am grateful to him.

While Chairman Bernanke was an inspiration for my vision and methodology, it is my students who helped me turn this vision into a reality. For over 12 years, I have taught students at New York University School of Law and at Fordham University. A number of my finest students helped me write this book, and I would like to thank each of them for their contribution. I would like this acknowledgment to serve as a recommendation to any one who might be fortunate enough to have the opportunity to work with them:

Colin Addy received his B.S., magna cum laude, from the University of Albany (2004) and earned his J.D. (magna cum laude, Order of the Coif) from Fordham University Law School (2008). His academic achievements translate into a well-reasoned and well-thought-out approach to culling through esoteric issues in the capital markets and applying them to actual transactions. Colin is an associate at Cahill Gordon & Reindel LLP.

Boriana A. Anguelova currently works in the finance group of WestLB AG. Originally from Bulgaria, she came to the United States to obtain her accounting and law degrees. The derivatives class at Fordham Law School is among the fondest memories of her school years for opening and demystifying the alluring world of derivatives transactions. She is honored to have had the opportunity to participate in the creation of this book.

Andrew Arons is an attorney in the corporate transactions group at Weil, Gotshal and Manges LLP, specializing in private equity, mergers and acquisitions, and corporate restructurings. Prior to joining Weil, Andrew attended Fordham University School of Law, where he graduated magna cum laude, and received his bachelor's degree from Yale University, where he was a member of the varsity men's tennis team. His competitive nature (probably a product of his tennis skills) helped him receive the highest recognition from me as his professor. Thank you, Andrew.

Alice Dullaghan is an associate in the corporate department of Proskauer Rose LLP. Alice gained an LL.M. in banking, corporate, and finance law (cum laude) from Fordham Law School in 2008. Alice previously practiced as a solicitor in Dublin, Ireland, and her insights into the operation of the capital markets have been as illuminating to me as I hope they will be to the reader. She brings a unique international background to her work, and I am pleased to include her contributions in this book.

Steven Eichorn has a prestigious academic background, having graduated summa cum laude from Touro College with a B.S. in finance (in 2003) and cum laude from Fordham Law School in 2008. His avid interest in the financial markets and their governance is a result of all the work he did for this book. His experience with regulatory filings and public offerings was very helpful in understanding how enterprises use the markets for capital. Thank you, Steven.

Lee J. Goldberg currently works as a judicial law clerk for the Honorable Arthur J. Gonzalez of the United States Bankruptcy Court, Southern District of New York. Lee will begin working as an associate in the business finance and restructuring department of a major international law firm that is extremely lucky to have him. Lee went out of his way to update me on new events in the capital markets and will be a resource to anyone with whom he has a professional relationship.

David E. Gravelle is a student at Fordham Law School. David has over 10 years of experience working in the financial services arena at firms such as Goldman Sachs & Co. and Lehman Brothers, Inc. David will begin his legal career as an associate at Fried, Frank, Harris, Shriver and Jacobson LLP, and I am extremely grateful for his insights. In my opinion, he will be a great success at whatever he works to achieve, and I am sure wherever his career path will always lead him to success.

Sarah Hayes has over a decade of experience in the commodities sector as a consultant, policy analyst, and attorney focusing on development and implementation of emissions trading programs and environmental regulations. She has worked to develop consensus responses to U.S. federal programs and has advised public- and private-sector clients on the development of emerging international energy markets. Ms. Hayes is a graduate of Fordham Law School, where she was a recipient of the Riker Danzig Environmental Law Award and was a Fordham Law Merit Scholar. We are lucky have her work as part of this book.

Robert A. Johnston was my student in the derivatives and risk management course. Robert is now employed in the litigation department of a major international law firm's New York office where he advises on complex commercial disputes, white-collar criminal defense, regulatory enforcement, and internal corporate investigations. His professional and academic background has been incorporated into his hard work on this book.

Jim Kelly worked as an executive director in investment banking at J.P. Morgan. Previously, Jim was an assistant director of homeland security for New York State. While working on this book, he was a managing director/ principle in global equities at Bear Stearns & Co. His professional experience at the center of the financial storm of 2008 has helped us gain insights into the capital markets. Jim has become a close friend, and I am honored that he was also my student. Jim, thank you for your friendship and your advice.

Michael Kuzmicz's work on the options chapter of this book was invaluable. He is a pleasure to work with and a valuable source of inspiration. His ideas are innovative and well thought out. He currently works at J.P. Morgan Chase Bank N.A., and I am grateful that he is available for me to call upon for guidance in my professional and academic pursuits.

Benchen Li has a unique background. He has a J.D. from Fordham University School of Law, a bachelor of science in computer science, magna cum laude, from the University of Bridgeport, and a bachelor of economics in tourism management from Fudan University. He is currently working as a senior software developer with Bloomberg LLP, and his insights have been a source of inspiration to me in assembling this book. Bingchen, I hope your team at Bloomberg is aware of the breadth of your knowledge and understanding of the capital markets.

Gabriel Mass's work on foreign exchange derivatives for this book was nothing short of brilliant—not surprising, considering his professional experience. Gabriel is a strategist and trader at Falcon Management Corporation, a global macro hedge fund.

Katie McDonald practices corporate and securities law in Calgary, Alberta, and through her participation in discussions about the final production of this book has been a source of ideas and analysis that have been incorporated both in whole and in part into this work. I am grateful to her for her wise counsel.

Robert Pierson, Jr., is an associate at the patent law firm Fitzpatrick, Cella, Harper & Scinto. He graduated cum laude from Fordham Law School and has a bachelor's in science and engineering from the University of Pennsylvania. His experience and background in science and engineering were very helpful in breaking down the rocket science of derivatives into terms we all can understand.

Justin Quinn graduated from the Johns Hopkins University with a B.S. in computer science and received a J.D. from the Fordham University School of Law. He currently works in the real estate department at Kaye Scholer LLP. The synthesis of his technical background and his legal skills will prove as invaluable to the reader as they have to me.

Joshua Riezman is currently an associate with Teigland-Hunt LLP, a boutique New York law firm that focuses on advising clients regarding trading in derivatives and commodities markets worldwide. His knowledge of the derivatives markets and his background in international affairs elucidated subtleties in our examination of financial instruments for which I am grateful.

Adam J. Tarkan is an associate in the investment management group at the law firm of Schulte Roth & Zabel LLP. His understanding of the investment landscape is a benefit to the reader, and I am specifically grateful to him for his intellect and insight.

Marshall Yuan is an associate in the corporate department of Paul, Weiss, Rifkind, Wharton & Garrison LLP. Marshall focuses his practice on general corporate matters, but his understanding of the attorney's role in the capital markets shines through in this work. Marshall, thank you.

In addition to the hard work of my students, I would like to acknowledge my personal editor Agnes Leyden for her contributions and guidance, as well as my editors and the staff at Oxford University Press for all their hard work bringing this treatise to the public at such an important juncture in the history and future of the capital markets.

INTRODUCTION

The year 2008 witnessed dramatic events affecting the global economy. Alan Greenspan called the 2008 market events a "once-in-a-century credit tsunami."[1] Kevin Warsh, a Member of the Board of Governors of the Federal Reserve System recently observed that, "if you have seen one financial crisis, you have seen one financial crisis."[2] It is the goal of this book to demonstrate the basic knowledge necessary to weather financial storms, providing the knowledge necessary to understand this and future financial crises and to participate in the capital markets.

Disruptions in the financial markets can be particularly disturbing to the global economy because these markets represent the opportunity for an enterprise to access capital. Ensuring the stability of the capital markets, therefore, is of paramount concern for the Federal Reserve and other financial market regulators in order to prevent systemic failure. By shoring up the capital markets, the Fed furthers its legislated goals of fostering an environment with maximum sustainable growth, maximum employment, and reasonable inflation.[3] In this book we will look at the steps the Fed has taken to meet its goals while attempting to save the financial system. In that context we will describe financial instruments and the capital markets.

The capital markets play an essential role in the world economy, providing a means for individuals and institutions to access capital and to enhance return on their investments. Financial instruments also allow market participants to manage risk by shifting unwanted risk to a counterparty who might be more willing or able to manage or capitalize on that risk. A number of enterprises facilitate capital market participation, including banks, brokers engaging in securities and derivatives transactions, and government-sponsored entities.

In the wake of the recent mortgage crisis, the Federal Reserve has actuated its role of preventing systemic failure. The liquidity crisis, which resulted in part from inefficient and inappropriate lending practices and the creation of financial instruments supported by those pools of loans, provided the backdrop for the Federal Reserve to flex its muscle in its operation within the capital markets. By providing liquidity, the Federal Reserve seeks to facilitate the function of the capital markets. A functioning capital market is essential to providing financing

---

1. Alan Greenspan (Testimony before the House of Representatives Committee on Oversight and Government Reform, October 23, 2008).

2. Kevin Warsh (Q&A Session, New York University School of Law Global Economic Policy Forum 2008, April 11, 2008).

3. *See* Federal Reserve Act §2a, 12 U.S.C. §225a.

opportunities and allowing counterparties to negotiate risk packaged in a variety of financial instruments. By understanding the Fed and its function the reader will gain the knowledge necessary to understand the implications of Fed action.

During the recent market turmoil, the Federal Reserve has navigated United States' interest rates lower. Lower interest rates affect the pricing of all assets—interest rates are a vital component of asset valuation. Economic pricing depends on incorporating certain pricing assumptions into valuation models in order to determine the "value" of an asset. Value is determined by the future expected cash flow discounted at a rate that reflects the riskiness of the cash flow.

The recent headlines publicize the dangers inherent in capital market trading activities. The credit crunch roiling the financial markets and the breakneck speed at which giants of the industry went from major financial firms to illiquidity demonstrate the state of readiness required by corporate fiduciaries in managing capital market activities during times of economic weakness and crises in confidence. When markets behave in unpredictable ways, corporate fiduciaries may be held responsible to stakeholders (i.e., shareholders, regulators, and unit holders) for not taking steps to control or manage risk. Derivatives-related losses have heightened the awareness of directors, senior managers, regulators, customers, and shareholders to the potential risks associated with inefficient or insufficient risk management practices. This book serves as a primer to corporate fiduciaries to help them to take steps to prevent liability.

The book also describes litigation issues that arise out of capital market participation. A variety of litigation issues may arise in the context of financial instruments and derivatives transactions. These issues can involve violations of federal securities laws, commodities laws, failure to follow the rules set down by self-regulated organizations, common-law theories such as fraud and negligence, and violations of state securities laws. This book looks at those litigation issues.

Much of the work contained in this treatise was adapted from outstanding research by others. Where a regulator, a judge, or an economist describes a financial instrument or a situation better than the author might have, that commentary has been included in its entirety or paraphrased for editorial consistency. In synthesizing materials such as the speeches of the Chairman of the Board of Governors of the Federal Reserve System, leading judicial rulings, descriptions of financial instruments, and government sources, the book is designed to immerse the reader in the world of the capital markets. This book is based on the lectures of the author, incorporating the outstanding directed research of a number of his students in the areas of derivatives, risk management, and financial instruments.

This treatise offers real world examples of how financial instruments actually work. The outline and methodology is unique. The treatise is designed to cover the functioning of the credit markets and the various applicable regulatory regimes. The subject matter cuts across a number of legal disciplines including securities, corporate finance, banking, financial institutions, and commodities.

The cases are drawn to describe the subject matter and to demonstrate to the reader the functioning of the capital markets. The pedagogical approach is to describe financial instruments in a way that everyone can understand them. As capital market events evolve, it is impossible to freeze time. The treatise seeks to serve as a foundation for understanding world economic events as they unfold.

This book begins with an analysis of the global economic events in the 2008 market. Using the American economic crisis and mortgage meltdown as a starting point, the book discusses how the Federal Reserve participates in the capital markets to prevent systemic and market failures. This book goes on to describe various financial instruments affected by changes in interest rates and indicates the regulatory impact of utilizing a particular instrument to further financial goals.

This book covers the basic issues affecting capital markets trading, regulation, litigation, financial instruments, risk management, or internal controls without delving in so deep that the author cannot accomplish his primary goal of making the reader comfortable with the basics of capital market trading activities. This work focuses on outlining the basic knowledge that every participant in the capital markets should have of the complexity of the role of the Federal Reserve in domestic capital markets, the use of financial instruments to manage risk and to enhance yield, the steps corporations take to prevent operational risk, and the steps regulators take to prevent systemic risk.

1. THE FINANCIAL CRISIS

The past year has witnessed dramatic events affecting the global economy. The world's current financial circumstance has been called by Alan Greenspan, the former Chairman of the Board of Governors of the Federal Reserve System, a "once-in-a-century credit tsunami."[1]

As the financial markets have evolved, financial instruments have taken on robust and sophisticated structures allowing returns to investors contingent on variables other than credit. Mortgage-backed bonds, for instance, are general obligations of the issuer, backed by the cash flow of underlying mortgages. The financial crisis currently affecting the world economy arose in large part as a result of "the complexity and sophistication of today's financial institutions and instruments and the remarkable degree of global financial integration that allows financial shocks to be transmitted around the world at the speed of light."[2]

Adair Turner, the Chairman of the Financial Services Authority,[3] explained that "[a]t the core of the crisis was an interplay between macroeconomic imbalances which have become particularly prevalent over the last 10–15 years, and financial market developments which have been going on for 30 years but which accelerated over the last ten under the influence of the macro imbalances."[4] Chairman Turner explained that very large current account surpluses pilling up in the oil exporting countries and corresponding deficits in the USA and other

---

1. Alan Greenspan, Testimony before the House of Representatives Committee on Oversight and Government Reform (October 23, 2008).

2. Ben S. Bernanke, "Stabilizing the Financial Markets and the Economy," (Speech at the Economic Club of New York, October 15, 2008), http://www.federalreserve.gov/newsevents/speech/bernanke20081015a.htm.

3. The Financial Services Authority (FSA) is an independent non-governmental body in the United Kingdom, given statutory powers by the Financial Services and Markets Act 2000. The UK Treasury appoints the FSA Board. The FSA is accountable to Treasury Ministers, and through them to Parliament. It is operationally independent of Government and is funded entirely by the firms it regulates.

4. Speech by Adair Turner, Chairman, FSA, The Economist's Inaugural City Lecture 21 January 2009.

countries led to a dramatic "reduction in real risk free rates of interest to histori-cally low levels."[5] Two effects of extremely low interest rates were: "[a] rapid growth of credit extension ... particularly but not exclusively for residential mortgages . . . and ... a ferocious search for yield."[6]

When the real estate market reversed, it carried securitized debt with it. Prices of securities which were purchased to enhance yield tumbled, and the dramatic reversal proved devastating for market participants creating and investing in debt. As a result of the implosion of the real estate and credit markets, firms like AIG who assumed market participant credit default risk were devastated as com-panies like Lehman declined from positions of financial supremacy to illiquidity in a matter of days.

I. ORIGINS

Recent events in the American real estate market and its closely related mortgage-backed securities markets culminated in the financial crisis. Mortgage-backed securities are financial instruments that derive their cash flow and or value from pools of mortgages and include mortgage-backed bonds. The ripple effect throughout the global economy resulted in diminished liquidity at finan-cial institutions and systemic threats to the broader capital markets. The under-tow created by mortgage foreclosures and deficiencies has rocked the financial world and changed the essential functioning of financial institutions in the global economy. Ben S. Bernanke, the current Chairman of the Board of Governors of the Federal Reserve System, explained that

> Large inflows of capital into the United States and other countries stimulated a reaching for yield, an underpricing of risk, excessive leverage, and the devel-opment of complex and opaque financial instruments that seemed to work well during the credit boom but have been shown to be fragile under stress. The unwinding of these developments, including a sharp deleveraging and a headlong retreat from credit risk, led to highly strained conditions in financial markets and a tightening of credit that has hamstrung economic growth.[7]

II. SUBPRIME LENDING

In 2007 and 2008 the high levels of delinquencies, defaults, and foreclosures among subprime borrowers led to the undoing of broad capital markets, the

---

5. *Id.*
6. *Id.*
7. *Id.*

shockwaves of which have been felt throughout the global economy. The effects of mortgage lending on the broader capital markets demonstrate how global banking systems and international economies are increasingly interconnected and what an effect a unique capital market disruption has on the broader U.S. economy. Today, more than ever before, improvements in communication and financial innovation have increased the effects of market disruptions anywhere in the world on the global capital market place.

The rise in real estate prices over the last ten years was encouraged, in large part, by low interest rates facilitating the purchase of homes and investment properties, mortgage brokers on commission, and federal policies encouraging home ownership. This increased real estate activity, and easy access to funding, allowed borrowers to access equity contained in their homes and speculators to make investments in property that would never have been possible without the availability of cheap money.

Banks lend money for, among other things, the funding of long-term purchases, such as a home, or to refinance those same purchases. In the years leading up to the mortgage meltdown, banks aggressively pumped capital into the economy, taking advantage of spreads between the rates at which banks borrow, and the mortgage rates they charge their customers. Cash was readily available to banks to lend to their customers because, once these loans were created, the loans were resold in the form of "mortgage-backed securities."

The concept of financing mortgages by issuing securities backed by the revenue stream generated from the mortgages is not new. Indeed the federal government sponsored the establishment of several enterprises specifically designed to provide liquidity to banks participating in the mortgage markets.

III. GOVERNMENT-SPONSORED ENTITIES

There are several entities that are sponsored by the federal government to refinance mortgages. Federal agencies are direct arms of the United States government; federally sponsored agencies were historically privately owned and publicly chartered organizations that were created by acts of Congress to support a specific public purpose (also referred to as government-sponsored entities or GSEs). The credit rating of many GSEs is AAA and, therefore, the credit spread between GSEs and treasuries is small. In 2008, after the U.S. government placed the two leading mortgage lenders, Fannie Mae and Freddie Mac, into conservatorship, the distinction between government and government agency has blurred beyond the implicit. GSEs are private entities with a public mandate to further public goals in housing, farming, and higher education. GSEs are competitors to other banking lenders and have therefore contributed to decreased margins on loans from other banks. GSEs benefit from favorable tax, credit, and implicit guaranties from the federal government. They serve as a source of securitization for a large pool of bank loans.

In the wake of recent financial events, two of the most well known government-sponsored agencies, the Federal National Mortgage Association (Fannie Mae) and the Federal Home Loan Mortgage Corporation (Freddie Mac) have been placed in federal conservatorship. This was done to avoid unacceptably large dislocations in the mortgage markets and the economy as a whole. The Treasury, drawing on authorities recently granted by the Congress, made financial support available.

The federal government created GSEs to meet the demands of borrowers where inadequacies were perceived in private initiatives. Investors generally perceived that the federal government offered implicit guarantees (although no such actual guaranty exists) of GSE debt. While equity holders have suffered under federal conservatorship, bond holders have benefited from the federal government's new and active role in overseeing Fannie Mae and Freddie Mac.

Until recent changes, several executive branches have overseen GSEs. The Department of Housing and Urban Development monitors the activities of Fannie Mae and Freddie Mac.[8] The Federal Housing Finance Board administers the FHLBs. The President of the United States appoints the minority of the board of the GSEs. The Department of the Treasury does not evaluate the capital adequacy of the GSEs. Because GSEs are government sponsored, investors inferred that the government had a "moral obligation" to guaranty the debt of these entities. Although no such guaranty existed, GSE's enjoyed a lower cost of doing business than private enterprises and certain tax exemptions giving them a competitive advantage. Indeed, after Fannie Mae and Freddie Mac were placed into federal conservatorship, investors' moral obligation inference seems to have been well placed as credit spreads tightened in the wake of government intervention into the ownership and operation of these entities.

GSEs were created to insure adequate credit flows. They were deemed necessary because the types of loans facilitated by the GSEs would not be adequately available in their absence. GSEs provide portfolio lending and financial guaranties and purchase or make loans directly. Their funding is accomplished through the issuance of debt to investors. The size of GSE loans is in the trillions of dollars. Much of the loans outstanding represent growth in the issuance of mortgage-backed securities by home-lending GSEs. Mortgage-backed securities are supported by mortgages the GSE purchases. Fannie Mae and Freddie Mac also purchase loans from banks and repackage the loans into debt securities called "residential mortgage-backed securities" (collateralized mortgage obligations or CMOs). By facilitating loans to homeowners, the GSEs help purchasers

---

8. Federal Housing Enterprises Financial Safety and Soundness Act of 1992. Fannie Mae and Freddie Mac are subject to supervision by a newly created regulator within HUD, called the Office of Federal Housing Enterprise Oversight (OFHEO).

realize the dream of home ownership. The GSEs also enhance liquidity by affording homeowners the opportunity to borrow money to spend in the economy. Mortgage-backed pass-through securities are created when mortgages are pooled together and sold as undivided interests to investors. Usually, the mortgages in the pool have the same loan type and similar maturities and loan interest rates.[9]

IV. THE LIQUIDITY CRISIS AND THE FED'S REACTION

The decision to purchase a home is probably the most interest-sensitive decision made by households. The balance sheets of most households must be analyzed in the context of the ratio of household net worth to income. A declining interest rate environment affords homeowners the ability to refinance their mortgages to reduce their exposure to short-term and high-interest debt. By fixing a long-term mortgage rate, homeowners are insulated from interest-rate increases.[10]

A number of Wall Street brokerage firms, including Bear Stearns, created private-label mortgage-backed securities to help lenders fund more purchases of real estate. The securities were backed by mortgages from borrowers who may have been "subprime," and when these borrowers were unable to meet the demands set by the mortgage pools, the securities derived from these mortgage pools became worthless, or where borrowers did not stop paying, securities may have reduced value, or firms did not know how to value them in the face of a changed economic environment. Because the issuance of these securities was so lucrative, a glut of mortgage-derived securities existed in the market place, many of which wound up on the balance sheets of a number of the leading Wall Street firms. As the securities declined in value, the liquidity of these securities declined leading to a liquidity crisis. So severe was this liquidity crisis that the Federal Reserve took the aggressive step of facilitating a buyout of Bear Stearns by J. P. Morgan to prevent the collapse of the Wall Street powerhouse.

In Chairman Bernanke's speech describing the build-up to the liquidity crisis and the steps the Federal Reserve took to shore up the system in facilitating the acquisition of Bear Stearns,[11] Bernanke confirmed the place of the Federal Reserve as the nation's central bank and the importance of its role in providing

---

9. FEDERAL RESERVE SYSTEM, TRADING AND CAPITAL-MARKETS ACTIVITIES MANUAL, (Board of Governors of the Federal Reserve System, 1998), §4110.1.

10. Ben S. Bernanke, "The economic outlook and monetary policy," (Remarks at the Bond Market Association Annual Meeting, New York, NY, NY, April 22, 2004).

11. Ben S. Bernanke, "Liquidity Provision by the Federal Reserve," Remarks at the Federal Reserve Bank of Atlanta Financial Markets Conference, Sea Island, Georgia, via satellite, May 13, 2008. Bernanke presented identical remarks to the Risk Transfer Mechanisms and Financial Stability Workshop, Basel, Switzerland, on May

liquidity to the banking system in a crisis. The duty of the central bank is to respond to a sharp increase in the demand for cash or equivalents by private creditors. The way to respond to a crisis in liquidity is for the central bank to lend freely.[12]

Chairman Bernanke commented that liquidity risks are always present for institutions—banks and nonbanks alike—that finance illiquid assets with short-term liabilities. However, mortgage lenders, commercial and investment banks, and structured investment vehicles have recently experienced great difficulty in rolling over commercial paper backed by subprime and other mortgages. Furthermore, a loss of confidence in credit ratings has led to a sharp contraction in the asset-backed commercial paper market as short-term investors have withdrawn their funds. Some financial institutions have even experienced pressures in rolling over maturing repurchase agreements (repos), which have traditionally been regarded as virtually risk-free instruments and thus largely immune to the type of rollover or withdrawal risks associated with short-term unsecured obligations. Markets can be severely disrupted when investors feel pressure to sell the underlying collateral in illiquid markets. Such forced asset sales can set up a particularly adverse dynamic, in which further substantial price declines fan investor concerns about counterparty credit risk, which then feed back in the form of intensifying funding pressures. These "fire sales," forced by sharp increases in investors' liquidity preferences, can drive asset prices below their fundamental value at significant cost to the financial system and the economy.[13]

This explains the basic logic of the central bank's prescription for crisis management:

A central bank may be able to eliminate, or at least attenuate, adverse outcomes by making cash loans secured by borrowers' illiquid but sound assets. Thus, borrowers can avoid selling securities into an illiquid market, and the potential for economic damage—arising, for example, from the unavailability of credit for productive purposes or the inefficient liquidation of long-term investments—is substantially reduced.[14]

This solution, however, while simple in theory, is far more complicated in practice. The central bank must "distinguish between institutions whose liquidity pressures stem primarily from a breakdown in financial market functioning and those whose problems fundamentally derive from underlying concerns about their solvency."[15] Moreover, "[c]entral banks provide liquidity through a

---

29, 2008 (via videoconference). *See* http://www.federalreserve.gov/newsevents/speech/bernanke20080513.htm for the complete text of the remarks.

12. *Id.*
13. *Id.*
14. *Id.*
15. *Id.*

variety of mechanisms, including open market operations and direct credit extension through standing lending facilities. The choice of tools in a crisis depends on the circumstances as well as on specific institutional factors."[16] Central banks in other countries have tools available to them that the Federal Reserve does not. "[T]he Federal Reserve has had to innovate in large part to achieve what other central banks have been able to effect through existing tools."[17] Because crises may involve large financial institutions operating across national borders and in multiple currencies, central banks must work closely together.[18]

Traditionally, the Federal Reserve has used open market operations to manage the aggregate level of reserves in the banking system and thereby control the federal funds rate."[19] The discount window has served as a source of reserves "when conditions in the federal funds market tighten significantly or when individual depository institutions experience short-term funding pressures."[20] However, this traditional framework for providing liquidity proved inadequate during the recent crisis, in part due to the reluctance of depository institutions to use the discount window as a source of funding due to a perceived "stigma" associated with it, arising "primarily from banks' concerns that market participants will draw adverse inferences about their financial condition if their borrowing from the Federal Reserve were to become known."[21]

The Federal Reserve took steps to make discount window borrowing more attractive by narrowing the spread of the primary credit rate over the target federal funds and by permitting depositories to borrow for as long as 90 days, renewable at their discretion so long as they remain in sound financial condition. Although these actions had some success in increasing depository institutions' willingness to borrow, new ways of providing liquidity were necessary. In December 2007, the Federal Reserve introduced the Term Auction Facility, or TAF, through which predetermined amounts of discount window credit are auctioned every two weeks to eligible borrowers for terms of 28 days. "The TAF, apparently because of its competitive auction format and the certainty that a large amount of credit would be made available, appears to have overcome the stigma problem to a significant degree."[22] In addition, the Federal Reserve expanded its ability to supply liquidity to primary dealers by initiating as part of its open-market operations a series of single-tranche repurchase transactions with terms of roughly 28 days and cumulating to up to $100 billion. Additionally, the Federal Reserve introduced the Term Securities Lending Facility (TSLF),

---

16. *Id.*
17. *Id.*
18. *Id.*
19. *Id.*
20. *Id.*
21. *Id.*
22. *Id.*

"which allows primary dealers to exchange less-liquid securities for Treasury securities for terms of 28 days at an auction-determined fee." The list of securities eligible for such transactions includes all AAA/Aaa-rated asset-backed securities.[23]

In mid-March 2008, Bear Stearns, a prominent investment bank, "advised the Federal Reserve and other government agencies that its liquidity position had significantly deteriorated, and that it would be forced to file for bankruptcy the next day unless alternative sources of funds became available."[24] In order to prevent a much broader liquidity crisis in the overall financial markets, the Federal Reserve Board "use[d] its emergency lending authorities under the Federal Reserve Act to avoid a disorderly closure of Bear. Accordingly, the Federal Reserve, in close consultation with the Treasury Department, agreed to provide short-term funding to Bear Stearns through J.P. Morgan-Chase. Over the following weekend, J.P. Morgan-Chase agreed to purchase Bear Stearns and assumed the company's financial obligations."[25]

In addition, the Federal Reserve used its emergency authorities to create the Primary Dealer Credit Facility (PDCF), which "allows primary dealers to borrow at the same rate at which depository institutions can access the discount window, with the borrowings able to be secured by a broad range of investment-grade securities. In effect, the PDCF provides primary dealers with a liquidity backstop similar to the discount window for depository institutions in generally sound financial condition."[26]

The provision of liquidity by a central bank can help mitigate a financial crisis, but raises the issue of "moral hazard."

[S]pecifically, if market participants come to believe that the Federal Reserve or other central banks will take such measures whenever financial stress develops, financial institutions and their creditors . . . have less incentive to pursue suitable strategies for managing liquidity risk and more incentive to take such risks. . . . [T]he problem of moral hazard can perhaps be most effectively addressed by prudential supervision and regulation that ensures that financial institutions manage their liquidity risks effectively in advance of the crisis. . . . [Institutions must] have "adequate processes in place to measure and manage risk, importantly including liquidity risk. . . ." In particular, future liquidity planning will have to take into account the possibility of a sudden loss of substantial amounts of secured financing. . . .

[I]f financial institutions and investors draw appropriate lessons from the recent experience about the need for strong liquidity risk management

---

23. *Id.*
24. *Id.*
25. *Id.*
26. *Id.*

practices, the frequency and severity of future crises should be significantly reduced.[27]

V. PROVIDING LIQUIDITY AND STABILIZING THE FINANCIAL MARKETS

The Federal Reserve provided large amounts of liquidity to the financial system to cushion the effects of tight conditions in short-term funding markets. In order to reduce the downside risks to growth emanating from the tightening of credit, the Fed, in a series of moves that began in September 2007, significantly lowered its target for the federal funds rate.[28]

Notwithstanding these and other efforts at increasing liquidity, the financial crisis intensified over the summer of 2008 as "mortgage-related assets deteriorated further, economic growth slowed, and uncertainty about the financial and economic outlook increased. As investors and creditors lost confidence in the ability of certain firms to meet their obligations, their access to capital markets as well as to short-term funding markets became increasingly impaired, and their stock prices fell sharply."[29] The investment bank Lehman Brothers and the insurance company American International Group (AIG) experienced this dynamic and were unable to weather the storm.[30]

Like the GSEs Fannie Mae and Freddie Mac, "both companies were large, complex, and deeply embedded in the American financial system." Private-sector solutions were not forthcoming for either entity. A public-sector solution for Lehman proved infeasible as well, "as the firm could not post sufficient collateral to provide reasonable assurance that a loan from the Federal Reserve would be repaid, and the Treasury did not have the authority to absorb billions of dollars of expected losses to facilitate Lehman's acquisition by another firm. Consequently, little could be done except to attempt to ameliorate the effects of Lehman's failure on the financial system."[31]

"In the case of AIG, the Federal Reserve and the Treasury judged that a disorderly failure would have severely threatened global financial stability and the performance of the U.S. economy."[32] The Federal Reserve granted emergency credit to AIG because it felt the credit would be adequately secured by AIG's assets,

---

27. *Id.*

28. Ben S. Bernanke, "Stabilizing the Financial Markets and the Economy," (Speech at the Economic Club of New York, NY, October 15, 2008), http://www.federalreserve.gov/newsevents/speech/bernanke20081015a.htm.

29. *Id.*

30. *Id.*

31. *Id.*

32. *Id.*

but "ensured that the terms of the credit extended to AIG imposed significant costs and constraints on the firm's owners, managers, and creditors."[33]

"AIG's difficulties and Lehman's failure, along with growing concerns about the U.S. economy and other economies, contributed to extraordinarily turbulent conditions in global financial markets [during the fall of 2008]. Equity prices fell sharply. . . . The cost of short-term credit, where . . . available, jumped for virtually all firms, and liquidity dried up in many markets."[34] The flow of credit to households, businesses, and state and local governments was severely restricted and posed a significant threat to economic growth.[35]

> The Treasury and the Fed have taken a range of actions to address financial problems. To address illiquidity and impaired functioning in commercial paper markets, the Treasury implemented a temporary guarantee program for balances held in money market mutual funds to help stem the outflows from these funds. . . [36] To address ongoing problems in interbank funding markets, the Federal Reserve has significantly increased the quantity of term funds it auctions to banks and accommodated heightened demands for temporary funding from banks and primary dealers. Also, to try to mitigate dollar funding pressures worldwide, [the Fed] greatly expanded reciprocal currency arrangements (so-called swap agreements) with other central banks.[37]

VI. THE EMERGENCY ECONOMIC STABILIZATION ACT

The expansion of Federal Reserve lending helped financial firms cope with reduced access to their usual sources of funding, and thus supported their lending to nonfinancial firms and households, but the intensification of the financial crisis during the late summer of 2008 made clear that a more powerful, comprehensive approach involving the fiscal authorities was needed.[38] On October 3, 2008, after a previously failed attempt at legislation, Congress passed and President George W. Bush signed the Emergency Economic Stabilization Act,[39] which provided important new tools for addressing the distress in financial markets and thus mitigating the risks to the economy. The act allows the Treasury to buy troubled assets, to provide guarantees, and to inject capital to strengthen the balance sheets of financial institutions.[40]

---

33. *Id.*
34. *Id.*
35. *Id.*
36. *Id.*
37. *Id.*
38. *Id.*
39. Pub. Law No. 110-343 (H.R. 1424).
40. *See* Ben S. Bernanke, "Stabilizing the Financial Markets and the Economy," (Speech at the Economic Club of New York, NY, NY, October 15, 2008) http://www. federalreserve.gov/newsevents/speech/bernanke20081015a.htm.

The Troubled Asset Relief Program (TARP) authorized by the legislation will allow the Treasury, under the supervision of an oversight board, to undertake two highly complementary activities: (1) using TARP funds to help recapitalize the banking system by purchasing nonvoting equity in financial institutions, and (2) using some of the resources provided under the bill to purchase troubled assets from banks and other financial institutions, in most cases using market-based mechanisms. Mortgage-related assets, including mortgage-backed securities and whole loans, will be the focus of the media attention surrounding the passage of the bill, although the law permits flexibility in the types of assets purchased as needed to promote financial stability. Specifically, the provision of equity capital to the banking system and the Act defines the term "Troubled Asset" as follows:

The term "purchase of troubled assets" means—
(A) residential or commercial mortgages and any securities, obligations, or other instruments that are based on or related to such mortgages, that in each case was originated or issued on or before March 14, 2008, the purchase of which the Secretary determines promotes financial market stability; and
(B) any other financial instrument that the Secretary, after consultation with the Chairman of the Board of Governors of the Federal Reserve System, determines the purchase of which is necessary to promote financial market stability, but only upon transmittal of such determination, in writing, to the appropriate committees of Congress.[41]

The flexibility resulting from the definition of "troubled asset" under the Act enabled the Treasury to purchase preferred equity of banks directly from the banks. Although TARP is evolving into direct government involvement in the banking activities of privately owned financial institutions, the manifest goal of the Act to provide equity capital to the banking system, thereby helping credit flow more freely, thus supporting economic growth.[42]

The funds allocated to the TARP program are not simple expenditures, but rather involve acquisitions of assets or equity positions, which the Treasury will be able to sell or redeem down the road. It is indeed possible that taxpayers could turn a profit from the program, although no assurances can be provided. The larger point, though, is that the economic benefit of these programs to taxpayers will not be determined primarily by the financial return to TARP funds, but rather by the impact of the program on the financial markets and the economy. If the TARP, together with the other measures that have been taken, is successful in promoting financial stability and, consequently, in supporting stronger

---

41. 122 Stat. 3766 Pub. Law No. 110–343—Oct. 3, 2008, Section 3.
42. *Id.* Furthermore, the Act itself describes its purpose as "provid[ing] authority for the Federal Government to purchase and insure certain types of troubled assets for the purposes of providing stability to and preventing disruption in the economy and financial system and protecting taxpayers."

economic growth and job creation, it will have proved itself a very good invest-ment indeed, to everyone's benefit.[43]

The Emergency Economic Stabilization Act also raised the limit on deposit insurance from $100,000 to $250,000 per account, effectively immediately.[44] In addition, the Federal Deposit Insurance Corporation (FDIC) has put forth a plan which will provide a broad range of guaranties of the liabilities of FDIC-insured depository institutions, including their associated holding companies. The costs of the FDIC guaranties are expected to be covered by fees and assessments on the banking system, not by the taxpayer.[45]

VII. RESULTS

The effort taken by Congress in enacting the Emergency Economic Stabilization Act was a critical first in stabilizing the capital markets. Economic recovery depends greatly on when and to what extent financial and credit markets return to more normal functioning.[46] Vital to improving the broader economy is the restoration of consumer and investor confidence, not limited to the credit and financial markets.

---

43. *Id.*
44. *Id.*
45. *Id.*
46. *Id.*

2. FINANCIAL INSTRUMENTS IN THE CAPITAL MARKETS

I. THE CAPITAL MARKETS

Kevin Warsh, a Member of the Board of Governors of the Federal Reserve System recently observed that, "if you have seen one financial crisis, you have seen one financial crisis."[1] His implication is that an understanding of a past crisis, such as the tumultuous events in Russia, Asia, and South America in 1997 and 1998, which led to global fears of systemic failure a decade ago, may have little impact on the course of action needed to negate the mortgage crisis of 2007 and 2008. Whatever lessons have been learned from past crises, central banks and market participants are now more aware than ever of the speed at which a problem in one part of the world can be transferred to healthy markets, creating a global systemic threat very quickly.

New innovations, the speed of information and transaction flow, and structured financial instruments can increase the resiliency of world markets, but also the speed at which problems are transferred from market to market. Regulators overseeing the capital markets must be prepared to react to severe

---

1. Kevin Warsh, (Q & A Session at New York University School of Law Global Economic Policy Forum 2008, April 11, 2008).

market conditions which can occur, in unexpected ways, literally instantaneously. Financial instruments provide the tools to fight the slings and arrows of financial fortunes. For instance, preferred securities, a class of financial instruments similar in structure to a bond although considered equity, have been used by the government as a tool to infuse liquidity into failing banks under the Term Asset Relief Program (TARP).

Access to capital through market participation allows companies to use financial instruments as a means of managing risk and making money. The capital markets provide a marketplace where persons with financial capacity can meet persons who have needs for long-term or short-term capital. The capital markets also provide a means for shifting risk from one party who is less willing or able to retain a financial risk to another party who is more willing or able to take on that risk.

Issuers, underwriters, regulators, and investors have a stake in the capital markets. There are two ways corporations access capital: issuing equity or issuing debt. These two means of capital access can be structured in complex and discreet ways furthering the simple goal of raising money. Equity issuers are generally private enterprises seeking venture participation in return for capital to expand operations or to buy out enterprise owners. (Although in the case of preferred equity, that participation may be limited to a "preferred" dividend.) Debt issuers can be private enterprises or sovereigns, municipalities or agencies seeking capital by borrowing money and retaining their equity interest. Underwriters are typically investment banks that sell the securities to investors and thereby earn a fee in return.

From an issuer's perspective, issuing debt means borrowing money from the investor. The issuer retains an obligation to pay back the principle at maturity and often the interest payments periodically as promulgated by the indenture. Issuing equity means selling an ownership interest to the investors. The issuer sometimes will pay periodic dividends to the common stock holders over and above dividends paid to "preferred" shareholders.[2,3]

Entities borrow and lend funds in the capital markets. Entities, such as banks, corporations and individuals, participate in the capital markets by trading financial instruments. Financial instruments, generally, are contractual agreements between parties regarding something of value. They are the primary vehicle for achieving two primary financial objectives: (1) making money; or (2) protecting the money already earned, in other words, hedging risk.[4] The type and specific structure of a particular financial instrument determines the magnitude of risk it poses or benefit it provides to the entity using it. Thus, in the example of a corporation, it is of paramount importance for the managers responsible for the

---

2. *See* Sec. II.B, *infra.*
3. *See* Sec. II.B, *infra.*
4. *See* Chapter 3, *infra.*

financial instruments to understand the impact those financial instruments have on the corporation.

A. Primary vs. Secondary Markets

The capital markets provide a forum for issuers and investors to meet to negotiate financial instruments. Within the context of the capital markets there are two subsidiary component markets reflecting whether an investor is purchasing a financial instruments directly from an issuer or its underwriter (the primary market) or from another investor who may or may not have purchased the instrument from the original issuer (the secondary market). It is conceptually similar to buying something new or used. It is important to consider that while some "used" items may be worth less than "new" ones, the "used" item may be something which has become scarce or rare (that is, more in demand or less in supply than when it was originally created). The item purchased "used" in the secondary market may, indeed, be worth significantly more than it was at creation or issue.

The primary market is the marketplace in which newly issued financial instruments are bought and sold. The basic parties in the primary market are: (1) the issuer and (2) a purchaser. The secondary market is the marketplace in which financial instruments are resold to other parties. The secondary market provides liquidity because it allows holders to resell their financial instruments.

An example of the distinction between the primary and secondary markets is where a private company decides to go public. When Google, for example, decided to access capital, it did so by issuing equity in a Dutch-auction initial public offering (IPO). It issued stock in the primary market at the highest price possible to meet the demands of all potential investors. The proceeds minus a small underwriting fee went to Google's coffers to use for corporate activities. The investors can sell their shares at a later date in the secondary market to other investors and will make a profit or incur a loss depending on the price of those shares in the secondary market.

B. Long-Term vs. Short-Term Marketplaces

The financial markets are also categorized into marketplaces for short-term obligations and long-term obligations. The money market is the marketplace for obligations lasting less than one year. The capital market is the marketplace for corporate equity and debt obligations lasting longer than one year.[5] These categories are subordinate to the notion of the primary and secondary market categories. For example, IPO shares are issued and sold in the primary capital market and then later resold in the secondary capital market. Treasury bills, which last one year or less, are issued and sold in the primary money market and then later

---

5. *See* the U.S. Federal Reserve Web site, http://www.federalreserveeducation.org/FRED/glossary/glossary.cfm.

resold in the secondary money market. The prospectus, indenture, or contractual agreement governing a financial instrument outlines its duration.

C. Case Study: The Auction Rate Securities Market (ARS)

Auction rate securities are generally long-term or perpetual debt instruments. The rate paid for capital is negotiated at a weekly auction. At that auction, the issuer is bound to pay the lowest rate at which all sellers might liquidate their positions in the security. Historically, because of the auction process, investors treated these instruments as short-term investment alternatives relying on the historical liquidity provided by the market place.

Unfortunately, investors ignored the reality (or arguably were not informed of the reality) that these instruments had extremely long durations, with a possibility that no bidder would be available when the investor needed its money. Because of the 2008 liquidity crisis in the banking industry, many auction participants were unwilling or unable to continue to bid in the auction rate securities market. Most auctions, therefore, "failed." When an auction fails, the investor is locked into the instrument until the auction process resumes. Most often this default interest rate is not attractive given the illiquidity of the instrument.

Prior to the recent auction failures, auction rate securities were used by many investors as cash management tools. While many investors and financial institutions approach the ARS auction failures as a monolithic challenge, there are two distinct categories of auction rate securities:

1. Auction Rate Certificates (ARCs)—Approximately $250 billion issued by United States public finance and $165 billion backed by student loans were issued. Many municipal ARCS have punitively high yields when auctions fail; there is some opportunity for market driven self-correction. Higher reset rates after failed auctions, coupled with credit issues, have impeded municipalities' access to capital.

2. Auction Rate Preferred Securities (ARPS)—Approximately $80 billion was issued by mutual funds, which generally have low maximum failure rates.

- ARPS are issued by mutual funds to leverage their portfolios.
- They are initially issued by prospectus, and subsequently traded by Dutch auction.
- The Investment Company Act of 1940 requires asset coverage of at least 200%.
- ARPS are rated AAA; a loss of that rating has implications on the security and its maximum yield as described in the prospectus.
- ARPS issuers have conflicting duties to preferred and common shareholders.
- Financial institutions represent ARPS as "Cash or Cash Equivalents" on client statements; many investors bought these instruments as "money market alternatives."

- Brokerage firms continue to earn fees on ARPS clients are forced to hold.
- There is evidence of pending litigation against banks, brokerage firms, and mutual funds relating to ARPS.

Many issuers have begun to retire their auction rate securities to fend off irate investors who claim to have been duped into purchasing long-term securities despite the investor's short-term risk appetite. Furthermore, a number of the underwriters of these securities have settled with state attorney generals and have agreed to return cash to investors.[6]

II. FINANCIAL INSTRUMENTS

A financial instrument is a contract involving a financial obligation.[7] Like all contracts, financial instruments grant a contractual right to one counterparty, impose a contractual obligation on the other counterparty, and must be supported by consideration. Thus, financial instruments are agreements to exchange something of value in return for something of value. A simple example of such an exchange is a loan—a lender provides the borrower an initial sum of money and in return the borrower pays the lender portions of the principal and interest over time.

A. Types of Financial Instruments

1. **Equity-Based Financial Instruments** The classic equity-based financial instrument is "common stock," or simply, "equity." The issuer carves out a piece of its equity and sells it to the purchaser. The purchaser, or shareholder, is part-owner of the corporation.[8] Equities can be tiered, giving some stock, such as "preferred stock," preference over other stocks, such as "common stock." While preferred stocks often include valuable rights that make those shares more valuable than common stocks, such as entitlement to a dividend,[9] they may not represent an ownership interest in the corporation, if, despite their designation

---

6. *See* Press Release Office of the Attorney General of the State of New York August 15, 2008, http://www.oag.state.ny.us/media_center/2008/aug/aug15a_08.html.

7. John Smullen and Nicholas Hand, eds., *Oxford Dictionary of Finance and Banking* (3d Ed. 2005), 154.

8. *See* U.S. Federal Reserve Web site, http://www.federalreserveeducation.org/FRED/glossary/glossary.cfm. *Equity* is defined as "ownership interest in an asset after liabilities are deducted;" *Stockholder* is defined as "a person who owns stock in a company and is eligible to share in profits and losses; same as shareholder."

9. *See, e.g.,* In re Nanovation Technologies, Inc., 364 B.R. 308, 347 (N.D.Ill., 2007). For a list of nuanced examples of equity instruments, *see* GLENN G. MUNN, F.L. GARCIA, CHARLES J. WOELFEL, THE ST. JAMES ENCYCLOPEDIA OF BANKING AND FINANCE (9th Ed. 1991), 401.

as "equity," they are functionally equivalent to a debt instrument—that is, they are issued as a means of accessing capital but, under their terms, do not represent any ownership interest in the company.

2. Debt-Based Financial Instruments The classic debt-based financial instrument is the "bond," which is basically an "I.O.U." issued by a borrower to a lender.[10] Bonds can be issued by sovereign entities, such as countries, states, or municipalities, or they can be issued by corporations. These financial instruments are essentially loans that contain terms for interest and repayment of principal.

Short-term debt obligations, obligations for one year or less, include: U.S. Treasury bills, commercial paper, certificates of deposit (CDs), repurchase agreements (REPOs), and federal funds. U.S. Treasury bills are federal government debt obligations that issue with maturities of three, six, or twelve months. Commercial paper is short-term debt issued by corporations in lieu of taking out a loan from a bank. CDs are short-term debt obligations issued by banks, although some CDs can have maturities longer than one year. A REPO is an agreement where one party sells assets to another party with the understanding that the initial party will *buy back* the assets at a later date. Federal funds are the overnight loans banks lend to each other and are kept on deposit at the Federal Reserve Bank.

Because of the extent to which companies rely on borrowing short-term capital, and because of the chilling effect on the economy of a disruption of that market, in February 2009, the government secured certain short-term corporate debt under the Temporary Liquidity Guarantee Program. The Federal Deposit Insurance Corporation (FDIC) has created this program to strengthen confidence in and encourage liquidity in the banking system by guaranteeing newly issued senior unsecured debt of banks, thrifts, and certain holding companies and by providing full coverage of non–interest bearing deposit transaction accounts, regardless of dollar amount.[11] The FDIC is an independent agency created by the Congress that maintains the stability of and public confidence in the nation's financial system, in part by insuring deposits at financial institutions. According to the FDIC,

> The FDIC adopted the Temporary Liquidity Guarantee Program on October 13th because of disruptions in the credit market, particularly the interbank lending market, which reduced banks' liquidity and impaired their ability to lend. The goal of the TLGP is to decrease the cost of bank funding so that bank lending to consumers and businesses will normalize. The industry

---

10. *See* John Smullen and Nicholas Hand, eds., OXFORD DICTIONARY OF FINANCE AND BANKING (3d Ed. 2005), 46.

11. http://www.fdic.gov/regulations/resources/TLGP/index.html.

funded program does not rely on the taxpayer or the deposit insurance fund to achieve its goals.[12]

As opposed to short-term obligations, long-term debt obligations are for longer than one year and include corporate bonds, U.S. Treasury notes and bonds, and municipal bonds. Corporate bonds are bonds issued by corporations and typically pay interest twice a year. U.S Treasury notes are bonds issued by the federal government lasting between one and ten years. U.S. Treasury bonds last longer than one year. Municipal bonds are issued by either the state or local governments and the interest paid out is usually free of federal income tax.

3. **Derivatives** In addition to straightforward equity or debt agreements, entities can use another form of financial instrument called a derivative to advance corporate goals in the capital markets. Derivatives are so called because they derive their value from another asset index or other investment. Derivatives are contractual agreements that obligate parties to exchange assets or cash flows.[13] A derivatives transaction is "a bilateral contract or payments exchange agreement whose value derives . . . from the value of an underlying asset or underlying reference rate or index." Derivatives transactions may be based on the value of foreign currency, U.S. Treasury bonds, stock indexes, or interest rates. The values of these underlying financial instruments are determined by market forces, such as movements in interest rates. Within the broad panoply of derivatives transactions are numerous innovative financial instruments whose objectives may include a hedge against market risks, management of assets and liabilities, or lowering of funding costs; derivatives may also be used as speculation for profit."[14] The U.S. Treasury distinguishes two categories of derivatives: (1) privately negotiated agreements, called over-the-counter derivatives; and (2) standardized agreements, called exchange-traded derivatives.[15]

Generally, derivatives are highly leveraged because they require little or no good faith deposit to secure the parties' obligations under the contract. There are four categories of derivatives: forwards, futures, options, and swaps.[16]

---

12. http://www.fdic.gov/news/news/press/2008/pr08122.html.

13. Procter & Gamble Co. v. Bankers Trust Co., 925 F. Supp. 1270 at 1275, Blue Sky L. Rep. (CCH) P74108, Comm. Fut. L. Rep. (CCH) P26700, Fed. Sec. L. Rep. (CCH) P99229 (S.D. Ohio 1996) citing Global Derivatives Study Group of the Group of Thirty, Derivatives: Practices and Principles 28 (1993).

14. *Id.*, citing Singher, *Regulating Derivatives: Does Transnational Regulatory Cooperation Offer a Viable Alternative to Congressional Action?* 18 FORDHAM INT'L. LAW J. 1405–06 (1995).

15. U.S. Treasury Web site, http://www.treas.gov/education/faq/markets/derivatives.shtml.

16. *See* Chapter 9, *infra*, for a detailed discussion of derivatives.

B. Distinction between Debt and Equity

The distinction between debt-based and equity-based financial instruments is an important one. One court noted that the distinction is one of investor intention: "Generally, shareholders place their money 'at the risk of the business' while lenders seek a more reliable return."[17] Whether a security is equity-based or debt-based affects whether the purchaser is guaranteed a return on her investment, whether the instrument is subordinate to other instruments in the case of bankruptcy, and whether the instrument receives favorable tax treatment.[18]

Moreover, the implications of issuing or buying equity-based financial instruments differ from those of debt-based financial instruments. When a corporation raises capital, it can do so by either issuing equity or debt. A corporation is not required to make distributions on equity shares it issues to shareholders, but must repay principal and interest to debt holders. Also, in the event of bankruptcy, equity claims are subordinate to debt claims. With regard to tax treatment, the type of instrument will determine the deductibility of interest paid, taxability of the return of principal, and the recognition of gain or loss upon exchange of property. Thus an entity must be cognizant of the implications of using equity-based versus debt-based financial instruments.

However, determining whether a financial instrument is equity-based or debt-based is not always easy, and the denomination of a financial instrument by the parties as one or the other is not always controlling. In *Fin Hay Realty v. United States*,[19] the Third Circuit applied an objective economic reality test to distinguish between debt and equity.[20] The issue in the case was whether funds paid by shareholders to a close corporation were "additional contributions to capital or loans on which the corporation's payment of interest was deductible under [the IRS Code]."[21] Two shareholders had created Fin Hay Realty with (1) capital contributions in exchange for stock, and (2) additional contributions in exchange for "unsecured promissory note[s] payable on demand and bearing [six percent interest]."[22] Years later, and after the deaths of the original shareholders, the IRS disallowed the corporation from deducting interest paid on the so-called loans.[23] Although other courts and commentators had analyzed several

---

17. Slappey Drive Indus. Park v. U.S., 561 F.2d 572, 581 (5th Cir. 1977). "Contributors of capital undertake the risk because of the potential return, in the form of profits and enhanced value, on their underlying investment. Lenders, on the other hand, undertake a degree of risk because of the expectancy of timely repayment with interest" (noting different risks associated with equity-instruments and debt-instruments).

18. *See generally* RICHARD A. BOOTH, FINANCING THE CORPORATION §1:5 (2007).

19. 398 F.2d 694 (3d Cir. 1968).

20. *Id.* at 697.

21. *Id.* at 694–95.

22. *Id.* at 695. The shareholders made subsequent additional contributions in exchange for "six per cent demand promissory notes."

23. *Id.* at 696.

factors to be considered in distinguishing debt from equity,[24] the court settled on an objective economic reality test.[25] The court considered the additional contributions as capital contributions because they did not dilute the shareholders' equity interests and were not called up during the shareholders' lifetimes.[26] The shareholders were in the position to structure contributions to receive the most favorable tax treatment without truly subjecting the corporation to the consequences of taking on debt.[27] Thus, the economic reality of the contributions was that they were capital contributions, or equity, rather than loans, or debt.

Courts also focus on the interpretation of the contract between the issuer and holders to determine if the financial instrument is debt or equity. In *Slappey Drive Industrial Park v. United States*,[28] the Fifth Circuit identified several factors to be considered in interpreting whether a financial instrument is debt or equity.[29] One of the issues in the case was whether certain transfers of property by shareholders to close corporations in exchange for financial instruments should be classified as debt or equity for tax purposes.[30] A representative transaction involved the transfer of land by one shareholder to the close corporation in exchange for a note from the corporation for "$65,000 five-year 3% installment[s]."[31]

---

24. *Id.* (Stating that factors for distinguishing debt and equity include: "(1) the intent of the parties; (2) the identity between creditors and shareholders; (3) the extent of participation in management by the holder of the instrument; (4) the ability of the corporation to obtain funds from outside sources; (5) the 'thinness' of the capital structure in relation to debt; (6) the risk involved; (7) the formal indicia of the arrangement; (8) the relative position of the obligees as to other creditors regarding the payment of interest and principal; (9) the voting power of the holder of the instrument; (10) the provision of a fixed rate of interest; (11) a contingency on the obligation to repay; (12) the source of the interest payments; (13) the presence or absence of a fixed maturity date; (14) a provision for redemption by the corporation; (15) a provision for redemption at the option of the holder; and (16) the timing of the advance with reference to the organization of the corporation.")

25. *Id.* at 697.

26. *Id.* at 697–98.

27. *See id.*

28. 561 F.2d, 572 (5th Cir. 1977).

29. 561 F.2d, at 582 (5th Cir. 1977). Listing factors for distinguishing debt and equity: "(1) the names given to the certificates evidencing the indebtedness; (2) the presence or absence of a fixed maturity date; (3) the source of payments; (4) the right to enforce payment of principal and interest; (5) participation in management flowing as a result; (6) the status of the contribution in relation to regular corporate creditors; (7) the intent of the parties; (8) "thin" or adequate capitalization; (9) identity of interest between creditor and stockholder; (10) source of interest payments; (11) the ability of the corporation to obtain loans from outside lending institutions; (12) the extent to which the advance was used to acquire capital assets; and (13) the failure of the debtor to repay on the due date or to seek a postponement." (citing Estate of Mixon v. U.S., 464 F.2d 394, 402 (5th Cir. 1972)).

30. *Id.* at 580.

31. *Id.* at 577.

The case involved several similar transactions by the same individuals; notably, the corporation did not meet the terms of repayment for any of the transactions. The court held the transactions should be considered equity transactions because the shareholders failed to insist on timely repayment,[32] the shareholders sought payment only when the corporation(s) had "plenty of cash,"[33] the proceeds went toward purchasing "capital assets,"[34] and the "proportionality" of the shareholder's equity interest equaled the shareholder's debt interests.[35] Thus, by examining the contract and behavior of the parties with respect to the contract the court determined the transactions should be treated like equity transactions rather than debt ones.

The Financial Accounting Standards Board (hereinafter "FASB") has issued guidelines to discerning equity from debt.[36] In a posting of project updates, the FASB identified three approaches to the problem. The approach favored by FASB is the "Basic Ownership Approach," under which a basic ownership instrument is considered equity. A basic ownership instrument is one that "(1) is the most subordinated interest in an entity and (2) entitles the holder to a share of the entity's net assets after all higher priority claims have been satisfied." All other financial instruments, such as "forward contracts, options and convertible debt," are to be classified either as assets or liabilities. Claims against an entity's assets are either (1) liabilities, or debt, if they reduce the net assets; or (2) assets if they increase the net assets available to the owner of the entity.[37]

The second approach is the "Ownership-Settlement Approach," which classifies financial instruments according to the return and settlement requirements. This approach considers as equity: (1) basic ownership instruments; (2) other perpetual instruments, such as preferred shares; and (3) indirect ownership instruments "settled by issuing related basic ownership instruments."[38] All other financial instruments are classified as either assets or liabilities.

---

32. *Id.* at 582 "When a corporate contributor seeks no interest, it becomes abundantly clear that the compensation he seeks is that of an equity interest: a share of the profits or an increase in the value of his shareholdings."

33. *Id.* at 582–83 stating that the intent to withdraw money only when the corporations were flush with cash was evidence that shareholders intended to treat the transactions as equity transactions rather than debt transactions.).

34. *Id.* at 583.

35. *Id.* at 583–84.

36. FASB Web site, http://www.fasb.org/project/liabeq.shtml.

37. *Id.* The U.S. Federal Reserve defines liabilities as "money an individual or organization owes; same as debt." U.S. Federal Reserve Web site, http://www.federalreserveeducation.org/FRED/glossary/glossary.cfm.

38. *Id.* Indirect ownership instruments are (1) not perpetual, (2) have terms that link value of the instrument to the "fair value of the basic ownership instrument," and (3) do not have contingent provisions linked to either market price of anything other than basic ownership instrument or unrelated price index. *Id.*

The third approach is the reassessed expected outcome, or "REO Approach," which considers financial instruments equity or non-equity depending on the direction of movement of fair value of the financial instrument compared to the direction of movement of fair value of the basic ownership instrument. The basic theme of each approach is that the FASB categorizes financial instruments as either (1) equity, or (2) nonequity; and nonequity as either an asset or a liability (i. e., debt).

C. Federal Regulation

Financial instruments are subject to regulatory oversight. There are two general governmental agencies that oversee financial instruments, the Securities Exchange Commission (SEC) and the Commodity Futures Trading Commission (CFTC). In addition, the Federal Reserve, which supervises the federal banking system, exerts some regulatory power over certain derivatives. Depending on how a transaction is structured, it may be subject to regulation by one or more of these agencies.[39]

The regulatory landscape will no doubt change as new governments and new realities become entrenched post-2008.[40] Recently President Obama promised "a sweeping overhaul of the financial regulatory system not seen since the reforms following the great depression." Prior to the Obama Administration, the Department of the Treasury, in its *Blueprint for a Modernized Financial Regulatory Structure*, under the leadership of Secretary Paulson, made the following observation during the early stages of the economic crisis:

> The capital markets and the financial services industry have evolved significantly over the past decade. These developments, while providing benefits to both domestic and global economic growth, have also exposed the financial markets to new challenges.
>
> Globalization of the capital markets is a significant development. Foreign economies are maturing into market-based economies, contributing to global economic growth and stability and providing a deep and liquid source of capital outside the United States.
>
> Unlike the United States, these markets often benefit from recently created or newly developing regulatory structures, more adaptive to the complexity and increasing pace of innovation. At the same time, the increasing interconnectedness of the global capital markets poses new challenges: an event in one jurisdiction may ripple through to other jurisdictions.
>
> In addition, improvements in information technology and information flows have led to innovative, risk-diversifying, and often sophisticated financial products and trading strategies. However, the complexity intrinsic to some

---

39. *See* Chapter 4, *infra*, for a complete discussion of the federal regulatory system.
40. *See* Preface, note 1.

of these innovations may inhibit investors and other market participants from properly evaluating their risks. For instance, securitization allows the holders of the assets being securitized better risk management opportunities and a new source of capital funding; investors can purchase products with reduced transactions costs and at targeted risk levels. Yet, market participants may not fully understand the risks these products pose.

The growing institutionalization of the capital markets has provided markets with liquidity, pricing efficiency, and risk dispersion and encouraged product innovation and complexity. At the same time, these institutions can employ significant degrees of leverage and more correlated trading strategies with the potential for broad market disruptions. Finally, the convergence of financial services providers and financial products has increased over the past decade. Financial intermediaries and trading platforms are converging. Financial products may have insurance, banking, securities, and futures components.

These developments are pressuring the U.S. regulatory structure, exposing regulatory gaps as well as redundancies, and compelling market participants to do business in other jurisdictions with more efficient regulation. The U.S. regulatory structure reflects a system, much of it created over seventy years ago, grappling to keep pace with market evolutions and, facing increasing difficulties, at times, in preventing and anticipating financial crises.

Largely incompatible with these market developments is the current system of functional regulation, which maintains separate regulatory agencies across segregated functional lines of financial services, such as banking, insurance, securities, and futures. A functional approach to regulation exhibits several inadequacies, the most significant being the fact that no single regulator possesses all of the information and authority necessary to monitor systemic risk, or the potential that events associated with financial institutions may trigger broad dislocation or a series of defaults that affect the financial system so significantly that the real economy is adversely affected. In addition, the inability of any regulator to take coordinated action throughout the financial system makes it more difficult to address problems related to financial market stability.

Second, in the face of increasing convergence of financial services providers and their products, jurisdictional disputes arise between and among the functional regulators, often hindering the introduction of new products, slowing innovation, and compelling migration of financial services and products to more adaptive foreign markets. Examples of recent interagency disputes include: the prolonged process surrounding the development of U.S. Basel II capital rules, the characterization of a financial product as a security or a futures contract, and the scope of banks' insurance sales.

Finally, a functional system also results in duplication of certain common activities across regulators. While some degree of specialization might be important for the regulation of financial institutions, many aspects of financial regulation and consumer protection regulation have common themes. For example, although key measures of financial health have different terminology in banking and insurance—capital and surplus respectively—they both serve a similar function of ensuring the financial strength and ability of financial institutions to meet their obligations. Similarly, while there are specific differences across institutions, the goal of most consumer protection regulation is to ensure consumers receive adequate information regarding the terms of financial transactions and industry complies with appropriate sales practices.[41]

III. THE EVOLVING ROLE OF THE ATTORNEY

A. Competent Representation
A thorough understanding of the structure and implications of various financial instruments is essential for the attorney who deals in these matters. The American Bar Association's *Model Rules of Professional Responsibility* require that an attorney be competent to handle any matter in which the attorney accepts representation. "A lawyer shall provide competent representation to a client. Competent representation requires the legal knowledge, skill, thoroughness and preparation reasonably necessary for the representation."[42] Furthermore, "competent handling of a particular matter includes inquiry into and analysis of the factual and legal elements of the problem, and use of methods and procedures meeting the standards of competent practitioners."[43] Thus the attorney has a legal and ethical obligation to understand the financial concepts that underlie the transactions on which he or she is working. If those transactions involve complicated financial structures and complex financial instruments, the attorney must acquire a knowledge of those.

B. Duty to Advise Client
The attorney, as in-house or outside counsel, has a duty to advise the corporate directors of the risks associated with various financial instruments. Corporate directors can be held liable for failing to exercise due care with regard to financial instruments if their decisions cause the corporation to suffer a loss. For example, in *Brane v. Roth*,[44] the shareholders of a grain cooperative sued the directors when the co-op lost money as a result of an unhedged grain position. The directors had relied on an accountant who suggested hedging the company's market

---

41. Department of the Treasury, *Blueprint for a Modernized Financial Regulatory Structure* 3–5, http://www.ustreas.gov/press/releases/reports/Blueprint.pdf.

42. ABA Model Rule 1.1.

43. ABA Model Rule 1.1 comment [5].

44. Brane v. Roth, 590 N.E. 587 (Ind. App. 1992).

exposure to grain. The directors hired a manager to implement a hedging strategy, but neglected to oversee the manager or his implementation of the hedging strategy. The manager, inexperienced in hedging, hedged only a small percentage of the co-op's total grain exposure; $20,000 of grain sales was hedged although the company had over $7,000,000 of potential exposure. As a result, the co-op suffered a substantial loss on the unhedged position.[45]

The court found that the directors had breached their fiduciary duties and were liable for the cooperative's losses. The court reasoned that the directors breached their duty to their shareholders by hiring a manager inexperienced in hedging, failing to maintain reasonable supervision over him, and failing to acquire knowledge of the basic fundamentals of hedging to be able to properly supervise the manager.[46]

In effect, the court was saying that the directors had an affirmative duty to become knowledgeable enough with regard to hedging strategy to be able to make an informed decision whether or not to follow such a strategy. It is a corollary, therefore, that the attorney who advises such directors must also be knowledgeable with regard to such financial instruments.

C. Drafting Financial Instruments

It is the responsibility of the attorney to draft legal documents that will meet the business needs of the client. Where financial instruments are involved, the attorney must thoroughly understand the basis of those instruments in order to draft a document that will maximize the benefits for the client and minimize the client's liability. The attorney must recognize the structure of the instrument, and be cognizant of any tax and other financial implications. Although many financial transactions use standardized agreements as their basis,[47] the attorney must be able to understand those agreements and have sufficient knowledge to be able to adapt them to the client's individual needs.

D. Regulatory Compliance

The attorney must be familiar with the various regulatory agencies that impose disclosure, registration, and other requirements on the issuers of financial instruments.[48] It is the responsibility of the attorney to draft such public disclosure documents, and to advise the client on how to comply with the requirements of all applicable laws. Plaintiffs who have sued corporations alleging fraud in the issuance of securities[49] have alleged that the attorneys advising those

---

45. *See* Chapter 15, *infra*, for a complete discussion of hedging.

46. Brane, 590 N.E. at 589.

47. *See, e.g.*, International Swaps and Derivatives (ISDA) Master Agreement, discussed in Chapter 9, *infra*.

48. *See* Sec. B, *supra*, and Chapter 4, *infra*.

49. *E.g.*, under SEC Rule 10b-5, discussed *infra* in Chapter 4.

clients "aided and abetted" the clients in the violation of those laws.[50] Courts have held lawyers potentially liable if a plaintiff can show, in addition to a violation of the law, that the lawyer knew of the violation and provided "substantial assistance" to the primary party with regard to the violation.[51] Therefore, to avoid potential liability, the attorney must understand the underlying structure of any transaction, and comply with any applicable disclosure and other requirements.

E. Liability to Third Parties

Attorneys may also have a responsibility to advise clients of their potential duties toward third parties—that is, the end-users who purchase their financial products. In both *Gibson Greetings, Inc. v. Bankers Trust Co.*[52] and *Proctor & Gamble Co. v. Bankers Trust Co.*,[53] an end-user bought a complex over-the-counter derivative product[54] from Bankers Trust. In both cases, the end-user alleged that Bankers Trust had a special relationship with the end-user, akin to that of a financial advisor, and that Bankers Trust had misled the end-user into buying the risky derivative product, which in turn caused the end-user to suffer a financial loss. In other words, the end-users alleged that Bankers Trust had a duty to explain the risks of the product and protect them from an unwise investment decision. Ultimately both cases were settled, but not without critics forming sharp opinions on both sides.[55] These cases, no matter what the ultimate outcome, illustrate the need for the attorney to understand complex financial instruments in order to properly advise the client regarding the client's potential liability to third parties.

Attorneys involved in financial transactions often issue opinion letters to their clients regarding the implications of those transactions. These letters provide conclusions regarding legal issues and are often for the benefit of third parties entering into a transaction.[56] An attorney for a securities issuer "assumes a duty to provide complete and nonmisleading information with respect to subjects on which he undertakes to speak [in an opinion letter]."[57] In *Mehaffy, Rider, Windholz & Wilson v. Central Bank Denver, N.A.*,[58] the court held that an attorney who prepares such a letter can be liable to a third party for any material misrepresentation

---

50. 22 Am. Jur. Proof of Facts 3d 559 §5 (2007).

51. *Id.*

52. Civ. No. 1-04-620 (S.D. Ohio 1994).

53. 925 F. Supp. 1270 (S.D. Ohio 1996).

54. An over-the-counter (OTC) derivative is a privately negotiated contract which is not traded on a national exchange. *See* Chapter 9, *infra,* for a complete discussion of these derivatives.

55. *See* Jerry W. Markham, *Protecting the Institutional Investor—Jungle Predator of Shorn Lamb?*, 12 YALE J. ON REG. 345, 365–67 (1995).

56. Steven L. Schwarcz, *The Public Responsibility of Structured Finance Lawyers*, working paper , (2006), 7 n.6.

57. Rubin v. Schottenstein, Zox & Dunn, 143 F.3d 263, 268 (6th Cir. 1998).

58. 892 P.2d 230, 236–37 (Colo. 1995).

contained in that letter. Thus the attorney has an affirmative duty to fully understand and accurately describe financial instruments in order to avoid personal liability as well.

F. The Attorney as Business Partner

For all the above reasons, it is crucial that the attorney have a solid understanding of the financial concepts that underlie the client's decisions, and of the financial instruments that effectuate the client's purposes. Only then can the attorney knowledgeably navigate the legal framework, properly fulfill his advisory role, and provide effective representation to the client.

It is the intention of this book to provide that necessary knowledge which will guide not only the attorney, but also the business professional, to an understanding of the interaction of law and economics in structuring financial instruments and participation in the capital markets.

3. USING FINANCIAL INSTRUMENTS

I. GOAL-ORIENTED INVESTING

While attorneys play an active role in memorializing transactions within a functioning capital markets, it is disruptions in the markets themselves that disturb the delicate equilibrium of the broader economy. The capital markets represent the opportunity for an enterprise to access capital to maintain its level of business activity. Ensuring the stability of the capital markets, therefore, is of paramount concern for the Federal Reserve and other financial market regulators in to prevent systemic failure. By shoring up the capital markets, the Fed furthers its legislated goals of fostering an environment with maximum sustainable growth, minimum unemployment, and reasonable inflation.[1]

Access to the capital markets is facilitated through the use of financial instruments that allow risk to be negotiated among market participants. Fundamentally, a corporation needs capital to run its daily operations or to pay for future endeavors. A corporation can use financial instruments to raise that capital by issuing either debt or equity instruments.[2] However, a corporation can use financial instruments for more than simply acquiring capital. A corporation can use financial instruments to achieve two other main goals: hedging risk and enhancing yield.

Financial instruments can serve two objectives: (1) providing stability in an unpredictable financial market; or (2) magnifying the swings of an unpredictable market.[3] To carry out the first objective, corporations can use financial instruments to hedge against adverse moves in commodity prices.[4] In furtherance of

---

1. *See* Federal Reserve Act §2a, 12 U.S.C. §225a.

2. *See* Chapter 2, Sec. II.A., *supra*.

3. *See* Proctor & Gamble Co. v. Bankers Trust Co, 925 F. Supp. 1270, 1275–76 (S.D. Ohio 1996). Citing Hu, *Hedging Expectations: "Derivative Reality" and the Law of Finance of the Corporate Objective,* 73 TEXAS L. REV. 985 (1995).

4. *Id.* at 1275.

the second objective, corporations seeking large profits can engineer financial instruments that are susceptible to dramatic increases in value.[5] Derivatives, which are risk-shifting agreements, the value of which are derived from the value of an underlying asset, can be used to facilitate both of these objectives. There are four categories of derivatives: forwards, futures, options, and swaps.[6]

Derivatives can be structured into complex financial instruments whose pricing is based on optionality and rocket science. However the basic structure of derivatives can be quite simple. In structuring derivative instruments designed to shift risk from one party who is less willing or able to assume that risk, to another who is more willing or able to assume that risk, market participants are able to utilize derivatives to maximize enterprise goals. Derivatives can be used to "facilitate identification, isolation, and separate management of fundamental risks."[7] Entities can employ derivatives to achieve various goals of cash flow, interest rate, and currency liquidity.[8] It is a fundamental premise, however, that although financial instruments can be used to generate profits, they are also accompanied by risk, and risk and reward are inversely proportional. Attorneys who engineer such financial instruments must recognize and prepare for such risks.[9]

When using financial instruments to achieve goals, a corporation must be aware of several considerations: the value of the asset underlying the financial instrument; duties or obligations the corporation owes to the other party to the contract; the implications and "worse case scenario" of the performance of the financial instrument; the risk of the transaction; and how the specific transaction can achieve the corporation's goals.

A. Using Financial Instruments to Hedge Risk

While derivatives have been vilified because of losses attributed to their misuse, in actuality they are neither good nor bad. They are tools of managing risk that can be used appropriately, or, indeed, misused. When used appropriately, they can be effective hedges against unwanted risk, thereby isolating the risk an enterprise wants to sustain. A hedge is a transaction or position designed to mitigate the risk of other financial exposure.[10] Hedgers trade to shift the risk of an unfavorable event to a counterparty that is better able or more willing to carry

---

5. *Id.* at 1275–76 .

6. Derivatives are discussed in detail in Chapter 9, *infra.*

7. Thomas C. Singher, *Regulating Derivatives: Does Transnational Regulatory Cooperation Offer a Viable Alternative to Congressional Action?* 18 FORDHAM INT'L L.J. 1397, 1405 (1995).

8. *Id.*

9. *See, e.g.,* In re BT Securities Corp., Securities Act Release No. 33-7124, Exchange Act Release No. 34-35136 (Dec. 22, 1994), http://www.sec.gov/litigation/admin/337304.txt.

10. John Smullen and Nicholas Hand, eds., OXFORD DICTIONARY OF FINANCE AND BANKING (3d Ed. 2005), 194.

that risk. The value of the contract being used to hedge a position will move in an opposite direction from the underlying asset being hedged. Hedging in effect balances a negative position with a positive one, and lowers the overall risk. Derivatives such as forwards, futures, and options can be used to hedge a transaction.[11]

B. Using Financial Instruments to Enhance Yield

Derivatives can also be used as a tool for enhancing yield, or making money. By assuming a counterparty's unwanted risk, market participants are afforded the opportunity to benefit form the reward attendant to that risk. The assumption of risk to enhance yield by speculating on the outcome of a contingent event allows market participants to achieve returns that might otherwise be impossible. The main contrary position to a hedge is speculation. The Federal Reserve defines *speculation* as: "The practice of buying or selling stocks, commodities, land, or other types of assets hoping to take advantage of an expected rise or fall in price."[12] Speculation is taking a greater risk in exchange for a possible greater return on the investment. Derivatives can also be used for speculative purposes.

Hedge funds are a good example of an end user using derivatives to shift risk or to enhance yield. Hedge funds are as diverse in their strategies as they are in their use of financial instruments. Some use highly sophisticated quantitative techniques with algorithms primarily driving the trading decisions, while others engage in more subjective trading based on analysis and interpretation of the market.[13]

To enhance yield, for instance, consider a hedge fund that might want to speculate that the gold price will rise. The fund can accomplish this by buying a "forward" position in gold. A forward is a class of derivatives that can be as simple in structure as a purchaser obliging himself to take delivery of an underlying commodity at some date in the future. The terms of that contract for delivery may require little or no good faith deposit; the contract is therefore highly leveraged. The seller of the contract has shifted the risk of gold prices falling from themselves to their counterparty, the hedge fund.[14]

Due to the wide variety of strategies, hedge funds are often classified according to their main investment strategy: whether global-macro, where managers take positions based on their forecasts of global macroeconomic trends and seek related assets that have deviated from some anticipated relationship; or event-driven, where funds invest in specific securities related to events such

---

11. *See* Chapter 9, *infra*

12. U.S. Federal Reserve Web site, http://www.federalreserveeducation.org/FRED/glossary/glossary.cfm.

13. *See* The President's Working Group on Financial Markets, *Hedge Funds, Leverage, and the Lessons of Long-Term Capital Management* (April 1999), 1.

14. *See* Chapter 9.

as bankruptcies, reorganizations, and mergers.[15] Other classifications include those focused on certain markets, such as healthcare or emerging markets.

Vital in the decision to invest in a hedge fund is an understanding of the strategy employed by that fund. Recent events regarding a pool of funds managed by the legendary Wall Street titan Bernard Madoff underscore the necessity of seeing beyond the black box of managed investing. The complaint filed by the SEC against Mr. Madoff alleged that his returns were based on a Ponzi scheme with little basis in transactional sophistication. According to the complaint:

> From an indeterminate period through the present [December 11, 2008], Madoff . . . has committed fraud through the investment adviser activities of BERNARD L .MADOFF INVESTMENT SECURITIES LLC, (BMIS) . . . Madoff admitted to one or more employees of BMIS that for many years he has been conducting a Ponzi scheme through the investment adviser activities of BMIS and that BMIS has liabilities of approximately $50 billion.[16]

On March 12, 2009 Madoff pled guilt to defrauding investors of as much as $65 billion in the biggest Ponzi scheme in history.

C. The Economy's Impact on Financial Instruments

The Madoff case fanned the flames of distrust seething within the capital markets. The crisis in confidence affecting the capital markets is, in part, due to fears of the credit worthiness and, indeed, the trustworthiness of counterparties. Because many financial instruments require counterparties to live up to their end of the bargain, if they are unwilling or unable to do so, the transactions are meaningless.

Financial instruments have two components in terms of their utility to shift risk or enhance yield: (1) the counterparties ability to meet their obligations under the terms of the financial instrument and (2) the underlying asset, the thing of value, upon which the obligations of the financial instrument depend. The valuation of the underlying asset, and therefore the value of the financial instrument, is dependent on numerous economic factors, including prevailing interest rates, which are the rates for borrowing money.[17]

Nationwide interest rates have historically been influenced by the federal funds rate, which is the rate at which banks lend money to each other for short-term, overnight loans.[18] The Federal Reserve affects interest rates by

---

15. *Id.* at 3.

16. http://sec.gov/litigation/complaints/2008/comp-madoff121108.pdf.

17. *See* Federal Reserve Web site, http://www.federalreserveeducation.org/Teachers/glossary/glossary.cfm.

18. Federal Reserve Web site, http://www.federalreserve.gov/fomc/fundsrate.htm.

implementing monetary policy,[19] and, post-2008, by taking extraordinary steps such as direct purchase of such securities as mortgage-backed bonds.

Prevailing interest rates directly affect decisions to hedge a risk or to speculate in order to enhance yield. What may be a prudent business decision at one point in time may seem otherwise when interest rates change. Because of the highly leveraged nature of financial instruments incorporating derivative components, a severe market capital market disruption such as in the events of 2008 has profound effects on the financial stability of enterprises throughout the broader economy.

II. ACHIEVING INVESTMENT GOALS

Firms that use financial instruments are classified by their market objectives. *End users* trade primarily to satisfy their own production, investment, or distribution needs. This can be accomplished by entering into derivatives contracts with the expectation of taking or making delivery. Recently, end users have become more aggressive and added strategic profit, or "yield enhancement" as an objective of their trading strategy.

Speculators trade with the specific intention of making profits from market movement. In its simplest form, speculating involves buying something cheap and selling it dear, for example, buying crude oil futures with the expectation of a slowdown in oil production and a corresponding price rise. Speculators hope to take advantage of an expected rise or fall in price.

A. The Investor's Perspective

The same financial instrument can be used both to hedge a risk and to speculate, depending on the party's perspective. For example, a forward contract, which is an agreement for delivery of an asset or commodity at some future date at a price agreed upon at the time the contract is made,[20] can be used to either speculate or hedge risk.[21] A manufacturer who wishes to ensure availability of a raw material at a given price can hedge against the risks of fluctuating prices by entering into a forward contract, agreeing to buy the raw material at a set price and ensuring its availability. The party selling the raw material is also hedging, guaranteeing against declining commodity prices.

---

19. *See* Chapter 5, *infra*, for a complete discussion of this topic.

20. John Smullen and Nicholas Hand, eds., Oxford DICTIONARY OF FINANCE AND BANKING (3d Ed. 2005), 168.

21. U.S. Commodity Futures Trading Commission "The Economic Purpose of Futures Markets and How They Work," http://www.cftc.gov/educationcenter/economicpurpose.html.

Consider, for example, a forward contract made between a wheat farmer and a cereal factory, regarding the future delivery of a set amount of wheat; the parties agree on a price and a delivery date. A forward contract is a contract between a purchaser and a seller for the delivery of an item at a forward date at a mutually agreed upon price. Since this agreement has terms, offer, acceptance, and consideration, it is a contract. Because the value of that contract will be affected by the changing value of the underlying item (i.e., wheat), this contract is a derivative. It also meets the functional definition of a derivative because it shifts the risk of an increase or decrease in the price of the underlying item from the seller to the buyer of the forward contract.

In terms of hedging risk, consider the wheat farmer who is concerned about a decline in wheat prices. By entering into a forward contract with a counterparty such as a cereal manufacturer, he has shifted the risk of declining wheat prices to the buyer of the contract.

If wheat rises in price over the six month life of the forward contract, the farmer will not benefit from an increase in the underlying price of wheat. A forward contract for wheat for $8, deliverable in six months, will give the wheat farmer $8 for one bushel of wheat six months from now even if the market price for one bushel of wheat six months from now is more or less than $8.

On the purchase side of the contract, the cereal manufacturer is establishing a wheat price of $8 regardless of where prices actually are in six months. The factory has contracted to purchase wheat for $8 even if the market price for one bushel of wheat six months from now is more than $8. Thus, in this example, both parties can use a forward contract to hedge against the future price of wheat moving in an unfavorable direction. The same forward contract protects the wheat farmer from a drop in wheat prices and protects the cereal factory from an increase in wheat prices.

In terms of speculating, a third party can purchase a wheat forward contract, hoping to profit from an increase in wheat prices. The speculator exchanges capital for the risk of an increasing wheat price. In contrast to the wheat farmer and the cereal factory, which have a specific risk that is being hedged using the wheat forward contract, the speculator has entered into a contract for wheat so that he might sell that contract or the physical wheat at a later date for a higher price. The speculator makes a profit on the forward contract when, in the future, the price of wheat increases and the forward contract (a contract for cheaper wheat) becomes valuable to a purchaser of wheat, for example, the cereal factory.

In the case of rising wheat prices, the cereal factory does not want to pay the higher, prevailing, market price of wheat and will look for cheaper ways of obtaining the same wheat. For example, if the prevailing price of wheat is $9 a bushel, the cereal factory can lock in that price. The speculator holding the forward contract can sell the forward contract to the cereal factory for some price higher than he originally paid for the contract, and the cereal factory can purchase the wheat it needs for less than the prevailing market price. Thus, the factory's interest in hedging against increasing wheat prices coincides with the speculator's interest in increasing wheat prices. Since forward contracts are privately negotiated financial instruments, it is essential that the terms reflect the objectives of both parties to the transaction. For example, in this case the wheat speculator will want to allow for novation in order to be able to extinguish his obligations to take delivery under the terms of the contract. In the alternative, the wheat speculator might ask for a forward contract structured as a cash-settled financial instrument, where changes in value are reflected in cash flows, rather than requiring actual delivery of the underlying commodity.

B. Financial Instrument Objectives

The Financial Accounting Standards Board (FASB) requires corporations to disclose the objectives for holding and issuing hedging instruments."[22] It is interesting to note the different ways financial instruments are intended to be used and the appropriateness for a specific stated objective. For instance, in *Fadem v. Ford Motor Co.*,[23] the Southern District of New York found that Ford did not misrepresent to shareholders its purpose for entering into palladium forward and futures contracts because Ford adequately stated its purpose for entering into such contracts.[24] Ford entered into palladium forward and futures contracts while prices were at a historic high; the price eventually settled and Ford sustained a loss on the contracts. However, in both of its 1999 and 2000 10-K filings, Ford stated that it entered into such contracts "to offset [Ford's/our] exposure to the potential change in prices mainly for various nonferrous metals [used in manufacturing automotive components]."[25] Thus, by identifying a risk and describing the management of that risk through the financial instruments it used, Ford adequately disclosed its objective for entering into the derivative financial instruments.

In *In re Ashanti Goldfields Securities Litigation*,[26] the Eastern District of New York denied in part a motion to dismiss a securities fraud complaint because shareholders sufficiently alleged facts that could support the claim that statements made by Ashanti regarding its use of gold futures were misleading.[27] Ashanti was in the business of mining and processing gold and regularly entered into gold futures contracts to protect itself from price fluctuation in gold. After gold prices rose dramatically, the value of Ashanti's futures contracts dropped

---

22. *See generally* FASB Statement 133, http://www.fasb.org/st/summary/stsum133.shtml.

23. 352 F. Supp.2d 501 (S.D.N.Y. 2005)

24. *Id.* at 508; Ford entered into such contracts "to lock in palladium supply at fixed prices."

25. *Id.* at 507.

26. 184 F. Supp. 2d 247 (E.D.N.Y. 2002).

27. *Id.* at 258.

from $290 million to negative $570 million.[28] The shareholders alleged that Ashanti misled them when Ashanti said it entered into the contracts for hedging purposes rather than speculation because Ashanti failed to fully disclose the extent of risk exposure to the rise in gold prices.[29]

Although Ashanti's actions could be used to hedge, the court noted the difference between hedging and speculating as one of magnitude risk/reward: "[a hedger's] primary financial interest is in the profit to be earned from the production or processing of the commodity. Those who seek financial gain by taking positions in the futures market generally are called 'speculators' or 'investors.'"[30] Because speculation takes on more risk than merely hedging, Ashanti misled shareholders by not fully disclosing the extent of its risk exposure from its derivative financial instruments.

In *Nationwide Life Insurance Co. v. St. Clair Mobile Home Parks LLC*,[31] the Eastern District of Missouri held that a client was not liable for "hedge losses" sustained by Nationwide when the client failed to close on a commercial loan because the client was not fully informed of Nationwide's hedging activity.[32] The court noted that it was standard industry practice for a commercial mortgage company to enter into a mirror-image ancillary agreement with a third party to act as hedge on any capital market loans it extended.[33] It was also standard industry practice to execute a hedge-loss agreement with any parties seeking a commercial loan, such that the borrower would be liable for any hedge losses sustained as a result of the borrower's failure to close on the loan.[34]

Nationwide, however, did not execute such an agreement with St. Clair.[35] After Nationwide and St. Clair agreed on terms for a mortgage application, Nationwide entered into a hedging arrangement with a third party, interest rates rose unfavorably for St. Clair, the closing was postponed repeatedly and Nationwide eventually cancelled the application.[36] Nationwide sought recovery for losses on the hedge it placed.[37] The court examined the language of the application and found no unambiguous language stipulating that St. Clair would be liable for any hedging losses.[38] Thus, Nationwide could not recover its hedge

---

28. *Id.* at 250.

29. *Id.* at 262 (discussing that Ashanti gave no warning of the extent of potential risks).

30. *Id.* at 254.

31. 2006 WL 3313786 (E.D.Mo. Nov. 14, 2006).

32. *Id.* at *1.

33. *Id.* at *2.

34. *Id.*

35. *Id.*

36. *Id.* at *9.

37. *Id.* at *10.

38. *Id.* at *12.

losses because it did not clearly disclose and inform its client of its hedging activity.

III. MANAGING RISK

Many financial instruments that are not labeled "derivatives" may contain a derivative component and function to shift risk (hedge) or to enhance yield to further corporate objectives. For example, when an oil company contracts to deliver fuel to a customer at a fixed price, and the customer retains contract termination rights, that contract termination clause is effectively an embedded derivative which may be classified as an "option."[39] It is therefore necessary to understand the risk components of any financial instrument or contracts.

Risk must be measured and managed comprehensively. That is, once the risk of a particular financial instrument is isolated and quantified, the holistic risk management focus should be on the dynamics of the investments in the context of an entire portfolio. Focusing on one instrument in a vacuum, ignoring the interplay among various instruments, can be costly if one financial instrument's ability to achieve its objective is offset by another financial instrument. Past crises have, in part, reflected a failure by some institutions to recognize and limit concentrations of risk within their portfolios which would have been revealed if the portfolio had been stress-tested and analyzed in a more comprehensive manner.[40]

Financial engineering can create derivative instruments that combine risks in very complex ways. Upon analysis, traditional cash instruments that appear simple may actually have greater risk than the complex instruments that are labeled "derivatives." Placing financial instruments into pigeonholes, without regard to their true underlying risks or economic functions, can create disincentives for prudent risk management, and often lead to disastrous results. Two instruments that have different names (*e.g.,* options and swaps) and entirely different treatment under existing legal and regulatory frameworks, might have identical financial, credit, liquidity, or operational risks.

Derivatives are by definition leveraged. For instance, if a speculator enters into a contract to purchase 5000 bushels of wheat at a fixed price of $9 a bushel six months hence, absent specific terms to the contrary, no margin is posted as a good faith deposit to insure performance of the contract. Therefore, the speculator has put up $0 to control a contract that's notional or underlying value is $45,000 ($9 times 5000 bushels). The assumption of risk or the control of assets far in excess of the capital invested is the definition of leverage.

---

39. *See* Chapter 9, *infra*, for a complete discussion of derivatives.
40. *See* Chapter 12, *infra*, for a complete discussion of risk management.

When privately negotiated, "over-the-counter" derivatives may be illiquid and therefore pose unique risks to portfolio managers and corporate fiduciaries. It should also be noted that in entering into an over-the-counter-derivatives contract, the counterparties take on the credit risk that the other side of the contract will be unwilling or unable to meet its obligations under the contract when those obligations come due. However, derivatives are neither good nor bad in themselves. The enterprise's overall business objective is the most important factor in determining their efficacy and value to the enterprise. Derivatives, thus, can be very valuable as a tool of risk management, but, if misused, can increase a firm's risks dramatically.[41]

---

41. *See* In re County of Orange v. Fuji Securities, Inc., 31 F. Supp. 2d 768 (C.D. Cal. 1998), for an illustration of the magnitude of leverage that can be achieved by entering into a series of derivatives based on debt-instruments, and the disastrous results that can ensue.

4. SECURITIES REGULATION

I. REGULATORY OVERVIEW

The capital markets play an essential role in the world economy, providing a means for individuals and institutions to access capital and to enhance return on their investments. Financial instruments also allow market participants to manage risk by shifting unwanted risk to a counterparty who might be more willing or able to manage or capitalize on that risk. A number of enterprises facilitate capital market participation, including banks, brokers engaging in securities and derivatives transactions, and government sponsored entities.

Within the capital markets, the Department of the Treasury ("Treasury") focuses on promoting economic growth and stability in the United States. Critical to this mission is a sound and competitive financial services industry grounded in robust consumer protection and stable and innovative market structure. To further its goals, the Treasury released, under the leadership of former Treasury Secretary Hank Paulson, a comprehensive "Blueprint for a Modernized

Financial Regulatory Structure" (Blueprint).[1] In this Blueprint, the Treasury analyzes the current regulatory structure for the domestic capital markets and makes specific suggestions for its improvement. The market conditions arising in 2007 and 2008 provided the impetus for reviewing the current regulatory regime. The implosion of the market for mortgage-backed securities and its impact on the broader financial markets encouraged the Department of the Treasury to review the concepts of functional regulation.

The Blueprint is an effective summary of the key participants and regulatory gaps in the current system. Under the current system, regulation is compartmentalized along lines of segmented financial instruments. In its Blueprint, The Treasury Department advances a hypothesis that such segmented regulatory authority creates an information void that in the event of crisis might be ineffective. By segmenting regulation, the risks to the system (systemic risk) are compounded by inefficient information flow among various financial regulators. The Obama administration has picked up on the regulatory reform initiatives outlined by Secretary Paulson. On March 26, 2009, Secretary Geithner outlined the administration's initiative for regulatory reform:

> On February 25, after meeting with the banking and financial services leadership from Congress, President Obama directed his economic team to develop recommendations for financial regulatory reform and to begin the process of working with the Congress on new legislation. The Treasury Department has been working with the President's Working Group on Financial Markets (PWG) to develop a comprehensive plan of reform. This effort has been and will be guided by principles the President set forth earlier this year and in his speech as a candidate at Cooper Union in March 2008.
>
> Financial institutions and markets that are critical to the functioning of the financial system and that could pose serious risks to the stability of the financial system need to be subject to strong oversight by the government. Our financial system and the major centralized markets must be strong and resilient enough to withstand very severe shocks and the failure of one or more large institutions. We need much stronger standards for openness, transparency, and plain, common sense language throughout the financial system. And we need strong and uniform supervision for all financial products marketed to consumers and investors, and tough enforcement of the rules to ensure full accountability for those who violate the public trust.
>
> Financial products and institutions should be regulated for the economic function they provide and the risks they present, not the legal form they take. We can't allow institutions to cherry pick among competing regulators, and shift risk to where it faces the lowest standards and constraints.[2]

---

1. The Department of the Treasury, *Blueprint for a Modernized Financial Regulatory Structure* (March 2008), http://www.treasury.gov.

2. March 26, 2009tg-71 Treasury Secretary Tim Geithner Written Testimony House Financial Services Committee Hearing.

In its white paper on regulatory reform, *Financial Regulatory Reform: A New Foundation*, the Department of the Treasury under Secretary Geithner outlines the need for regulatory reform:

> While this crisis had many causes, it is clear now that the government could have done more to prevent many of these problems from growing out of control and threatening the stability of our financial system. Gaps and weaknesses in the supervision and regulation of financial firms presented challenges to our government's ability to monitor, prevent, or address risks as they built up in the system. No regulator saw its job as protecting the economy and financial system as a whole.[3]

Currently, the regulation of futures and securities is bifurcated along product lines between the Securities and Exchange Commission and the Commodity Futures Trading Commission. The original reason for the regulatory bifurcation reflected the market conditions as they existed at the time of the enactment of the Commodity Exchange Act and the federal securities laws in the 1930s. This bifurcation operated effectively until the 1970s when futures trading expanded beyond agricultural commodities to encompass the rise and eventual dominance of nonagricultural commodities.[4] Recently the SEC and the CFTC have begun the process of establishing a coordinated approach to regulating certain derivatives as regulation evolves.

A. The Securities and Exchange Commission

1. **Jurisdiction** The Securities and Exchange Commission was established by Congress under the Securities Exchange Act of 1934.[5] The SEC is vested with regulatory jurisdiction over securities markets, the companies issuing securities, and purchasers and sellers of securities pursuant to the Securities Act of 1933 (the "Securities Act")[6] and the Securities Exchange Act of 1934 (the "Exchange Act."[7] The jurisdiction of the SEC extends to all financial instruments that are covered by the definition of a "security" under these statutes. According to the Securities Act:

> The term "security" means any note, stock, treasury stock, security future, bond, debenture, evidence of indebtedness, certificate of interest or participation in any profit-sharing agreement, collateral-trust certificate, preorganization certificate or subscription, transferable share, investment contract, voting-trust certificate, certificate of deposit for a security, fractional undivided interest in oil, gas, or other mineral rights, any put, call, straddle, option,

---

3. The Department of the Treasury, *Financial Regulatory Reform: A New Foundation* (June 17, 2009) at page 2, http://www.financialstability.gov/docs/regs/FinalReport_web.pdf.

4. *Id.*

5. 15 U.S.C. §78(d)(a).

6. 15 U.S.C. §77a *et seq.*

7. 15 U.S.C. §78a *et seq.*

or privilege on any security, certificate of deposit, or group or index of securities (including any interest therein or based on the value thereof), or any put, call, straddle, option, or privilege entered into on a national securities exchange relating to foreign currency, or, in general, any interest or instrument commonly known as a "security," or any certificate of interest or participation in, temporary or interim certificate for, receipt for, guarantee of, or warrant or right to subscribe to or purchase, any of the foregoing.[8]

The definition of security is "sufficiently broad to encompass virtually any instrument that might be sold as an investment."[9] The definition of security is quite broad because it was adopted to restore investors' confidence in the financial markets; it includes not only the typical instruments that fall within the ordinary concept of a security but also any uncommon and irregular instruments.[10] The securities laws cannot be avoided by calling a security by a term that is not listed in the statute because "Congress' purpose in enacting the securities laws was to regulate investments, in whatever form they are made and by whatever name they are called."[11] However, "it is also important to bear in mind that Congress, in enacting the securities laws, did not intend to provide a federal remedy for all common law fraud."[12]

B. What Constitutes a "Security"

In every securities case, it is necessary to prove that the financial instruments sold are securities as defined in the Act.[13] That proof may come from the face of the financial instrument itself (which shows it to be a stock, note, or other security), or it may need to be proven with external information.[14] Proof from the face of the instrument itself is appropriate with notes, stocks, and bonds; these instruments are generally standardized and the name alone has a well-settled meaning.[15] External proof is appropriate where the financial instrument embodies some of the significant characteristics associated with a type of security but is

---

8. 15 U.S.C. §77(b)(1). The definition under the Exchange Act, 15 U.S.C. §78(c)(a)(10), is identical except that the Exchange Act exempts notes having a maturity of less than nine months. The Supreme Court has treated the two definitions as functionally indistinguishable in virtually all cases. See Reves v. Ernst & Young, 494 U.S. 56, 61 n. 1 (1990); Tcherepnin v. Knight, 389 U.S. 332, 335 (1967).

9. SEC v. Infinity Group Co. 212 F.3d 180, 186 (3d Cir. 2000), quoting Reves.

10. Marine Bank v. Weaver, 455 U.S. 551, 555 (1982).

11. Reves.

12. Rivanna Trawlers Unlimited v. Thompson Trawlers, Inc., 840 F.2d 236, 241 (4th Cir. 1988); see also Marine Bank 551, 556, which states that Congress did not "intend to provide a broad federal remedy for all fraud."

13. SEC v. Joiner, 320 U.S. 344, 355 (1943).

14. Id.

15. Id. at 351.

not called by its standard name.[16] Regardless, the legal terminology describing the financial instrument is not determinative of whether it is considered a security.[17] A financial instrument may be a security if, under its terms, or through the course of business, its character is established as "any interest or instrument commonly known as a security."[18] In determining whether a particular financial instrument is a security, the focus is on the substance of the transaction, and an emphasis is placed on the economic reality.[19]

1. Stocks A financial instrument does not become a "security" simply by being called one.[20] For example, even though the statutory definition includes "any . . . stock," the "stock" purchased by tenants of a low-income cooperative housing project that gave them the right to lease a state subsidized and supervised apartment was found not to be a security because the court focused on the economic reality of the transaction and substance triumphed over form.[21] The sole purpose of the "stock" was to enable the purchaser to obtain an apartment—the shares were explicitly tied to the apartment, they were not transferable, did not possess any voting rights, and only descended to a surviving spouse. Moreover, upon termination of occupancy, a tenant could only resell the shares to the managing company at the initial selling price.[22] It is the economic reality, not the label attached to the financial instrument, which determines whether it falls within the reach of the federal securities laws.[23] Purchasers intending to acquire a residential apartment in a state-subsidized housing project do not believe they are purchasing securities simply because the transaction instrument is called a "stock."[24]

The economic reality of the transaction is determinative, but it is not necessary to conduct a case-by-case analysis of every financial instrument.[25] Some instruments, like stock, are investments by their nature and are securities if they have the normal characteristics associated with stock.[26] "Stock" has a limited meaning and refers to a narrow set of instruments with a common name

---

16. United Housing Foundation v. Forman, 421 U.S. 837, 850 (1975).

17. Joiner, 320 U.S. at 351. *See also* Nat'l Bank of Yugoslavia v. Drexel Burnham Lambert, Inc., 768 F.Supp. 1010, 1015 (S.D.N.Y. 1991).

18. Joiner, 320 U.S. at 351.

19. *See* Tcherepnin 389 U.S. 332, 336. As one would assume, all financial instruments are analyzed as they existed at the time of the original agreement. *See* El Khadem v. Equity Securities Corp., 494 F.2d 1224, 1228 (9th Cir. 1974).

20. Robinson v. Glynn, 349 F.3d 166, 172 (4th Cir. 2003).

21. United Housing Foundation v. Forman, 421 U.S. 837, 848 (1975).

22. *Id.* at 842.

23. Robinson, 349 F.3d at 172.

24. United Housing Foundation, 421 U.S. at 851.

25. Reves, 494 U.S. 56, 62 (1990).

26. Reves, 494 U.S. at 62.

and common characteristics.[27] The traditional common features of stock are (1) the right to receive dividends upon an apportionment of profits, (2) negotiability, (3) the ability to be hypothecated or pledged, (4) the conferring of voting rights in proportion to the stock owned, and (5) the capacity for value appreciation.[28] For example, purchasers of all the outstanding stock of a lumber business in a privately negotiated transaction were entitled to bring a federal securities claim.[29] It did not matter that the purchasers intended to purchase the whole business and operate it themselves.[30] The financial instrument was called "stock," it plainly fell within the statutory definition, and there was no need to analyze the economic reality to determine if the Securities Acts should apply.[31] Stock, providing it has the normal characteristics of stock, is *per se* a security regardless of the manner and transaction in which it is used.[32] Indeed, stock is viewed in a category by itself when interpreting the scope of a security under the Securities Acts.[33] For example, a note that is a unique agreement negotiated on a one-to-one basis will not be a security; however, a paradigm security (like those on the level of stock) can be offered to only one person and still be a security.[34]

The plain language of the statute expressly covers instruments that bear both the name "stock" and possess all of its normal characteristics because such instruments represent to people the paradigm of a security which obtains the full protection of the Securities Acts.[35] Although the name given to a financial instrument is not dispositive, it is relevant where the traditional name "stock" justifiably leads the purchaser to conclude that he is purchasing a security.[36] In a similar vein, warrants are *per se* securities, regardless of the transaction and manner in which they are used.[37] Thus, a purchase warrant on common stock

---

27. Robinson, 349 F.3d at 173.

28. United Housing Foundation, 421 U.S. at 85, which notes that the touchstone of an investment is the reasonable expectation of profits from the efforts of others; therefore, in scenarios where the purchaser is motivated by a desire to use or consume the item, the securities laws will not apply. *See also* Landreth Timber Co. v. Landreth, 471 U.S. 681, 686 n. 2 (1985), which clarifies that these are the usual characteristics of common stock but that various types of preferred stock may have different characteristics and still be covered by the Act.

29. Landreth Timber Co., 471 U.S. at 692, in which the buyers wanted to rescind the purchase because the business was not as profitable as the sellers led them to believe.

30. *Id.* The court applied the Securities Acts where control passed to the purchaser and explicitly rejected the sale of business doctrine that held the securities laws do not apply to the sale of 100% of the stock of a closely held corporation.

31. *Id.* at 690.

32. Bass v. Janney Montgomery Scott, Inc., 210 F.3d 577, 586 (6th Cir. 2000).

33. Landreth Timber Co., 471 U.S. at 694.

34. *See* Bass, 210 F.3d at 585.

35. Landreth Timber Co., 471 U.S. at 693.

36. United Housing Foundation v. Forman, 421 U.S. 837, 850 (1975).

37. Bass, 210 F.3d at 586.

that was part of the consideration for a bridge loan subjected the transaction to the securities laws.[38] The court noted that the parties could have structured the transaction as a straight loan which would not have triggered the securities laws, but once a warrant (with the label warrant and its associated characteristics) is used, that is *per se* a security and the securities laws apply.[39] Options, like warrants, have likewise been held to be *per se* securities.[40] Other courts have suggested that "debentures" and "bonds" are traditional securities, and when they have the associated characteristics, are *per se* securities.[41]

2. Notes While common stock is considered the quintessence of a security and investors may justifiably assume a stock is protected by the Securities Acts, this same assumption may not be made regarding notes, which are used in a wide variety of settings and do not necessarily involve investments.[42] The Supreme Court has adopted a modified version of the "family resemblance" test developed by the Second Circuit to determine whether a note is a security (the "*Reves* test").[43] The *Reves* test starts with the presumption that every note is a security.[44] This presumption is rebuttable by proving a strong resemblance to the family of notes that are not securities.[45] The four factors used to rebut the presumption are:

1. What is the reasonable motivation that prompts a reasonable buyer and seller to enter into the transaction? If the seller's purpose is to raise money for a general business purpose or to finance its investments and the buyer's purpose is primarily for profit, then it is likely a security.[46]

---

38. *Id.* at 581–82.

39. *Id.* at 586.

40. *See* One-O-One Enters., Inc. v. Caruso, 848 F.2d 1283, 1288 (D.C. Cir. 1988).

41. *See* Developer's Mortgage Co. v. TransOhio Sav. Bank, 706 F.Supp. 570, 577 (Dist. Ohio 1989).

42. Reves 494 U.S. 56, 62 explains that a note is not *per se* a security, despite the statutory language "any note"). *See also id.* at 63, where the court rejected the investment versus commercial approach, which distinguishes notes that are securities based on the circumstances surrounding the transaction (i.e., whether they are issued in a commercial or consumer context).

43. Reves, 494 U.S. at 63.

44. *Id. See also id.* n. 3, where the court declined to decide whether that presumption extends to notes with a payout term of less than nine months which appear to be exempt under the literal language of the statute. Many circuits, including the Second Circuit, have not applied the literal language of the nine-month exemption and have limited the nine-month exemption to certain prime-quality commercial paper. *See, e.g.,* Nat'l Bank of Yugoslavia v. Drexel Burnham Lambert, Inc., 768 F.Supp. 1010, 1017 (S.D.N.Y. 1991).

45. Reves, 494 U.S. at 65.

46. However, if the purpose of the note was to facilitate the purchase or sale of a minor asset or consumer good, or for some other commercial or consumer purpose, then it is not likely to be a security. *Id.* at 66.

2. What is the plan of distribution and is it an instrument for which there is common trading for speculation or investment?[47]

3. Whether the reasonable expectations of the investing public are that it is a security, and

4. Whether there exists a factor, such as an alternative regulatory scheme, that significantly reduces the riskiness of the investment and makes the protection of the Securities Acts unnecessary.[48]

The types of notes that are not securities are: notes delivered in consumer financing, notes secured by a home mortgage, short-term notes secured by a lien on a small business or some of its assets, notes evidencing a "character" loan to a bank customer,[49] short-term notes secured by accounts receivable, notes given in connection with loans by a commercial bank for the current operations of a business,[50] or notes that formalize an open-account debt incurred in the ordinary

---

47. This factor is easily satisfied when the notes are offered to a broad segment of the public, but the exact boundaries of this requirement are unclear. For instance, an offering and sale to thirteen customers was held not to be a broad segment of the public. Stoiber v. SEC, 161 F.3d 745, 751 (D.C. Cir. 1998). However, an employee of a broker-dealer firm who sold promissory notes to only six individuals may have sold securities because they were sold to private individuals who needed the protection of the Act. McNabb v. SEC, 298 F.3d 1126, 1132 (9th Cir. 2002). See also Nat'l Bank of Yugoslavia, 768 F.Supp. at 1015, which notes that other courts have held that a distribution to one investor may still cause the instrument to be a security; Resolution Trust Corp. v. Stone, 998 F.2d 1534, 1539 (10th Cir. 1993) holds that notes sold to sophisticated market weighs against finding the existence of common trading. Thus, it appears that both the breadth of the offering and the sophistication of the purchasers are factored into determining whether there was common trading. Cf. Marine Bank v. Weaver, 455 U.S. 551, 559–560 (1982), which explains that Congress intended the securities laws to cover those instruments that are ordinarily considered securities (even in a private transaction) and that the unusual instruments found to be securities involved offerings to a large number of potential investors.

48. Reves, 494 U.S. at 66.

49. Generally, these bank character loans are loans that a bank makes to cement or maintain its commercial relationship with a customer. See McNabb v. SEC, 298 F.3d 1126, 1131 (9th Cir. 2002).

50. These commercial loans are made to allow the borrower to smoothly continue its business operations during periods where cash inflows and outflows do not match up. See id. The reason they are exempted is because normally the bank obtains extensive documentation, scrutinizes the business' operations, and even obtains some control over the operations, thereby reducing the riskiness of the loans and eliminating the need for the protection of the Securities Acts. See, e.g., Nat'l Bank of Yugoslavia, 768 F.Supp. at 1014-15 (citing cases). See also Payable Accounting Corp. v. McKinley, 667 P.2d 15, 20 (Utah 1983), which explains that commercial loans are usually private transactions between a few individuals while securities are usually open to a general class of investors). In addition, the lender is usually a bank that has substantial lending expertise and has less of a need for protection from fraud than the average individual investor.

course of business (especially if it is collateralized).[51] If the note is not sufficiently similar to one of the nonnote classes, then the same four-factor test is applied to decide if a new class of nonnote should be added.[52] None of the four factors are dispositive; rather, they are considered as a whole.[53]

For example, a Farmers Co-Op sold promissory notes that were payable on demand of the holder in order to raise money for its general business operations.[54] The notes were offered both to members and nonmembers, were marketed as an "Investment Program," were supposedly backed by the assets of the Farmers Co-Op (but in reality were uncollateralized and uninsured), and paid a variable interest rate that was above the prevalent local interest rate.[55] After the bankruptcy of the Farmers Co-Op, the note holders sued under the securities laws.[56] Applying the *Reves* test, the court found that the promissory demand notes were securities because they did not strongly resemble any of the nonnote classes and the four factors did not suggest the demand notes should be a new category of nonnotes.[57] The Farmers Co-Op sold the notes for its general business purposes and the purchasers bought them to earn a profit at higher interest rates (indeed, that rate was constantly revised to keep it above the prevalent local interest rate), which signifies an investment rather than a commercial or consumer transaction.[58] Additionally, the plan of distribution was to a broad segment of the public; it was unnecessary for the notes to be traded on an exchange in order for them to be considered securities.[59] The public's reasonable perception was that the note constituted an investment and it was thus advertised to the public.[60] Lastly, no risk-reducing factor was present.[61]

In another case, a company that factored medical accounts receivable offered "investment agreements" which the court found to be notes.[62] The "investment

---

51. Reves, 494 U.S. at 65. It is important to realize that no labels are dispositive and the court looks at the economic realities to see if it fits into one of the nonnote categories. SEC v. Wallenbrock, 313 F.3d 532, 538 (9th Cir. 2002).

52. *Id.* at 67. Although this is technically a two-step analysis (i.e., whether it strongly resembles a non-note category and whether a new category should be added), both steps involve the same four-factor test and it is essentially a single inquiry. *See* SEC v. Wallenbrock, 313 F.3d 532, 537 (9th Cir. 2002).

53. *See, e.g.,* SEC v. Wallenbrock, 313 F.3d 532, 537 (9th Cir. 2002).

54. Reves 494 U.S. 56, 58 (1990).

55. *Id.* at 58–59.

56. *Id.* at 59.

57. *Id.* at 67.

58. *Id.* at 67–68.

59. *Id.* at 68.

60. *Id.*

61. *Id.* at 69.

62. SEC v. Current Financial Services, 100 F.Supp.2d 1, 4–5 (D.D.C. 2000). The company purchased the discounted receivables from various health care providers and planned on collecting all or most of the face value. *See id.* at 3. In order to raise capital, the company

agreements" were offered to the public to raise capital to finance the purchase of the accounts receivable (which was its general business purpose), the purchasers earned profits in the form of high interest rates, the reasonable expectation was that they were securities, and there was no risk-reducing factor present.[63]

In a case involving privately negotiated promissory notes which provided operating capital for the debtor to continue his business operations, the court applied the *Reves* test and found they were not securities.[64] There were two factors in favor of a finding that the notes were securities: the notes were investments in a business venture rather than commercial or consumer transactions, and the notes were uncollateralized and uninsured. Two factors argued against the finding that the notes were securities: there was no offering to a broad segment of the public, and the reasonable expectation was that they were only promissory notes and not securities.[65] Based largely on the fact that there was no plan of distribution to a broad segment of the public, the court found the promissory notes not to be securities.[66]

Similarly, the Ohio Supreme Court adopted the *Reves* test for state law matters and held that an unconditional promissory note to provide funds for a sports arena with an obligation to pay a specified sum on a certain date was a security.[67] Interestingly, the first *Reves* factor was inconclusive because the motivations of the parties were different—the lender entered into the transactions as an investment, while the borrower entered into it as a commercial transaction.[68] Regarding the

---

entered into "investment agreements" with public investors, which were essentially debt securities with a high interest rate. There were also separate companies formed with the sole purpose of purchasing the original company's debt and then issuing its own debt to the public.

63. *Id.* at 5. *See also* Majors v. S.C. Securities Comm'n, 644 S.E.2d 710, 712 (S.C. 2007), which holds that an investment contract existed where a company entered into agency contracts with investors to purchase tax lien certificates (which the company reasonably believed would not be redeemed), the company did all the work and exercised full control, and the company and investors split the profits when the tax lien certificates were not redeemed; Payable Accounting Corp. v. McKinley, 667 P.2d 15, 16–17 (Utah 1983), which holds that an investment contract existed where investors contributed funds to the company, the funds were used to run its business, the investors received profits in the form of a fixed monthly payment, and the profits were derived from the company's managerial skills. Thus a company must be wary of raising funds for its general business purposes through issuing notes and through contractual agreements.

64. LeBrun v. Kuswa, 24 F.Supp.2d 641, 642 (D. La. 1998).

65. *Id.* at 647–49.

66. *Id.* at 649. *See also* Bass v. Janney Montgomery Scott, Inc., 210 F.3d 577, 585–86 (6th Cir. 2000), which applies the *Reves* test and finds that a bridge loan is not a security because it was a unique privately negotiated transaction (no plan of distribution) and there was significant collateral (risk-reducing factor is present).

67. Perrysburg Twp. v. City of Rossford, 814 N.E.2d 44, 47–49 (Ohio 2004).

68. *Id.* at 50. *See also* Bass, 210 F.3d at 585, which explains that the first *Reves* factor does not help decide whether it is a security if on one side of the transaction the motivation is

second *Reves* factor, there was a private agreement between two sophisticated parties and no evidence of common trading, which implied the note should not be a security.[69] However, the promissory notes were called investments, the reasonable public would have believed they were securities, and there was no alternative risk-reducing regulatory scheme present. Therefore, the presumption that a note is a security held.

The fourth factor of the *Reves* test is whether there exists a factor, such as an alternative regulatory scheme, which significantly reduces the risk of the financial instrument.[70] The mere existence of an alternative regulatory scheme is not sufficient, however; it must be a scheme that is quite comprehensive and significantly reduces the risk of the financial instrument, thereby making it unnecessary to have the protections of the securities laws.[71] For example, certificates of deposit ("CDs") offering a fixed rate of return were insured by the Federal Deposit Insurance Corporation and subjected to the comprehensive regulations of the banking system; therefore, the notes were not securities because the comprehensive regulatory and insurance schemes already in place eliminated the risk of loss to the investor.[72] Likewise, pension plans are already federally regulated by ERISA and such existing comprehensive regulation weighs against extending the Securities Acts to cover pension plans.[73]

Reinsurance contracts were also found not to be securities because they are subject to the comprehensive regulation of the insurance laws.[74] However, a federal regulatory scheme may be required to satisfy the risk-reducing factor of the *Reves* test; the presence of state law relief may be insufficient.[75] Collateral, such as a note secured by a mortgage on the property, significantly weighs against the

---

for a typical commercial loan (like raising interim funds for a new enterprise) and on the other side of the transaction the motivation is for an investment (i.e., to make a profit).

69. Perrysburg Twp., 814 N.E.2d at 50.

70. This factor is important because the foremost threat to the investor is to lose his investment, but the factor is still not dispositive because many commercial transactions are extremely risky and are not governed by the securities laws.

71. *See* SEC v. Wallenbrock, 313 F.3d 532, 540 (9th Cir. 2002); *accord* LeBrun v. Kuswa, 24 F.Supp.2d 641, 649 (D. La. 1998), which requires a federal regulatory scheme that affords investors with a sufficient level of protection.

72. Marine Bank v. Weaver, 455 U.S. 551, 557–58 (1982). The CD was different from long-term debt because the investors were "abundantly protected under the federal banking laws." *Id.* at 559.

73. Int'l Brotherhood of Teamsters, Chauffeurs, Warehousemen & Helpers of America v. Daniel, 439 U.S. 551, 569–570 (1982).

74. *See* American Mut. Reinsurance Co. v. Calvert Fire Ins. Co., 367 N.E.2d 104 (Ill. App. 1977).

75. *See, e.g.*, LeBrun v. Kuswa, 24 F.Supp.2d 641, 649 (D. La 1998). *See also* Manns v. Skolnik, 666 N.E.2d 1236, 1246 (Ind. 1996), which specifically requires another federal regulatory scheme, despite the existence of a state civil remedy; SEC v. Wallenbrock, 313 F.3d 532, 540 (9th Cir. 2002) comments that a "patchwork of state regulation" cannot displace the federal regime).

note being found to be a security because the collateral is a risk-reducing factor.[76] The securing of an investment by collateral does not automatically remove the investment from regulation under the securities laws, but if an instrument is not clearly a security then the presence of collateral can be a probative factor because the collateral may be seized in case of default.[77] Lastly, a note that promises a fixed rate or is short term may have a reduced risk, but the note may still be a security if it is not afforded protection comparable to the safeguards of the securities laws.[78]

The case of *SEC v. Wallenbrock*[79] illustrates the presence of all four *Reves* factors in a transaction. A company issued promissory notes that supposedly were secured by accounts receivable of Malaysian latex glove manufacturers. The goal of the company was to use its cash and the funds raised from the sale of the promissory notes to purchase the accounts receivable at a discount.[80] Ostensibly the company and the holders of the promissory notes would hold equal ownership of the receivables and split the profits upon collection of the full amount from the buyers. In fact, the entire transaction was a high-stakes pyramid scheme and the funds from the promissory notes went to pay off earlier investors or to finance other risky start-up companies.[81] The Ninth Circuit held that the promissory notes were securities because the lenders/investors invested to earn a profit, they provided the company with cash for its general business enterprise, the notes were offered to a broad segment of the public (there were over 1,000 investors and the company even wanted to broaden its marketing plan), a reasonable investor would think this was an investment, and there was no risk-reducing factor present.[82]

---

76. *See* Eagle Trim, Inc. v. Eagle-Picher Indus., Inc., 205 F.Supp.2d 746, 753 (D. Mich. 2002); although the mortgage did not cover the full amount claimed, the court still considered it to satisfy the fourth factor because it did reduce the overall risk of the investment; Bass v. Janney Montgomery Scott, Inc., 210 F.3d 577, 585 (6th Cir. 2000), in which the existence of collateral is significant as a risk-reducing factor; SEC v. Wallenbrock, 313 F.3d 532, 539 (9th Cir. 2002), in which collateral does mitigate the risk of the investment, but where the collateral is a fiction it cannot be a risk-reducing factor.

77. *See* State v. Crofters, 525 F.Supp 1133, 1137 (S.D. Ohio 1981)

78. *See* Nat'l Bank of Yugoslavia v. Drexel Burnham Lambert, Inc., 768 F.Supp. 1010, 1015–16 (S.D.N.Y. 1991), which notes that short-term instruments may still contain substantial risk and that many notes undoubtedly covered by the Securities Acts have fixed rates. *See also* SEC v. Wallenbrock, 313 F.3d 532, 539–40 (9th Cir. 2002), which explains possible risks, such as default because of a lack of funds, which exist under fixed rate instruments also).

79. 313 F.3d 532 (9th Cir. 2002).

80. *Id.* at 535.

81. *Id.* at 536.

82. *Id.* at 538–39. Note that the promissory notes here seem to fall into one of the non-security categories, "short-term notes secured by a lien on a small business or some of its assets," yet the court found them to be securities because the collateral promises were

3. Investment Contracts—The *Howey* Test The fundamental purpose of the Securities Acts is to eliminate serious abuses in the financial markets.[83] Congress enacted broad statutes to cover the "virtually limitless scope of human ingenuity, especially in the creation of 'countless and variable schemes devised by those who seek the use of the money of others on the promise of profits.'"[84] Congress intended catch-all phrases like "investment contracts" to encompass the wide range of novel and unusual instruments created by individuals where the economic realities of the transaction lend themselves to the application of the federal securities laws.[85] "Nevertheless, we do not believe every conceivable arrangement that would fit a dictionary definition of an investment contract was intended to be included within the statutory definition of a security."[86]

Whether a particular financial instrument constitutes an "investment contract," and therefore also a security, is determined using the "*Howey* test."[87] The *Howey* test is a tripartite test:[88] (1) the investment of money, (2) in a common enterprise, and (3) with an expectation of profits to be derived solely from the

---

largely a fiction. However, one could question whether the test for a security should be applied to the financial instrument that was promised (what the parties thought the transaction involved) or to the financial instrument that was the reality of the transaction. *See also* SEC v. Pickney, 923 F.Supp 76, 80–81 (E.D. N.C. 1996), which holds that the analysis of whether a financial instrument is a security is dependent on the reality of the investment, and not on the promised instrument, if the promises are found to be false.

83. Reves 494 U.S. 56, 60–61.

84. *Id.*, quoting SEC v. W. J. Howey Co., 328 U.S. 293, 299 (1946).

85. Robinson v. Glynn, 349 F.3d 166, 172–173 (4th Cir. 2003).

86. Milnarik v. M-S Commodities, Inc., 457 F.2d 274, 275–76 (7th Cir. 1972).

87. SEC v. W.J. Howey Co., 328 U.S. 293 (1946). The *Howey* test is both necessary and sufficient to determine if a financial instrument is an investment contract. *See* Developer's Mortgage Co. v. TransOhio Sav. Bank, 706 F.Supp. 570, 575–76 (S.D. Ohio 1989).

88. Some courts have interpreted Landreth Timber Co. v. Landreth, 471 U.S. 681 (1985), as requiring an initial two-part analysis for an investment contract: whether a security has (1) a title traditionally associated with securities and (2) its typical associated characteristics; if not, then the court should apply the *Howey* test which would be dispositive. *See, e.g.,* Developer's Mortgage Co. v. TransOhio Sav. Bank, 706 F.Supp. 570, 577 (Dist. Ohio 1989); All Seasons Resorts, Inc. v. Abrams, 68 N.Y.2d 81, 88 (N.Y. 1986) (applying federal securities law to state blue sky laws). However, this analysis appears to be wrong. The *Landreth* test is reserved for traditional securities like stock. *See supra* notes 23–34 and accompanying text. Investment contracts are determined using the *Howey* test exclusively. *See infra* notes 98–166 and accompanying text, which cites many cases applying the *Howey* test; however, no case holds an investment contract that may be *per se* a security and those courts do not invoke the *Landreth* test. Moreover, it is possible that the two courts cited above required a two-part analysis only because the Supreme Court had not yet created the *Reves* test (*see supra* notes 41–46 and accompanying text). In the post-*Reves* world, it is clear the *Howey* test is used for investment contracts, the *Reves* test is used for notes, and the *Landreth* test is used only for traditional securities like stocks.

efforts of others (a promoter or other third party).[89] In compliance with the spirit of the securities laws, the *Howey* test must be applied in light of the economic reality of the transaction.[90]

In *Howey*, a Florida citrus company sold land interests in citrus groves that were coupled with management service contracts, pursuant to which the promoters retained complete control over the land, cultivated and marketed the citrus crops, and allocated net profits to the purchasers. The company used the proceeds from the sales to finance its citrus growing operation.[91] The court held this was an investment contract because the investors provided the investment capital, the sellers managed and controlled the enterprise for the benefit of all the investors, and the investors' expectation was that they would receive the profits (as evidenced by the fact the investors had a claim only for their percentage of the net profits and not to the actual produce).[92] The court explained that the purchasers were attracted solely by the opportunity for profits and the land sales were merely a "convenient method" by which to apportion profits.[93]

The Court had previously held that the sales of leasehold rights were investment contracts where the purchasers obtained leasehold rights and also shares in the discovery value of well-drilling explorations for oil that were currently being conducted by the promoters, which was the real economic enterprise being offered for investment.[94] The court found it was not a mere sale of a leasehold; rather the exploration enterprise was woven into the leasehold in an economic and legal sense.[95]

The *Howey* test embodies a flexible principle that is capable of adaptation to meet the virtually limitless scope of human ingenuity, especially in the creation of "countless and variable schemes devised by those who seek the use of the money of others on the promise of profits."[96] To demonstrate the flexibility of the *Howey* test, it has been applied to the purchase of a life partnership in an

---

89. Howey, 328 U.S. at 298–99. When analyzing these factors, the court considers both the actual agreement between the parties and any promotional materials. *See, e.g.,* SEC v. Professional Assoc., 731 F.2d 349, 354 (6th Cir. 1984); Hocking v. Dubois, 885 F.2d 1449, 1457 (9th Cir. 1989), in which the court must examine all the representations of the promoter, such as the promotional materials, merchandising approaches, oral assurances, and contractual arrangements.

90. United Housing Foundation, Inc. v. Forman, 421 U.S. 837, 851–52 (1975).

91. Howey, 328 U.S. at 295–97.

92. *Id.* at 300–301.

93. *Id.* at 300.

94. SEC. v. Joiner Corp., 320 U.S. 344, 348–49 (1943).

95. *Id.* at 349 (the land itself was purely an incidental consideration in the transaction; the financial instruments sold contained all the evils inherent in the securities transactions that the Securities Acts sought to end).

96. Howey, 328 U.S. at 299.

evangelical community,[97] a cattle-feeding and consulting agreement,[98] and a chinchilla breeding and resale agreement.[99]

The first prong of the *Howey* test requires the investment of money, which means only that the investor must commit his assets to the enterprise in such a manner that the assets are subject to a monetary loss.[100] This does not mean the investors must actually incur the monetary loss; it is sufficient that they were subject to the risk of monetary loss.[101]

The second prong of the *Howey* test requires an investment in a common enterprise. There is broad disagreement over what degree of commonality is required.[102] One approach requires horizontal commonality, meaning the fortunes of each investor in the pool of investors must be tied to the success of the overall venture.[103] The other approach, vertical commonality, requires only a tying of fortunes between the investor and the promoter, as in a one-on-one arrangement between a lender and a customer.[104] Horizontal commonality focuses on the relationship between multiple investors; vertical commonality focuses on the relationship between the promoter and the individual investor.[105] Some circuits have adopted the narrower horizontal commonality requirement because the vertical commonality approach effectively excises the common enterprise requirement; it does not require a link between multiple investors and allows, for example, the relationship between a stockbroker and customer in a discretionary trading account[106] to satisfy the common enterprise

---

97. Teague v. Bakker, 35 F.3d 978, 981, 990 (4th Cir. 1994).

98. Long v. Shultz Cattle Co., 881 F.2d 129, 132 (5th Cir. 1989).

99. Miller v. Central Chinchilla Group, 494 F.2d 414, 415, 418 (8th Cir. 1974). For a listing of varied transactions that were held to be investment contracts, *see* SEC v. Glenn W. Turner Enters., Inc., 474 F.2d 476, 481 n. 6 (9th Cir. 1973) (citing cases).

100. *See* SEC v. Rubera, 350 F.3d 1084, 1090 (9th Cir. 2003); *accord* SEC v. Pickney, 923 F.Supp 76, 80 (E.D. N.C. 1996); SEC v. The International Mining Exchange, Inc., 515 F.Supp 1062, 1067 (D. Colo. 1981).

101. Rubera, 350 F.3d at 1090.

102. *See, e.g.*, SEC v. SG LTD., 265 F.3d 42, 49–50 (1st Cir. 2001) (citing cases); Majors v. S.C. Securities Comm'n, 644 S.E.2d 710, 716–17 (S.C. 2007) (citing cases).

103. Deckebach v. La Vida Charters, Inc. of Florida, 867 F.2d 278, 282 (6th Cir. 1989). Another court explained horizontal commonality as the pooling of interest and funds among the investors only. Majors v. S.C. Securities Comm'n, 644 S.E.2d 710, 716 (S.C. 2007).

104. Deckebach, 867 F.2d at 282. Another court explained vertical commonality as the pooling of interests between the promoter and the investor only. *See* Majors, 644 S.E.2d at 716.

105. SEC v. Pickney, 923 F.Supp. 76, 80–81 (E.D. N.C. 1996). It is important to realize that horizontal commonality would exclude from the securities laws a case of multiple, parallel frauds between investors and the promoter.

106. *See* Milnarik v. M-S Commodities, Inc. 457 F.2d 274 (7th Cir. 1972), which holds that a broker who entered into discretionary trading arrangements with many customers

requirement.[107] Notably, the Second Circuit has adopted a strict[108] vertical commonality requirement because it has reasoned that a broad vertical commonality renders the third prong of *Howey* superfluous: the "common enterprise and profits derived from the efforts of others" requirements would be merged into a single inquiry, that is, whether the success of the enterprise collectively is dependent on the promoter's expertise.[109]

The case of *Deckebach v. La Vida Charters, Inc. of Florida*[110] illustrates the difference in the commonality level required. In *Deckebach*, investors purchased a yacht and entered into a management service agreement which gave the management company significant day-to-day control over the yacht.[111] The management company had a number of yachts that it managed together, but the income generated from each yacht was segregated and applied to its own maintenance and expenses.[112] There was no pooling of funds among the various yacht owners.[113] The court noted that only vertical commonality was satisfied and not horizontal commonality, because there was no pooling of funds, even though the company attempted to uniformly allocate income among all the yacht owners through sequential chartering, and some expenses were divided pro rata.[114] The purchasers were essentially hiring an independent contractor to perform management services and to produce rental income.[115]

The third prong of the *Howey* test appears to require investors to expect profits "solely" from the efforts of others; however the courts generally do not

---

had not created investment contracts because the success or failure of one account had no effect on the other accounts and was lacking commonality.

107. Deckebach, 867 F.2d at 281 notes that the vertical approach would effectively mean the adoption of an expansive "risk capital" approach. *See also* SEC v. Lauer, 52 F.3d 667, 670 (7th Cir. 1995) (adopting horizontal commonality); Salcer v. Merrill Lynch, Pierce, Fenner & Smith, Inc., 682 F.2d 459, 460 (3d Cir. 1982) (adopting horizontal commonality).

108. Broad vertical commonality only requires a showing that all the investors' fortunes are dependent on the expertise and efforts of the promoter. Pickney, 923 F.Supp. at 81. Strict vertical commonality requires that the investor's profits are directly related to the promoter's profits (the fortunes of the investor and promoter are linked). *Id.* at 80–81.

109. Revak v. SEC Realty Corp., 18 F.3d 81, 87–88 (2d Cir. 1994).

110. 867 F.2d 278 (6th Cir. 1989).

111. *Id.* at 279. Note that the agreement was structured as a purchase rather than as an investment of funds in a charter business, which would have triggered the securities laws.

112. *Id.* at 280.

113. *Id.*

114. *Id.* at 282.

115. *Id.* at 283. The court did acknowledge that a de facto "tie-in" of the management services with the purchase of the yachts would constitute an investment contract (similar to the situation in *Howey*).

interpret "solely" literally[116] because the Supreme Court has omitted the word "solely" from its restatements of the *Howey* test, and a literal compliance would exclude from the protection of the securities laws any agreement that involved the slightest efforts of the investors.[117] A number of courts have phrased the question as whether the efforts of the promoter are the undeniably significant ones and are the essential managerial efforts that affect the failure or success of the enterprise.[118] Moreover, one court has held that even if the investors' own efforts could produce limited profits from certain activities, but the profit-generating business that is essential to the business' success must come from the efforts of others, then it is an investment contract.[119]

The "expectation of profits" required by the *Howey* test is satisfied by the returns that investors seek on their investments, such as dividends, other periodic payments, or the increased value of their original investment.[120] Profits may be capital appreciation from the development of the initial investment or from earnings contingent on the profits earned from the investors' funds.[121] Furthermore, profits from an investment may also come in the form of tax benefits.[122] An example that did not satisfy "expectation of profits" was a company that marketed memberships in outdoor resort campgrounds for the personal enjoyment of the members; there were significant restrictions on the transferability of the memberships, and the members were not entitled to share in any

---

116. *See, e.g.,* Robinson 349 F.3d 166, 170, which notes that no federal circuit has required "solely"; Bailey v. J.W.K. Prop., Inc., 904 F.2d 918, 920 (4th Cir. 1990): "a program requiring some effort from the investor may still constitute an 'investment contract,' but the most essential functions or duties must be performed by others and not the investor."

117. *See id. See also* Long v. Shultz Cattle Co., Inc., 881 F.2d 129, 133 (5th Cir. 1989) (citing cases).

118. *See, e.g.,* SEC v. Rubera, 350 F.3d 1084, 1091–92 (9th Cir. 2003), which follows the modification of "solely" as construed in SEC v. Glenn W. Turner Enterprises, 474 F.2d 476 (9th Cir. 1973); *accord* Majors v. S.C. Securities Commission, 644 S.E.2d 710, 718 (S.C. 2007).

119. Ball v. Volken, 741 P.2d 958, 959–60 (Utah 1987). A purchaser of a district license agreement was allowed to sell franchises for area sales offices, but the purchaser was not allowed to make sales directly to the public (which constituted the bulk of his potential profits) and had to rely on the seller to generate the sales to the public.

120. SEC v. Edwards, 540 U.S. 389, 394 (2004).

121. SEC v. Infinity Group Co., 212 F.3d 180, 189 (3d Cir. 2000); *accord* SEC v. Rubera, 350 F.3d 1084, 1093 (9th Cir. 2003).

122. *See, e.g.,* Long v. Shultz Cattle Co., Inc., 881 F.2d 129, at 132 n.2 (5th Cir. 1989) (citing cases). *See also* SEC v. The Int'l Mining Exch., Inc., 515 F.Supp. 1062, 1068–69 (D.Colo. 1981), which notes that a 500% tax write-off was the linchpin of the investment program and that tax consequences may be the sole inducement to enter into an investment so it satisfies "expectation of profits."

gain of the company's business.[123] This arrangement did not constitute an investment contract because there was no potential for financial gain.[124]

Regarding expectation of profits, there is no difference between promises of fixed returns or of variable returns because that would allow any promoter to evade the securities laws by promising a fixed rate of return.[125] "The definition of security does not turn on whether the investor receives a variable or fixed rate of return."[126] In one fixed-return case, investors loaned money to a corporation in exchange for a high fixed interest rate and the return of the principal after three years.[127] The court found it was an investment contract because the investors risked losing all of their investments if the company was not profitable.[128] Other examples of fixed-return investments that were considered investment contracts are: an investment that promised guaranteed profit of 30% per year with no chance of loss,[129] a sale and lease-back arrangement where investors received a fixed return of 2% each month for ten years,[130] and time deposits made for investment purposes in exchange for a fixed rate of interest.[131] Indeed, investments promising fixed returns (e.g., those marketed as a low-risk, guaranteed return) often are especially attractive to individuals who are particularly vulnerable to investment fraud, such as the elderly and less sophisticated investors.[132]

In another case, a company that offered a bonus to open an account was found not to have created an investment contract, even though there was a risk of nonpayment of the bonus (i.e., the risk of insolvency), because the expectation of profits from the efforts of others means the successful investment of the investors' funds and is not just based on the solvency of a company.[133] Similarly, a company that offered silver bars for sale, guaranteed their purity,

---

123. *See* All Seasons Resorts, Inc. v. Abrams, 68 N.Y.2d 81, 85–86 (NY 1986).

124. *Id.* at 92.

125. SEC v. Edwards, 540 U.S. 389, 394–95 (2004). *See also* Payable Accounting Corp. v. McKinley, 667 P.2d 15, 19 (Utah 1983) (citing cases where a promise for a fixed return was an investment contract).

126. SEC v. Infinity Group Co., 212 F.3d 180, 189 (3d Cir. 2000).

127. Suave v. K.C., Inc., 591 P.2d 1207, 1208 (Wash. 1979).

128. *Id.* at 1210 (Wash. 1979), which applies the *Howey* test for state securities law. The court adopted the reasoning of the Ninth Circuit in *El Khadem v. Equity Securities Corp.*, 494 F.2d 1224 (9th Cir. 1974), that even if only the risk of loss is dependent on the promoter's management skills and the gain is fixed, that is sufficient for the expectation of profits requirement of the *Howey* test. The court reasoned that a risk of loss or a possible gain is the difference between a corporate bond and a common stock, yet both are considered securities. *Id.* at 1229.

129. *See* SEC v. Universal Serv. Assn., 106 F.2d 232, 234, 237 (7th Cir. 1939)

130. *See* SEC v. Amer. Trailer Rentals Co., 379 U.S. 594, 598 (1965).

131. *See* Nat'l Bank of Yugoslavia v. Drexel Burnham Lambert, Inc., 768 F.Supp. 1010, 1016 (S.D.N.Y. 1991).

132. SEC v. Edwards, 540 U.S. 389, 394 (2004).

133. *See* Reiswig v. Dep't of Corp. for State of California, 144 Cal. App. 327, 339 (2006).

offered free storage for one year, agreed to delivery upon full payment, and represented that it would buy back the silver bars at any time at the current spot market price of silver was not offering an investment contract because the investors profits depended on the fluctuations of the market price of silver and not on the company's managerial expertise or efforts.[134] The insolvency risk did not create an investment contract because the solvency of a company is a risk that any buyer takes when he pays in advance expecting delivery at a later date, and the viability of a company is not enough to create an investment contract.[135]

a. *Control and Splitting the Transaction* The degree of control exercised by an investor may determine whether the transaction is found to constitute an investment contract. In one case,[136] an investor in a limited liability company ("LLC") sued the LLC and its chairman for misrepresentations made to convince the investor to purchase a membership interest in the LLC. The court held there was no investment contract because "profits derived solely from the efforts of others" means the investor (whether as a result of the investment agreement or from the factual circumstances) is unable to exercise meaningful control over his investment. The investor in the LLC was an active and knowledgeable investor and had negotiated for a level of control (regarding incurring additional indebtedness, diluting shares, etc.) that was antithetical to the passive investor required for an investment contract. The managerial control was sufficient to prevent the transaction from being an investment contract, even though the investor lacked the technical knowledge to understand the business and also lacked decisive control over major decisions, because the investor had the type of influence that provided access to information and protection against a dependency on others.[137] Thus, this was an ordinary commercial venture and it would be an unjustifiable expansion of the securities laws to consider it an investment contract.[138]

In contrast, investors who purchased pay telephones from a corporation and leased them back to the corporation to manage on their behalf in exchange for a

---

134. Noa v. Key Futures, Inc. 638 F.2d 77, 79 (9th Cir. 1980). *See also* Reiswig, *supra*, which holds that the fluctuation of interest rates of CD's was not dependent on the efforts of others.

135. Noa, 638 F.2d at 79.

136. Robinson 349 F.3d 166.

137. A lack of specialized knowledge alone will not create an investment contract; rather a lack of specialized knowledge and a lack of control causing the investors to rely on the efforts of others will create an investment contract, as opposed to the present case where the investor obtained sufficient control over the LLC despite his lack of technical expertise. *See id.* at 172. The investor's expertise must be considered in light of the venture, and generalized business experience does not preclude a finding that the investor lacked the knowledge or ability to exercise meaningful control over the venture. Long v. Shultz Cattle Co., Inc. 881 F.2d 129, 134–35 (5th Cir. 1989)

138. Robinson, 349 F.3d at 168.

monthly payment were considered to have entered into investment contracts.[139] The investors possessed limited contractual rights under the lease, were inactive in the company's operation, were inexperienced in that business, and lacked access to important information.[140] The investors retained minimal control over their investments, and relied on the corporation to provide all the essential managerial functions (such as phone placement, collection, and maintenance). Therefore, those investors were dependent on the efforts of others in a manner that the investor in the LLC was not dependent.[141]

Therefore, the more control the investor retains, the less likely the contract will be a security.[142] Despite contractual terms that appear to retain control for the investor, the court will consider who has discretion over the investment funds and the focus will be on the actual relationship between the parties.[143] If the investor has legal control, then he must prove practical dependence and an inability to exercise meaningful control or find another person to manage his investment.[144]

In a case with similar facts, investors purchased pay telephones from a corporation and simultaneously entered into service agreements whereby the corporation agreed to manage and maintain the pay telephones.[145] The corporation offered various packages with different levels of service and approximately 90% of the investors chose the package with the highest service level (which made themselves passive investors and left operation of the telephones solely in the corporation's control). This constituted an investment contract: the court refused to split the transaction into two distinct transactions (a purchase of assets (the pay telephones) and a service agreement for the telephones, which would remove

---

139. SEC v. ETS Payphones, Inc., 408 F.3d 727, 732 (11th Cir. 2005).

140. SEC v. ETS Payphones, Inc. 300 F.3d 1281, 1282 (11th Cir. 2002).

141. *See* Robinson, *supra* note 134, 349 F.3d at 175 n.4.

142. Similarly, a general partnership is typically not an investment contract because the partners have sufficient power to protect their own interests and do not need the protection of the securities laws. *See* SEC v. Profess'l Assoc., 731 F.2d 349, 356 (6th Cir. 1984). In addition, the profits in a general partnership require each partner's efforts and are not dependent on the efforts of others.

143. *See* SEC v. ETS Payphones, Inc., 408 F.3d 727, 732–33 (11th Cir. 2005), which calls the control retained by investors under contractual terms "illusory" and finds that an investment contract existed.

144. Hocking v. Dubois, 885 F.2d 1449, 1460 (9th Cir. 1989). *See also* Long v. Shultz Cattle Co., Inc. 881 F.2d 129, 131 (5th Cir. 1989), which holds that theoretical control does not suffice if the investors did not exercise that power of control and instead relied on the promoters to make the management decisions.

145. SEC v. Rubera, 350 F.3d 1084, 1087 (9th Cir. 2003). The profit split was 70% for the corporation and 30% for the investor; however, the corporation agreed to reduce its share to ensure the investors would receive a base amount equaling a 14% annualized return.

it from the securities laws) because they were marketed as one package.[146] The court pointed out that *Howey* also involved an investment scheme which could have been characterized as a purchase of land and a management service agreement, but the Supreme Court refused to separate the transactions because the investors were attracted solely by the returns on their investments and the transaction satisfied the requirements for an investment contract.

Likewise, an investment package that offered a contract to purchase a condominium along with a service agreement (the promoter would maintain and rent out the condominium) was held to be an investment contract and the two transactions were not separated.[147] However, the court noted the condominium was offered as a package with the service agreement; it would not be an investment contract if someone already owned a condominium and wanted to purchase a service agreement for the condominium.

b. Prepurchase Efforts The question also arises whether pre-purchase efforts by the promoters can satisfy the "expectation of profits to be derived solely from the efforts of others" prong of the *Howey* test. One court has held viatical settlements[148] contracts purchased from a promoter are not investment contracts because the posttransaction ministerial functions did not affect the investors' profits; therefore, the "expectation of profits" prong was missing since prepurchase efforts by themselves do not satisfy the expectation of profits that arise predominantly from the efforts of others.[149] Other courts have disagreed and held that significant prepurchase activities that ensure the success of the enterprise may satisfy the "expectation of profits" prong.[150] However the prepurchase activities must consist of significant efforts that require the expertise or specialized skill of the promoters in selecting an asset or negotiating its price.[151] For example, the prepurchase activities in viatical settlements were sufficient because they required substantial skills to identify terminally ill patients, select insurance

---

146. *Id.* at 1090–91.

147. Hocking v. Dubois, 885 F.2d 1449, 1458 (9th Cir. 1989).

148. "A viatical settlement is a transaction in which a terminally ill or chronically ill insured ("viator") sells the benefits of his life insurance policy to a third party in return for a lump-sum cash payment equal to a percentage of the policy's face value. Viatical settlement providers purchase the policies from individual viators. Once purchased, these viatical settlement providers typically sell fractionalized interests in these policies to investors." SEC v. Mut. Benefits Corp., 323 F.Supp.2d 1337, 1338 (S.D.Fla. 2004). This appears similar to how mortgage-backed securities and other collaterized debt obligations operate and raises the same concern as to whether their prepurchase activities suffice to create an investment contract.

149. SEC v. Life Partners, Inc. 87 F.3d 536, 548 (D.C. Cir. 1996).

150. SEC v. Mut. Benefits Corp., 408 F.3d 737, 743 (11th Cir. 2005); *accord* SEC v. Eurobond Exch., Ltd. 13 F.3d 1334 (9th Cir. 1994).

151. Mutual Benefits Corp., 408 F.3d at 744.

policies, negotiate and pay premiums, and perform the critical life expectancy evaluations.[152]

In another case which further illustrates the significant prepurchase activities required, a company offered yields on certificates of deposit (CDs) greater than any other bank, but the investor had to first personally meet a company representative and the offer was limited to a $5,000 investment.[153] The goal was to entice customers and then convince them to purchase annuities from the company. If the customer insisted on purchasing the CD, the company provided a list of institutions offering the current highest CD yields that were FDIC-insured and told the customer to apply for a CD directly to one of the institutions on the list. The company would then pay the customer the difference between the yield advertised by the company and the yield paid by the institution. The difference was paid in the form of a bonus check that was issued within seven days after the customer submitted proof that he had opened a CD with one of the institutions. In this case the bonus checks were not paid from the profits earned from investor funds because the bonus checks were paid by the company (as an inducement to hear its sales pitch for the annuities) and the profits from investor funds were earned by the institution who offered the CD.[154] The passive task of compiling the daily list of institutions paying the highest CD rates was not a significant prepurchase effort nor was the profit dependent on the company's expertise or efforts; rather, it was dependent on the fluctuation in interest rates for CDs.[155]

Although the *Howey* test constitutes a flexible approach to determining what is a security, it is not without limitations.[156] As in the case of the *Reves* test,[157] the existence of a comprehensive alternative federal regulatory scheme that obviates the need for the protection of the federal securities laws will weigh against creating an investment contract.

---

152. *Id.* at 744–45.

153. Reiswig v. Dep't of Corp. for State of California, 144 Cal. App. 327, 332 (2006).

154. *Id.* at 338–39. The court distinguished this case from a seemingly factually similar case, *Safeway Portland Employees' Fed. Credit Union v. C.H. Wagner & Co., Inc.*, 501 F.2d 1120 (9th Cir. 1974), because in that case the investors' profit was dependent on the success of the broker (who solicited both the CD purchasers and the borrowers willing to pay the above market rates), the investment was not guaranteed by any bank, and the CD funds were fully integrated into the enterprise.

155. *Id.* at 341. *See also* Noa v. Key Futures, Inc. 638 F.2d 77, 79 (9th Cir. 1980), which holds that the fluctuation of the market price of silver is not dependent on the efforts of others.

156. Payable Accounting Corp. v. McKinley, 667 P.2d 15, 19 (Utah 1983).

157. Reves 494 U.S. 56 (1990); *see supra* n. 38–40 and accompanying text. *See also* SEC v. Infinity Group Co. 212 F.3d 180, 189 (3d Cir. 2000); *accord* Reiswig v. Dep't of Corp. for State of California, 144 Cal. App. 327, 336 (2006).

c. State Regulation and the Hawaii Market *Test* It is important to note that the federal securities laws were not intended to preempt a state's blue sky laws.[158] The "*Hawaii Market* test"[159] is a test used by many states to determine whether a financial instrument is an investment contract for purposes of state securities laws.[160] The *Hawaii Market* test is based on an earlier state test, the risk capital test, which requires that risk capital be invested with a reasonable expectation of a valuable benefit, but without the right to control the enterprise.[161] The *Hawaii Market* test requires four prongs for an investment contract to exist: (1) the offeree furnishes an initial value to the offeror, (2) a portion of the initial value is subject to the risk of the enterprise, (3) the initial value was given over because of the offeror's representations which led to the reasonable expectation of the offeree that there would be an additional valuable benefit, above the initial value, accruing to the offeree from the enterprise, and (4) the offeree has no practical and actual control over the management decisions of the enterprise.[162] In comparing the *Hawaii Market* test to the *Howey* test: (1) the first prong is similar to the investment prong of the *Howey* test, (2) the second prong focuses on a risk

---

158. *See* 15 U.S.C. §77(r). Additionally, the federal and state securities laws were enacted to serve different purposes. *See* King v. Pope, 91 S.W.3d 314, 319 (Tenn. 2002). The states enacted securities laws to protect their investors (so a broader, more protective test is warranted); federal securities laws were enacted for the broader purpose of protecting the integrity of the financial markets. *See id.* at 320. This presumption that the federal and state securities laws serve different purposes is questionable. *See, e.g.,* Payable Accounting Corp. v. McKinley, 667 P.2d 15, 18 (Utah 1983): "The federal securities acts were adopted and designed to restore investors' confidence in the financial markets, as was the Utah Act." *See also* United Housing Foundation v. Forman, 421 U.S. 837, 849 (1975): "The focus of the Acts is on the capital market system: the sale of securities to raise capital for profit-making purposes, the exchanges on which securities are traded, and the need for regulation to prevent fraud *and to protect the interest of investors*" (italics added); El Khadem v. Equity Securities Corp., 494 F.2d 1224, 1227 (9th Cir. 1974): "The Acts must be interpreted liberally to ensure their purpose of ensuring full and fair disclosure to purchasers of securities *and protecting the public from speculative or fraudulent schemes of promoters.*" (italics added), and quoting the Senate Report of the 1933 Act, "The aim is to prevent further exploitation of the public by the sale of unsound, fraudulent, and worthless securities through misrepresentation; to place adequate and true information before the investor; to protect honest enterprise, seeking capital by honest presentation, against the competition afforded by dishonest securities offered to the public through crooked promotion."

159. *See* State v. Hawaii Market, 485 P.2d 105 (Haw. 1971).

160. *See, e.g.,* State v. Brewer, 932 S.W.2d 1, 13 n. 13 (Tenn. Crim. App. 1996), notes that seventeen jurisdictions had adopted the *Hawaii Market* test.

161. *See* SEC v. Glenn W. Turner Enterprises, Inc., 474 F.2d 476 (9th Cir. 1973); *see also* All Seasons Resorts, Inc. v. Abrams, 68 N.Y.2d 81, 93–94 (N.Y. 1986) lists various states following the risk capital approach. Under this test, the risk capital cannot be invested for immediate benefits, a portion of the risk capital must be at risk, and the expectation is for future benefits in excess of the original investment. *Id.* at 93.

162. *See* Hawaii Market, 485 P.2d at 109.

capital concept while the *Howey* test focused on commonality (vertical or horizontal), (3) the third prong allows an expectation of "benefits" (a more liberal concept) as opposed to the stricter "profits" required by the *Howey* test, and (4) the fourth prong explicitly requires that the investor does not exercise managerial control, which is also true according to the subsequent court interpretations of the *Howey* test.[163]

The *Hawaii Market* test was applied to a company which offered a pay telephone sale-leaseback program, which consisted of executing three documents simultaneously: a purchase agreement, a telephone lease agreement, and an option to sell agreement.[164] The investors purchased the pay telephones from the company, entered into the lease agreement (which gave the company exclusive control over managing the payphones and its profits in exchange for a fixed monthly fee), and also entered into the option to sell agreement (which gave the investors the right to sell the payphone to the company with the appropriate notice, less any termination fee). The court applied the *Hawaii Market* test and found it was an investment contract.[165] The first prong was satisfied by the purchase of the telephones, which was furnishing initial value for an investment and was not the ordinary purchase of consumer goods.[166] The second prong was satisfied because the promoter relied on the investors for a substantial portion of the capital necessary to launch the enterprise and the investors expected a return on their investment.[167] The third prong was satisfied because the investors reasonably expected a benefit from the successful operation of the enterprise.[168] The fourth prong was satisfied because the investors had no managerial control and their right to termination is not the equivalent of exercising practical control.[169]

---

163. *See, e.g.,* Brewer, 932 S.W.2d at 13–14. *See also* All Seasons Resorts, Inc., 68 N.Y.2d at 93, which differentiates between the *Howey* test that requires an expectation for financial gain (profits) and the risk capital test that requires only an expectation of future benefits in excess of the initial value. *See supra* Section I.B.3.a., explaining control under the *Howey* test.

164. King v. Pope, 91 S.W.3d 314, 316 (Tenn. 2002).

165. *See id.* at 316.

166. *See id.* at 326. Initial value has been explained as value "given in consideration for the right to receive future income from the corporation." State v. Hawaii Market, 485 P.2d 105, 110 (Haw. 1971).

167. *See id.* at 324. *See also id.* at 324–25, which explains that a performance bond that was essentially worthless does not reduce the riskiness and the court focuses on substance over form.

168. *See id.* at 325.

169. *See id.* at 325. *See also* In the Matter of Trivectra v. Ushijima, 144 P.3d 1 (Haw. 2006), which applies the *Hawaii Market* test and finds an investment contract existed where an Internet-based company marketed and sold online "shopping malls" that allowed individuals to host a customized Web site that contained links to brand-name retailers. The potential profits were from commissions of the Internet sales and from

C. Sellers' Representations

The validity of the sellers' representations regarding the proposed instrument must also be examined, because if those representations turn out to be false then the instrument may be a security even though as proposed it would not have been a security. For example, in one case[170] where the promoters contractually promised to keep the investors' funds in a guaranteed bank account[171] so the funds would not be at risk (and thus appear not to be a security), the contract was a security because the representations were false and the funds, in truth, were at risk.[172]

Similarly, investors gave their funds to a trust and in exchange received a property transfer agreement that was purportedly risk free and guaranteed extremely high rates of return (the promised rates ranged from 138% to 181% annually).[173] The guarantee was supposedly based on the trust's superior historical returns on its investment, financial connections, and the ability to pool large amounts of money. However, the trust operated like a Ponzi scheme[174] and substituted new investor's money as a return on old investor's money. There was no prudent investment strategy and the funds were used for the personal expenses of the trust (and its officers) or in ill-advised investments. The court held the property transfer agreements, which in reality were subject to substantial risk, satisfied the *Howey* test, and were investment contracts.[175]

Moreover, virtual shares in fictional companies that were sold on a virtual stock exchange may be considered securities.[176] The virtual stock exchange was created and operated as an investment game for the personal entertainment of

---

recruiting additional mall owners, which was by far the more lucrative method to earn profits.

170. SEC v. Pickney, 923 F.Supp 76 (E.D. N.C. 1996).

171. These were called "prime bank instruments," which are nonexistent according to the SEC, and purported to be bank letters of credit or bank guarantees that could be traded for a profit. *See* Pickney, 923 F.Supp. at 78. This particular scheme promised to yield a 9% weekly return and to be guaranteed by a "top five U.S. bank" which made it a virtually risk-free investment.

172. *See id.* at 80–81.

173. SEC v. The Infinity Group Co., 212 F.3d 180, 184–85 (3d Cir. 2000).

174. There are two common financial arrangements employed by scheming individuals, which essentially rob Peter to pay Paul, and they are both dependent on a continuous influx of new money. *See* SEC v. SG LTD., 265 F.3d 42, 51 n.3 (1st Cir. 2001). A Ponzi scheme, named after the notorious swindler Charles Ponzi, is run by using the money tendered by later investors to pay the returns for the earlier investors. In contrast, pyramid schemes run by using a recruiting element in which earlier investors are paid based on their ability to recruit new members who pay fees to enter the scheme.

175. The Infinity Group Co., 212 F.3d at 191.

176. *See* SEC v. SG LTD., 265 F.3d 42 (1st Cir. 2001). Obviously, the investors in the virtual stocks invested real money which provided the necessary investment of funds to satisfy the first prong of the *Howey* test.

Internet users and the company emphasized its game-like nature.[177] However, if the transaction fits the criteria of a security, then placing an emphasis on the game-like nature of transacting in virtual shares will not remove them from the long reach of the securities laws. "It is equally immaterial whether the promoter depicts the enterprise as a serious commercial venture or dubs it a game."[178] The securities laws contain no exception for games.

D. Consequences of Securities Violations[179]

It is possible for a promoter to have offered or sold a security without realizing that the promoter was offering a security, or what the consequences of that offering would be. If financial instruments are determined to be securities, then their offer or sale will be a violation of Section 5 of the Securities Act[180] (assuming they were not registered securities).[181] Section 5 of the Securities Act is the linchpin of the Securities Acts and requires all securities to be registered unless they qualify for an exemption.[182] The requirements of the Securities Acts are intended to prevent fraud before it arises; therefore, it is possible to violate the Securities Acts even if no investor has been harmed.[183]

Moreover, section 5 is a strict liability statute and the promoter is liable even though he did not believe that he was selling a security.[184] For example, one defendant relied on an opinion letter from a senior attorney in the state securities division that he was not selling a security, yet the court held that the reliance on the opinion letter was irrelevant because Section 5 is a strict liability statute.[185] The prima facie case of a Section 5 violation is: (1) the defendant, directly or indirectly, offered or sold securities, (2) the offer or sale used interstate transportation, communication, or the mails, and (3) no registration statement was effective.[186] The individual is considered to have sold securities if the individual

---

177. *Id.* at 44–45.

178. *Id.*at 48.

179. This section is only meant to provide a brief overview of the ramifications of SEC regulation. A more extensive discussion of the litigation issues may be found in Chapters 13 and 14, *infra.*

180. 15 U.S.C. §77e.

181. *See, e.g.,* SEC v. Professional Associates, 731 F.2d 349, 358 (6th Cir. 1984). Note that there may also be state securities violations and sanctions. *See, e.g.,* Manns v. Skolnik, 666 N.E.2d 1236, 1246–51 (Ind. 1996).

182. *See, e.g.,* SEC v. Current Financial Services, Inc., 100 F.Supp.2d 1, 5 (D.D.C. 2000).

183. *See* SEC v. Life Partners 87 F.3d 536, 538–39 (D.C. Cir. 1996), which holds that a Section 5 violation may occur even though no individual is claimed to have been harmed.

184. SEC. v. Calvo, 378 F.3d 1211, 1215 (11th Cir. 2004).

185. SEC v. Current Financial Services, Inc., 100 F.Supp.2d 1, 5 (D.D.C. 2000).

186. *Calvo,* 378 F.3d at 1214.

is a "necessary participant" or "substantial factor" in the sale.[187] Additionally, there is joint and several liability when there is a close relationship between two parties in conducting the illegal transaction.[188]

There are various consequences as a result of an intended or unintended securities violation.

1. Preliminary Injunction A federal court may not issue an asset freeze (as in the form of a preliminary injunction) in an action for money damages; however, in an action under the Securities Acts a court may issue an asset freeze to preserve funds for the disgorgement claim (an equitable remedy).[189] Despite a concurrent civil damages claim, the court may issue the asset freeze to preserve funds for the equitable remedy. The inclusion of a civil remedy does not render it a legal action and not an equitable action. The amount and scope of the asset freeze extends to a reasonable approximation of the ill-gotten gains and exactitude is not required.[190]

2. Disgorgement Disgorgement is an equitable power of the court to disgorge any profits obtained through a violation of the Securities Acts.[191] The purpose of disgorgement is to deprive the wrongdoer of his ill-gotten gains, rather than to compensate investors who lost their investments. The reach of the disgorgement is to any profit, with interest, that the defendant gained by his wrongdoing.[192] The amount of the disgorgement need only be a reasonable approximation of the ill-gotten gains and exactitude is not required.[193] "So long as the measure of the disgorgement is reasonable, any risk of uncertainty should fall on the wrongdoer whose illegal conduct created that uncertainty."[194]

3. Permanent Injunction The SEC also has the power to sue for injunctive relief.[195] Permanent injunctive relief is granted when the SEC establishes a prima facie case of prior violations of the securities laws and a reasonable likelihood of future violations.[196] The critical question is whether the defendant's past conduct

---

187. *Id.* at 1215.

188. *Id.* which notes that joint and several liability will apply even though one party was more culpable than the other party.

189. SEC v. ETS Payphones, Inc., 408 F.3d 727, 734 (11th Cir. 2005).

190. *Id.* at 735.

191. SEC v. Blatt, 583 F.2d 1325, 1335 (5th Cir. 1978).

192. *Id.* notes that disgorgement is a remedial remedy and not punitive.

193. SEC. v. Calvo, 378 F.3d 1211, 1217 (11th Cir. 2004).

194. *Id.*, which quotes SEC v. Warde, 151 F.3d 42, 50 (2d Cir. 1998).

195. 15 U.S.C. §77(t) (b) (under the Securities Act) and 15 U.S.C. §78(u) (d) (under the Exchange Act) (granting the power to sue for an injunction when it appears a person has engaged or will engage in a violation of the Securities Acts).

196. SEC. v. Calvo, 378 F.3d 1211, 1216 (11th Cir. 2004). Unlike a private litigant who is seeking an injunction, the SEC is not required to show an irreparable injury or a balance of equities in its favor. *See* SEC v. Unifund SAL, 910 F.2d 1028, 1035 (2d Cir. 1990). The burden on the SEC is to show a strong likelihood of success if the goal of the injunction is

indicates a reasonable likelihood of a future violation, and the proof must come from something other than the mere fact of past violations.[197] The courts evaluate the likelihood of a future violation by considering the totality of the circumstances, which includes the "egregiousness of the defendant's actions, the isolated or recurrent nature of the infraction, the degree of scienter involved, the sincerity of the defendant's assurances against future violations, the defendant's recognition of the wrongful nature of the conduct, and the likelihood that the defendant's occupation will present opportunities for future violations."[198] Additionally, even a single violation may be so reprehensible that a likelihood of committing future violations can be inferred and an injunction may be warranted.[199]

The collateral consequences of an injunction can be severe. For example, an injunction can cause the loss of employment for an officer of a public company.[200] An injunction may also serve as the basis for an enforcement action by a self-regulatory organization.

4. Antifraud Statutes The antifraud statutes of the Securities Acts prohibit fraudulent conduct in connection with the offer or sale of securities. Injunctions for violations of the antifraud statutes of the securities laws, section 17(a)(1) of the Securities Act[201] and sections 10(b)[202] (and Rule 10b-5)[203] and 14(e) of the Exchange Act[204] require proof of scienter and materiality.[205] Scienter is "a mental state embracing intent to deceive, manipulate, or defraud."[206] Scienter requires

---

to preserve the status quo and a more substantial likelihood of success if the injunction is likely to have "grave consequences." *See id.* at 1039.

197. SEC v. Blatt, 583 F.2d 1325, 1334 (5th Cir. 1978).

198. Calvo, 378 F.3d at 1216, which quotes SEC v. Carriba Air, Inc., 681 F.2d 1318, 1322 (11th Cir. 1982).

199. Blatt, 583 F.2d at 1335.

200. SEC v. Ginsburg, 362 F.3d 1292, 1306 (11th Cir. 2004) (footnote in concurrence).

201. 15 U.S.C. §77q.

202. 15 U.S.C. §78j.

203. 17 C.F.R. §240.10b-5.

204. 15 U.S.C. §78n.

205. SEC v. Ginsburg, 362 F.3d 1292, 1297 (11th Cir. 2004). *See also* Aaron v. SEC, 446 U.S. 680, 702 (1980), holds that scienter is required for an injunction under §17(a) (1) of the Securities Act and §10(b) (and Rule 10b-5) of the Exchange Act, but not for §§17(a) (2) and (3) of the Securities Act. Note that scienter is not required for Section 5 violations because it is a strict liability statute. *See, e.g.,* SEC v. Current Financial Services, Inc., 100 F.Supp.2d 1, 5–6 (D.D.C. 2000).

206. Ernst & Ernst v. Hochfelder, 425 U.S. 185, 194 n. 12 (1976). Scienter may also be established by proving extreme recklessness. *See* SEC v. Rubera, 350 F.3d 1084, 1094–95 (9th Cir. 2003), which explains the level of recklessness needed to satisfy the scienter requirement.

the possession of material nonpublic information that was used in a trade.[207] The test for materiality is whether there is a substantial likelihood that a reasonable investor would consider the missing information an important representation when making the decision to invest.[208]

5. **Attorney's Potential Liability** Attorneys as well as promoters can be found liable for securities violations if due care is not exercised. In one cautionary case, a lawyer serving as bond counsel for a school district was found liable under Sections 17(a)(2) and 17(a)(3) of the Securities Act for his negligence in misrepresenting the risk of the bond issue, and the SEC sanctions were upheld by the court.[209] The lawyer, an experienced bond counsel, served as bond counsel and wrote the bond opinion letter. The lawyer examined the documents regarding the proposed projects from the Board of the school district and found they mostly consisted of the Board's "wish list." The lawyer gave the impression to the Board of the school district that to ensure the tax-exempt status of the bonds they only needed to *intend* to complete the proposed projects (a subjective test), rather than to have a reasonable need for the funds (an objective test). The lawyer also wrote an unqualified opinion letter to be sent to the investors that the bonds would be exempt from federal taxes. The lawyer further warranted that nothing came to his attention that would lead him to change his opinion about the federal tax-exempt status of the bonds. There was no reasonable basis to conclude the Board had decided to undertake any projects. An opinion letter implies that there was a reasonable investigation into the underlying facts that provided a reasonable basis for the opinion. Thus, the lawyer was negligent in writing the opinion letter and that suffices for liability under Sections 17(a)(2) and 17(a)(3) of the Securities Act.[210]

The goals of the securities laws were to provide investors with accurate information and to protect them from the misrepresentations of other parties that would induce them to purchase worthless securities. If a lawyer does his due diligence and the investors receive fair disclosure and are aware of the risks, then the courts will be less likely to find a violation of securities laws.

E. HEDGE FUNDS

The term "hedge fund" has become the umbrella term used to describe a type of loosely regulated private investment vehicle engaged in a variety of

---

207. Ginsburg, 362 F.3d at 1297–98.

208. *See* Basic v. Levinson, 485 U.S. 224, 231 (1988).

209. Weiss v. SEC, 468 F.3d 849, 850, 856 (D.C. Cir. 2006). Sections 17(a)(2) and 17(a)(3) require proof only of negligence and not scienter. *See* Aaron v. SEC, 446 U.S. 680, 697 (1980).

210. Weiss, 468F.3d at 354–56.

complex investment strategies with the goal of producing absolute returns for its investors.[211] The term encompasses "any pooled investment vehicle that is privately organized, administered by professional money managers, and not widely available to the public."[212] Hedge funds are often defined by their legal status; they are somewhat unique in that they are investment companies that do not register their securities offerings under the Securities Act and that are not registered as investment companies under the Investment Company Act.[213] Historically, hedge funds are granted these exemptions because they deal exclusively with a certain level of sophisticated investor the legislature considers not to be in need of protection by the Securities and Exchange Commission.

Hedge funds exist in a peculiar regulatory atmosphere as a result of their historical focus on wealthy individual and institutional investors. This permits them certain exemptions from the registration and disclosure requirements of the federal financial regulatory agencies on the principle that the federal government is primarily concerned with shielding unsophisticated investors. Hedge funds enjoy exemptions from the somewhat interlocking reporting and registration requirements of the Securities Act, the Exchange Act, the Investment Advisers Act of 1940 ("Advisers Act") and the Investment Company Act of 1940 ("Investment Company Act"). This is significant, because hedge funds are thus not prohibited from engaging in aggressive investment activity and allow for new levels of financial innovation. The legal status of hedge funds allows them to engage in highly leveraged trading, short selling, and risky hyperconcentrated investments. The issue of whether the lack of specific regulatory oversight of hedge funds increases systemic risk is a matter of debate. Indeed, Chairman Bernanke observed in April 2007 at The NYU Global Economic Policy Forum:

> Regulatory oversight of hedge funds is relatively light. Because hedge funds deal with highly sophisticated counterparties and investors, and because they have no claims on the federal safety net, the light regulatory touch seems largely justified. However, the growing market share of hedge funds has raised concerns about possible systemic risk. The complexity and rapid change inherent in the strategies of many funds make them relatively opaque to outsiders, and so the concern arises that the collapse of a hedge fund might come with little warning. In addition, many hedge funds are either highly leveraged or hold positions in derivatives or other assets that make their net asset positions very sensitive to changes in asset prices (the functional

---

211. "Absolute return" refers to producing a positive return regardless of market conditions and not as compared to an index.

212. The President's Working Group on Financial Markets, *Hedge Funds, Leverage, and the Lessons of Long-Term Capital Management* 1 (April 1999).

213. U.S. Securities and Exchange Comm'n, *Implications of the Growth of Hedge Funds*, at viii (September, 2003) [hereinafter "SEC Report"], available at http://www.sec.gov/news/studies/hedgefunds0903.pdf.

equivalent of high leverage). Highly leveraged investors are intrinsically more vulnerable to market shocks, of course, but leverage also increases the risks to the broader financial system. The failure of a highly leveraged fund holding large, concentrated positions could involve the forced liquidation of those positions, possibly at fire-sale prices, thereby imposing heavy losses on counterparties. In the worst scenarios, these counterparty losses could lead to further defaults or threaten systemically important institutions. In addition, market participants that were not creditors or counterparties of the defaulting firm might be harmed indirectly through changes in asset prices, liquidity strains, and increased market uncertainty.[214]

The term "hedged fund" was first applied to Alfred Winslow Jones's private investment fund, widely described as the first hedge fund. By combining both long and short positions in stocks that would rise faster than the market would in strong markets and fall slower than the market in declining markets, this would, in theory, ensure that the investment fund would always make a profit while at the same time minimizing, or "hedging" against the risk of loss.

1. **The Investment Company Act** The Investment Company Act[215] defines and regulates typical investment companies, including mutual funds. While hedge funds fall within the definition of an "investment company," they are able to avoid registration and substantive regulation under the Act by relying on one of two exclusions from the definition of investment company.[216] The first exclusion, under Section 3(c)(1) of the Investment Company Act,[217] is available to hedge funds that have 100 or fewer investors, while the second exclusion, under Section 3(c)(7) of the Investment Company Act,[218] applies to hedge funds that sell their interests only to highly sophisticated investors who are recognized as "qualified purchasers"—individuals with over $5,000,000 in investments.[219] Therefore, a Section 3(c)(1) fund cannot have more than 100 investors, while a Section 3(c)(7) fund can have an unlimited number of investors.[220]

Section 3(c)(1) reflects Congress's view that private investment companies owned by a limited number of investors do not rise to the level of federal interest under the Investment Company Act.[221] Section 3(c)(7) conveys Congress's

---

214. Chairman Ben S. Bernanke At the New York University Law School, New York, New York April 11, 2007 *Financial Regulation and the Invisible Hand.*

215. 15 U.S.C. §80a-1 *et seq.*

216. SEC Report, *supra* note 317, at ix.

217. 15 U.S.C. §80a-3(c)(1).

218. 15 U.S.C. §80a-3(c)(7).

219. Investment Company Act §2(a)(51)(A), 15 U.S.C. §80a-2(a)(51)(A).

220. SEC Report, *supra* note 317, at 13: ("In practice, however, most funds relying on Section 3(c)(7) have no more than 499 investors in order to avoid the reporting and registration requirements of the Exchange Act.").

221. *Id.*

contention that "certain highly sophisticated investors do not need the protections of the Investment Company Act because those investors are in a position to appreciate the risks associated with pooled investment vehicles."[222] To rely on either exclusion, the hedge fund must restrict its offerings so that they meet the requirements for nonpublic offerings.[223]

Exemption under either section of the Investment Company Act allows hedge funds to engage in more aggressive investing behavior than their mutual fund counterparts. While mutual funds must register with the Commission and must therefore disclose their investment positions and financial condition, hedge funds are able to remain secretive about their positions and strategies. This is the cause of much consternation among policymakers, who argue that this lack of comparable transparency makes hedge fund investors more susceptible to fraud. While hedge fund investors may not be unable to obtain basic information such as the daily net asset value of their investment or even the actual investment positions, investors will often accept such risk in return for the promise of outsized returns.[224]

2. Investment Advisers Act Hedge fund advisers are further exempt from regulation flowing from the Investment Advisers Act,[225] which was issued as a companion statute to the Investment Company Act.[226] The Advisers Act is primarily a registration and antifraud statute that allows the SEC to "better respond to, initiate, and take remedial action on complaints against fraudulent advisers."[227] Nearly all hedge fund managers fall under the definition of an "investment adviser"[228] who would be required to register under the Act,[229] but most rely on the "private adviser exemption" from registration.[230] The section exempts those advisers that have fewer than fifteen "clients," that do not hold themselves out

---

222. *Id.* at 13. *See also* Goldstein v. SEC, 451 F.3d 873, 875 (D.C. Cir. 2006): "Investment vehicles that remain private and available only to highly sophisticated investors have historically been understood not to present the same dangers to public markets as more widely available investment companies, like mutual funds."

223. *Id.*

224. *See generally* Goldstein v. SEC, 451 F.3d 873 (D.C. Cir. 2006).

225. 15 U.S.C. §80b-1 *et seq.*

226. *Goldstein*, 451 F.3d at 876 ("Enacted by Congress to 'substitute a philosophy of *caveat emptor*' in the investment advisory profession," quoting SEC v. Capital Gains Research Bureau, Inc., 375 U.S. 180, 186 (1963)).

227. *Id.*

228. *See* Advisers Act §202(a)(11), 15 U.S.C. §80b-2(a)(11) (defining "investment adviser" as "any person who, for compensation engages in the business of advising others, either directly or through publications or writings, as to the value of securities or as to the advisability of investing in purchasing, or selling securities, or who, for compensation and as part of a regular business, issues or promulgates analyses or reports concerning securities").

229. Advisers Act §203(a), 15 U.S.C. §80b-3(a).

230. Advisers Act §203(b)(3), 15 U.S.C. §80b-3(b)(3).

generally to the public as an investment adviser, and that are not investment advisers to registered entities.

While it might seem that most hedge funds would naturally have more than fifteen "clients," the Commission originally permitted investment advisers to count "legal organization(s)" such as a hedge fund, as a single client. This was altered under the "hedge fund rule," discussed below, in an attempt to force hedge fund managers to register under the Advisers Act, but the rule was overturned in a landmark federal appeals case.[231] Nonexempt "investment advisers" must register with the Commission, and all advisers, including hedge fund managers, are prohibited from engaging in fraudulent or deceptive practices under federal securities law.[232]

3. Securities Act Under the Securities Act,[233] any company that offers or sells its securities must register with the SEC or find an exemption from the registration requirement in order to fulfill the Act's primary objective of providing full and fair disclosure in securities transactions.[234] The Securities Act, however, provides hedge funds with a number of exemptions that allow a company to sell its securities to what are known as "accredited investors" under the safe harbor exemption, as long as it is under a private offering.

Section 4(2)[235] exempts qualifying entities from the registration and prospectus delivery requirements of Section 5[236] as long as the transaction does not involve a public offering.[237] The Supreme Court has defined a private offering as an "offering to those who are shown to be able to fend for themselves."[238] The Securities Act defines "accredited investors,"[239] who are intended to be those investors with the sophistication to "fend for themselves;" a company does not have to register with the SEC if the entity is able to limit the number of investors to fewer than 100 "accredited investors."[240] An accredited investor is a natural person who earns in excess of $200,000 a year (or has joint income with his/her spouse above $300,000) or who has $1 million in net worth, or a company with more than $5 million in assets.[241] These exempted transactions may not use any form of "general solicitation or general advertising."[242]

---

231. Goldstein v. SEC, 451 F.3d 873 (D.C. Cir. 2006).

232. See 15 U.S.C. §§80b-3, 80b-4.

233. 15 U.S.C. §77a et seq.

234. "Accredited Investors," available at http://www.sec.gov/answers/accred.htm. See also SEC Report, supra note 317, at 13.

235. 15 U.S.C. §77d(2).

236. 15 U.S.C. §77e.

237. SEC Report, supra note 317, at 14.

238. Id., which cites SEC v. Ralston Purina Co., 346 U.S. 119, 125, 126–127 (1953).

239. 15 U.S.C. §77b(a)(15).

240. 15 U.S.C. §77d(6).

241. Regulation D, Rule 501, 17 C.F.R. §230.501.

242. Regulation D, Rule 501, 17 C.F.R. §230.506. See SEC Report, supra note 317, at 16: "[I]ssuers and persons acting on their behalf cannot find investors through, among other things, advertisements, articles, notices or other communications published in a newspa-

4. Other Regulations While this list of exemptions might make it seem that hedge funds are able to operate in a regulatory-free environment, this is far from the case. In 2006, 86 percent of hedge funds were registered with some regulatory body (such as the SEC or the CFTC).[243] Some hedge funds choose to register for competitive purposes, as increased transparency can lead to more confidence from the investment community.

Hedge funds face reporting and registration requirements due to their investment activity. While the funds are not required to make periodic reports under the Exchange Act, hedge funds must still report to the SEC all nontrivial holdings in public companies.[244] Further, many hedge funds trade commodity options and futures, which bring them under the purview of the CFTC. To the extent that a hedge fund trades exchange-traded derivatives, the fund is considered a commodity pool, and its operator is subject to regulation under the Commodity Exchange Act.[245] Such fund advisers are required to register as a "Commodity Pool Operator" (CPO) or a "Commodity Trading Adviser" (CTA), and registered CPOs are "subject to periodic reporting, recordkeeping, and disclosure requirements."[246] The Commission does not directly regulate the commodity pools, but rather the advisers.[247]

---

per, magazine or similar media, cold mass mailings, broadcasts over television or radio, material contained on a Web site available to the public or an e-mail message sent to a large number of previously unknown persons."

243. Houman B. Shadab, *The Challenge of Hedge Fund Regulation*, 30 Regulation 1 (Spring 2007) (quoting a Hennessey Hedge Fund Manager Survey).

244. *See* 15 U.S.C. §78m(d), (g), which (requires entities that own greater than five percent of the class of equity securities of any equity security registered under Section 12 of the Exchange Act to file a beneficial ownership statement); 15 U.S.C. §78p (disclosures required of directors, officers, and principal stockholders).

245. Jane Kang Thorpe, *Assessment of the Current Regulatory Framework*, Director, Division of Clearing and Intermediary Oversight, CFTC, (address at the SEC Hedge Fund Roundtable; Panel 7: "Assessment of the Current Regulatory Framework," Washington D.C., (May 15, 2003).

246. The President's Working Group on Financial Markets, *Hedge Funds, Leverage, and the Lessons of Long-Term Capital Management* 3 (April 1999).

247. Thorpe, *supra* note 348: ("[T]he regulatory scheme for CPOs and CTAs is based on investor protection—it is designed to protect investors against fraud and other abuses. To achieve this purpose the CFTC sets forth registration and other requirements for CPOs and CTAs designed to ensure their qualifications and fitness. . . . This will normally include information on the investment program, principal risk factors, past performance, fees and expenses, and conflicts of interest. CPOs also must provide periodic account statements as well as an annual audited financial statement for any pool they operate, and both CPOs and CTAs must comply with sales practice requirements as well as various reporting and recordkeeping requirements. Finally, they are subject to requirements on antifraud and anti-manipulation.").

Furthermore, CPOs and CTAs must complete an annual self-audit and must submit to periodic audits conducted by the National Futures Association.[248] However, many hedge fund managers can now qualify for exemptions from CPO and CTA registration if they engage in limited commodity futures activities and sell interests solely to "accredited investors" as defined in the Securities Act or "qualified purchasers" as defined in the Investment Company Act.[249] Further, the CEA provides a *de minimis* exemption from CTA registration very similar to that of the Advisers Act's exemption.[250] Therefore, fund managers exempt under the Advisers Act's *de minimis* exemption are likely exempt from registration as a CTA.[251]

Hedge fund managers are also considered fiduciaries under the Investment Advisers Act, the same as mutual fund advisers, which requires fund managers to put the interests of their funds above their personal interests. Thus, hedge funds are actually required to make substantial disclosures to investors in order to discharge fiduciary duties and avoid violating antifraud rules prohibiting "misleading statements and omissions." Managers typically fulfill this obligation by providing investors with "a private placement memorandum that discloses information about the investment strategies the hedge fund is permitted to use and an overview of how the hedge fund operates."[252]

APPENDIX A

CHECKLIST FOR STOCKS, NOTES, AND INVESTMENT CONTRACTS

The following is a helpful checklist for a lawyer who is representing a company to determine if financial instruments used in a transaction are governed by the securities laws.

- Remember that the focus is on the substance of the transaction and its economic reality and not the legal terms that define the financial instruments.

Stocks
- Is it called "stock" and does it have the traditional characteristics of stock to be considered a *per se* security?
- Is the justifiable expectation of investors that it is a security and has the protection of the Securities Acts?

---

248. SEC Report, *supra* note 317, at 23–24.
249. *See* CFTC Rule 4.13(a)(3), (4).
250. SEC Report, *supra* note 317, at 24–25.
251. *Id.* at 25.
252. *Id.* at ix.

- Warrants to purchase stock, options, bonds, and debentures may also be *per se* securities.

Notes
- Apply the four-factor *Reves* test, beginning with the presumption that a note is a security.
- Presumption is rebuttable by proving a strong resemblance to a category of notes that is not a security.
- Is there an alternative comprehensive regulatory scheme that makes the protection of the Securities Acts unnecessary?

Investment Contracts
- Apply the tripartite *Howey* test, which is a very flexible test.
- Determine the level of commonality required in the jurisdiction.
- Fixed profit may also support the finding of an investment contract.
- Strong investor control may prevent it from being an investment contract.
- Pre-purchase efforts may suffice to create an investment contract.
- Check if it is an investment contract under state law.

APPENDIX B

DERIVATIVE PRODUCT REGULATION

The following table summarizes various derivatives products and the regulators to which they are subject.

Derivatives Products	Product Sub-category	General Descriptions	Regulators
Forward Contracts	Forward contracts on excluded commodities and exempted commodities	Forward contracts on financial instruments and nonagricultural commodities (crude oil, gold, etc.) or off-exchange future contracts	Exempted from the CEA; not regulated by the CFTC

Derivatives Products	Product Sub-category	General Descriptions	Regulators
	Forward contracts on agricultural commodity	Contracts regarding the sale of any cash commodity for deferred shipment or delivery	Depending on the distinction between a cash-forward contract and a future contract: if treated as cash-forward, generally exempted from the CEA and not regulated by the CFTC
Options	Commodity options	Options on domestic or foreign agricultural commodities and other physicals	CFTC
	Options on securities and indexes	Publicly tradable put and call options for securities and indexes	SEC
Futures Contracts	Security futures and futures on narrow-based securities indexes	Futures on a single security or futures on "narrow-based securities indexes" as defined by CEA 1a(25)	Coregulated by the CFTC and the SEC; tradable on both securities markets and commodity markets; cross-registration needed
	Futures on broad-based security index	A broad-based security index should be found by meeting the safe harbor definition in CEA 1a(31)	Regulated by the CFTC exclusively

Derivatives Products	Product Sub-category	General Descriptions	Regulators
Swap Contracts	Non–security-based swap agreements	A transaction between two parties, in which payments or rates are exchanged over a specified period and according to specified conditions, based on nonsecurity index or asset price.	Exempted from the CEA; the CFTC has no jurisdiction.
	Security-based swap agreement	Swap agreements based on the value of a security	Regulated by the SEC, but limited to insider trading, fraud and market manipulation; the CFTC has no jurisdiction.
	Covered bank swap agreements	Swap agreements entered into banks.	Exempted from the CEA; the Federal Reserve retains certain regulatory power
Hybrid Instruments	Securities or banking products	A security or banking product with a payment indexed to a commodity value or rate or providing for delivery of a commodity	Exempted from the regulation of the CEA; may still be subject to the regulation of the SEC or the Federal Reserve depending on the nature
Foreign Exchange Products	Foreign currency futures	Futures on foreign currencies	CFTC (if the counterparty is not a bank, broker-dealer, futures commission merchant, or other specified regulated entity)
	Options on foreign currencies	Options on foreign currencies	

Derivatives Products	Product Sub-category	General Descriptions	Regulators
Credit Derivatives	Credit default swaps	A private contract in which private parties bet on the probability of a debt issuer becoming default	Generally unregulated; the Federal Reserve retains some regulatory power
	Collateralized debt obligation	An asset pool consisting of numerous debt obligations held by a special purpose entity whose interests are divided and resold into different tranches based on differences in credit quality of the assets in the pool	

5. UNDERSTANDING INTEREST RATES AND THE ECONOMY

I. THE FEDERAL RESERVE

The Federal Reserve system was created by Congress under the Federal Reserve Act[1] "to provide for the establishment of Federal reserve banks, to furnish an elastic currency, to afford means of rediscounting commercial paper, to establish a more effective supervision of banking in the United States, and for other purposes."[2]

---

1. Ch. 6, 38 Stat. 251 (1913).

2. *See The Federal Reserve System, Purposes and Functions* 2 (Board of Governors of the Federal Reserve System, 9th Ed. 2005), available at http://www.federalreserve.gov/pf/pdf/pf_1.pdf.

The Federal Reserve's duties include:

- Conducting the nation's monetary policy by influencing the monetary and credit conditions in the economy in pursuit of maximum employment, stable prices, and moderate long-term interest rates;
- Supervising and regulating banking institutions to ensure the safety and soundness of the nation's banking and financial system and to protect the credit rights of consumers;
- Maintaining the stability of the financial system and containing systemic risk that may arise in financial markets; and
- Providing financial services to depository institutions, the U.S. government, and foreign official institutions, including playing a major role in operating the nation's payments system.[3]

A. Recent Market Turmoil and the Fed's Reaction

In the wake of the recent mortgage crisis, the Federal Reserve has actuated its role of preventing systemic failure. The liquidity crisis referenced in Chapter 1 of this treatise, which resulted from inefficient lending practices and the creation of financial instruments supported by those pools of loans, provided the backdrop for the Federal Reserve to flex its muscle in its operation within the capital markets. By providing liquidity, the Federal Reserve seeks to facilitate the function of the capital markets. A functioning capital market is essential to providing financing opportunities and allowing counterparties to negotiate risk packaged in a variety of financial instruments.

Federal Reserve Chairman Ben S. Bernanke recently described the mortgage crisis and the Fed's reaction in creating a new Term Auction Facility to provide liquidity for the financial markets in the United States.[4] Bernanke noted the strain that the financial markets in the United States and a number of other industrialized countries have been under since the summer of 2007. This turmoil has affected the broader economy, principally through its effects on the availability and terms of credit to households and businesses. This has made it difficult for investors to assess future earnings and asset values, and has made forecasting the course of the economy even more difficult than usual.

In June 2006, the target for the federal funds rate was 5.25 percent—a level that, in the judgment of the Federal Open Market Committee (FOMC), would best promote the policy objectives given to it by Congress.[5] The economy continued to perform well into 2007, but was faced with a challenge in the form of a

---

3. *Id.* at 1.

4. Ben S. Bernanke, *Financial Markets, the Economic Outlook, and Monetary Policy*, (Remarks at the Women in Housing and Finance and Exchequer Club Joint Luncheon, Washington, D.C., January 10, 2008.) The complete text of the remarks can be found at http://www.federalreserve.gov/newsevents/speech/bernanke20080110a.htm.

5. *See* Sec. IV, *infra*.

sharp and protracted correction in the housing market, which followed a multi-year boom in housing construction and house prices. This housing contraction would have been considerably milder had it not been for adverse developments in the subprime mortgage market, in particular the high and rising delinquency rates of subprime mortgages, especially those with adjustable interest rates (subprime ARMs):

> Although poor underwriting and, in some cases, fraud and abusive practices contributed to the high rates of delinquency . . . in the subprime ARM market, the more fundamental reason for the sharp deterioration in credit quality was the flawed premise on which much subprime ARM lending was based: that house prices would continue to rise rapidly. When house prices were increasing at double-digit rates, subprime ARM borrowers were able to build equity in their homes during the period in which they paid a (relatively) low introductory (or "teaser") rate on their mortgages. Once sufficient equity had been accumulated, borrowers were often able to refinance, avoiding the increased payments associated with the reset in the rate on the original mortgages. However, when declining affordability finally began to take its toll on the demand for homes and thus on house prices, borrowers could no longer rely on home-price appreciation to build equity; they were accordingly unable to refinance and found themselves locked into their subprime ARM contracts. Many of these borrowers found it difficult to make payments at even the introductory rate, much less at the higher postadjustment rate. The result . . . has been rising delinquencies and foreclosures, which will have adverse effects for communities and the broader economy as well as for the borrowers themselves.[6]

As a result, the availability of credit for nonprime borrowers has disappeared, and few new loans are being made. The loss of this source of demand for housing has exacerbated the downturn, adding to the sharp decline in new home-building and putting downward pressure on house prices. The addition of foreclosed properties to the inventories of unsold homes is further weakening the market. These losses in the subprime mortgage market have triggered a substantial reaction in other financial markets. Following a period of more aggressive risk-taking, the subprime crisis has led investors to reassess credit risks more broadly and, perhaps, to become less willing to take on risks of any type. Investors have also been concerned that, by further weakening the housing sector, the problems in the subprime mortgage market may lead overall economic growth to slow. Moreover, the subprime mortgage crisis has contributed to a considerable increase in investor uncertainty about the appropriate valuations of a broader range of financial assets, not just subprime mortgages.

---

6. Bernanke, *supra* note 1.

Even as their balance sheets expanded, banks began to report large losses, reflecting the sharp declines in the values of mortgages and other assets. Thus, banks too became subject to valuation uncertainty. . . . The combination of larger balance sheets and unexpected losses also resulted in a decline in the capital ratios of a number of institutions. Several have chosen to raise new capital in response, and the banking system retains substantial levels of capital. However, on balance, these developments have prompted banks to become protective of their liquidity and balance sheet capacity and thus to become less willing to provide funding to other market participants, including other banks. As a result . . . banks have become more restrictive in their lending to firms and households. More expensive and less available credit seems likely to impose a measure of financial restraint on economic growth.[7]

Market strains have been serious, and they continue to pose risks to the broader economy. The Federal Reserve has responded with two courses of action: (1) efforts to support market liquidity and functioning, and (2) the pursuit of macroeconomic objectives of maximum sustainable employment and price stability through monetary policy.[8] In order to support market liquidity, the following has occurred:

The Federal Reserve [has] cut the discount rate—the rate at which it lends directly to banks—by 50 basis points, or 1/2 percentage point, and it has since maintained the spread between the federal funds rate[9] and the discount rate at 50 basis points, rather than the customary 100 basis points. The Fed also adjusted its usual practices to facilitate the provision of discount window financing for as long as thirty days, renewable at the request of the borrower. Loans through the discount window differ from conventional open market operations in that the loans can be made directly to individual banks. In contrast, open market operations are arranged with a limited set of dealers of government securities. In addition, whereas open market operations involve lending against government and agency securities, loans through the discount window can be made against a much wider range of collateral.

The changes to the discount window were designed to assure banks of the availability of a backstop source of liquidity. Although banks borrowed only moderate amounts at the discount window, they substantially increased the amount of collateral they placed with Reserve Banks. This and other factors suggest that these changes to the discount window facility, together with the

---

7. *Id.*

8. *See* Sec. IV, *infra,* for more detailed discussion of how the Federal Reserve achieves these objectives.

9. *See* Sec. II.C., *infra.*

statements and actions of the FOMC, had some positive influence on market conditions.[10]

In addition, the Federal Reserve recently introduced a term auction facility, or TAF, through which prespecified amounts of discount window credit can be auctioned to eligible borrowers.[11] This and other liquidity-related actions appear to have had some positive effects.

The Federal Reserve continues to use monetary policy (that is, the management of the short-term interest rate) as its best tool for pursuing its macroeconomic objectives, namely to promote maximum sustainable employment and price stability.[12] In total, the FOMC has brought the funds rate down by several percentage points from its level just before financial strains emerged. By lowering short-term interest rates, the Fed hopes to stimulate the economy. As interest rates approach zero, however, the Fed has found it necessary to take extraordinary measures in its monetary policy by purchasing longer term securities such as U.S. Treasury bonds and mortgage-backed debt in order to influence the rates that matter most—those that affect the purchase of longer-term assets (i.e., longer-term interest rates).

> The Federal Reserve took these actions to help offset the restraint imposed by the tightening of credit conditions and the weakening of the housing market. However, in light of recent changes in the outlook for and the risks to growth, additional policy easing may well be necessary. The Committee will, of course, be carefully evaluating incoming information bearing on the economic outlook. Based on that evaluation, and consistent with our dual mandate, we stand ready to take substantive additional action as needed to support growth and to provide adequate insurance against downside risks.[13]

B. Background

Providing liquidity to the market allows continued participation and transactions in the myriad of financial instruments that are the backbone of a healthy economy. Financial instruments are economic tools allowing users to manage risk or to enhance yield (make money). Financial instruments are also used as a means of accessing capital from investors. Individuals and institutions use financial instruments as a means of furthering economic goals. Central banks use these same financial instruments as tools for implementing monetary policy.

---

10. Bernanke, *supra* note 1.

11. *See* the complete text of Bernanke's remarks, http://www.federalreserve.gov/newsevents/speech/bernanke20080110a.htm, for a complete discussion of TAF and its effects.

12. *See* Sec. IV.B., *infra*.

13. Bernanke, *supra* note 1.

The first step to understanding an individual financial transaction or a financial instrument is to determine its economic purpose and the goal that particular financial transaction or instrument is designed to achieve. Changes in the economy have a significant impact on the value of a particular financial instrument. Federal governments and private industry release data describing changes in the economy. Each economic data point gives capital market participants insight into the direction of interest rates.

Wall Street focuses on the myriad of financial reports to recalibrate interest variables in financial formulas. Central Banks influence interest rates to control economies. By making money more expensive (raising interest rates) economies slow because there is less money available to invest. Central banks will readjust interest rates to the best of their ability as a clearer picture of the economy emerges.

The United States economy is the sum of all the assets, liabilities, and investment decisions made by investors in the United States. Asset pricing is based on mathematical valuation models and market perceptions. Incorporated into these models are certain assumptions about the future direction of the economy. These assumptions might be as simple as how many iPods Apple will sell next year, or as complex as the repercussions of an inverted yield curve.

Underpinning any formula for the determination of the value of a particular asset are the prevailing interest rates in the market for capital. The simplest component of this variable is the risk free interest rate, to which all other returns on capital might be compared. The risk free interest rate is determined by an analysis of the interest paid by the United States Government on its short-term obligations. Theses Federal IOU's are considered virtually risk free because they are of short duration, are extremely liquid, and have virtually no credit risk.

During the recent financial market crises, rates on these short-term U.S. Government IOU's have reached historic lows. Indeed, auctions for new treasury bills have been effectuated at a return of absolute zero to the investor, and Treasury securities in the secondary market are trading at negative interest rates. A negative interest rate means that the purchaser is willing to *pay* for the privilege of owning treasury securities to assure as close to absolute credit security as possible. The crisis in confidence in the broader financial markets has caused investors to gravitate to absolute safety in terms of credit risk. Within the credit markets, that absolute safety can only be achieved in the form of short term Treasury obligations. So serious has the crisis in confidence become that investors have, in the waning months of 2008, been willing to accept negative yields on Treasury securities, thereby paying the seller for the privilege of owning treasury bills.

Historically, prior to the crisis of 2008, the yields on the shortest-term interest bearing financial instruments were most directly affected by the activities of the Federal Open Market Committee of the Federal Reserve in its targeting of the federal funds rate. In November 2008 the Federal Reserve announced that it will begin a process of purchasing longer term instruments issued by Government Sponsored Entities (GSEs). The Fed described this decision as a means to reduce the cost and increase the availability of credit for the purchase of houses, which in turn should support housing markets and foster improved conditions in financial markets more generally. On March 18, 2009, the Fed announced that it would be purchasing U.S. Treasury bonds to influence longer-term rates and loosen credit conditions:

> In these circumstances, the Federal Reserve will employ all available tools to promote economic recovery and to preserve price stability. The Committee will maintain the target range for the federal funds rate at 0 to ¼ percent and anticipates that economic conditions are likely to warrant exceptionally low levels of the federal funds rate for an extended period. To provide greater support to mortgage lending and housing markets, the Committee decided today to increase the size of the Federal Reserve's balance sheet further by purchasing up to an additional $750 billion of agency mortgage-backed securities, bringing its total purchases of these securities to up to $1.25 trillion this year, and to increase its purchases of agency debt this year by up to $100 billion to a total of up to $200 billion. Moreover, to help improve conditions in private credit markets, the Committee decided to purchase up to $300 billion of longer-term Treasury securities over the next six months. The Federal Reserve has launched the Term Asset-Backed Securities Loan Facility to facilitate the extension of credit to households and small businesses and anticipates that the range of eligible collateral for this facility is likely to be expanded to include other financial assets. The Committee will continue to carefully monitor the size and composition of the Federal Reserve's balance sheet in light of evolving financial and economic developments.[14]

The Fed uses its open-market operations to affect the broader economy. To understand how the Fed affects the economy through its open market operations, it is necessary to understand how federal funds work. Federal reserves are traded in the form of Federal Funds between banks, as they are needed to meet Federal Reserve Capital Requirements. By targeting the rate at which transactions in these reserves are conducted between member institutions, the Federal Reserve can affect the amount of money flow in the economy. By studying economic data, the Federal Reserve makes determinations on the amount of money flow it believes will be best for consistent economic expansion while limiting inflation. The process of targeting the federal funds rate is fluid and will adjust as economic conditions change.

When the Federal Reserve changes the target rate at which federal fund transactions are conducted between participant depository institutions, asset

---

14. Federal Reserve Press Release: March 18, 2009.

valuations are affected. A change in perception as to the direction of the Federal Reserve's approach can have a ripple effect on all asset valuation models; these effects are not limited to the yield on short-term, risk-free investments. Since all long-term investments are really a series of short-term investments melded together, a subtle change in short term interest rates can affect the value of stock prices, a house, a car or even a complex long term derivative financial instrument.

Because of the almost immediate effect on the underlying assumptions underpinning the valuation of assets, the Federal Reserve has unique and far-reaching control over the growth of the economy. The mere expectation of lower interest rates at the Federal Reserve can have an immediate and profound impact on investment decisions. Therefore, the capital markets are uniquely focused on the activities of the Federal Reserve, not only on the ultimate decisions taken at meetings of the Federal Open Market Committee, but also on the myriad of data points released in the economy that might affect the Federal Reserve's interest rate bias. This near obsession with the Federal Reserve's interest rate posture leads capital market participants to closely scrutinize the speeches of Federal Reserve officials and the data upon which their decisions are made. It is for these reasons that market participants closely follow economic data releases.

Generally, economic news or statements by officials have the greatest effect on short-term interest rates; the effect of a change in Federal Reserve posture directly and immediately affects short-term financial instruments.[15] Historically, the effects on longer-term investments are visible as market participants change their underlying assumptions about market valuations. By direct intervention in longer-term capital market trading through the purchasing securities issued by treasuries and GSEs, the Federal Reserve hopes to be able to directly affect longer-term interest rates and directly impact the market through market participation. The Fed described its decision to purchase longer-term securities as follows:

> The Federal Reserve announced on Tuesday that it will initiate a program to purchase the direct obligations of housing-related, government-sponsored enterprises (GSEs)—Fannie Mae, Freddie Mac, and the Federal Home Loan Banks—and mortgage-backed securities (MBS) backed by Fannie Mae, Freddie Mac, and Ginnie Mae. Spreads of rates on GSE debt and on GSE-guaranteed mortgages have widened appreciably of late. This action is being taken to reduce the cost and increase the availability of credit for the purchase of houses, which in turn should support housing markets and foster improved conditions in financial markets more generally.

---

15. See THE FEDERAL RESERVE SYSTEM, PURPOSES AND FUNCTIONS 17 (Board of Governors of the Federal Reserve System, 9th Ed. 2005), http://www.federalreserve. gov/pf/pf.htm.

Purchases of up to $100 billion in GSE direct obligations under the program will be conducted with the Federal Reserve's primary dealers through a series of competitive auctions and will begin next week. Purchases of up to $500 billion in MBS will be conducted by asset managers selected via a competitive process with a goal of beginning these purchases before year-end. Purchases of both direct obligations and MBS are expected to take place over several quarters. Further information regarding the operational details of this program will be provided after consultation with market participants.[16]

II. THE ROLE OF THE FEDERAL RESERVE IN DOMESTIC CAPITAL MARKETS

A. The Federal Reserve Banking System

The United States Constitution (Article I, Section 8) gives Congress the power over money and the regulation of the value of the American currency. As a result of financial panics in the nineteenth and early twentieth centuries, which led to bank failures and business bankruptcies that severely disrupted the economy, Congress created the Federal Reserve and delegated those responsibilities to it. [17] Congress passed the Federal Reserve Act[18] in 1913 "to provide for the establishment of Federal reserve banks, to furnish an elastic currency, to afford means of rediscounting commercial paper, to establish a more effective supervision of banking in the United States, and for other purposes." A network of twelve Federal Reserve banks and their branches currently carry out a variety of Federal Reserve System functions, including operating a nationwide payments system. Each Reserve bank also acts as a depository for the banks in its own District.[19] These banks, although heavily regulated, are independent, privately owned, and locally controlled corporations.[20]

1. **Composition** The Federal Reserve System comprises a central Board of Governors and twelve regional Reserve banks. Monetary policy is set by the Federal Open Market Committee, which consists of the members of the Board of Governors, the president of the Federal Reserve Bank of New York, and presidents of four other Federal Reserve Banks, who serve on a rotating basis.[21] Monetary policy is implemented through open market operations, that is,

---

16. Federal Reserve Press Release, November 25, 2008. *See* Appendix B, *infra,* for further information regarding this program.

17. *See* THE FEDERAL RESERVE SYSTEM, PURPOSES AND FUNCTIONS 1–2.

18. *See* 12 U.S.C. §221 *et seq.*

19. *See* THE FEDERAL RESERVE SYSTEM, PURPOSES AND FUNCTIONS 6.

20. Lewis v. United States, 680 F.2d 1239 (9th Cir. 1982).

21. *See* THE FEDERAL RESERVE SYSTEM, PURPOSES AND FUNCTIONS 3.

the purchase and sale of government securities.[22] Open market operations are funded with reserves supplied by participating banks, and these operations are profitable for the Federal Reserve. The Federal Reserve banks also provide check clearing and other banking services to financial institutions.[23]

2. Purpose When the System was founded, its principal legal purpose was to provide "an elastic currency," by which was meant a supply of credit that could fluctuate as needed to meet seasonal and other changes in credit demand. In this regard, the Federal Reserve was an immediate success. The seasonal fluctuations that had characterized short-term interest rates before the founding of the Federal Reserve were almost immediately eliminated, removing a source of stress from the banking system and the economy. The Federal Reserve today retains important responsibilities for banking and financial stability, but its formal policy objectives have become much broader. Its current mandate, set formally in law in 1977 and reaffirmed in 2000, requires the Federal Reserve to pursue three objectives through its conduct of monetary policy: maximum employment, stable prices, and moderate long-term interest rates.[24]

The Federal Reserve has the responsibility to issue paper money. It serves as banker for both the government and commercial banks, and acts as lender of last resort.

As the lender of last resort, the bank has regulatory responsibilities. The Federal Reserve requires member banks to maintain reserve deposits. The Federal Reserve, in managing Reserve Deposits, manages monetary policy.[25]

3. Responsibilities The Federal Reserve has two broad sets of responsibilities. First, it has a mandate from the Congress to promote a healthy economy—specifically, maximum sustainable employment, stable prices, and moderate long-term interest rates. Second, since its founding, the Federal Reserve has been entrusted with the responsibility of helping to ensure the stability of the financial system. The Federal Reserve likewise has two broad sets of policy tools. First, it makes monetary policy, mainly by targeting the overnight interest rate, that is, the federal funds rate.[26] Second, the Federal Reserve has a range of powers with respect to financial institutions, including rule-making powers, supervisory oversight, and a lender-of-last resort function made operational by the its ability to lend through its discount window. The Federal Reserve focuses its monetary policy instruments on achieving its macro goals—price stability

---

22. *See* Sec. IV, *infra,* for more detailed discussion.

23. *See generally* 12 U.S.C. §§221 *et seq.*

24. Ben S. Bernanke, *The Benefits of Price Stability,* (remarks at the Center for Economic Policy Studies and on the Occasion of the Seventy-Fifth Anniversary of the Woodrow Wilson School of Public and International Affairs, Princeton University, Princeton, New Jersey, February 24, 2006).

25. *See* Sec. IV, *infra,* for more detailed discussion.

26. *See* Sec. IV, *infra,* for more detailed discussion.

and maximum sustainable employment—while using its regulatory, supervisory, and lender-of-last resort powers to help ensure financial stability.[27]

B. Federal Funds Transactions

Federal Reserve depository institutions actively trade balances (federal funds) held in their accounts at an interest rate known as the "federal funds rate."[28] Federal funds market participants include commercial banks, thrift institutions, agencies and branches of banks in the United States, federal agencies, and government securities dealers. Transactions in federal funds are conducted directly between banks and through brokers. Either the borrower or the lender may initiate the transaction. Community banks find willing counterparties in the form of regional correspondents. Therefore, selling banks are able to easily shift excess funds to borrowing institutions.

Since banks are not always able to predict the amount of excess reserves they will have each day, federal fund transactions are generally conducted on an overnight basis. The duration of a contract in federal funds ranges between overnight ("continuing contracts") to one year ("term federal funds"). Term federal funds are subject to a 15 percent lending limit with anyone counterparty.

Continuing contracts are automatically renewed unless either the buyer or the seller terminates the contract. Correspondents who purchase overnight federal funds from respondent banks typically employ this type of arrangement. Unless notified to the contrary by the respondent, the correspondent will continually roll the interbank deposit into federal funds, creating a longer-term instrument of open maturity. A bank may sell overnight federal funds to any counterparty without limit. Sales of federal funds with maturities of one day or less or under continuing contract have been specifically excluded from lending limit restrictions.[29]

The interest payments on continuing-contract federal funds loans are computed from a formula based on each day's average federal funds rate. Federal funds transactions are generally unsecured loans and expose the lender to credit risk. Banks purchase federal funds up to the line limits set by the selling bank. Since these line limits are not generally disclosed, purchasing banks might test line limits to establish parameters for transactions when they are actually needed. The Federal Reserve bank examiners look to see that banks evaluate the credit quality of any bank to whom they sell federal funds and set a maximum line for each potential counterparty. If the "lender" is not comfortable with the

---

27. Ben S. Bernanke, *Asset-Price "Bubbles" and Monetary Policy*, (remarks before the New York Chapter of the National Association for Business Economics, New York, New York, October 15, 2002).

28. *See* THE FEDERAL RESERVE SYSTEM, PURPOSES AND FUNCTIONS 16.

29. 12 CFR 32.

creditworthiness of the borrower, the correspondent bank selling the reserves may require collateral from its counterparty.

Transactions in federal funds are accomplished exclusively using Federal Reserve Bank accounts. The Federal funds are transferred between the transacting institutions when the selling bank authorizes its district Federal Reserve Bank to debit its reserve account and credit the reserve account of the buying institution. The lender bank informs its correspondent that it intends to sell funds. In response, the correspondent bank purchases funds from the lender by reclassifying the respondent's demand deposits as federal funds purchased. The respondent does not have access to its deposited money as long as it is classified as federal funds on the books of the correspondents. The banks then use the Federal Reserve's electronic funds and securities transfer system "Fedwire" to complete the transaction. Upon maturity of the loan, the respondent's demand deposit account is credited for the total value of the loan plus interest. On the maturity date, the buying institution uses Fedwire to return the funds purchased plus interest.

The federal funds rate is a key rate for the money market because all other short-term rates are linked to it. The difference between the bid and offer prices of federal funds is usually small because of the liquidity of the market place. The overnight market is highly liquid. As there is no secondary market for term federal funds rates, their liquidity is directly related to their maturity.

Since federal funds are generally of a short-term duration, banks rarely hedge exposure to federal fund contacts. There is a derivatives market for federal funds and, where necessary, a bank wishing to hedge its federal funds exposure might use the federal funds futures market.

C. The Federal Funds Rate
The Federal Reserve implements its control over the federal funds interest rate by affecting the market for deposits held at the Federal Reserve banks. The "targets" the Federal Reserve uses to affect the desired interest rate outcome have evolved over time. During the 1970s, the Federal Reserve had as its objective affecting the growth of the monetary aggregate. The monetary aggregate represents the amount of money in the economy; by affecting the monetary aggregate, the Federal Reserve believed that it could control how much money was available for investment and spending. It was believed that the amount available to the economy had a direct and ongoing relationship to economic activity. Raising and lowering the fed fund target interest rates can effectively control this aggregate by affecting the amount of money financial institutions have on deposit with the Federal Reserve banks. Lowering interest rates, for example, makes having money on deposit less attractive, thereby influencing the investor's decision whether to keep money in the bank.

The problem with the monetary aggregate goal-oriented approach was that the Federal Reserve was often forced to make large rate movements to bring the monetary aggregate back into line. Because of the profound impact of substantial changes in the federal funds rate, the Federal Reserve was often unable to react to inflationary pressures resulting from oil price shocks and excessive monetary growth over the decade.[30]

By the end of the 1970s, the Federal Reserve began to focus on controlling the amount of reserves held in the vaults of depository institutions. The goal of the Federal Reserve was no longer to affect the amount of aggregate money in the economy but to affect the money held on deposit. By targeting a specific amount of unborrowed money, banks would be required to pay higher interest to shore up their reserves, thereby affecting prevailing interest rates. The Federal Reserve could influence the rate that the market would bear for borrowing funds by affecting the discount window borrowing rate.

The discount window is the means of extending credit from the Federal Reserve to financial institutions when all other borrowing opportunities have been exhausted. During the 2008 crisis, the discount window has been opened to primary dealers of government securities in order to flood the capital markets with liquidity. When, however, market uncertainties discouraged financial institutions from borrowing from the discount window, the Federal Reserve sought a more direct means of influencing the interest rates financial institutions used to borrow funds from each other. In July 1995, the Federal Reserve announced that it would directly target the rate banks charge each other to borrow deposits held at Federal Reserve Banks.[31]

In the wake of recent market turmoil caused by the mortgage crisis, the Federal Reserve opened up a program similar to the discount borrowing offered to member banks to its primary dealers. Primary dealers are banks and securities broker-dealers that trade in U.S. Government securities with the Federal Reserve Bank of New York. To reduce the potential for counterparties and creditors to make a run on other primary dealers, the Federal Reserve used its emergency lending authority to create a new Term Auction Facility that provided the primary dealers with a liquidity backstop similar to the discount window available to banks in generally sound financial condition.[32]

D. Banks and Federal Funds

Control over the banking system generally and over federal funds in particular allows the Federal Reserve to influence interest rates and implement monetary

---

30. *See* THE FEDERAL RESERVE SYSTEM, PURPOSES AND FUNCTIONS 28.

31. *Id.* at 29.

32. *See* Sec. I.A., *supra*.

policy. Influence over capital market liquidity allows the Federal Reserve to inject liquidity into its member banks and now to its primary dealers. The effect of providing access to liquidity can be seen in the following example:

Assume, for example, a hypothetical bank, USA First America Bankcorp (USAFB) offering depositors two options to attract their money:

1. Depositors can buy a six month CD paying 2.5 percent on an annualized basis, or
2. Depositors can deposit funds in an interest-bearing checking account paying 0.5 percent.

USAFB has two customers: Big Money Incorporated and Able Lotsamoney. Big Money Incorporated (BMI) deposits three million dollars into the CD and ten million dollars into the checking account. USAFB uses the money from BMI to make loans. The bank offers two options for borrowers who are taking on a mortgage:

1. A fixed-rate mortgage at 7 percent for ten years or
2. A floating rate mortgage at the Federal Funds Rate plus 1 percent (100 basis points).

Able Lotsamoney, a successful Chicago trader, decides to buy a number of condo apartments on Lake Shore Drive for fifteen million dollars. Able takes a thirteen million dollar loan to be able to purchase the condos and agrees to pay the floating rate.

To USAFB, the loan is an asset and represents capital of the bank, similar to other assets such as its building, computers, and desks. The Federal Reserve requires that USAFB maintain sufficient capital to meet obligations should depositors like BMI wish to withdraw their funds from their checking account.

In addition to capital requirements, the Federal Reserve Act requires "each depository institution [to] maintain reserves against its transaction accounts as the Board may prescribe by regulation solely for the purpose of implementing monetary policy."[33] In order to comply with this requirement, known as "Regulation D," USAFB must maintain in vault cash or on deposit with its local Federal Reserve Bank 3 percent of its current liabilities on checking account deposits between 8.5 million and 10 million dollars.[34] Since the CD is a time deposit, it is not subject to Regulation D. USAFB, therefore, must maintain

---

33. 12 U.S.C. §461.

34. *Regulation D: Reserve Requirements of Depository Institutions,* 12 CFR 204 §204.9. This regulation specifies the reserve ratios for net transaction accounts, nonpersonal time deposits, and eurocurrency liabilities, and also identifies the amount of net transaction deposits reservable at three percent and the amounts of reservable liabilities that are exempt from reserve requirements. These amounts are subject to adjustment every year to reflect changes in the monetary aggregate.

$45,000 (3% of 1.5 million dollars) on deposit with its local Federal Reserve Bank or in cash in its vault in order to meet its Regulation D reserve requirements.[35]

USAFB profits by collecting the difference between the amount of interest it pays to BMI and the amount of interest it collects from the loan to Lotsamoney. Since all its cash is committed to the transaction with Lotsamoney, USAFB will need to purchase Federal Funds ($45,000 dollars worth) to meet its Regulation D requirements. That purchase will function as a loan of Federal funds and will be acquired at the current Federal funds rate.

III. ECONOMIC INDICATORS AND INTEREST RATES

A. The Economic Calendar

The Federal Reserve targets and maintains the federal funds rate based on its perception of the economy. Banks use this targeted rate to loan each other excess federal reserves. The Federal Reserve and markets participants carefully watch the release of economic data in order to gauge how the Federal Reserve will adjust the target federal funds rate. The economic calendar includes Federal Reserve meeting dates, release of market sensitive data, and important economic information affecting our economy.

A typical week of financial information releases is represented in the next section.

B. Key Economic Statistics

Date	Statistic	For	Actual	Forecast	Market Expects	Prior
13-Jul	Export Prices ex-ag.	Jun	−0.10%	NA	NA	−0.40%
13-Jul	Import Prices ex-oil	Jun	−0.40%	NA	NA	−0.30%
13-Jul	Trade Balance	May	−$55.3B	−$56.0B	−$57.0B	−$56.9B
13-Jul	Treasury Budget	Jun	$22.4B	$21.0B	$28.0B	$19.1B

---

35. Regulation D requirements have nothing to do with the safety of the bank. The Federal Reserve has other requirements regarding sufficient working capital, which are not relevant to a discussion of Regulation D or federal funds. The exclusive purpose of the Regulation D requirement is to allow the Federal Reserve to affect interest rates by targeting the Federal funds rate and by participating in open market operations to achieve that rate.

Date	Statistic	For	Actual	Forecast	Market Expects	Prior
14-Jul	Core CPI	Jun	0.10%	0.20%	0.20%	0.10%
14-Jul	CPI	Jun	0.00%	0.10%	0.30%	−0.10%
14-Jul	Initial Claims	Jun	336K	325K	322K	320K
14-Jul	Retail Sales	Jun	1.70%	0.90%	0.90%	−0.30%
14-Jul	Retail Sales ex-auto	Jun	0.70%	0.60%	0.50%	0.00%
15-Jul	Business Inventories	May	–	0.20%	0.40%	0.30%
15-Jul	Core PPI	Jun	–	0.20%	0.10%	0.10%
15-Jul	NY Empire State Index	Jul	–	10	9	11.6
15-Jul	PPI	Jun			–	0.20%
15-Jul	Capacity Utilization	Jun	–	79.70%	79.60%	79.40%
15-Jul	Industrial Production	Jun	–	0.50%	0.40%	0.40%
15-Jul	Michigan Sentiment	Jul	–	95	94.5	96

Each economic data point provides a picture of the health of the economy. By analyzing this data, the Federal Reserve determines the current domestic economic condition. In response to each data release, the market will adjust its perception of how assets should be valued. There are several key economic releases that economists use to analyze the economy:

Import Price Indexes. Import price indexes measure the average change in import prices of a fixed basket of goods. The prices are generally either "free on board" (f.o.b.) foreign port or "cost, insurance, and freight" (c.i.f.) United States port transaction prices, depending on the practices of the individual industry.[36]

Balance of Trade. The balance of trade reflects the difference in the value of exports and imports in the American economy. Where exports exceed imports there is a trade surplus; the reverse is a trade deficit. The United States Census Bureau and the United States Bureau of Economic Analysis, through the Department of Commerce, release the statistics of the total monthly exports and imports.[37]

---

36. *See* U.S. Bureau of Labor Statistics definition at http://data.bls.gov/.
37. *See* Bureau of Economic Analysis at www.bea.gov.

Treasury Monthly Budget. Issued by the United States Treasury, the Treasury Monthly Budget contains information on the monthly budget deficit. Generally, a growing deficit will increase the yield on United States Government bonds. The effect of a trade deficit is that the Treasury will have to issue more bonds to finance its operations. As the government issues more bonds, the new supply pressures bond price, thereby pushing interest rates higher.

Consumer Price Index (CPI). The Consumer Price Index, issued by The Bureau of Labor Statistics (BLS) demonstrates changes in retail prices that American consumers paid for a basket of goods. This report provides a measure of domestic economic activity. The BLS gathers price information from selected department stores, supermarkets, service stations, doctors' offices, rental units, and so forth. About 80,000 prices are recorded in 87 urban areas. The information contained in the CPI provides an accurate picture of the increase or decrease in prices that consumers are paying for their goods.[38]

Initial Jobless Claims. The United States Department of Labor reports on the number of people who have filed for unemployment insurance or unemployment benefits during the prior week. By analyzing these statistics, the Federal Reserve and the capital markets are better able to understand the employment picture in the United States on a weekly basis. Because maximum unemployment is a key goal of the Federal Reserve, these statistics provide valuable insight into the health of the economy and the resulting direction of interest rates.

Retail Sales. A monthly report issued by the United States Census Bureau measures the cost of all goods sold by retailers based on a sampling of various retail stores. This report is a solid indication of the Consumer Confidence Index, a monthly survey of 5,000 households designed to measure Americans' optimism about their current and future situation, which is issued by the Conference Board, a research organization for businesses. Since automobile sales can be quite volatile but are nonetheless included in the weekly retail sales report, many economists look at the retail sales report but exclude automobile sales.

Business Inventories. A monthly report issued by the United States Department of Commerce measures the change on a month-to-month basis in manufacturers,' retailers,' and wholesalers' inventories. These changes are reflected on a percentage basis. The ratio of inventories to sales is particularly important because an increase in the ratio of inventory to sales might indicate a slow down in the economy.

Producer Price Index (PPI). Released monthly by the Bureau of Labor Statistics, this index measures changes in prices on the wholesale level. Included in the PPI are prices of food, certain commodities, and energy products. The PPI, therefore, is a direct measure of inflation on a wholesale level. Increases in wholesale prices are likely to carry over into the consumer market place and may

---

38. *See* U.S. Department of Labor Bureau of Labor Statistics at http://www.bls.gov.

have an impact on consumer spending and the CPI. The core CPI that excludes food and energy (components which are generally more price volatile) is usually more indicative of macroeconomic inflationary trends. When inflation increases, yields rise, and the market will confirm its reaction to the release of the PPI data when the CPI is released.

New York Empire State Index. The New York Federal Reserve Bank's New York Empire State Index reflects the results of a monthly survey of 175 manufacturing CEO's and presidents regarding certain business indicators. Respondents give their views regarding the likely direction of these same indicators six months ahead. This index is seasonally adjusted using the Philadelphia Federal Reserve's seasonal factors because there is insufficient historical data of its own to make a meaningful adjustment. Market participants follow the economic indicators reflected in this index to better understand the direction of regional economic activity. Excessive growth in these indicators may indicate inflationary pressure on the markets for capital.

Capacity Utilization. The Capacity Utilization report, released by The Board of Governors of the Federal Reserve System, measures the operating capacity of resources in the economy. This report gauges the use of economic resources throughout the economy and measures the amount of current productive capacity utilized. Industrial production data gives data watchers an indication of actual output relative to potential economic output throughout the domestic economy. These rates will generally rise during economic expansions and fall during recessions. Where capacity utilization is increasing month to month, the market may infer that the economy is expanding, resulting in increased inflation and higher interest rates.

Industrial Production. The report on industrial production, issued by The Federal Reserve, measures the total output of United States factories and mines. It is considered a key economic indicator measuring the all of the goods produced by the economy. Industrial production rises during economic expansions and falls during recessions. Higher levels of industrial production signal growth in the economy. Bond yield will often rise in response to higher industrial production numbers, reflecting capital market inflation concerns.

The University of Michigan's Consumer Survey. The University of Michigan's *Consumer Survey* reports on the results of a survey of 500 American households conducted monthly by the University of Michigan. The sentiment of American consumers is directly correlated to consumer spending. Consumer spending has a great influence on asset valuation in that it is a strong influence on demand for goods and services throughout the economy. Consumer spending accounts for more than two-thirds of the economy, so the markets are constantly examining the consumer attitude towards spending. The more confident consumers are about their personal economic situation, the more likely they are to spend money to increase economic productivity.[39]

---

39. *See* http://www.nasdaq.com/econoday/reports/.

C. Asset Pricing and Short-Term Interest Rates

As economic data changes, the Federal Reserve and the capital markets react by affecting prevailing interest rates. As asset prices revalue in response to changes in short-term rates, the prices of stock as well as other asset classes will advance or decline. As the assets are revalued, there is a global change in perception and wealth. When stock or housing prices rise in reaction to lower interest rates, people are richer and thus are more willing to spend money to fuel economic growth. When people have more money they buy more cars, employ more laborers, and fuel economic growth in a meaningful way.

Changes in interest rates also directly affect the value of the dollar as compared to other currencies. As interest rates rise in the United States, the return on dollar-based investments (investment in American capital markets) becomes more attractive. The increasing value of the dollar thereby affects the global economic relationship of the United States to its trading counterparties. A stronger dollar may mean cheaper Japanese imports and therefore a higher living standard for those who benefit from using the latest and greatest imported Japanese technology. However, this increasing strength of the dollar, which allows for Americans to import more goods, has the unfortunate consequence of affecting exports by American companies. As dollar-denominated goods become more expensive to foreigners, American companies are less able to sell their goods abroad, thereby limiting expansion for the American manufacturer. This limiting quality of a strong dollar can reduce domestic expansion and cause economic contraction. The Federal Reserve watches and is aware of the balance of trade and includes this statistic in its formulation of monetary policy.

Each interest rate move at the Federal Reserve has a profound effect on asset valuation and domestic spending. For example, a company may not be willing to make an investment in a new plant because its cost to borrow money is too high. However, a change in the prevailing interest rate might allow it to make an investment that would otherwise have been untenable. Similarly, lower mortgage rates allow homebuyers to purchase more expensive homes than they would have otherwise, thereby increasing housing activity and prices in the housing market. Such an increase in housing prices increases the consumer wealth, allowing the consumer to spend more money. Indeed, when housing prices rise, homeowners may withdraw equity from their homes to buy cars, expand businesses, and to otherwise fuel the economy. A similar effect occurs from higher stock prices, where increased consumer wealth leads to increased spending in the economy.

During the recent credit crisis, however, low interest rates have done little to spur the economy. Banks' inability or unwillingness to part with cash for credit had made low interest rates somewhat meaningless to borrowers who are unable to access capital. In response, the Federal Reserve has become a direct short term lender by participating in the short-term commercial paper market in order to keep those windows of borrowing open where no cash has been forthcoming from normal market participants and to facilitate short term spending by the borrowers of that capital.

The aggregate spending and investing activities of Americans and corporations fuels the domestic economy. While lower interest rates will ordinarily spur the economy, a rising interest rate environment can have the opposite effect, thereby causing a reduction in economic spending and activity. Where economic data leads the Federal Reserve to conclude that there is a general slowdown in the economy, the Federal Reserve can ease monetary policy by lowering interest rates, thereby stimulating growth. The increased access to capital facilitated by lower interest rates stimulates demand. This will ordinarily be effective when credit markets are functioning normally, which has not been the case in 2008.

By contrast, in a period of broad economic growth, where the economy grows unfettered, inflation pressures begin to seep into the supply and demand equation. As demand increases in an expanding economy, the price of goods rises as supply is unable to absorb the increased demand in consumer spending. As prices increase, consumers will buy less consumer goods. When inflation begins to affect economic growth, the Federal Reserve steps in to forestall that growth by raising interest rates.

For example, when everyone has lots of money and wants to buy cars, those car prices will rise. Once those prices rise to a level where the car is no longer an attractive purchase, consumers will stop buying. Reduced demand for American goods and services can result in an economic bust. In this example, the automobile manufacturer will stop selling cars, close plants, and eliminate labor. These unemployed laborers will no longer have money to spend in the economy and the economy might quickly reverse course. In response to an economy where the Federal Reserve perceives inflationary pressures, the Federal Reserve will be inclined to tighten the availability of money by raising interest rates and slowing growth to a more sustainable level. By doing so, the Federal Reserve is able to bring supply back in line with demand, thereby maintaining growth.

Another source of inflation may stem from too much liquidity in the system. That is to say, as the Fed prints more dollars the dollar loses value. A major concern stemming from the steps the Fed has taken in 2008 and from any subsequent liquidity efforts it may undertake is when the line is crossed that will lead to creating inflation from the glut of dollars in the system. Tempering this concern is the fact that as stock markets and assets decline in value, the domestic impact on wealth may be so deflationary that the influx of excessive liquidity may be unimportant until the economy begins to improve.

D. Monetary Policy Decisions

In forming monetary policy, the Federal Reserve is faced with numerous and often contradictory data points, which make the job of setting interest rates subtle and often quite difficult. The Federal Reserve studies data points reflecting *past* economic activity; it is sometimes difficult to determine what is going on in the economy at a given moment in the *present*. Policy makers must rely on economic assumptions and reasonable projections in steering the economy;

Federal Reserve economists analyze data using statistical probabilities to determine likely outcomes. The actions of the Federal Reserve reflect the best efforts of the central bank to determine the correct course of action for the American economy; however, the Federal Reserve cannot guaranty that its adjustments in the target federal funds rate will in fact have the desired impact on economic expansion or contraction.

IV. THE ROLE OF THE FEDERAL OPEN MARKET COMMITTEE

The Federal Reserve sets United States monetary policy. It has a mandate from Congress to determine and implement monetary policy "so as to promote effectively the goals of maximum employment, stable prices, and moderate long-term interest rates."[40]

A. Affecting the Federal Funds Rate
The Federal Reserve currently implements monetary policy by directly affecting the federal funds rate, that is, the market rate for deposits held at Federal Reserve Banks as negotiated between financial institutions. By announcing a target federal funds rate, and then participating in the marketplace while setting reserve requirements to manifest those rates, the Federal Open Market Committee directly affects the federal funds rate. The Federal Reserve exercises control over the supply and demand for federal funds and thereby implements its policy targets and objectives.

The Federal Reserve accomplishes its monetary policy objectives, in part, by targeting the federal funds rate. By adjusting the target for the federal funds rate the Federal Reserve hopes to influence liquidity in the economy. To achieve its mandated objectives of sustainable growth with maximum employment, the Federal Open Market Committee influences the course of the United States economy, helping it to grow rapidly enough to make full use of available resources but not so rapidly as to stoke inflation.

Historically, it was somewhat of a misconception to assume that the Federal Reserve "controls interest rates." The funds rate is the rate needed to achieve equality between the demand for and the supply of reserves held at the Federal Reserve, and that is a market rate, not an administered rate set by fiat. As the Fed increases its involvement in direct market participation by purchasing longer term obligations, the interest rates that affect the economy most, those of longer duration, will be directly affected. The Federal Open Market Committee's main goal is to take the appropriate actions, and set policy that will steer the economy on a sustainable path of growth while preventing risk to the system.

---

40. 12 U.S.C. §225a.

According to a 2004 speech by Governor Bernanke, "[t]he current funds rate imperfectly measures policy stimulus because the most important economic decisions, such as a family's decision to buy a new home or a firm's decision to acquire new capital goods, depend much more on longer-term interest rates, such as mortgage rates and corporate bond rates, than on the federal funds rate. Long-term rates, in turn, depend primarily not on the current funds rate but on how financial market participants expect the funds rate and other short-term rates to evolve over time. For example, if financial market participants anticipate that future short-term rates will be relatively high, they will usually bid up long-term yields as well; if long-term yields did not rise, then investors would expect to earn a higher return by rolling over short-term investments and consequently would decline to hold the existing supply of long-term bonds. Likewise, if market participants expect future short-term rates to be low, then long-term yields will also tend to be low, all else being equal. Monetary policy makers can affect private-sector expectations through their actions and statements, but the need to think about such things significantly complicates the policymakers' task."[41]

Federal funds are reserves held in a bank's Federal Reserve Bank account. If a bank holds more federal funds than is required to cover its Regulation D reserve requirement, those excess reserves may be lent to another financial institution with an account at a Federal Reserve Bank. To the borrowing institution, these funds are federal funds purchased. To the lending institution, they are federal funds sold.

Federal funds purchases are not government insured and are not subject to Regulation D reserve requirements or insurance assessments. They can be borrowed only by those depository institutions that are required by the Monetary Control Act of 1980 to hold reserves with Federal Reserve Banks: commercial banks, savings banks, savings and loan associations, and credit unions. These transactions generally occur without a formal, written contract, which is a unique feature of federal funds.[42]

It was only after the passage of the Monetary Control Act of 1980 that state chartered banks were required to join the Federal Reserve System and to maintain non–interest-bearing reserves with the central bank; prior to 1980, state-chartered banks could elect to join, but their participation in the system was not mandatory. When inflation rates rose in the late 1970s and interest rates increased, voluntary participation of state-chartered banks in the Federal Reserve System declined, as did the level of reserve deposits.

---

41. Remarks by Governor Ben S. Bernanke, "The Logic of Monetary Policy" Before the National Economists Club, Washington, D.C. December 2, 2004.

42. Board of Governors of the Federal Reserve System, TRADING AND CAPITAL-MARKETS ACTIVITIES MANUAL §4005.1.

B. Treatment of Federal Funds

The Monetary Control Act of 1980 required that all depository institutions hold "sterile" reserves with the Federal Reserve as deposits earning no interest. These deposits are held in the form of currency known as "vault cash."[43] The Federal Reserve recently implemented a program for the payment of market-rate interest on these reserves in order to increase bank liquidity and to take up the slack resulting from banks that were unwilling to engage in counterparty transactions with banks whose fortunes could change overnight. The Federal Reserve described its decision in an October 6, 2008, press release:

> The Federal Reserve Board on Monday announced that it will begin to pay interest on depository institutions' required and excess reserve balances. The payment of interest on excess reserve balances will give the Federal Reserve greater scope to use its lending programs to address conditions in credit markets while also maintaining the federal funds rate close to the target established by the Federal Open Market Committee. . . .
>
> These actions should encourage term lending across a range of financial markets in a manner that eases pressures and promotes the ability of firms and households to obtain credit. The Federal Reserve stands ready to take additional measures as necessary to foster liquid money market conditions. . . .
>
> The Financial Services Regulatory Relief Act of 2006 originally authorized the Federal Reserve to begin paying interest on balances held by or on behalf of depository institutions beginning October 1, 2011. The recently enacted Emergency Economic Stabilization Act of 2008 accelerated the effective date to October 1, 2008.
>
> Employing the accelerated authority, the Board has approved a rule to amend its Regulation D (Reserve Requirements of Depository Institutions) to direct the Federal Reserve Banks to pay interest on required reserve balances (that is, balances held to satisfy depository institutions' reserve requirements) and on excess balances (balances held in excess of required reserve balances and clearing balances).
>
> The interest rate paid on required reserve balances will be the average targeted federal funds rate established by the Federal Open Market Committee over each reserve maintenance period less 10 basis points. Paying interest on required reserve balances should essentially eliminate the opportunity cost of holding required reserves, promoting efficiency in the banking sector.
>
> The rate paid on excess balances will be set initially as the lowest targeted federal funds rate for each reserve maintenance period less 75 basis points. Paying interest on excess balances should help to establish a lower bound on the federal funds rate. The formula for the interest rate on excess balances may be adjusted subsequently in light of experience and evolving market conditions.

---

43. 12 U.S.C. §461(c).

The payment of interest on excess reserves will permit the Federal Reserve to expand its balance sheet as necessary to provide the liquidity necessary to support financial stability while implementing the monetary policy that is appropriate in light of the System's macroeconomic objectives of maximum employment and price stability.

The Board also approved other related revisions to Regulation D to prescribe the treatment of balances maintained by pass-through correspondents under the new rule and to eliminate transitional adjustments for reserve requirements in the event of a merger or consolidation. In addition, the Board approved associated minor changes to the method for calculating earnings credits under its clearing balance policy and the method for recovering float costs.[44]

Historically, the United States Treasury had opposed the paying of interest on these deposits because it views the payment if interest as an unwarranted use of "taxpayer resources."[45]

The Federal Reserve has taken the position that

noninterest-bearing reserve requirements represent a tax on depository institutions that is not borne by other suppliers of financial services [and which] impairs the efficiency of resource allocation. . . . Paying such interest would circumvent the ill effects of reserve requirements while preserving their advantages for monetary policy. . . . Reserve requirements provide for a reasonably predictable demand for overall reserve balances [which] is essential for the effective implementation of open market operations.[46]

With the crisis of 2008 in full swing, the Federal Reserve has begun to pay interest of federal funds.

C. Implementing Monetary Policy

The Federal Open Market Committee oversees open market operations, which is the main tool used by the Federal Reserve to implement monetary policy.[47] The FOMC meets eight times each year to discuss monetary policy and implement change when necessary. The FOMC can also meet by conference call if necessary in between scheduled meeting dates. As a result of these deliberations,

---

44. Federal Reserve Press Release, October 6, 2008.

45. Testimony of Treasury Acting Undersecretary Donald V. Hammond before the Subcommittee on Financial Institutions and Consumer Credit of the Committee on Financial Services, U.S. House of Representatives, March 13, 2001.

46. Texas State Bank v. United States, 423 F.3d 1370 (Fed. Cir 2005), citing Letter from Alan Greenspan, Chairman, Board of Governors of Federal Reserve System, to Rep. Stephen Neal, Chairman, Subcommittee on Domestic Monetary Policy of House Committee on Banking, Finance, and Urban Affairs (March 6, 1992).

47. See THE FEDERAL RESERVE SYSTEM, PURPOSES AND FUNCTIONS 3, http://www.federalreserve.gov/pf/pf.htm.

monetary policy is set and Federal Reserve open market participation is determined. Congress mandates that the FOMC works to ensure price stability and the greatest sustainable employment. The FOMC works to encourage sustained growth in the economy without fostering inflation. The Federal Reserve, through open market operations, can affect short-term interest rates.

The Federal Open Market Committee's main goal is to take appropriate actions and set policy which will steer the economy on a sustainable path of growth. At times, when the economy is slowing down, the FOMC might lower its target on Federal Fund Rates to provide financial stimulus for the economy. By making money cheaper to borrow, more money is available to be used for endeavors stimulating economic growth. "Financial stimulus" is not an exact science, but its target is to encourage households, consumers, and corporations to spend money more freely. A good example of the stimulating effect of lower interest rates may be seen in the United States housing market, which has grown immensely since 2002 as a result of lower mortgage rates. The increased value in homes allows consumers to feel richer, to borrow more money on their home equity, and to spend more money. This spending helps the economy to grow. The Federal Reserve walks a fine line between maintaining growth while not fostering inflation.

To increase the supply of reserves, the Federal Reserve will purchase securities, crediting the seller with an increase in reserve balances on deposit with the Federal Reserve corresponding to the amount of the purchase. If the seller is not a bank, the Federal Reserve credits the reserve account of the seller's correspondent bank. Similarly, a sale of securities from the Federal Reserve's portfolio results in debits of the counterparty to the transactions, thereby draining reserve balances from the system. In practice the Federal Reserve does not sell securities but will allow its own securities to mature without replacing them when it wants to drain reserves from the system.

The manager of the open market desk of the Federal Reserve bears the responsibility of adjusting Federal funds to maintain the funds rate at or near the target rate established by the FOMC. Open market operations are set in motion to achieve that target rate. In addition the Federal Reserve stands ready to lend depository institutions federal funds at a rate of proximately 100 basis points over the target federal funds rate.

D. Open Market Operations

In a March 2005 speech on "Implementing Monetary Policy" then Governor Ben S. Bernanke offered a unique look into the targeting of the federal funds market rate:

> The funds rate is a market rate, not an administered rate set by fiat—that is, the funds rate is the rate needed to achieve equality between the demand for and the supply of reserves held at the Fed . . . [T]he demand for reserve balances arises both because banks must hold required reserves and because

reserve balances are useful for facilitating transactions. Because of the scale of and volatility in daily payments flows, the demand for reserve balances can vary substantially from one day to the next.

The supply of reserve balances is largely determined by the Federal Reserve—at the operational level, by the specialists at the Federal Reserve's Open Market Desk, located in the Federal Reserve Bank of New York in the New York financial district. For example, to increase the supply of reserves, the Open Market Desk purchases securities (usually government securities) on the open market, crediting the seller with an increase in reserve balances on deposit at the Fed in the amount of the purchase, thus, a purchase of a billion dollars' worth of securities by the Open Market Desk increases the supply of funds available to lend in the fed funds market by the same amount. Similarly, sales of securities from the Fed's financial portfolio result in debits against the accounts of commercial banks with the Fed and thus serve to drain reserve balances from the system. Collectively, these transactions are called open-market operations. Factors outside the control of the Open Market Desk can also affect the supply of reserve balances. For example, when the Federal Reserve receives an order for currency from a bank, it debits the reserve account of the bank in payment when the currency is shipped, thereby reducing reserve supply. When deciding upon open market operations to control the supply of reserves, the Open Market Desk must take account of these external factors.

In practice, the Open Market Desk uses several methods of performing open-market operations. In some cases it purchases securities outright, that is, with the intention of holding the securities in its portfolio indefinitely. Outright purchases are used to offset long-lasting changes in factors affecting the demand for and supply of reserves. For example, long-term increases in the private sector's demand for currency have largely been met by outright purchases of securities. Over the years, the Fed has accumulated a portfolio of more than $700 billion of Treasury securities, mostly as an offset to its issuance of currency. In contrast, in cases in which variations in the demand for reserves or in external factors affecting reserve supply appear likely to be temporary, the Desk typically prefers to conduct open-market operations through short-term or long-term repurchase agreements, known as repos. Under a repurchase agreement, the buyer and seller of a security agree to reverse the transaction after a certain fixed period. Thus, when the Open Market Desk purchases securities under a repo agreement, the resulting increase in reserve balances lasts only until the time at which the transaction is reversed. Over the course of a year, the value of repos on the Fed's books on any given day may range from a few billion dollars to $30 billion or more. In the period before the millennium date change (Y2K), when the demand for currency was temporarily very high, the daily value of repos peaked at nearly $150 billion.

The manager of the Open Market Desk and his team bear the responsibility of adjusting the supply of fed funds to maintain the funds rate at or near the target established by the FOMC. Meeting this objective on a daily basis is technically challenging. To hit the funds rate target, the Desk staff must forecast the daily demand for balances as well as changes in external factors affecting reserves supply. Open-market operations are then set in motion to balance the supply of and demand for reserves at the target funds rate.

Shortly after 9 a.m. each morning, the Desk staff and staff members at the Board of Governors confer over the phone to discuss their respective estimates of the day's demand for balances as well as to consider factors that may affect supply. The Desk manager and his staff also keep in close touch with fed funds brokers and other market participants so as to be able to assess general market conditions. The Desk's market contacts are useful not only for controlling the funds rate but also for obtaining broader financial-market information for the use of Fed policymakers.

At 9:20 a.m., a conference call is held between the Desk staff, Board staff, and the President of a Reserve Bank. The Desk staff summarize the projections for reserves demand and supply, report on conditions in the federal funds market and global financial market developments, and present to the President their plans for open-market operations for his or her comment.[48]

E. Targeting the Federal Funds Rate

As an additional means for managing the federal funds, the Federal Reserve stands ready to lend reserves to depository institutions that request them. Financially sound banks are eligible to borrow from the Fed at what is called the "primary credit rate," which to date has been set at 100 basis points (1 percentage point) above the target funds rate. Historically, reserve shortages occasionally caused the funds rate to "spike" well above its target, once even hitting 100 percent (in 1991). The primary credit facility is designed to avoid such spikes by providing an elastic supply of reserves at a rate not far above the funds rate target.

The Federal Reserve recently announced its intention to target interest rates at or near zero. In observing the weakness in the economy, the Federal Reserve has taken unprecedented steps to spur growth. The Federal Reserve Open Market Committee explained its decision as follows:

> The Federal Open Market Committee decided today to establish a target range for the federal funds rate of 0 to 1/4 percent.
>
> Since the Committee's last meeting, labor market conditions have deteriorated, and the available data indicate that consumer spending, business

---

48. Governor Ben S. Bernanke, Implementing Monetary Policy, Remarks at the Redefining Investment Strategy Education Symposium (March 30, 2005).

investment, and industrial production have declined. Financial markets remain quite strained and credit conditions tight. Overall, the outlook for economic activity has weakened further.

Meanwhile, inflationary pressures have diminished appreciably. In light of the declines in the prices of energy and other commodities and the weaker prospects for economic activity, the Committee expects inflation to moderate further in coming quarters.

The Federal Reserve will employ all available tools to promote the resumption of sustainable economic growth and to preserve price stability. In particular, the Committee anticipates that weak economic conditions are likely to warrant exceptionally low levels of the federal funds rate for some time.

The focus of the Committee's policy going forward will be to support the functioning of financial markets and stimulate the economy through open market operations and other measures that sustain the size of the Federal Reserve's balance sheet at a high level. As previously announced, over the next few quarters the Federal Reserve will purchase large quantities of agency debt and mortgage-backed securities to provide support to the mortgage and housing markets, and it stands ready to expand its purchases of agency debt and mortgage-backed securities as conditions warrant. The Committee is also evaluating the potential benefits of purchasing longer-term Treasury securities. Early next year, the Federal Reserve will also implement the Term Asset-Backed Securities Loan Facility to facilitate the extension of credit to households and small businesses. The Federal Reserve will continue to consider ways of using its balance sheet to further support credit markets and economic activity.[49]

F. How the Federal Reserve Talks Up the Market

Central banks around the world have become noticeably more open and transparent over the past fifteen years or so.[50] Policymaking committees have adopted various mechanisms to enhance their communication with the public, including more informative policy announcements, postmeeting press conferences, expanded testimony before the legislature, the release of the minutes of policy meetings, and the regular publication of reports on monetary policy and the economy.

This increased openness is a welcome development, for many reasons. Perhaps most importantly, as public servants whose policy actions affect the lives of every citizen, central bankers have a basic responsibility to give the public full and compelling explanations of the rationales for those actions. Besides satisfying the principle of democratic accountability, a more open policymaking

---

49. Federal Reserve Press Release, December 16, 2008.

50. Ben S. Bernanke (remarks at the Meetings of the American Economic Association, San Diego, California January 3, 2004).

process is also likely to lead to better policy decisions, because engagement with an informed public provides central bankers with useful feedback in the form of outside views and analyses. Yet another benefit of full and timely release of information about policy decisions and their rationales is a reduced risk that market-sensitive information will dribble out through inappropriate channels, giving unfair advantage to some financial market participants.[51]

The fact that market expectations of future settings of the federal funds rate are at least as important as the current value of the funds rate in determining key interest rates such as bond and mortgage rates suggests a potentially important role for central bank communication. If effective communication can help financial markets develop more accurate expectations of the likely future course of the funds rate, policy will be more effective and risk in financial markets should be reduced as well.[52]

G. Inflation Targeting

A rich recent literature on learning and macroeconomics has emphasized that actual inflation and inflation expectations may to some degree evolve independently, and that effective monetary policy stabilizes inflation expectations as well as inflation itself.[53] It is far easier to make sense of the term structure of Treasury yields if one assumes that expectations about long-run inflation adjust in a reasonable adaptive manner.[54]

The Federal Reserve has become increasingly more open about its processes and about its decision making. The Federal Reserve has an important responsibility to maintain strong and sustained employment growth and continues to use the federal funds targeting approach to implement monetary policy. In recent years, a promising new approach to effecting monetary policy has emerged: inflation targeting. This approach has been adopted by a number of European Central Banks, and has been considered by Federal Reserve Chairman Ben S. Bernanke and other leading economists as a potential course for United States monetary policy.

Inflation targeting is a process whereby the central bank publicly announces and pursues specific targets for the rate of inflation. Inflation targeting is a framework for monetary policy characterized by the public announcement of official quantitative targets (or target ranges) for the inflation rate over one or

---

51. *Id.*

52. *Id.*

53. Ben S. Bernanke, *Inflation Targeting: Prospects and Problems*, (Remarks at the 28th Annual Policy Conference: Federal Reserve Bank of St. Louis, St. Louis, Missouri, October 17, 2003).

54. Ben S. Bernanke, *Monetary Policy Modeling: Where Are We and Where Should We Be Going?* (remarks at the Federal Reserve Board Models and Monetary Policy Conference, Washington, D.C. March 27, 2004).

more time horizons, and by explicit acknowledgement that low, stable inflation is monetary policy's primary long-run goal. Among other important features of inflation targeting are vigorous efforts to communicate with the public about the plans and objectives of the monetary authorities, and, in many cases, mechanisms that strengthen the central bank's accountability for attaining those objectives. Inflation targeting can be described as a form of "constrained discretion." Under a constrained discretion approach, central banks adhere to a conceptual structure while maintaining flexibility.

Inflation targeting represents continuity with the existing approach of the Federal Reserve System. The existing approach of the Federal Reserve System focuses on maintaining medium- and long-term inflation stability as the primary contribution that the Federal Reserve can make to maintaining stability of the general economy.

The inflation targeting ideas simply are an attempt to perhaps codify or strengthen this important commitment of the Federal Reserve to maintaining low inflation. One of the best ways is to maintain, in the medium and long term, low and stable inflation and inflation expectations. To the extent that naming a long-term inflation objective can help to stabilize those expectations and keep inflation under control, it actually significantly advances the Federal Reserve's ability to meet the dual mandate and to increase employment growth.[55]

Inflation targeting, at least in its best-practice form, consists of two parts: a policy framework of constrained discretion and a communication strategy that attempts to focus expectations and explain the policy framework to the public. Together, these two elements promote both price stability and well-anchored inflation expectations; the latter in turn facilitates more effective stabilization of output and employment. Thus, a well-conceived and well-executed strategy of inflation targeting can deliver good results with respect to output and employment as well as inflation.[56] With the recent events creating a crisis mode at the Fed, discussions of inflation targeting have taken a back seat to implementing specific steps to preventing economic collapse.

55. Hearing Regarding Ben Bernanke's Nomination to be Chairman of the Board of Governors of the Federal Reserve, November 15, 2005, U.S. Senate Committee on Banking, Housing and Urban Affairs.

56. Ben S. Bernanke, *A Perspective on Inflation Targeting*, (remarks at the Annual Washington Policy Conference of the National Association of Business Economists, Washington, D.C., March 25, 2003).

APPENDIX A

SAMPLE FOMC MINUTES

The FOMC holds eight regularly scheduled meetings during the year, and other meetings as needed. It is required by the Federal Reserve Act to keep records of these meetings and to include them in its annual report to Congress. The Federal Reserve releases the minutes of regularly scheduled meetings three weeks after the date of the policy decision.

The release of Federal minutes is only one of the means by which the FOMC communicates with the public. When the FOMC meets, they release a statement on the same day they make a policy decision. Also, through speeches by members of the FOMC and through the Chairman's testimony the FOMC communicates biases and impressions of the capital markets.[57]

The minutes try to explain in plain language what happened at a particular FOMC meeting, and follow a standard organizational structure. Following are annotated minutes from the meeting of the FOMC held on May 9, 2007. These minutes reflect a calmer time in America's economic history than the latter half of 2007 and 2008 and are presented here to demonstrate how the Fed observes data under "normal" circumstances.

MINUTES OF THE FEDERAL OPEN MARKET COMMITTEE[58]

May 9, 2007
A meeting of the Federal Open Market Committee was held in the offices of the Board of Governors of the Federal Reserve System in Washington, D.C., on Wednesday, May 9, 2007 at 8:30 A.M.

> *Section I:* Lists the Attendees at the meeting. "Members" are the twelve voting Members of the FOMC. "Participants" includes voting and nonvoting Bank Presidents. "Staff" refers to those economists and other Federal Reserve staff members attending the meeting. The comments of all the participants at the meeting are reflected in the minutes. This section will also describe any organizational changes and approval of any FOMC documents.

---

57. Deborah J. Danker and Matthew M. Luecke, *Background on FOMC Meeting Minutes,* Federal Reserve Bulletin, p. 175 (Spring 2005).

58. Available at www.federalreserve.gov.

Present:

Mr. Bernanke, Chairman
Mr. Geithner, Vice Chairman
Mr. Hoenig
Mr. Kohn
Mr. Kroszner
Ms. Minehan
Mr. Mishkin
Mr. Moskow
Mr. Poole
Mr. Warsh
Mr. Fisher, Ms. Pianalto, and Messrs. Plosser and Stern, Alternate Members of the Federal Open Market Committee

Messrs. Lacker and Lockhart, and Ms. Yellen, Presidents of the Federal Reserve Banks of Richmond, Atlanta, and San Francisco, respectively

Mr. Reinhart, Secretary and Economist
Ms. Danker, Deputy Secretary
Ms. Smith, Assistant Secretary
Mr. Skidmore, Assistant Secretary
Mr. Alvarez, General Counsel
Mr. Baxter, Deputy General Counsel
Ms. Johnson, Economist
Mr. Stockton, Economist
Messrs. Connors, Evans, Kamin, Madigan, Rasche, Slifman, Tracy, and Wilcox, Associate Economists

Mr. Dudley, Manager, System Open Market Account

Messrs. Clouse and English, Associate Directors, Division of Monetary Affairs, Board of Governors

Ms. Liang and Mr. Struckmeyer, Associate Directors, Division of Research and Statistics, Board of Governors

Messrs. Leahy and Wascher, Deputy Associate Directors, Divisions of International Finance and Research and Statistics, respectively

Mr. Dale, Senior Adviser, Division of Monetary Affairs

Mr. Blanchard, Assistant to the Board, Office of Board Members, Board of Governors

Mr. Small, Project Manager, Division of Monetary Affairs, Board of Governors

Mr. Luecke, Senior Financial Analyst, Division of Monetary Affairs, Board of Governors

Mr. Carlson, Economist, Division of Monetary Affairs, Board of Governors

Ms. Low, Open Market Secretariat Specialist, Division of Monetary Affairs, Board of Governors

Ms. Green, First Vice President, Federal Reserve Bank of Richmond

Mr. Rosenblum, Executive Vice President, Federal Reserve Bank of Dallas

Mr. Hakkio, Ms. Perelmuter, Messrs. Rolnick, Rudebusch, Sniderman, and Weinberg, Senior Vice Presidents, Federal Reserve Banks of Kansas City, New York, Minneapolis, San Francisco, Cleveland, and Richmond, respectively

Messrs. Dotsey, Tallman, and Tootell, Vice Presidents, Federal Reserve Banks of Philadelphia, Atlanta, and Boston, respectively

The Manager of the System Open Market Account reported on recent developments in foreign exchange markets. There were no open market operations in foreign currencies for the System's account in the period since the previous meeting. The Manager also reported on developments in domestic financial markets and on System open market transactions in government securities and federal agency obligations during the period since the previous meeting. By unanimous vote, the Committee ratified these transactions.

By unanimous vote, the Committee extended for one year beginning in mid-December 2007 the reciprocal currency ("swap") arrangements with the Bank of Canada and the Banco de Mexico. The arrangement with the Bank of Canada is in the amount of $2 billion equivalent and that with the Banco de Mexico is in the amount of $3 billion equivalent. Both arrangements are associated with the Federal Reserve's participation in the North American Framework Agreement of 1994. The vote to renew the System's participation in the swap arrangements maturing in December was taken at this meeting because of the provision that each party must provide six months' prior notice of an intention to terminate its participation.

Section II: Describes the current economic conditions, economic forecasts based on recent data, and any topics that might come before the FOMC. In this section the FOMC will refer to the economic reports described in Section III.B., above.

The information reviewed at the May meeting suggested that economic activity had expanded at a below-trend pace in recent months. Gains in payroll employment had moderated, and the unemployment rate appeared to have sta-bilized after a period of decline. Housing construction remained under pressure from weak demand and large inventories of unsold homes, and consumer spend-ing appeared to have slowed in recent months. Business fixed investment remained subdued. Manufacturing production, however, showed signs of strengthening after a period of considerable softness. Rising energy prices pushed up total PCE price inflation in March, while the twelve-month increase in core PCE prices was just slightly above its year-earlier pace.

The average monthly increase in payroll employment through the first four months of this year was well below the relatively strong pace recorded in the fourth quarter of 2006. In April, the construction industry continued to shed jobs, manufacturing employment declined further, and retailers reduced hiring after a large gain in March. The unemployment rate stood at 4.5 percent in April, similar to its average in the first quarter, and the labor force participation rate moved down.

Industrial production increased at a modest annual rate of 1.4 percent in the first quarter, with the monthly pattern reflecting fluctuations in the output of utilities, which was influenced importantly by swings in weather conditions. Manufacturing output declined, on net, over the six months ending in February as a result of inventory-related adjustments in a number of industries. However, factory production turned up in March. The output of high-tech industries rose briskly; the production of consumer goods increased; and the output of business equipment, construction supplies, and materials picked up. The limited infor-mation available on industrial production for April suggested that output had been boosted by the scheduled pickup in motor vehicle assemblies.

Real consumer expenditures increased at a brisk pace in the first quarter, although monthly gains in spending slowed over the course of the quarter, in part because of swings in weather-related outlays on energy goods and energy services. Retail sales of both autos and light trucks moved up in the first quarter, but eased a bit in April. Real spending on goods other than motor vehicles, which had shown exceptional vigor late last year, was broadly flat between December and March. However, outlays on non-energy services were reported to have posted solid gains, especially in March. Real disposable personal income rose smartly in the first quarter. Wages and salaries increased solidly, on average, and the Bureau of Economic Analysis estimated that income in January was boosted by unusually large bonus payments and stock option exercises. The household wealth-to-income ratio likely ticked down in the first quarter, as the stock market rose only a little and house prices remained soft. However, given the surge in stock prices in April, much of the lost ground had probably since been made up.

Residential construction activity remained soft as builders attempted to work off elevated inventories of unsold new homes. Single-family housing starts moved up in March, almost certainly boosted by unusually warm and dry weather; single-family permit issuance also increased. Although existing home sales declined in March, the level of sales was only slightly below the steady pace that had prevailed in the second half of 2006. By contrast, new home sales fell sharply in the first two months of the year and had recovered only a bit in March. All told, recent readings on home sales suggested that housing demand had weakened further. House-price appreciation continued to slow, and some measures were again showing declines in home values.

Real spending on equipment and software rose modestly in the first quarter after having fallen in the fourth quarter of 2006. Spending on high-tech equipment, boosted by a surge in outlays on computers, posted a substantial increase in the first quarter. In addition, purchases of communications equipment—which tend to be volatile quarter to quarter—rebounded strongly after a fourth-quarter dip. By contrast, spending on transportation equipment declined significantly: Although domestic spending on aircraft jumped after three weak quarters, purchases of medium and heavy trucks dropped sharply, largely as a consequence of a pull-forward of truck purchases in the latter part of last year in anticipation of the tighter emissions standards that took effect in January. Business investment in equipment other than high-tech and transportation dropped in the first quarter, although the weakness in this broad category appeared to have been especially pronounced around the turn of the year and to have lessened somewhat over the course of the quarter. Robust corporate cash reserves and continuing declines in the user cost of high-tech goods remained supportive of equipment and software spending going forward. Real outlays for nonresidential construction regained some momentum in the first quarter of this year after having hit a lull in late 2006.

Real nonfarm inventory investment excluding motor vehicles increased at a slower pace in the first quarter of 2007 than in the previous quarter. The down-shift in inventory investment had helped to reduce the apparent overhangs that had emerged in late 2006. In the motor vehicle sector, the sharp decline in the pace of assemblies over the past few quarters appeared to have brought inventories back into line with sales. In April, surveys indicated that the net number of firms who viewed their customers' inventory levels as too high had dropped back from elevated readings over the previous two quarters.

The U.S. international trade deficit narrowed in February, reflecting a steep drop in imports, which more than offset a sizable decline in exports. Within imports, the value of oil imports plunged, reflecting decreases in both prices and quantities, and imports of industrial supplies, capital goods, and automotive parts also fell. The lion's share of the February decline in exports was of capital goods. Smaller decreases occurred in exports of industrial supplies, consumer goods, and services.

Economic activity in advanced foreign economies appeared to have grown at a steady rate in the first part of the year. Canada's growth seemed to have rebounded from a disappointing fourth quarter. Renewed household demand in

Japan pointed to further strong growth in the first quarter, while investment demand seemed to be underpinning growth in the United Kingdom. Although euro-area exports had slowed from the rapid pace set in the fourth quarter and the hike in the German value-added tax likely depressed consumption, overall economic conditions remained solid. Economic activity in the emerging market countries appeared to have continued to advance at a robust pace in the first quarter. Surging growth in China was a highlight of the strong performance of most countries in Asia. In Latin America, indicators pointed to further lackluster growth in Mexico and some weakening in Argentina, but in other countries, especially Brazil, conditions appeared more positive.

The total PCE price index rose substantially in both February and March. The advance in February was distributed across a broad range of categories, while the March increase was driven largely by a jump in the index for energy. Core PCE prices were unchanged in March after an upswing in February. Smoothing through the high-frequency movements, the twelve-month change in the core PCE price index in March was just a touch higher than the increase over the year-earlier period. Accelerations in the costs of housing and medical services were major contributors to both core CPI and core PCE inflation over the past year. Household surveys conducted in April indicated that the median expectation for year-ahead inflation had moved up, consistent with the recent pickup in head-line CPI inflation. Median expectations of longer-term inflation had edged higher but were still in the narrow range seen over the past few years. Average hourly earnings for production or nonsupervisory workers, which had accelerated noticeably over the past couple of years, posted moderate increases in March and April.

At its March meeting, the Federal Open Market Committee (FOMC) maintained its target for the federal funds rate at 5.25 percent. The Committee's accompanying statement noted that recent economic indicators had been mixed and that the adjustment in the housing sector was ongoing. Nevertheless, the economy seemed likely to expand at a moderate pace over coming quarters. Recent readings on core inflation had been somewhat elevated. Although inflation pressures seemed likely to moderate over time, the high level of resource utilization had the potential to sustain those pressures. The Committee's predominant policy concern remained the risk that inflation would fail to moderate as expected. Future policy adjustments would depend on the evolution of the outlook for both inflation and economic growth, as implied by incoming information.

Market participants had largely anticipated the FOMC's decision at its March meeting to leave the target federal funds rate unchanged. Nevertheless, the expected path for monetary policy moved lower on the announcement, as investors apparently interpreted the accompanying statement as suggesting that the Committee's economic outlook had become somewhat more balanced. However, subsequent FOMC communications—including the Chairman's testimony before the Joint Economic Committee, speeches by various FOMC members, and the minutes from the March meeting—were generally seen as emphasizing the Committee's concern about upside risks to inflation. Over the intermeeting period, yields on nominal Treasury securities edged up at all maturities. Measures of inflation compensation based on inflation-indexed Treasury securities were little changed despite a significant rise in oil prices. Yields on investment-grade corporate bonds rose in line with those on comparable-maturity Treasury securities, leaving their spreads little changed at fairly low levels. Spreads on speculative-grade corporate bonds narrowed. Equity prices climbed steeply amid solid earnings reports and improved sentiment, more than reversing the declines in the previous intermeeting period. The foreign exchange value of the dollar against other major currencies moved lower, on balance.

Gross bond issuance by nonfinancial businesses slowed from its torrid first-quarter pace in April, but acquisition-related financing continued to fuel the issuance of both investment- and speculative-grade corporate bonds. Commercial paper outstanding declined, but bank lending accelerated. In the household sector, the rise in home mortgage debt likely slowed a bit further in the first quarter, as home-price appreciation appeared to have remained sluggish. Consumer credit continued to expand at a moderate pace early in the year. M2 accelerated during March and April, primarily reflecting faster growth in liquid deposits, which were likely boosted in April by tax-related flows.

In its forecast prepared for this meeting, the staff expected the pace of economic activity to pick up from weak first-quarter growth to a rate a little below that of the economy's long-run potential for the remainder of this year and to increase at a pace broadly in line with potential output in 2008. The projected gradual acceleration in economic activity largely reflected the expected waning of the drag from residential investment, although recent readings on sales and inventories of new homes had been interpreted by the staff as suggesting that the ongoing contraction in residential investment would continue for longer than previously expected. In response to data received over the past year, the staff had marked down slightly its estimate of structural productivity growth and nudged up its estimate for the increase in labor supply—leaving its estimate of the overall growth of potential GDP broadly unchanged. The increases in energy and other commodity prices over the intermeeting period had led the staff to revise up its forecast for headline PCE inflation during the first half of the year. Nonetheless, the staff continued to expect core inflation to edge lower over the course of the next two years.

Section III: Describes individual participants' evaluation of current economic data and the macroeconomic situation. This section will vary from meeting to meeting based on the ensuing consideration of the topics at hand.

In their discussion of the economic situation and outlook, participants noted that their assessments of the medium-term prospects for economic growth and inflation had not changed materially from the previous meeting. The pace of economic expansion had slowed in the first part of this year, but the recent sub-par performance probably exaggerated the weakness of underlying demand, and the rate of economic growth was expected to pick up in coming quarters. Meeting participants anticipated that real GDP would advance at a pace a little below the economy's trend rate of growth through the remainder of this year and then pick up to a rate broadly in line with the economy's trend rate in 2008. Most participants continued to expect core inflation to slow gradually, although considerable uncertainty surrounded that judgment and the Committee's predominant concern remained the risk that inflation would fail to moderate as expected.

The incoming data on new home sales and inventories suggested that the ongoing adjustment in the housing market would probably persist for longer than previously anticipated. In particular, the demand for new homes appeared to have weakened further in recent months, and the stock of unsold homes relative to sales had increased sharply. That said, participants also noted that sales of existing homes appeared to have held up somewhat better since the beginning of the year. Moreover, the turmoil in the subprime market evidently had not spread to the rest of the mortgage market; indeed, mortgage rates available to prime borrowers remained well below their levels of last summer. Nevertheless, most participants agreed that, although the level of inventories of unsold homes that homebuilders desired was uncertain, the correction of the housing sector was likely to continue to weigh heavily on economic activity through most of this year—somewhat longer than previously expected.

Growth in consumer spending appeared to have slowed over the past few months. Real spending on goods had flattened out, and contacts in both the retail sector and the consumer credit sector reported a softening in the expansion of demand. In contrast to the rapid gains of recent years, meeting participants expected household expenditure to grow at a more moderate pace in coming quarters. Consumption was likely to be supported by continued advances in employment and incomes, as well as gains in stock prices; but the recent increases in gasoline prices probably would damp households' spending power in the near term, and the effect of the anticipated leveling out in home-price appreciation on household wealth was expected to contribute to a gradual increase in the personal saving rate over the medium run. Participants remained concerned that the housing market correction could have a more pronounced impact on consumer spending than currently expected, especially if house prices were to decline significantly.

The growth of business fixed investment seemed most likely to move higher in coming quarters, supported by strong corporate balance sheets and profits, favorable financial conditions, and a gradual strengthening in business output. The downside risks to business capital spending appeared to have diminished somewhat since the previous meeting. In particular, participants took note of the upturn in orders and shipments of capital goods, and of more upbeat surveys of business conditions. However, participants cautioned against drawing too much comfort from the most recent few data observations, and recognized that the current sluggishness of equipment outlays could persist for longer than currently anticipated, especially if financial market conditions became less supportive. Participants were also encouraged that, outside of the construction sector, the correction of inventories to more comfortable levels appeared well advanced, thus reducing the possibility that going forward this adjustment process could trigger shortfalls in business spending and output.

Economic activity in the rest of the world continued to advance briskly. Participants noted that strong foreign expansion should help to underpin demand for U.S. exports, but expressed some concern that the strength of global demand could contribute to price pressures at home. Prices of non-energy commodities, especially metals, had moved up markedly since the previous meeting. Moreover, inflationary pressures in a number of overseas economies appeared to have increased of late, perhaps partly in response to heightened levels of capacity utilization in those countries, and this development had the potential to add to the prices of U.S. imports. In that regard, several participants noted that the decline in the foreign exchange value of the dollar over the intermeeting period could reinforce the upward pressure on import prices.

Participants discussed how best to reconcile the slowdown in output growth over the past year with the relatively strong performance of the labor market. This apparent tension could partly reflect measurement issues; in particular, participants noted that the more-rapid gains in estimates of gross domestic income over this period might better capture the pace of activity than the modest advances in measured GDP. Aside from measurement problems, a possible explanation was that these differing trends largely related to the lagged adjustment of employment to the slowing pace of expansion. In that regard, several participants observed that the recent moderation in economic growth had been concentrated in the construction sector, but that measured employment in construction had not yet declined by a corresponding amount. This suggested that increases in overall employment in coming quarters may possibly be held down by notable declines in construction employment as the adjustment of the labor force in that sector played out. A slowing in employment could then occur in conjunction with a strengthening in productivity growth. Alternatively, some of the recent weakness in measured productivity growth could reflect a decline in the underlying trend in productivity and so might persist. Although this explanation might help account for some of the downshift in measured productivity growth, participants agreed that there appeared to be little other evidence pointing to a significant slowing of advances in structural productivity. In the context of this discussion, many participants commented that their view of potential output growth was somewhat more optimistic than that of the staff.

Labor markets appeared to remain relatively tight. Unemployment continued around the low levels seen since last fall, and many business contacts reported difficulties in recruiting suitably qualified workers, especially for certain types of professional and skilled positions. However, several participants observed that aggregate measures of labor compensation had so far increased only modestly, perhaps suggesting that the labor market might be less stretched than it appeared. Moreover, even if wages and salaries did accelerate, the resulting cost pressures might be absorbed by a narrowing in firms' profit margins from current elevated levels, rather than being passed on in the form of higher prices. On the other hand, some participants reported that their business contacts appeared very resistant to any squeeze in profit margins. All told, for most participants, the apparent tightness of the labor market remained a significant source of upside risk to inflation.

Nearly all participants viewed core inflation as remaining uncomfortably high and stressed the importance of further moderation. Although readings on core inflation in March had been more favorable, this followed several months of elevated inflation data and price pressures were not yet viewed as convincingly on a downward trend. Most participants expected core inflation to moderate gradually, fostered in part by stable inflation expectations and a likely deceleration in shelter costs. Some participants also expected the anticipated slight easing of pressures on resources to help nudge inflation lower, although others felt that small movements in resource utilization were unlikely to have discernible effects on inflation. All participants agreed that the risks around the anticipated moderation in inflation were to the upside; and some noted that a failure of inflation to moderate could entail significant costs particularly if it led to an upward drift in inflation expectations.

In the Committee's discussion of monetary policy for the intermeeting period, all members favored keeping the target federal funds rate at 5.25 percent. Recent developments were seen as supporting the Committee's view that maintaining the current target rate was likely to foster moderate economic growth and a gradual ebbing in core inflation. Members continued to view the risks to economic activity as weighted to the downside, although with turmoil in the subprime market appearing to have remained relatively well contained and business spending indicators suggesting a more encouraging outlook, these downside risks were judged to have diminished slightly. Members agreed that considerable uncertainty attended the prospects for inflation, and the risk that inflation would fail to moderate as desired remained the Committee's predominant concern.

In light of the recent economic data and anecdotal information, the Committee agreed that the statement to be released after the meeting should acknowledge that economic growth had slowed in the first part of the year. The Committee thought that the statement should reiterate the view that the adjustment in the housing market was ongoing, but that nevertheless the economy seemed likely to expand at a moderate pace over coming quarters. While readings on core inflation were lower in March, members felt that it was appropriate to emphasize that core inflation remained somewhat elevated. The Committee agreed that the statement should continue to note that their predominant policy concern was the risk that inflation would fail to moderate as expected, and that future policy adjustments would depend on the evolution of the outlook for both inflation and economic growth.

> *Section IV:* Describes any policy decisions taken at the meeting and the result of any votes. This section further announces the date of the next FOMC meeting and the result of any actions that were taken between meetings.

At the conclusion of the discussion, the Committee voted to authorize and direct the Federal Reserve Bank of New York, until it was instructed otherwise, to execute transactions in the System Account in accordance with the following domestic policy directive:

"The Federal Open Market Committee seeks monetary and financial conditions that will foster price stability and promote sustainable growth in output. To further its long-run objectives, the Committee in the immediate future seeks conditions in reserve markets consistent with maintaining the federal funds rate at an average of around 5.25 percent."

The vote encompassed approval of the text below for inclusion in the statement to be released at 2:15 P.M.:

"In these circumstances, the Committee's predominant policy concern remains the risk that inflation will fail to moderate as expected. Future policy adjustments will depend on the evolution of the outlook for both inflation and economic growth, as implied by incoming information."

Votes for this action: Messrs. Bernanke, Geithner, Hoenig, Kohn, and Kroszner, Ms. Minehan, Messrs. Mishkin, Moskow, Poole, and Warsh.

Votes against this action: None.

Meeting participants briefly discussed the next steps in their review of communication issues and agreed to consider them at the next FOMC meeting, confirmed for June 27–28, 2007.

The meeting adjourned at 1:15 P.M.

Notation Vote

By notation vote completed on April 10, 2007, the Committee unanimously approved the minutes of the FOMC meeting held on March 20–21, 2007.

Vincent R. Reinhart
Secretary

APPENDIX B

FAQs: MBS PURCHASE PROGRAM

The following frequently asked questions (FAQs) provide further information about the program to purchase agency mortgage-backed securities (agency MBS) that was announced by the Federal Reserve on November 25, 2008. This agency MBS program will be managed at the direction of the Federal Open Market Committee (FOMC) by the Federal Reserve Bank of New York (New York Fed). The New York Fed has selected four investment managers to help implement the agency MBS program.

Effective December 30, 2008

Q. What is the policy objective of the Federal Reserve's program to purchase agency mortgage-backed securities?

A. The goal of the program is to provide support to mortgage and housing markets and to foster improved conditions in financial markets more generally.

Q. Why is it necessary for the Federal Reserve to transact in the agency MBS market via external investment managers?

A. The operational and financial characteristics of MBS purchases are significantly more complicated than those associated with the assets that have traditionally been purchased by the Federal Reserve. The Federal Reserve has chosen external investment managers as a means of implementing the MBS program quickly and efficiently while at the same time minimizing operational and financial risks.

Because of the size and complexity of the agency MBS program, a competitive request for proposal (RFP) process was employed to select four investment managers and a custodian. The investment managers are BlackRock Inc., Goldman Sachs Asset Management, PIMCO and Wellington Management Company, LLP. The selection criteria were based on the institution's operational capacity, size, overall experience in the MBS market and a competitive fee structure. The contract for a custodian is not yet final.

Q. What securities are eligible for purchase under the program?

A. Only fixed-rate agency MBS securities guaranteed by Fannie Mae, Freddie Mac and Ginnie Mae are eligible assets for the program. The program includes, but is not limited to, 30-year, 20-year and 15-year securities of these issuers. The program does not include CMOs, REMICs, Trust IOs/Trust POs and other mortgage derivatives or cash equivalents. Eligible assets may be purchased or sold in specified pools, in "to be announced" (TBA) transactions, and in the dollar roll market.

Q. What is the investment strategy that will be employed?

A. Investment managers will employ a passive buy and hold investment strategy in accordance with investment guidelines prescribed by the Federal Reserve.

Purchases will be guided by commonly referenced market indices. The agency MBS program will involve the outright purchase of up to $500 billion in agency MBS by the investment managers on behalf of the Federal Reserve by the end of the second quarter of 2009. The New York Fed will adjust the pace of its purchases based on input from the investment managers about market conditions and the impact of the program. The investment managers will be required to purchase securities frequently and to disclose the Federal Reserve as principal.

The investment strategy may involve the use of dollar rolls as a supplemental tool to smooth market supply and demand. A dollar roll is a transaction involving the sale of agency MBS for delivery in the current month and the simultaneous agreement to repurchase substantially similar (although not the same) securities on a specified future date.

Q. Does the agency MBS program expose the Federal Reserve to increased risk of losses?
A. Assets purchased under this program are fully guaranteed as to principal and interest by Fannie Mae, Freddie Mac, and Ginnie Mae, so the Federal Reserve's exposure to the credit risk of the underlying mortgages is minimal. The market valuation of agency MBS can fluctuate over time based on the interest rate environment; however, the Federal Reserve's exposure to interest rate risk is mitigated by the conservative, buy and hold investment strategy of the agency MBS purchase program.

Q. When will the purchases begin?
A. Purchases are expected to begin in early January, 2009.

Q. Who will the investment managers trade with and who is eligible to sell agency MBS to the Federal Reserve under the program?
A. Initially, the investment managers will trade only with primary dealers who are eligible to transact directly with the Federal Reserve Bank of New York. Primary dealers are encouraged to submit offers for themselves and for their customers.

Q. Will the agency MBS held by the Federal Reserve through this program be eligible for lending through the Treasury Securities Lending Facility (TSLF) or the daily System Open Market Account (SOMA) securities lending operations conducted by the New York Fed?
A. There are no plans for the agency MBS held by the SOMA to be available for borrowing through the TSLF or the daily securities lending program.

Q. How will purchases under the agency MBS program be financed?
A. Purchases will be financed through the creation of additional bank reserves.

Q. What is the legal basis for the agency MBS purchase program?
A. Purchases of agency MBS in the open market, under the direction of the FOMC, are permitted under section 14(b) of the Federal Reserve Act.

Q. How is the Federal Reserve's agency MBS purchase program related to the U.S. Treasury's efforts to purchase agency MBS?

A. The Federal Reserve's agency MBS program is separate and distinct from the U.S. Treasury's program but both programs are aimed at fostering improved conditions in mortgage markets.

Q. How will holdings under the agency MBS program be reported?

A. Balance sheet items related to the agency MBS purchase program will be reported after settlement occurs on the H.4.1. statistical release titled "Factors Affecting Reserve Balances of Depository Institutions and Condition Statement of Federal Reserve Banks." There will be an explanatory cover note on the release when the new items appear for the first time. However, these data may be published well after trade execution due to agency MBS settlement conventions. In addition, the New York Fed will publish the SOMA agency MBS activity in more detail on its external website on a weekly basis.

Q. What measures will the Federal Reserve take to ensure that an investment manager implementing the MBS program will not have an unfair advantage relative to other market participants due to the information it receives about the MBS program?

A. Each investment manager will be required to implement ethical walls that appropriately segregate the investment management team that implements the Federal Reserve's agency MBS program from other advisory and proprietary trading activities of the firm. The New York Fed will monitor each investment manager's compliance with this requirement.

Q. Where should questions regarding the MBS purchase program be directed?

A. Questions regarding the MBS program should be directed to the New York Fed's Public Affairs department: 212-720-6130.

6. ASSET VALUATION

During the recent market turmoil, the Federal Reserve has navigated U.S. interest rates lower. Lower interest rates affect the pricing of all assets, as interest rates are a vital component of asset valuation. Economic pricing depends on incorporating certain pricing assumptions into valuation models in order to determine the "value" of an asset. Value is determined by the future expected cash flow discounted at a rate that reflects the riskiness of the cash flow. In determining what discount rate to incorporate in a valuation formula, the cost of capital is adjusted for the risk taken in making the investment; applicable interest rates will vary based on investors' perception of risk.

I. THE USE OF INTEREST RATES IN ASSET VALUATION

Interest rates play a vital role in the pricing of assets throughout the economy. Changes in interest rates have an effect on the valuation of the various financial instruments that are used to increase opportunity or to reduce risk for investors. Investors incorporate a basic understanding of the cost of capital into their investment decisions in order to rationally deploy their capital. In evaluating a particular investment, an investor is able to determine whether to assume the risks associated with that investment in order to achieve profit. It is the amalgam of these investment decisions that the Federal Reserve considers when making interest rate decisions affecting the macroeconomy by raising or lowering the target for the federal fund rate.[1]

Economic pricing depends on incorporating certain pricing assumptions into valuation models in order to determine the "value" of an asset. Investors deploy capital in order to maximize profit and to minimize the risk of loss. The risk an investor takes should be related to the related expected reward from making an investment. An investor's perception of risk reflects her perception of the possibility of loss. Portfolio Theory assumes that a rational investor seeks to minimize

---

1. *See* Chapter 5, *supra* for a complete discussion of the Federal Reserve and the federal funds rate.

risk while maximizing reward.[2] The true value of an asset is determined by discounting the value of an asset by its attendant risk. In making an investment decision, investors incorporate a "hurdle rate" into their analysis of whether to make an investment. The hurdle rate is the rate of return an investor requires, above which the investment makes sense and below which it does not. The hurdle rate may be a function of the investors' cost of capital adjusted for risk.

Value is determined by "the future expected cash flow discounted at a rate that reflects the riskiness of the cash flow."[3] The relationship of risk and reward are manifest in pricing models by discounting the cash flow or return from an investment by the prevailing interest rate. The present value of an asset is calculated by incorporating the discount rate (i.e., what is a dollar worth at some point in the future). The cost of capital as demonstrated in the discount rate incorporates risk variability. Cost of capital is the essence of risk analysis. What banks charge for capital demonstrates the risk that bank determine in loaning out money. Determining the value of an asset, then, requires an analysis of the return generated by the asset discounted by the cost of money tied up in that investment. Value or pricing of an asset is the sum of risk-adjusted return.

II. INTEREST RATE YIELD CURVE

In determining what discount rate to incorporate in a valuation formula, the cost of capital must be adjusted for the risk taken in making the investment. Any hurdle rate will consider the risk-free return on investments as manifest in the pricing of obligations issued by the United States Treasury. Affecting that risk-free return is the current federal funds rate.[4] The federal funds rate affects other interest rates but is not the most direct influence on asset valuation and investment decision-making.

As discussed in the previous chapter, Ben Bernanke explained that "[t]he current funds rate imperfectly measures policy stimulus because the most important economic decisions, such as a family's decision to buy a new home or a firm's decision to acquire new capital goods, depend much more on longer-term interest rates, such as mortgage rates and corporate bond rates, than on the

---

2. Harry Markowitz, *Portfolio Selection*, 7 J. FIN. 77 (1952); Robert C. Merton, *Theory of Rational Option Pricing*, 4 BELL J. ECON. & MGMT. SCI. 141 (1973); William F. Sharpe, *Capital Asset Prices: A Theory of Market Equilibrium Under Conditions of Risk*, 19 J. FIN. 425 (1964).

3. *See* Robert J. Rhee, *The Effect of Risk on Legal Valuation*, 78 U. COLO. L. REV. 193 (Winter 2007), citing THOMAS E. COPELAND, ET AL., VALUATION: MEASURING AND MANAGING THE VALUE OF COMPANIES 73 (2d ed. 1995).

4. *See* Chapter 5, *supra*, for a complete discussion of the federal funds rate.

federal funds rate. Long-term rates, in turn, depend primarily not on the current funds rate but on how financial market participants expect the funds rate and other short-term rates to evolve over time. For example, if financial market participants anticipate that future short-term rates will be relatively high, they will usually bid up long-term yields as well; if long-term yields did not rise, then investors would expect to earn a higher return by rolling over short-term investments and consequently would decline to hold the existing supply of long-term bonds. Likewise, if market participants expect future short-term rates to be low, then long-term yields will also tend to be low, all else being equal. Monetary policy makers can affect private-sector expectations through their actions and statements . . ."[5]

A. Types of Yield Curves

The yield curve is a graphical representation of a specific type of financial instrument and its corresponding yield over a specified period. Expectations of future monetary policy affect the shape of the yield curve. The horizontal axis of the graph represents the duration of a financial instrument; the vertical axis represents the yield of that instrument. There are three types of yield curves: normal sloping, flat, and inverted, depending on the relationship between the short-term yield and the long-term yield.

A normal sloping yield curve (Figure 6.1) represents an interest rate environment where interest rates in the short term are lower than those in the long term:

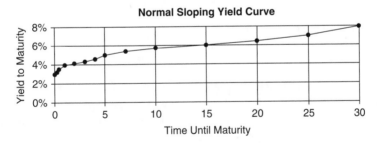

FIGURE **6.1 NORMAL SLOPING YIELD CURVE**

A flat yield curve (Figure 6.2) reflects an interest rate environment where there is little difference between long-term and short-term interest rates. In other words, investors are not rewarded proportionately for holding longer-term assets, as they would be in a normal yield curve environment.

5. Ben S. Bernanke, *The Logic of Monetary Policy*, (remarks before the National Economists Club, Washington, D.C., December 2, 2004).

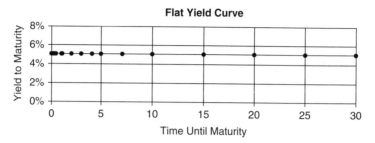

FIGURE 6.2 FLAT YIELD CURVE

An inverted yield curve (Figure 6.3) reflects economic conditions where investors are paid a higher return on short-term assets than they are on longer-term assets.

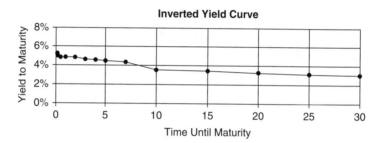

FIGURE 6.3 INVERTED YIELD CURVE

Interest rates vary based on investors' perception of risk. There is a school of thought that it may be possible to gauge investors' perception of the economy base on the yield curve. The normal yield may reflect a healthy economy where investors perceive normal growth over the specified time horizon. The flat yield curve may reflect a market environment where investors perceive little or no economic growth. A flat yield curve can reflect the market perception of a transitional phase, where investors perceive a shift from positive to negative growth or vice versa. The inverted yield curve may reflect a negative outlook on the economy. Investors may perceive an economic slow down or a recession on the horizon. While there is some credible historical evidence that the yield curve may portend economic growth, stagnation, or recession, there are other interpretations offered to the shape of the yield curve.[6]

---

6. Ben S. Bernanke, *The Logic of Monetary Policy*, (remarks before the National Economists Club, Washington, D.C., December 2, 2004).

B. Why the Yield Curve May Be Flat or Inverted

Dr. Ben S. Bernanke, Chairman of the Board of Governors of the Federal Reserve System, has spoken on the shape of the yield curve and why a yield curve might be flat or inverted. He offered one set of explanations that focus on special factors that may have influenced market demands for long-term securities per se, independent of the macroeconomic outlook.[7] The following discussion is a summary of his remarks.

1. Increase in Market Demand for Long-Term Securities Each long-term interest rate has two components: (1) the spot interest rate that market participants currently expect to prevail at the corresponding date in the future, and (2) the additional compensation that investors require for the risk of holding longer-term instruments, known as the "term premium." With the economic outlook held constant, changes in the net demand for long-term securities have their largest effect on the term premium. In particular, if the demand for long-dated securities rises relative to the supply, then investors will generally accept less compensation to hold longer-term instruments—that is, the term premium will decline.

There are four possible reasons why the net demand for long-term issues may have increased, lowering the term premium.

(1) Longer-maturity obligations may be more attractive because of more stable inflation, better-anchored inflation expectations, and a reduction in general economic volatility. If investors have come to expect this past performance to continue, they might believe that less compensation for risk—and thus a lower term premium—is required to justify holding longer-term bonds.

(2) Increased intervention in currency markets by a number of governments, particularly in Asia, have put downward pressure on yields, as foreign official institutions, primarily central banks, have invested the bulk of their greatly expanded dollar holdings in United States Treasuries and closely substitutable securities.

(3) Reforms have been proposed that encourage pension funds to be more fully funded and to take steps to better match the duration of their assets and liabilities. These changes may have increased the demand for longer-maturity securities, as pension funds tilt the composition of their portfolios toward long-duration bonds substantially over time.

(4) As investors' demands for long-duration securities may have increased over the past few years, the supply of such securities seems not to have kept pace. The average maturity of outstanding Treasury debt, for example, has dropped by 1.5 years since its peak in 2001.

---

7. Ben S. Bernanke, (remarks before the Economic Club of New York, NY, March 20, 2006).

2. Long-Term Yield Affected by Federal Reserve Monetary Policy Since longer-term investments can be viewed as a series of short-term investments strung together, short-term monetary policy of the Federal Reserve will have a relative effect on longer-term asset valuation. Therefore the Federal Reserve will watch the yield curve in order to make adjustments to its monetary policy. Chairman Bernanke has further described the erosion of term premium on monetary policy:[8]

If the decline in forward rates can be traced to a decline in the term premium, perhaps for one or more of the reasons articulated above, the effect is financially stimulative and argues for greater monetary policy restraint, all else being equal. Specifically, if spending depends on long-term interest rates, special factors that lower the spread between short-term and long-term rates will stimulate aggregate demand. Thus, when the term premium declines, a higher short-term rate is required to obtain the long-term rate and the overall mix of financial conditions consistent with maximum sustainable employment and stable prices.

However, if the behavior of long-term yields reflects current or prospective economic conditions, the implications for policy are quite the opposite. When low or falling long-term yields reflect investor expectations of future economic weakness investors will mark down their projected path of future spot interest rates, lowering far-forward rates and causing the yield curve to flatten or even to invert. Indeed, historically, the slope of the yield curve has tended to decline significantly in advance of recessions.

When drags on the growth of spending do materialize, then a lower real interest rate will be needed to sustain aggregate demand and keep the economy near full employment. To be consistent with a lower long-term real rate, the short-term policy rate might have to be lower than it would otherwise be as well.

After the events of 2008, the Fed has taken specific steps to effect long term interest rates to improve asset pricing throughout the economy. By increasing the size of the Federal Reserve's balance sheet and buying Treasury and Agency securities, the Fed seeks "to promote economic recovery and to preserve price stability."[9]

---

8. *Id.*
9. Federal Reserve Press Release March 17, 2009.

7. UNITED STATES TREASURY SECURITIES

I. PURPOSE AND GOALS

The impact of lower interest rates facilitated by the Fed's reaction to market turmoil is that prices of treasury securities have risen, and thus interest rates have fallen. This price rise is due to the perception that treasuries are a risk-free investment (the risk-free premium), the Fed's direct purchase of treasury securities, and the impact of lower interest rates on the pricing of bonds generally.

Treasury securities are a type of financial instrument designed to provide an investor with limited credit risk in the form of a debt investment. United States Treasury bills, notes, and bonds (collectively known as "Treasuries") are issued by the Treasury Department and represent direct obligations of the United States government. Treasuries are issued in various maturities of up to thirty years. Treasury securities are offered by the United States Treasury Department to meet the needs of investors who wish to "loan" money to the Federal Government and in return receive a fixed or floating interest rate. The United States Treasury Yield curve is a benchmark for fixed income securities across the spectrum of debt securities.

The United States began issuing debt in 1776 to finance the Revolutionary War. In 1789, President George Washington appointed Alexander Hamilton to serve as the first Secretary of the Treasury. As Secretary, Hamilton established three goals for the Treasury that still guide the Department today:

- Achieve the lowest possible debt service cost,
- Ensure access to unlimited credit in times of war or emergencies, and
- Promote efficient capital markets.

Alexander Hamilton's plan for the United States economy has allowed Treasury securities to become the world's safest, most liquid financial instruments. Treasury securities are unique in their virtually nonexistent default risk and their tight bid offer spreads. Treasuries have evolved to be the investment of choice for safety. It is because of their universal appeal as a credit risk–free investment that they have facilitated the expansion of the United States economy. Given the size and success of the American economy and the Government's taxing power, financial markets regard treasuries to be default risk-free.[1] Financial market participants use treasury securities to approximate the risk-free rate of return.

A. Risk-Free Nature

Treasuries are backed by the full faith and credit of the United States government and have little or no credit risk, (the risk that a debtor will be unwilling or unable to meet its obligations under the terms of a loan when that obligation matures). The risk-free nature of United States Treasuries allows them to be utilized as the linchpin of many economic functions in the United States and abroad. The universal appeal of Treasuries allows them to be used in the following ways:

- by the Federal Reserve to carry out monetary policy,
- by foreign currency boards as reserves for dollar-linked currencies,
- as the default risk free United States benchmark
- as the yield determinate for pension funding adequacy
- by portfolio managers to hedge risk, and
- as a benchmark in determining the required return from riskier investments.[2]

---

1. Garry J. Schinasi, Charles F. Kramer, and R. Todd Smith, Financial Implications of the Shrinking Supply of United States Treasury Securities 12 (Washington, D.C.: International Monetary Fund, 2001).

2. See Federal Debt: Market Structure and Economic Uses For United States Treasury Debt Securities, (Joint Economic Committee United States Congress, August 2001).

B. Primary Dealers

Newly issued Treasuries are auctioned by the United States Treasury through the primary market, and subsequently trade over the counter in the secondary market. Primary dealers are banks and securities brokerages that trade in United States Government securities directly with the Federal Reserve System.[3] As of September 2008, there were 19 primary dealers. Primary dealers' daily average trading volume in United States Government securities was approximately $570 billion during 2007.[4]

Primary dealers trade United States Treasuries with the Federal Open Market Committee trading desk at the Federal Reserve Bank of New York. It is this desk that engages in open market operations to effectuate monetary policy.[5] Open market transactions occur through a competitive bidding process among the primary dealers.

The Federal Reserve ("the Fed") requires primary dealers to participate meaningfully in both the Fed's open market operations and Treasury auctions and to provide the Fed's trading desk with market information and analysis that are helpful in the formulation and implementation of monetary policy. In 1992, the New York Fed changed its criteria for administering its counterparty (primary dealer) relationships. One change eliminated a standard for trading volume with customers. Another disbanded the Bank's dealer surveillance unit and shifted its focus to market surveillance.[6]

According to the New York Fed's current criteria, bank-related primary dealers must be in compliance with Tier I and Tier II capital standards under the Basel Capital Accord, with at least $100 million of Tier I capital. Registered broker-dealers must have at least $50 million in regulatory capital and must not be in violation of the regulatory "warning levels" for capital set by the Securities and Exchange Commission and the Treasury.[7] The minimum absolute levels of capital are designed to help insure that primary dealers are able to enter into transactions with the Fed in sufficient size to maintain the efficiency of trading desk operations. Should a firm's capital position fall below these minimum standards, the Federal Reserve Bank of New York (FRBNY) may suspend its trading relationship until the firm's capital position is restored to levels corresponding to these minimum standards. In making such determinations, the FRBNY will look to the firm's primary Federal regulator for guidance as to whether the firm

---

3. *See* List of the Primary Government Securities Dealers Reporting to the Government Securities Dealers Statistics Unit of the Federal Reserve Bank of New York, www.newyorkfed.org/newsevents/news/markets/2007/an070208.html.

4. http://www.newyorkfed.org/aboutthefed/fedpoint/fed02.html.

5. *See* Chapter 5, *supra.*

6. http://www.newyorkfed.org/aboutthefed/fedpoint/fed02.html.

7. Federal Reserve Bank of New York Operating Policies as of January 22, 1992, http://www.newyorkfed.org/markets/pridealers_policies.html.

has in place an acceptable plan to restore its capital position in a reasonable period of time. However, in no circumstances will the Bank maintain a trading relationship with a primary dealer that is unable to restore its capital position to the stipulated minimum level within a year. Over time, the maximum grace period of one year may be shortened and would not apply in any event if a firm's capital position were seriously impaired.

II. DESCRIPTION OF U.S. TREASURY SECURITIES

A. Types of Treasury Securities

1. Treasury Bills Treasury bills are short-term investments offered by the United States government, they are offered at a discount to their face value and mature in less than one year. They are offered to the public via an auction system. Treasury bills (T-bills) are:

> negotiable, noninterest-bearing securities with original maturities of three months, six months, and one year. T-bills are offered by the Treasury in minimum denominations of $10,000, with multiples of $5,000 thereafter, and are offered only in book-entry form. T-bills are issued at a discount from face value and are redeemed at par value. The difference between the discounted purchase price and the face value of the T-bill is the interest income that the purchaser receives. The yield on a T-bill is a function of this interest income and the maturity of the T-bill. The returns are treated as ordinary income for federal tax purposes and are exempt from state and local taxes.[8]

The Treasury department determines how much of a particular treasury bill it wishes to issue on a weekly basis. T-bills are issued at regular intervals on a yield-auction basis. The three-month and six-month T-bills are auctioned every Monday. The one-year T-bills are auctioned in the third week of every month. The amount of T-bills to be auctioned is released on the preceding Tuesday, with settlement occurring on the Thursday following the auction. The auction of T-bills is done on a competitive-bid basis (the lowest-yield bids are chosen because they will cost the Treasury less money). Noncompetitive bids may also be placed on purchases of up to $1 million. The price paid by these bids (if allocated a portion of the issue) is an average of the price resulting from the competitive bids. Treasury bills are zero coupon instruments; they pay no interest and are issued at a discount to face value. They can be redeemed from the Treasury at maturity, or sold in the secondary market.

2. Treasury Notes and Bonds Unlike treasury bills, treasury notes and bonds are fixed income, interest-bearing securities with a fixed coupon payable

---

8. TRADING AND CAPITAL-MARKETS ACTIVITIES MANUAL §4020.1 (Board of Governors of the Federal Reserve System).

semiannually until maturity. Treasury notes and bonds can be held until maturity or sold before maturity in the secondary market. Treasury notes are currently issued in maturities of two, three, five and ten years on a regular schedule, and are not callable. The term "Treasury Bonds" is usually associated with the 30-year bond.

The "par value" of a Treasury note or bond is its face amount, which usually differs from the price at which it is trading in the market. For example, a bond with a par value of $1,000 ($1,000 is the lowest denomination sold and is referred to as one bond) may sell for more or less than $1,000 depending on market factors. Treasury bonds are quoted and priced as a percentage of par value to the nearest 1/32 of one percent. For example if a $1,000 Treasury bond were priced at "100," it would actually sell at $1,000. A bond that sold at 102:16 would bring 102 16/32 percent for each $100 of par value, or $1,025.

B. Pricing

There is a secondary market for Treasury bills and notes once they have been issued. There is also a market for treasuries trading on a "when-issued" basis. Bonds trade based on a "yield-to-maturity."

1. **Discounts and Premiums** Treasury bills are priced at a discount to their face value. For example, a $1 million treasury bill maturing in six months, trading at a 5% discount (to face value) would be priced at approximately $975,000 dollars ($1 million x 5% is $50,000 for one year of interest and $25,000 for six months of interest). The Treasury bill is said to be trading at a "5% discount." The discounted value is different than the Treasury bill's "yield-to-maturity." That is to say, since the investor is earning $25,000 on a $975,000 investment, the investor's yield or return is higher than 5% ($25,000 annualized/$ 975,000 is approximately 5.20%).

Treasury notes trade based on their yield to maturity, and are issued and traded as a percentage of face value. For instance, an investor who buys a two-year treasury note from the United States Treasury might pay 100% of face value for a note paying a semiannual interest payment of 5% (annualized). The note is therefore deemed to be trading at a "5% yield." The dollar price is easily determined by virtue of the yield in considering its 5% coupon. A 5% coupon note trading at a 5% yield is obviously trading at 100% (of face value). A note trading at 100% of face value is called a "par" bond.[9]

2. **Factors Affecting Yield** Numerous factors influence the yield and therefore the pricing of treasury notes. The Fed's activities in targeting the federal funds rate[10] influence the direction of short-term interest rates but also influence

---

9. *See* Chapter 6, Sec. I, *supra,* for further discussion of interest rates and asset valuation.

10. *See* Chapter 5, Sec. IV.D, *supra,* for further discussion of targeting the federal funds rate.

longer-term investments as well. The ten-year Treasury yield, for instance, can be viewed as a weighted average of the current one-year rate and nine one-year forward rates, with the weights depending on the coupon yield of the security. Current and near-term forward rates are particularly sensitive to monetary policy actions, which directly affect spot short-term interest rates and strongly influence market expectations of where spot rates are likely to stand in the next year or two.

Short-term interest rates influence long-term rates because any investor has the choice of holding either a long-term security or a series of short-term securities, reinvesting his or her funds in a new short-term security as the old short-term security matures. Since both short-term and long-term Treasury securities are willingly held in the marketplace, investors must be roughly indifferent between short-term and long-term securities, implying that (on average and abstracting from any term premiums) expected future short-term rates must be similar to the current long-term yield.

When market participants aggressively buy treasuries, the price will rise and the associated yield on that financial instrument will fall.

The inverse relationship between treasury prices and yield can be best understood by thinking of an investment in treasuries as an investment in a machine generating cash flow every year at a fixed production rate. The machine lasts for a fixed duration and then can be redeemed for a fixed amount of money. If that machine generates $5 bills twice per year, and it costs $100, it is a "10% machine." If that machine can be redeemed in ten years for $100, it is similar to the structure of a ten-year treasury note with a 10% coupon. If the Treasury Department (the inventor of the machine) creates a new improved device that generates $10 bills twice a year, the old $5 machines will become worthless. No one will want to own a 10% machine in a 20% machine environment unless they can pick one up at a significant discount. Therefore the prices of money machines and bonds are inversely related to their yield. This is also true if the inventor of the money

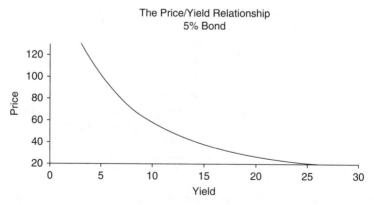

The Price/Yield Relationship
5% Bond

FIGURE 7.1 THE PRICE/YIELD RELATIONSHIP ON A 5% BOND

machine stops making money machines. The price will go up as more people want the money machines and there are less available. Bonds that pay a fixed rate of return and are now worth more than 100% of face value are said to be trading at a "premium." Bonds trading under face value are described as trading at a "discount."

III. BOND AUCTIONS AND THEIR EFFECT ON PRICE

The United States Treasury issues securities by auction. Primary dealers and individuals bid on bonds of particular durations at the auction held by the United States Treasury at regular intervals. The Treasury creates the financial instruments. These instruments are subsequently traded between and among counterparties in the secondary market. The amount of treasuries issued affects the pricing of outstanding issues in the secondary market; therefore, the Treasury's issuance and forbearance of issuing securities affects the yields of outstanding securities trading in the secondary market. As yields rise and fall on a particular security, the price of that security moves inversely to the direction of the yield.

A. Interruption of Supply: *SEC v. Davis et al.*

On October 31, 2001, the United States Treasury announced that they would no longer issue thirty-year bonds in the auction process. In August of 2005, Treasury announced the reintroduction of the thirty-year bond. Treasury held its first auction of the bond in five years on February 9, 2006. The prior thirty-year bond auction took place on August 9, 2001.

The Securities and Exchange Commission (SEC) alleged that when the announcement was made that the Treasury would stop issuing the thirty-year bond, a consultant tipped a number of secondary market traders that the thirty-year bond would be eliminated. As a result, traders who were "tipped" made money on this "inside information." The SEC sued all those involved claiming that they had benefited illegally form nonpublic information. In *SEC v. Davis et al.,*[11] the SEC filed a complaint against Peter J. Davis, Jr., John M. Youngdahl, and Steven E. Nothern, for insider trading based on the events of October 31, 2001.[12] The case, which was subsequently settled,[13] illustrates the effect of the Treasury's decision to discontinue the thirty-year bond on the price of those bonds in the secondary market.

According to the complaint, Davis, a Washington, D.C.-based consultant, Youngdahl, formerly a Vice President and Senior Economist at Goldman Sachs & Co., Inc. (Goldman Sachs), a New York broker-dealer; and Nothern, formerly

---

11. Civ. Act. No. 03-CV6672 (NRB) (S.D.N.Y, Sept. 4, 2003).

12. http://www.sec.gov/litigation/complaints/comp18322.htm.

13. http://www.sec.gov/litigation/litreleases/lr18322.htm.

a mutual fund manager at Massachusetts Financial Services Company (MFS), violated the Federal securities laws' prohibition against insider trading.

Davis was a paid consultant to Goldman Sachs and MFS, among others. According to the SEC, Davis tipped off Youngdahl and Nothern with material nonpublic information that the Treasury would suspend issuance of the thirty-year bond. Davis received this information at a Treasury quarterly refunding press conference; these conferences are held at the Treasury to notify the public how much debt will be issued by the Treasury in the coming quarter. This information was announced at 9:25 A.M., and embargoed until 10:00 A.M., when it would be released to the public. Nevertheless, Davis violated the embargo and notified Youngdahl and Nothern between 9:28 and 9:41 A.M. Before the suspension of the thirty-year bond was announced publicly at 10:00 A.M., Youngdahl, Nothern, and other portfolio managers to whom they communicated this information purchased large quantities of the thirty-year bonds.

Public announcement that Treasury will suspend issuance of a particular maturity Federal Government bond drives up the price of outstanding bonds with that maturity because traders anticipate a shortage. Traders who know about the suspension in advance of the public announcement can realize enormous profit by purchasing the bonds before the announcement and selling immediately afterwards. The Treasury Department's announcement had a dramatic market impact, causing the largest one-day price movement in the thirty-year bond since October 1987. As a result of their bond purchases, made before the Treasury's announcement was made public, Nothern and the three other MFS portfolio managers made profits of $3.1 million for the portfolios they managed.

B. Manipulation of the Auction Process: *United States v. Salomon Brothers*

The Treasury sells Treasury securities through periodic auctions conducted mainly by and through the Federal Reserve System, especially the Federal Reserve Bank of New York. At each such auction, the Treasury awards securities to the bidders willing to accept the lowest yield levels (effectively, interest rates) on their cash.

When the size of an auction is announced, trading in the securities to be issued begins. These trades are done for securities on a "when-issued" basis. This trading continues until the day the securities are actually issued by the Treasury. After settlement, trading in the issued Treasury security continues in the secondary market until the maturity date, when the issue is redeemed.

With every "when-issued" transaction, the buyer agrees to buy a specified quantity of the security to issue at an agreed upon price from the seller. The seller is said to be "short" the issue, and the buyer "long." On settlement day, the buyer pays for the security it has agreed to purchase and the seller delivers the security by purchasing it from the Treasury in the auction or by borrowing it to deliver to the purchaser. Each Treasury security is unique. If a seller does not purchase a sufficient amount of a particular security in the auction to meet its obligations from "when issued" transactions, that seller must go into the secondary market to meet its demand for the particular security. When there is a substantial "short" position in a security, the demand for that security causes its price to rise in the secondary market.

There have been attempts to manipulate the auction process to affect the secondary market for treasury securities. On May 20, 1992, the United States filed a civil antitrust forfeiture complaint[14] alleging that Salomon Brothers Inc. ("Salomon") and others had conspired to restrain competition in markets for United States Treasury securities, in violation of the Sherman Act.[15] The complaint sought forfeiture of property owned by Salomon pursuant to the alleged conspiracy of the Sherman Act.[16]

As charged in the complaint, in or about June 1991, Salomon and its coconspirators agreed on a scheme to coordinate their transactions in May 1991 United States Treasury notes. This scheme had the effect of limiting the supply of May two-year notes available in the secondary markets, thereby ensuring that persons who had sold May two-year notes short in the when-issued market could not obtain such notes without purchasing them in the secondary market at artificially inflated prices. Through purchases at the auction and in the when-issued market, Salomon and its coconspirators obtained substantial positions in the May two-year notes. As part of the alleged scheme, Salomon and its coconspirators agreed to coordinate limiting the supply of May two-year notes made available for short selling, also artificially inflating their price in the secondary market.

The United States Government alleges that these anticompetitive actions by Salomon and its coconspirators caused substantial damages to sellers and to the United States. As noted in the Joint Report on the Government Securities Market issued by the Treasury, the SEC and the Federal Reserve Board, an acute, protracted squeeze resulting from illegal coordinated conduct, such as the one alleged here, "can cause lasting damage to the marketplace, especially if market participants attribute the shortage to market manipulation. Dealers may be more reluctant to establish short positions in the future, which could reduce liquidity and make it marginally more difficult for the Treasury to distribute its securities without disruption."[17]

Salomon and the Department of Justice reached a settlement in this case. Pursuant to the settlement, Salomon paid $27.5 million plus interest to the

14. United States v. Salomon Bros. Inc., 57 Fed. Reg. 29,743 (July 6, 1992).

15. 15 U.S.C. §1.

16. 15 U.S.C. §6.

17. *See* DEPARTMENT OF THE TREASURY, SECURITIES AND EXCHANGE COMMISSION, BOARD OF GOVERNORS OF THE FEDERAL RESERVE SYSTEM; JOINT REPORT ON THE GOVERNMENT SECURITIES MARKET at 10 (January 1992).

United States. On the same date the Department of Justice and the Securities and Exchange Commission reached a global settlement with Salomon to resolve the firm's liability under the securities laws and the common law for its conduct. The terms of that settlement provide that Salomon paid $290 million in fines and forfeitures including $100 million to establish a fund to be used to compensate victims of its misconduct.[18]

IV. INTEREST RATES

A. Fixed vs. Floating Rate Securities

Treasury notes can be either fixed income securities or floating rate securities. Fixed rate securities will pay a fixed rate of return for a set period of time. The set coupon is fixed at the time of issuance. Yields on fixed income financial instruments change as interest rates rise and fall; the attendant price of the underlying financial instrument changes in accord with the interest rate market. The coupon payment, however, remains constant.

The Treasury also issues floating rate securities in the auction process. Unlike fixed income securities, floating rate instruments have coupons that fluctuate based on terms described by the issuer. A floating rate note will have a coupon linked to an index or a market interest rate. The coupon of the floating rate financial instrument changes as the index or market-linked interest rate adjusts to market conditions. For example, corporate bonds may have a coupon linked to the United States Treasury Bill or federal funds rate. The bond itself might mature in ten years but the coupon on that bond will readjust as short-term rates fluctuate. Floating rate notes offer some protection in a rising interest rate environment in that their coupon rises when the interest rate on the benchmark index rises. Floating rate notes are often subject to a maximum or minimum rate of interest.

B. Treasury Inflation-Protected Securities (TIPS)

Treasury Inflation-Indexed Securities (TIIS), more popularly known as Treasury Inflation-Protected Securities (TIPS), are securities whose principal is linked to the Consumer Price Index (CPI). The coupon on TIPS is fixed while the principal fluctuates as the CPI rises or falls. The United States Treasury began issuing TIPS in January 1997. TIPS are a hedge against inflation; as inflation increases the investor is rewarded with greater principal. At maturity the investor receives the greater of the original or adjusted principal. TIPS, like other treasury notes, pay interest two times per year and are backed by the full faith and credit of the

---

18. *See* U.S. Dep't of Justice, *Department of Justice and SEC Enter $290 Million Settlement with Salomon Brothers in Treasury Securities Case* (Press Release, May 20, 1992), http://www.usdoj.gov/atr/public/press_releases/1992/211182.htm.

United States Government. The interest is a fixed rate calculated based on the adjusted principal. TIPS promise a yield-to-maturity that is guaranteed in real terms. To provide the promised real yield, TIPS coupon and principal payments are escalated based on increases in the Consumer Price Index from the time at which the security was issued.[19]

The following example illustrates how TIPS work:

Suppose an investor purchases a $1,000 note in January. The interest rate set at the time of the auction is 3%. Suppose the inflation rate for the first year of the life of the note is 3%. At the end of the December of the first year of the life of the note, the $1,000 principal will be $1,030 reflecting the 3% inflation rate. The investor does not receive the increase in principal until maturity. The investor will, however, receive a 3% interest payment reflecting the interest determined at the time of the note's original auction. After the first year, the note will continue to pay interest on the increased principal amount of the note (3% of $1,030 as opposed to 3% of the initial issue price of par). The note's principal amount is adjusted each year based on the increase or decrease in the inflation rate.[20]

Although clues about inflation expectations abound in financial markets, inflation-indexed securities would appear to be the most direct source of information about inflation expectations and real interest rates. The difference between the real yield guaranteed by an inflation-linked security and the nominal yield provided by a conventional security of the same maturity is known as the breakeven inflation rate or, alternatively, as inflation compensation. The breakeven rate of inflation is often treated as a direct reading of investors' expectations of inflation.[21]

An investor might use TIPS as a means of hedging against the erosion of principal due to increases in inflation. Banks also use TIPS for investing, hedging, and speculating. An investor in TIPS is taking a position that benefits when real interest rates fall. Real interest rates reflect the return on an investment minus inflation. Real interest rates are defined as the nominal rate of interest less the rate of inflation. If nominal rates fall, but inflation does not (that is, a decline in real interest rates), TIPS will appreciate because their fixed coupon will now represent a more attractive rate relative to the market. If inflation rises, but nominal rates rise more (that is, an increase in real interest rates), the security will decrease in value because it will only partially adjust to the new interest rate environment.[22]

---

19. Ben S. Bernanke, *"Constrained Discretion" and Monetary Policy*, (remarks before the Money Marketeers of New York University, New York, NY, February 3, 2003).

20. TRADING AND CAPITAL-MARKETS ACTIVITIES MANUAL §4030.1.

21. Ben S. Bernanke, *What Policymakers Can Learn from Asset Prices* (remarks before The Investment Analysts Society of Chicago, April 15, 2004).

22. *Id.*

V. STRIPS

A. Description

STRIPS—an acronym for "separate trading of registered interest and principal securities,"—are zero coupon bonds of the United States treasury created by physically separating the principal and interest cash flows. This process is known as "coupon stripping." Prior to 1985, investment banks had created similar securities by purchasing Treasury securities and depositing them in a trust, which then issued receipts representing separate ownership interests in the coupon and principal payments of the underlying security. In 1985, the treasury developed its own program for turning their coupon securities into STRIPS. All new Treasury bonds and notes with maturities of ten years or more are eligible to be stripped under this program and become direct obligations of the United States government. The holder of any eligible security can request that the Treasury create separate book-entry instruments for all of the principal and interest cash flows.[23]

The coupon and principal components of a United States Treasury STRIPS can be reassembled back into a coupon bond. This is possible because the Federal Reserve Board, acting as agents for the United States Treasury, stands ready at any time to exchange a treasury coupon bond for individual STRIPS, or in turn to exchange all of the STRIPS components for a bond. Reassembly of STRIPS into a coupon bond is known as a "reconstitution" or "recon."

B. Valuation

Like treasury bills, United States treasury STRIPS trade at a discount to their face value. Zero coupons are considered to have an absolute duration of their maturity date. As opposed to coupon securities, which return money to the investor as time marches forward, the zero coupon bond only pays at maturity.

Assume, for example, that the United States issues a ten-year bond with a 5 percent coupon. If the size of the issue is $100 million, the government will have to pay to all its investors $5 million per year, for a total payout of $50 million. The treasury will allow the coupon part of the bond to be "stripped" off the $100 million dollar principal component of the bond, thereby creating several new zero coupon securities. One security will be the $100 million dollar principal zero coupon STRIPS. The other securities will be zero coupon bonds representing the interest payments with maturities corresponding to interest payment dates.

The market for bonds affects the discounted value of the new $100 million zero coupon bond. The government will pay $100 million at maturity on the principal strip; to determine the current value of the zero coupon bond the

---

23. TRADING AND CAPITAL-MARKETS ACTIVITIES MANUAL §4025.1.

prevailing interest rates and the lack of cash flow attached to the security must be taken into account.

A valuable tool for understanding the compounding effects of STRIPS investments is the "rule of 72." The rule of 72 states that a bond will double in value at the rate of 72 divided by the interest rate. For instance, a zero coupon bond which compounds at a rate of 7.2% will double the investors' money in ten years (72 divided by 7.2 equals 10). If prevailing interest rates dictate that the discounted value of a ten-year zero coupon STRIPS is 7.2%, that bond will trade at 50% of face value. In other words a $50,000 investment will mature to be $100,000 ten years hence. Although the investor is not earning any spendable income along the way (since the interest is merely accruing to the bond) the accrual is treated as income for tax purposes even though the money has not reached the pocket of the investor in the form of cash.

The prices of STRIPS are quoted on a discount basis, as a percentage of par. Eligible securities can be stripped at any time. For a book-entry security to be separated into its component parts, the par value must be an amount which, based on the stated interest rate, will produce a semiannual interest payment of $1,000 or a multiple of $1,000. Quotes for STRIPS are quoted in yields-to-maturity.[24]

C. Uses

STRIPS have a known cash-flow value at specific future dates. Zero coupon bonds have the beneficial effect for an investor of allowing him to receive the same return on interest earned as that which was originally promised by the issuer, thereby eliminating "reinvestment risk." Reinvestment risk is the risk that an investor will not be able to reinvest income at the same rate as the bond that paid him the interest. STRIPS are a means of restructuring an income security to meet the needs of someone who might wish to purchase a zero coupon bond, such as an investor who wishes to have a certain amount of money at retirement.

A financial institution might wish to purchase zero coupon government bonds to structure within other securities. For example, consider a bank structuring a certificate of deposit with a guarantee of principal at maturity. The bank might issue a ten-year CD with a return linked to the stock market. The financial instrument would be structured as follows: the bank collects $100,000 from an investor. The bank then buys a zero coupon STRIPS with a 7.2% yield at a cost of $50,000 and invests the balance in stocks. If the stock market goes up 7.2% a year as well, the bank can return to the **investor** $200,000. If the stock market goes down, the bank returns to the investor $100,000, representing the investment in the STRIPS (minus any fees the bank has built into the security).

---

24. *Id.*

The bank, therefore, issues the CD while guaranteeing the principal with additional upside potential. A number of mutual funds and futures funds have adopted this strategy in guaranteeing principal and allowing for additional returns. This type of structure is composed of two parts: the zero coupon bonds, and the investment in another asset class.

D. Abuses: *In the Matter of Orlando Joseph Jett*

The case of *In re Kidder Peabody Securities Litigation*[25] describes the infamous story of Joseph Jett, an employee of Kidder Peabody, who was allegedly responsible for reporting inflated prices on his trading of STRIPS. This was a class action by investors who lost money by relying on certain information released in public documents regarding the profitability of Kidder Peabody. This information reflected Jett's misreported trading, thereby allegedly violating the Securities Act of 1934.

According to the opinion in a separate Securities and Exchange Commission proceeding,[26] Joseph Jett entered into hundreds of millions of dollars of "forward recons" of STRIPS, agreements to exchange a full set of STRIPS for the underlying bond from which they were originally stripped. By devising what he called a "carefully planned trading strategy," Jett was able to manipulate Kidder's computer system to create the illusion of profitable securities trading. This strategy brought Jett rich rewards at the firm, including promotions and millions of dollars in bonuses, but in fact, Jett's "trading strategy" caused the firm a large loss.

The decision in *Kidder Peabody* describes STRIPS trading as follows:

> Due to the time value of money, in trading with consumers, a STRIPS security will sell for less than its final payment value. This is because the present value of the right to receive a future payment is less than the value of receiving that payment immediately. Generally, the greater the length of time between purchase date and final payment date, the greater the gap between current price and final value. The converse is also true: As the payment date approaches the price of a STRIPS security will increase, until payment date, when the two values converge.
>
> Purchasers and dealers of STRIPS seek to profit on shifts in interest rates and demand that occur between the sale date of a STRIPS security and its payment date. Dealers also can make profits through "arbitrage," exploiting small, temporary price discrepancies between bonds and the component STRIPS. Thus, if the demand for individual STRIPS on any given day is higher than their current market value as a fully reconstituted bond, a dealer

---

25. In re Kidder Peabody Sec. Litig., 10 F.Supp.2d 398 (S.D.N.Y. 1998).
26. In the Matter of Orlando Joseph Jett, Admin. Proc. File No. 3-8919 http://www.sec.gov/litigation/opinions/33-8395.htm#P45_1761.

may be able to make a profit by stripping a bond and selling the individual components.

To facilitate the trading of government bonds, the Federal Reserve Board ("Federal Reserve"), acting as agent for the United States Treasury, stands ready at any time to exchange a bond for its individual STRIPS, or vice versa. The exchange of a full set of STRIPS for a bond is known as a "reconstitution" or "recon." The opposite exchange, of a bond for its individual STRIPS, is known as a "strip."

Unlike the sale of STRIPS or bonds to consumers, the exchange of STRIPS for bonds (or bonds for STRIPS) between a broker-dealer and the Federal Reserve has no economic significance. Such an exchange is merely a non-cash trade of economically equivalent securities, much like the exchange of one $100 bill for five $20 bills. Only the Federal Reserve can execute a strip or recon exchange and the Federal Reserve does not arrange, agree to, or confirm such exchanges in advance.[27]

According to the complaint, when Joseph Jett entered into a "recon," the accounting system treated the transaction as a sale of the STRIPS. Since STRIPS accrue interest daily, a sale of STRIPS would necessarily be at a higher dollar price than the day on which the transaction was made. Simply put, the accounting system at Kidder Peabody offset the future recon against the current price of the STRIPS and therefore recorded a false profit.

The Kidder accounting system was allegedly set up so that STRIPS recons were treated as a sale of the underlying securities. This accounting for a forward recon would appear as a profit in the accounting system because the computer would immediately record the difference between the future value of the STRIPS, which, of course would be higher because of the accrual of interest, and the current price of the recon which would inevitably be lower. The difference between the two prices was recorded as an immediate profit while no actual transaction had occurred in the recon process. Depending on the size of the STRIPS and the settlement, the system would record profits that were illusory. There was no economic reality or risk in the transaction since the recon of STRIPS does not involve the exchange, receipt, or risk of capital. On the settlement date, the accounting system would record a loss to offset the false profit. The court describes what a trader would have to do to profit from this anomaly in the accounting system:

> In other words, as the current value of the STRIPS converged with its payment value, the apparent profit decreased, generating an offsetting false loss. By settlement date, the original false profit would be eliminated. As a result,

---

27. *Kidder Peabody*, 10 F.Supp.2d at 403.

to continue the illusion of profits, a trader would have to continue to enter more and more forward recons, with more and more distant settlement dates.[28]

This is just what Jett allegedly did, for a period of over two years, until April 1994, when Kidder Peabody acknowledged that his trading had generated $350 million in false profits.[29] The SEC subsequently found that Jett, with intent to defraud, booked hundreds of millions of dollars in illusory profits, thereby deceiving the firm about his trading performance and obtaining large bonuses and other benefits, and had violated several recordkeeping provisions of the Securities Exchange Act.[30] Jett was barred from association with a broker or dealer, and was ordered to cease and desist from committing or causing any violations of the recordkeeping provisions he was found to have violated. He was also ordered to disgorge $8.21 million (plus prejudgment interest) and to pay a $200,000 civil penalty. This penalty was upheld on appeal.[31] The appellate opinion contains a detailed discussion of how STRIPS function and are traded, and how Jett was able to capitalize on the anomaly in the Kidder trading system to create such huge false profits through the use of phantom trades.

---

28. *Id.* at 404.

29. *Id.* at 405.

30. Orlando Joseph Jett, Initial Decision Rel. No. 127 (July 21, 1998), 67 SEC Docket 1901.

31. In the Matter of Orlando Joseph Jett, Admin. Proc. File No. 3-8919 http://www.sec.gov/litigation/opinions/33-8395.htm#P45_1761; http://www.sec.gov/litigation/litreleases/2007/lr20273.htm.

8. DEBT SECURITIES

I. DESCRIPTION

While Treasury securities provide a credit risk-free investment vehicle which have become uniquely desirable in the wake of recent market events, debt securities are issued by a wide range of issuers throughout the capital markets. Fixed-income securities are debt instruments that obligate the issuer to make fixed interest payments and repay the principal amount to the buyer upon maturity of the security.[1] Also known as bonds, these instruments are attractive to investors because they provide a reliable stream of cash flows in the form of interest payments, and also provide for repayment of principal upon maturity. Furthermore, because bond holders are creditors to the issuer, they have claims to assets upon bankruptcy that are superior to the claims of shareholders. Bonds carry less risk

---

1. The Bond Market Association, available at: www.investinginbonds.com.

than equities but also offer a lower potential for returns. For issuers, bonds are an attractive way of raising capital because they do not dilute the equity or ownership interests in a company and because voting rights are not attached to bonds, so purchasers of these securities do not participate in control of the issuer in any way.

A. Features of Bonds

Bonds have several important characteristics that affect their structure and therefore their yield. These include the face or par value, interest or coupon rate, maturity, and any special redemption options that may be attached to the bond. The *par value* is the principal amount of the debt obligation. *Coupon rate* refers to the rate of interest that will be paid on the principal amount. A bond's *maturity* is the date on which the principal will be repaid to the buyer. Bonds are generally classified into short (thirty days to five years), medium (five to twelve years) and long term (twelve years or longer). A bond can carry redemption features that provide benefits to either the issuer or the buyer.

For example, a *call option* allows the issuer to "call" the bond and repay the principal prior to the maturity date, whereas a *put option* allows the buyer to redeem his principal prior to maturity. The value of a bond is also affected by the issuer's credit quality. Credit quality is assessed by various agencies, including Moody's, Standard & Poor's, and Fitch. These agencies consider and evaluate the financial position of the issuer of the specific bond in order to rate them from highest credit quality to lowest.

B. Types of Bonds

There are four main types of bonds: government bonds (discussed in Chapter 6), corporate bonds, municipal bonds, and federal agency bonds.

1. *Corporate bonds.* These are debt instruments issued by a corporation as a means of raising capital. If offered for sale to the public, they are subject to federal securities laws.
2. *Municipal bonds.* Municipal bonds are fixed-income securities issued by municipal governments as a mechanism for raising revenue to finance public expenditures. A prime feature of these securities is that interest or other investment earnings on them is usually excluded from gross income of the holder for federal income tax purposes.[2] Issuers of municipal securities are exempt from most federal securities laws.
3. *Federal agency bonds.* Federal agency bonds are securities issued by wholly-owned government corporations. These include Ginnie Mae, Fannie Mae, and Freddie Mac, which are described below. They are considered

---

2. Municipal Securities Rule Making Board, http://www.msrb.org/msrb1/glossary/glossary_db.asp?sel=m.

to be low risk debt instruments because some are backed by the full faith and credit of the United States government (Ginnie Mae); those that are not backed by full faith and credit are nevertheless safe investments as a result of their special priority for borrowing from the United States government.

4. *Mortgage-backed and asset-backed securities*: Mortgage-backed securities (MBS) are debt obligations that represent claims to the cash flows from pools of mortgage loans, most commonly on residential property.[3] Most MBSs are issued by government sponsored enterprises.

These different types of fixed-income securities and their regulatory frameworks are described in more detail below.

C. The Indenture

A trust indenture is a contract entered into between a corporation issuing bonds or debentures and a trustee for the holders of the bonds or debentures that delineates the rights of the holders and the issuer.[4] The Trust Indenture Act of 1939[5] sets minimum standards for the content of indentures and the qualifications and responsibilities of trustees. The indenture sets out the rights and responsibilities of the trustee. In general, the trustee's responsibilities are ministerial and involve little to no action until an event qualifying as default occurs. At this time, the trustee is generally required to collect all money owed to bond holders. The trustee has a legal duty to effectively protect the rights of bond holders and may not contract out of liability for failure to do so.[6]

The indenture should include, at a minimum, the following terms: the maturity date of the bonds; the interest rate; redemption, subordination, and convertibility features; registration, transfer and exchangeability of ownership provisions; covenants of the trust; default definitions, provisions, and remedies; and procedures for amending the indenture.

II. BOND RATING AGENCIES

Bond rating agencies "disseminate information about the relative creditworthiness of financial obligations of corporations, banks, government entities and pools of assets collected in structured finance transactions."[7] These agencies

---

3. Securities and Exchange Commission, http://www.sec.gov/answers/mortgagesecurities.htm.

4. UPIC & Co. v Kinder-Care Learning Centers, Inc., 793 F. Supp 448 (S.D.N.Y. 1992).

5. 15 U.S.C. §77aaa–§77bbbb.

6. 15 U.S.C. §77ooo.

7. Michael Kanef (Moody's Investor Service), (testimony before the United States Senate Committee on Banking, Housing and Urban Affairs, September 26, 2007).

track debt covering corporate issuers, public finance issuers, sovereign nations, and structured finance obligations.[8] Their ratings are available to the public free of charge.

In the wake of recent market events, rating agencies have come under scrutiny for their role in the mortgage-backed securities meltdown. At least six government or global industry bodies have been examining the rating agencies' role in the crisis.[9] New York Attorney General Andrew Cuomo announced an agreement with Wall Street's three major credit rating agencies that would greatly affect their processes for analyzing mortgage-backed debt.[10] Cuomo announced new guidelines that will have "a dramatic effect on the industry." The Cuomo initiative targets, in particular, "ratings shopping" on mortgage-backed securities by altering how the agencies are paid. In the past, rating agencies would propose a rating and an investment bank was free to choose the best rating. This process created a conflict as rating agencies sought to get business from the debt issuers who sought their rating. "If the investment bank didn't like where the process was going, they would just go to another rating agency. The rating agencies will now undertake new standards," Cuomo said. Instead of being paid at the end of the process once a rating has been submitted to the investment bank for review, the new plan will pay rating agencies at four different points during the process. This will "level the playing field," Cuomo said. The three ratings agencies will continue to review their processes with the Attorney General while the SEC is investigating these matters as well.

Bond ratings focus on the likelihood that debt will be repaid in accordance with the terms of the security. More specifically, the rating "reflects an assessment of the probability that a debt instrument will default and the amount of loss the debt-holder will incur in the event of default."[11] This information helps investors understand the risk associated with a given security, which is a key element in the valuation of bonds. All else being equal, bonds with a higher credit rating will be more expensive than those with a lower credit rating. The "discount" on lower-rated bonds serves to compensate the investor for the increased risk that the investor takes on in purchasing the bond. It is important to remember that credit ratings reflect only the likelihood of repayment and the expected credit loss and do not reflect various other key indicators in the "value" of a bond, such as price, maturity, and interest rate.

Ratings are expressed on a scale using letters and numbers that vary from agency to agency. In general, bonds that exhibit the least likelihood of credit loss

---

8. Moody's Investor Service, www.moodys.com.

9. THE ECONOMIST, (June 5, 2008).

10. Joe Bel Bruno, *Cuomo, rating agencies agree on mortgage reforms,* (AP NEWSWIRE, June 5, 2008).

11. Michael Kanef (Moody's Investor Service), (testimony before the United States Senate Committee on Banking, Housing and Urban Affairs, September 26, 2007).

are assigned a AAA rating, and as this likelihood increases, the rating declines down the scale to AA, A, B, and so forth.

A. Independence and Conflicts of Interest

Credit rating agencies have been subject to allegations that their impartiality and independence is compromised by their relationships with issuers of fixed-income securities. Because credit rating agencies are paid by issuers for their ratings, there is an inherent conflict of interest that arises from this relationship. The Credit Agency Reform Act of 2006[12] was passed in an attempt to address some of these concerns. Rules issued pursuant to that Act attempt to regulate this issue through the prohibition of unfair, coercive, or abusive practices.[13] However, managing conflicts of interest is primarily up to the credit rating agency.

B. Regulation of Bond Rating Agencies

Credit rating agencies wishing to be have their ratings used by issuers for the purposes of federal securities laws can apply under the Credit Rating Agency Reform Act of 2006 to be recognized as Nationally Recognized Statistical Rating Organizations (NRSROs). This designation permits the agency's ratings to be used by issuers of securities for certain regulatory purposes.

The SEC administers the Credit Rating Agency Reform Act and oversees NRSROs. The purpose of the Act is "to improve ratings quality for the protection of investors and in the public interest by fostering accountability, transparency and competition in the credit rating agency industry."[14] It provides guidelines for the SEC to use in assessing which agencies qualify for NRSRO status and provides some disclosure requirements for the agencies themselves. The concept is to provide more regulatory oversight in an attempt to improve transparency. The SEC rules implementing the Credit Agency Reform Act contain various disclosure and registration requirements, rules for managing conflicts of interest, and prohibitions of unfair, coercive, or abusive practices.[15]

III. SPECIAL TYPES OF FIXED-INCOME SECURITIES

A. Repos

1. **Description** A repurchase agreement ("repo") is a financial instrument that provides a method of short-term borrowing. It involves the sale and repurchase

---

12. Pub. Law No. 109-291, 120 Stat. 1327–1339, amending the Securities Exchange Act of 1934.

13. Credit Rating Agency Reform Act of 2006, SEC Rule 17g-6.

14. Credit Rating Agency Reform Act of 2006, Preamble.

15. SEC Rules 17g-1 through 17g-6.

of securities. A reverse repo is the term used to describe the opposite perspective of the same transaction—the purchase and resale of securities. Repos are often used by governments. They can be used as a means of short term borrowing or for speculative purposes. A party speculates when it reinvests the proceeds from a repo in a different security in an attempt to profit on a positive spread. When used for such speculative purposes, repos can be used to enter highly leveraged complex financial transactions.

Economically, a repo is substantively similar to a secured loan, since the sale of securities serves as collateral in the event of default. However, a repo differs from a loan in that legal title to the securities passes from the seller to the buyer. This has implications in bankruptcy proceedings, since bankruptcy stays loans but does not stay securities sold that create a legal claim to the assets of the seller. The bankruptcy of Orange County, California, in 1994 provides an example of repos used for speculative purposes and the legal implications of taking on such high degrees of risk.

2. Orange County Case Study In the early 1990s the treasurer of Orange County, California, entered into several reverse repos that, while successful for some time, ultimately resulted in a loss of $1.7 billion and bankrupted the county. The treasurer's strategy involved the use of reverse repos to finance floating rate notes, specifically "inverse interest only" mortgage-backed securities (inverse IOs).[16] While interest rates stayed low, this strategy proved highly profitable for the county. At times, the $7.6 billion portfolio was leveraged to a book value of more than $20.6 billion. However, when interest rates began to rise, the treasurer's investment strategy resulted in a massive loss.

The County's loss arose from the highly leveraged positions that the treasurer took on the inverse IOs. Inverse IOs have a set principal amount and earn interest at a rate that moves inversely to a specified index rate.[17] When leveraged, as they were in the case of Orange County, a small increase in interest rates can cause a significant decrease in the inverse floating rate. When interest rates fall or remain low, inverse IOs earn high returns, but if interest rates rise, they can incur substantial losses.

The County's investment strategy involved the sale of its portfolio of securities through reverse repos with maturity dates of less than 180 days. The proceeds of the repos were then reinvested in inverse IOs with much longer maturity dates—between two and five years. Furthermore, the treasurer "rolled over" new repo transactions to pay his obligations on old ones (rolling over means issuing new securities at the new interest rate to repay existing obligations). Finally, the repo transactions were "stacked" by using earlier reverse repos as collateral for subsequent reverse repos. As interest rates rose, the County's

---

16. In re Orange County v. Fuji Securities Inc., 31 F. Supp. 2d 768 (C.D. Cal. 1998).

17. *See* Banca Cremi v. Alex Brown & Sons, 132 F. 3d 1017, 1037 (4th Cir. 1997).

debt grew since it had to pay more interest on there reverse repos. At the same time, the return on its inverse IOs was falling as a result of the rise in interest rates. Since the investments made by Orange County were backed by mortgages, another effect of rising interest rates was that the duration of the lower interest rate mortgages became extended as homeowners became less willing to pay down or refinance their "cheap" mortgage rates. In other words, as interest rates rose, the return to the investor declined and the time horizon of the investment extended.

By December 1994, the County had lost over $1.6 billion and eventually went into Chapter 9 bankruptcy. In an attempt to void the repo transactions which contributed to the County's need to seek Chapter 9 bankruptcy protection, the County brought a lawsuit against Fuji Securities Inc., a counterparty in some of the reverse repo transactions. The County argued that its former treasurer did not have the authority to enter into these transactions since they exceeded the California constitutional debt limit and as such, they should be considered void. In order to be successful in the lawsuit, the County had to first convince the court that a repo is a structured loan for the purposes of the constitutional debt limit.

The California Constitution placed restrictions on the amount of indebtedness a county could incur. This created an incentive to find alternative means of leveraging speculative investments. There was also a state law in place that authorized the County to enter into repo transactions.[18] However, the County argued that a repo was, in substance, a structured loan and should qualify as "indebtedness or liability" under the constitutional debt limit, which states the following:

> No county, city, town . . . shall incur any indebtedness or liability in any manner or for any purpose exceeding in any year the income and revenue provided for such year, without the assent of two-thirds of the qualified electors thereof, voting at an election to be held for that purpose . . . [19]

The court examined the economic substance and ultimately held that the repos did not create liability or indebtedness because the transactions were not essentially collateralized loans in the context of the constitutional debt limit. While repos share various characteristics with collateralized loans, they differ in important ways. Specifically, in a loan transaction, there is no transfer of title, whereas in a repo transaction, a buyer acquires title of securities and as such, no loan takes place.

Furthermore, the court ruled that within the meaning of the debt limit, the relevant time frame from which to analyze the transaction is at the outset,

---

18. Cal. Gov't Code. §16480.4: "The State Treasurer may enter into repurchase agreements or reverse repurchase agreements of any securities described in Section 16430."
19. Cal. Const. Art. XVI, §18.

because the debt limit does not set performance standards, it only regulates how much may be incurred up front. At the time the transaction was entered into, there were sufficient funds to repurchase the underlying securities, and as such, the acts were within the grant of authority by law and were not ultra vires and void.[20]

In response to the bankruptcy of Orange County, the California State Legislature enacted various amendments to the law that placed restrictions on repo transactions. Specifically, under the new rules, the proceeds of reverse repos can only be used to purchase other securities with maturities of less than 92 days from the settlement date of the "reverse" repo agreement, unless the agreement contains a written codicil guaranteeing a minimum earning or spread for the entire term of the purchased securities.[21] Furthermore, reverse repos cannot exceed 20% of the base value of the entire portfolio.[22] Finally, "stacking" is no longer permitted; only securities which have been owned for a minimum of 30 days may act as collateral for a reverse repo agreement.[23] The amendments also now hold a trustee to a "prudent person" standard.[24]

B. Mortgage-Backed Securities

Mortgage-backed securities (MBSs) are financial products that use pools of mortgages as collateral for the issuance of securities.[25] Most commonly, these are collateralized by residential properties. An important feature of mortgage-backed securities is their backing by three government sponsored agencies: The Government National Mortgage Association (GNMA or Ginnie Mae), the Federal Home Loan Mortgage Corporation (FHLMC or Freddie Mac) and the Federal National Mortgage Association (FNMA or Fannie Mae). Because MBSs are backed by these government related agencies, their credit risk is low compared to other fixed-income securities.

Mortgage-backed securities exhibit a unique form of risk known as prepayment risk. This is the risk that the mortgagee will pay off the remaining amount of the loan prior to its maturity date, thereby reducing the amount of interest payments the issuer, or investor, will receive. Therefore, in contrast to most other fixed-income securities, the value of fixed rate mortgages falls when interest rates fall. This happens because when interest rates fall, home owners often refinance their homes at the new lower rate. When a mortgage is prepaid, the mortgagee must reinvest funds at the new lower rate of interest.

---

20. The court did note, however, that repos may be characterized differently under different statutes and regulations.

21. Cal. Gov't Code. §53601(j)(3)(D).

22. Cal. Gov't Code. §53601(j)(3)(B).

23. Cal. Gov't Code. §53601(j)(3)(A).

24. Cal. Gov't Code. §53600.3.

25. TRADING AND CAPITAL-MARKETS ACTIVITIES MANUAL §4110.1.

There are various types of mortgage-backed securities exhibiting different structures. The simplest structure entitles the investor to a pro rata share of all principal and interest payments that are made on a pool of loan assets. These are called "pass-through participation certificates."[26] More complex structures are created to allow investors to expose themselves to varying levels of risk. A collateralized mortgage obligation (CMO) is an example of such an instrument.

CMOs are securities derived from pools of private home mortgages backed by United States Government Sponsored Enterprises.[27] These securities attempt to reduce prepayment risk by pooling mortgages and creating two streams of income from the underlying mortgages: interest and principal streams. These income streams are then divided into "tranches," which are classes of bonds/securities that are purchased by investors. Each tranche has a specific interest rate and priority ranking on the principal repayment stream. High priority tranches are paid out first when principal payments are made on the underlying mortgages, whereas "support" tranches are paid out last. Investors can choose how much and what type of risk to take on by selecting an appropriate tranche.

1. **Structuring Mortgage-Backed Securities** The originator of the MBS begins by pooling a large number of residential mortgage loans. The risk associated with the portfolio of mortgages is then assessed by an investment bank. At this stage, any mortgages that do not conform to the underwriter's standards are "kicked out."[28] Next, a trust, LLC, or corporation is created, and the originator then sells its legal right to receive monthly payments on the mortgages to the trust, LLC, or corporation, which becomes the securitization issuer.[29] The trust then issues and sells bonds to investors (typically institutional investors) in separate "tranches." Each tranche exhibits a different degree of risk and payout structures. When mortgage borrowers make payments on their loans, these payments are funneled to the trust's bond holders. If the issuer wishes to enhance the credit of the securities, there are measures that can be taken to protect against the loss that any given investor is likely to incur. For example, a subordination feature provides that losses be borne unequally, in reverse order of seniority. Likewise, the securities can be overcollateralized, meaning that the total amount of the mortgage loans exceeds the amount of bonds issued. As such, any default by a mortgage borrower will be borne by the investor in a disproportionately smaller amount. These are simply two of the various mechanisms an issuer can use to reduce the likelihood of loss to the investor.

---

26. Securities and Exchange Commission, http://www.sec.gov/answers/mortgagesecurities.htm.

27. Trading and Capital-Markets Activities Manual §4110.1.

28. Michael Kanef, (testimony before the United States Senate Committee on Banking, Housing and Urban Affairs, September 26, 2007).

29. *Id.*

2. Recent Subprime Mortgage Crisis In mid 2007, the United States experienced a sharp rise in home foreclosures, resulting in what is referred to as a "subprime mortgage crisis." This crisis led to the decline of many lending institutions and sparked a global credit crisis.

Subprime mortgages are those mortgages that are issued to borrowers with relatively poor credit ratings. These investments are labeled as "subprime" by lending institutions and entail more risk than "prime" mortgages. Mortgages are issued based on the value of the house, and the income and credit history of the borrower. As house prices rise, subprime borrowers can borrow more money since they have more "collateral" in the form of increased value in their home. However, if house prices fall, this is no longer possible. In 2007, house prices began falling while at the same time, interest rates were rising. This resulted in a situation in which borrowers faced rising interest payments (because many loans were adjustable rate mortgages) while the value of their houses was declining, removing the ability to refinance or to sell the house and use the proceeds to pay off mortgage loans. Thousands of borrowers were forced to default on their mortgages, and lenders had no means of collecting on the billions of dollars lent out to fund the pool of subprime mortgages.

The availability of subprime mortgages was significantly increased through the use of collateralized mortgage obligations. Because of the increased risk associated with subprime mortgages, a single investor faces a lower probability that the mortgage will be repaid and thus faces a lower expected return. CMOs based on these mortgages allow risk to be spread among investors with different risk tolerance levels, offering a greater potential for high returns. When the CMO is divided into tranches with varying risk profiles, investors with low risk tolerance (pension funds, banks) purchase CMOs that ensure that they will be a repaid first while those with higher risk tolerance (hedge funds) purchase CMOs that are paid out last. Because financial instruments like CMOs enable lending practices that might not otherwise occur in the absence of a mechanism for spreading risk, some commentators have called for more government regulation on lending practices in order to avoid a recurrence of the events of the 2007 subprime mortgage crisis.

IV. EXEMPTION FROM SECURITIES ACT REGISTRATION

Fixed-income securities are regulated by various federal and state laws. The type of security will determine which agency has jurisdiction to regulate a given security or issuer.[30] The Securities and Exchange Commission regulates many fixed-income securities in implementing the Securities Act of 1933 (Securities

---

30. *See* Chapter 4, *supra*, for a complete discussion of this topic.

Act),[31] the Securities and Exchange Act of 1934 (Exchange Act),[32] and the Trust Indenture Act of 1939 (Trust Indenture Act).[33]

The Securities Act determines which financial issuers are required to register their instruments with the commission.[34] All those that are required to register are also subject to the rules and regulations of the SEC, including all disclosure requirements and antifraud provisions. The registration requirement applies to debt securities in the same manner as it applies to equity securities. It is primarily corporate debt securities that are subject to the requirements of the Securities Act.

Some securities are exempt from the Securities Act registration requirements. In some cases, these securities are unregulated and in other cases, they are regulated by another source, often by a self-regulatory organization (SRO). The exemption may arise from the issuer's status, or it may arise from the type of transaction at issue. Exempt securities include United States government securities, GSE securities, securities of domestic banks or trust companies, commercial paper, municipal securities, and private placements.[35] While these are exempt from disclosure requirements, they are subject to the antifraud provisions of the Securities Act.[36] As such, any material misrepresentation contained in any documents exposes the issuer to liability.

A. Government Securities

Government securities, such as treasury bills, are exempt from the registration and disclosure requirements under the Securities Act and the Exchange Act. They are regulated by the Government Securities Act of 1986.[37] This act provides a framework to regulate all government securities brokers and dealers. It grants authority to the United States Treasury Department to issue and implement rules to regulate transactions involving government securities. The Government Securities Act also added a section to the Exchange Act, requiring broker-dealers who trade only in government securities to register with the SEC as government securities broker-dealers.[38]

B. Government Agency Securities

Government agency securities, such as those offered by Fannie Mae, Freddie Mac and Ginnie Mae, are exempt from the registration and disclosure requirements

---

31. 15 U.S.C. §77a et seq.
32. 15 U.S.C. §78a et seq.
33. 15 U.S.C. §77aaa–§77bbbb.
34. See 15 U.S.C. §77e.
35. See 15 U.S.C. §77c.
36. See 15 U.S.C. §77q.
37. Pub. Law No. 99-571, 100 Stat. 3208.
38. See 15 U.S.C. §78o-5.

under the Securities Act and the Exchange Act.[39] For the purposes of regulation, they are considered "government securities."[40] Since they do not need to be registered in order to be sold to the public, they do not typically file offering documents with the SEC. They do provide offering documents and make financial statements available to investors via their Web site.[41]

C. Municipal Securities

Municipal securities are regulated by the Municipal Securities Rulemaking Board (MSRB), a self-regulatory organization that operates under the oversight of the SEC to develop rules governing municipal securities activities.[42] All rules issued by the MSRB must be approved by the SEC.[43] While the MSRB is highly involved in the regulation of municipal securities, the SEC thus has the ultimate enforcement authority.

    1. SEC Disclosure Requirements SEC rules require that underwriters making primary offerings of municipal securities of $1 million or greater obtain an "official statement," which is a type of disclosure document, disclosing no more than the following information: the offering price, interest rate, selling compensation, aggregate principal amount, principal amount per maturity, delivery dates, any other terms or provisions required by an issuer of such securities to be specified in a competitive bid, ratings, other terms of the securities depending on such matters, and the identity of the underwriter.[44] Unlike many other types of securities, the disclosure obligation here is on the underwriter and not the issuer.

    2. MSRB Disclosure Requirements The MSRB disclosure rule[45] requires, among other things, that the underwriter of a primary securities offering file the official statement required by the SEC with the MSRB. The official statement is subject to the antifraud provisions of the Exchange Act[46] and as such must provide complete and true information. The SEC has the ultimate enforcement authority in this situation.

---

    39. *See* 15 U.S.C. §77c.

    40. FRIEDMAN, FELICE B., REGULATION OF FIXED INCOME SECURITIES MARKETS IN THE UNITED STATES (April 21, 2004). World Bank Policy Research Working Paper No. 3283. http://ssrn.com/abstract=610328.

    41. *Id.*

    42. Municipal Securities Rule Making Board, http://www.msrb.org/msrb1/glossary/glossary_db.asp?sel=m.

    43. *See* 15 U.S.C. §78o-4.

    44. SEC Rule 15c-12(b).

    45. MSRB Rule G-32.

    46. 15 U.S.C. §78j(b).

D. Corporate Debt Securities

Corporate debt securities are subject to the registration and disclosure requirements under the Securities Act, and the regulatory framework for debt securities is substantially the same as for equity securities.

1. Securities Act Requirements All corporate debt securities sold to the public must be registered with the SEC. Registration requires the filing of the following documents, which together form the "registration statement" required by the Securities Act:[47]

1. *Prospectus:* this is a document that contains the offer of securities and is delivered to each purchaser of securities. An issuer can be sued in federal court for any omission or misrepresentation of material fact in the prospectus and that the CEO, CFO, chief accountant and directors can also be held personally liable for any such misrepresentations.
2. *Supplementary Information:* this information is filed with the SEC and is available to the public but does not form part of the prospectus which all purchasers of the security receive.

Before issuing securities to the public, the SEC must complete its review of the registration statement. However, prior to this, a preliminary prospectus may be circulated to potential purchasers. This may contain most of the same information as the final prospectus but is not official. Once registered, the prospectus and registration statements, along with other filings, are available to the public on EDGAR databases.

2. Trust Indenture Act Requirements The Trust Indenture Act is administered by the SEC and is designed to regulate the trust indenture and the appointment of trustees acting for the benefit of holders of securities in principal amounts of $10 million or more.[48] It requires that issuers file an indenture with the SEC with an "indenture qualification statement."[49] The purpose of the Trust Indenture Act is to ensure that the indenture, which is the agreement between the issuer and the bond holder setting out their respective rights and obligations, conforms to the standards set by the SEC.

E. Private Placements of Debt Securities

Securities not offered to the public or listed on a public exchange—private placements—are exempt from the registration requirements under the Securities Act. Smaller issuers often choose to make private placements. By exempting small offerings from the registration process, the SEC seeks to foster capital

---

47. *Cf.* 15 U.S.C. §77e.
48. 15 U.S.C. §77ddd.
49. 15 U.S.C. §77eee.

formation by lowering the cost of offering securities to the public.[50] While debt securities issued in a private placement are generally not eligible for resale since they are not registered with the SEC, Rule 144A provides an exception. Adopted pursuant to the Securities Act, Rule 144A provides a safe harbor by which private placement securities can be resold to "qualified institutional buyers" (QIBs). QIBs must be certified as such by the SEC and generally include large institutional buyers. This rule is designed to increase liquidity in the corporate debt market. Trading in the Rule 144A market has been significantly enhanced by the introduction of the Private Offerings, Resales, and Trading through Automated Linkates (PORTAL) system, created and administered by the National Association of Securities Dealers, Inc. (NASD). This is an automated trading system which facilitates the quoting and trading of unregistered securities eligible to be resold pursuant to SEC Rule 144A.[51]

Making a private placement under Rule 144A is particularly attractive to foreign issuers who wish to avoid the complications and cost of filing the necessary documents for a public offering, particularly given the necessity that all SEC filings must conform to United States Generally Accepted Accounting Principles (GAAP) standards. However, foreign issuers of private placements are required to supply the SEC with information that is required by the issuer's home country for a public offering of securities there.[52] In addition, all Rule 144A issuers must provide basic information to the SEC, including a description of their business, and financial statements for the previous two years.

Whatever the structure of a particular debt instrument, its primary function is to allow the issuer to access the capital markets. The purchaser of the instrument uses debt security as a means of investing capital and receiving a return on that investment.

---

50. Securities and Exchange Commission, available at: http://www.sec.gov/about/laws.shtml#trustinact1939.

51. NASDAQ PORTAL, available at: http://www.nasdaqportalmarket.com.

52. SEC Rule 12g3-2.

9. DERIVATIVES

I. INTRODUCTION

A. Description

Derivatives provide a means for shifting risk from one party to a counterparty that is more willing or better able to assume that risk. The counterparty's motivation for assuming that risk might be to manage its own risk or to enhance yield (make money). A derivatives transaction is "a bilateral contract or payments exchange agreement whose value derives . . . from the value of an underlying asset or underlying reference rate or index."[1] Derivatives transactions may be based on the value of foreign currency, U.S. Treasury bonds, stock indexes, or interest rates. The values of these underlying financial instruments are determined by market forces, such as movements in interest rates. Within the broad

---

1. Procter & Gamble Co. v. Bankers Trust Co., 925 F. Supp. 1270 at 1275, Blue Sky L. Rep. (CCH) P74108, Comm. Fut. L. Rep. (CCH) P26700, Fed. Sec. L. Rep. (CCH) P99229 (S.D. Ohio 1996) citing Global Derivatives Study Group of the Group of Thirty, Derivatives: Practices and Principles 28 (1993).

panoply of derivatives transactions are numerous innovative financial instruments whose objectives may include a hedge against market risks, management of assets and liabilities, or lowering of funding costs; derivatives may also be used as speculation for profit.[2] There are four types of derivatives contracts: forwards, futures, swaps, and options.[3] Derivatives are used to manage risk by enabling a user to isolate, trade, and transfer one or more distinct risks. Generally they are highly leveraged because they require little or no good faith deposit to secure the counterparties' obligations under the contract. Many financial institutions are now implementing stricter margin requirements due to the deteriorating credit quality of counterparties, the general tightness in credit conditions, and the wariness of financial market participants.

B. Counterparty Credit Risk

In March 2008 the Federal Reserve facilitated the sale of the investment bank Bear Stearns (which was reported on the verge of insolvency), to J. P. Morgan Chase. A major motivating factor for the Federal Reserve's initiative with regard to Bear Stearns was fear of the effect the implosion of Bear Stearns would have on its counterparties throughout the capital markets. Counterparties rely on the financial ability of the other side of the transaction to meet its obligations under the terms of the contract. If a counterparty fails, the derivative contract is meaningless. If Bear Stearns had disappeared, risk that had been shifted to it through derivatives contracts would have reverted back to its counterparties. This risk dislocation would have had a profound impact throughout the capital markets.

The threat posed to the financial system by the interconnectivity of counterparties was previously made apparent in the wake of losses experienced in 1998 at a mammoth hedge fund, Long Term Capital Management (LTCM). Concerns by the Federal Reserve about the impact of a major counterparty's failure, and the responsibility of the Federal Reserve to ensure that the financial system is not at risk, were the incentives for the Federal Reserve in negotiating the bail out of LTCM. The General Accounting Office, in analyzing the events surrounding the demise of LTCM, provided insight into the factors motivating the Federal Reserve to act to prevent systemic risk:

> The Federal Reserve's decision to facilitate the private sector recapitalization of LTCM was based on its concern that LTCM's failure might pose systemic risk. Although a systemic crisis can result from the spread of difficulties from one firm to others, in this case the potential threat was to the functioning

---

2. *Id.*, citing Singher, *Regulating Derivatives: Does Transnational Regulatory Cooperation Offer a Viable Alternative to Congressional Action?* 18 FORDHAM INT'L. LAW J. 1405–06 (1995).

3. *See* Sec. III, *infra.*

of financial markets. According to Federal Reserve officials, they were concerned that rapid liquidation of LTCM's very large trading positions and of its counterparties' related positions in the unsettled market conditions of September 1998 might have caused credit and interest rate markets to experience extreme price moves and even temporarily cease functioning. This could have potentially harmed uninvolved firms and adversely affected the cost and availability of credit in the U.S. economy.

LTCM's creditors and counterparties would have faced sizeable losses if LTCM had failed. Estimates are that individual firms might have lost from $300 million to $500 million each and that aggregate losses for LTCM's top 17 counterparties might have been from $3 billion to $5 billion. However, according to financial regulators, these losses were not large enough to threaten the solvency of LTCM's major creditors. Among the eight U.S. firms that participated in the recapitalization, equity capital at the end of fiscal 1998 ranged from $4.7 billion to $42.7 billion. The Basel Committee on Banking Supervision noted that these losses could have increased further if the repercussions had spread to markets more generally.

According to Federal Reserve officials, LTCM's failure, had it occurred in the unsettled market conditions of September 1998, might have disrupted market functioning because of the size and concentration of LTCM's positions in certain markets and the related sales of other market participants. As noted previously, the firm had sizeable trading positions in various securities, exchange-traded futures, and OTC derivatives markets. Moreover, LTCM's counterparties might have faced the prospect of "unwinding" their own large LTCM-related positions in the event of that firm's default. Unwinding these positions could have been difficult: according to LTCM officials, about 20,000 transactions were outstanding between LTCM and its counterparties at the time of its near-collapse.

The LTCM crisis illustrated that potential systemic risk can exist in large trading positions. According to Federal Reserve officials, a default by LTCM on its contracts might have set off a variety of reactions. For example, most of LTCM's creditors and counterparties held collateral against their current credit exposures to LTCM. In the event of LTCM's default, however, the exposures might have risen in value by the time the collateral was sold, resulting in considerable losses. Also, derivatives counterparties, faced with sudden termination of all their contracts with LTCM, would have had to rebalance their firms' overall risk positions; that is, they would have had to either purchase replacement derivatives contracts or liquidate their related positions. In addition, firms that had lent securities to LTCM might have had to sell the collateral held and buy replacement securities in the marketplace at prevailing prices. In considering the prospect of these developments, Federal Reserve officials said that a "fire sale" of financial instruments by LTCM's creditors and counterparties might have set off a cycle of price declines, losses, and further liquidation of positions, with the effects spreading to a wider group of uninvolved investors.[4]

In part, since, like LTCM, Bear Stearns was the counterparty to numerous transactions, its demise posed a risk to the economic system. Since derivatives are bilateral contracts, in each transaction there is a winner and a loser and the incremental increase in value on one side of a derivatives contract is offset by a corresponding decrease in value to the opposite side of the contract. If a major financial institution such as Bear Stearns were to disappear, its counterparties would need to stand in line with other unsecured creditors to recover the value of any outstanding derivatives contracts. Counterparties would likely sustain huge losses. Moreover, uncertainty about whether counterparties would be made whole would have an adverse "ripple effect" on all actors in the financial system. The government applied a similar rationale to the bailout of AIG, a counterparty to numerous credit derivatives transactions. AIG's failure may have caused a chain reaction of failed derivatives transactions, endangering the solvency of the entire financial system.

Counterparty credit risk is the risk of economic loss from the failure of an obligor to perform according to the terms and conditions of a contract or agreement.[5] In a free market, it is hoped that counterparties can effectively monitor each other's credit risk. Chairman Bernanke explains that, "in many situations, regulation that relies on the invisible hand of market-based incentives can complement direct government regulation. For market-based regulation to work, the incentives of investors and other private actors must align with the objectives of the government regulator. In particular, private investors must be sophisticated enough to understand and monitor the financial condition of the firm and be persuaded that they will experience significant losses in the event of a failure. When these conditions are met, market discipline is a powerful and proven tool for constraining excessive risk-taking.[6] When certain unpredictable forces affect market positions, however, regulators may be forced to take action.

C. Over-the-Counter vs. Exchange-Traded Derivatives

The United States Treasury distinguishes two categories of derivatives: (1) privately negotiated and traded agreements, called over-the-counter derivatives, (hereinafter "OTC"); and (2) standardized agreements, called exchange-traded derivatives, which are traded through an organized exchange.[7] OTC derivatives are

---

4. United States General Accounting Office, GAO/GGD-00-3 Long-Term Capital Management October 1999.

5. Trading and Capital-Markets Activities Manual §2020.1.

6. Ben S. Bernanke, (remarks at the New York University School of Law, New York, NY, April 11, 2007).

7. U.S. Treasury Web site, http://www.treas.gov/education/faq/markets/derivatives.shtml (last visited Dec. 3, 2007).

contracts directly negotiated by counterparties on a principal-to-principal basis. As such, OTC derivatives permit counterparties to negotiate specific contract terms and thus allow a firm to tailor a contract to its individual needs. However, OTC derivatives tend to be illiquid and subject to counterparty or credit risk.

Exchange-traded derivatives are designed to virtually eliminate counterparty risk. An organized exchange addresses the counterparty credit risk inherent in bilateral contracting by standardizing derivatives contracts to create a liquid market in the contracts themselves. Essentially, the buyer is entering into a derivative contract with the exchange itself as counterparty. Furthermore, an exchange imposes margin requirements on all open contracts, requiring each market participant to maintain a certain balance with the exchange over the life of an open position.

The exchange takes steps to minimize its own counterparty credit risk by regulating its market participants to ensure their financial integrity. First, an exchange's clearinghouse serves as counterparty to every trade. That is, the clearinghouse guarantees each contract. Thus individual traders never need to conduct individual credit evaluations of a counterparty. The individual counterparty credit risk of OTC derivative contracting is replaced by the risk of a clearinghouse default. The clearinghouse itself is less likely to default than any individual trading partner. This is true because of exchange-imposed margin and mark-to-market requirements, as well as the loss-sharing provisions an exchange requires of its members.

Exchange-traded and OTC derivatives can be compared as follows:

Exchange-traded[8]	OTC
Centralized marketplace	Bilaterally negotiated
Standardized terms	Flexible terms
Daily mark-to-market	Collateral agreements
Constant maturity	Mature over time

II. SHIFTING RISK

A firm uses derivatives instead of direct "spot" transactions in the underlying asset for a number of reasons. For example, when a firm does not have the immediate need or ability to transact in an underlying commodity, but contemplates a future transaction in that underlying asset, it may find it desirable to lock in the price of that commodity today, thereby hedging the risk that changes in the market price of the underlying asset will make a planned future transaction costlier than originally contemplated. Moreover, due to the leveraged nature

---

8. *See* Chapter 11, *infra*, for further discussion of exchange-traded derivatives.

of derivatives, a firm may lock in the future price of an expected spot transaction without expending the entire cost of the notional value of the underlying.

A. The Concept of Leverage

Leverage refers to the concept of making an investment with a small up-front monetary commitment using borrowed funds. Both OTC and exchange-traded derivatives may be leveraged. For example, an OTC derivative may not require any transfer of funds until a contemplated performance or maturity date. Likewise, exchange-traded derivatives require only a good faith margin deposit at the time a position is opened. This concept of leverage—obtaining future control over an asset that has not yet been purchased—has a number of important implications for derivatives as a tool for risk management. An exchange-traded derivative's market price includes more than just the spot price of the derivative's underlying. Because the derivatives contract essentially transfers the right to future ownership of an underlying before the actual transaction occurs, its market price also reflects the various "carry" costs that would be incurred in holding the underlying until the future transaction. For example, if the underlying asset is a physical commodity, one such carry cost would be that of storing and protecting the commodity until delivery. Further, because ownership is effectively transferred leveraged in a derivative transaction, the derivative essentially incorporates a loan extending from contract formation to maturity. A derivative's value thus changes with prevailing interest rates.

The carry costs reflected in a derivative's contract price above the spot price of its underlying will decrease as the contract approaches maturity. As a derivatives contract approaches expiry, carry costs converge toward zero and the market price converges toward the spot market price of the derivative's underlying. A firm choosing not to offset its position in an exchange-traded derivative prior to maturity thus effectively holds its position in the underlying at expiry.

B. Basis Risk

Exchanges standardize contract terms to promote liquidity and reduce the transaction costs associated with finding a counterparty. An exchange's value, both to its users as well as to its owners, lies in its trading volume. However, standardized contract terms trading on a dynamic exchange implicate basis risk to a greater degree than their OTC counterparts.

Basis risk is the risk arising from possible changes in the difference between the spot and futures price of a particular underlying.[9] Basis risk exists to the extent that changes to a derivative's value do not completely offset the risk exposure a firm is trying to hedge. Anytime a derivative is based on an underlying that is not the exact risk a firm is trying to hedge, basis risk exists. *Thrifty Oil Co. v.*

---

9. John Smullen and Nicholas Hand, eds., OXFORD DICTIONARY OF FINANCE AND BANKING 37 (3d Ed. 2005).

Bank of America Nat'l Trust and Savings Assn.[10] provides an example of basis risk introduced in an OTC derivative. A subsidiary of Thrifty Oil, looking to secure a medium term loan at a fixed rate, found that its cheapest option was to obtain a floating-rate loan and then enter into an interest rate derivative to effectively convert that floating-rate loan into a fixed-rate obligation. Because the firm used an interest rate swap based off LIBOR (the London Inter Bank Offered Rate) to hedge against the risk of unpredictable cash flow requirements stemming from its floating Federal Funds Rate loan, it was exposed to the (heretofore nominal) risk of divergence between LIBOR and the Federal Funds Rate.[11] The firm, in identifying a risk (in this case, the market risk of interest rate exposure) first considered a non-derivative solution (simply securing a fixed-rate loan) and then ultimately determined that the use of a derivatives contract more efficiently achieved its risk management objective.[12]

C. Market Risk

Since derivatives are contracts whose value is derived from something else, they are inherently forward-looking, allowing firms to manage market risks associated with the passage of time. Market risk, also known as "financial risk," is the potential for changes in market price of an item. The four most common market-risk factors are interest rates, foreign-exchange rates, equity prices, and commodity prices.[13] Indeed, derivatives are most commonly used to manage these four market risks.

D. Effective Tools of Risk Management

Since derivatives are creatures of contract, they are extremely flexible, and can be used to accomplish a broad array of risk management objectives. For example, firms use derivatives to guarantee periodic cash flows or to "synthetically" trade in an underlying. In order to effectively use derivatives as a tool of risk management, a firm must be cognizant of the risks inherent in their use. Indeed, the leveraged nature of derivatives often comes with increased exposure to ordinary business risks, such as the operational risk of a "rogue trader," magnifying the potential for financial harm. The following sections discuss risks commonly associated with particular forms of derivatives.

III. TYPES OF DERIVATIVES

Different derivative structures allow an investor to address a single risk in a number of ways. While each structure is capable of addressing the same risks, the

---

10. 322 F.3d 1039 (9th Cir. 2002).

11. *See id.* at 1045 n. 7.

12. *See id.* at 1044.

13. TRADING AND CAPITAL-MARKETS ACTIVITIES MANUAL §2010.1.

associated transaction costs differ. Certain structures may be more or less favorable depending upon the circumstances. In order to effectively use derivatives as a tool for risk management, the investor must examine the costs of any particular derivatives structure in light of the risk it would like to transfer. Moreover, the regulatory impact of using a particular financial instrument is also an important consideration in selecting the most suitable particular derivative structure.[14]

A. Forwards

Forwards are financial contracts in which two counterparties agree to exchange a specified amount of a designated product for a specified price on a specified future date or dates. Forwards differ from futures in that their terms are not standardized and they are not traded on organized exchanges. Because they are individually negotiated between counterparties, forwards can be customized to meet the specific needs of the contracting parties.[15] The risks associated with the use of forwards are generally those associated with OTC derivatives contracts, the most significant being counterparty credit risk.[16]

A typical forward contract is a "privately negotiated bilateral contract" that is not executed in a standardized marketplace or on an exchange.[17] Like any privately negotiated bilateral agreement, the forward contract has an obvious drawback: the forward seller must find a counterparty willing to enter the contract. Because forwards are not executed on an anonymous exchange where brokers match up buyers to sellers, forwards may not be the most reliable and efficient financial instruments for hedging risk.

A forward's "primary purpose is to facilitate the sale and delivery of [a] physical commodity and, in particular, to assure the commodity's availability at a date in the future when it will be needed."[18] Actual delivery of the underlying is contemplated, so there is generally "no established mechanism for offset or cash settlement."[19] In re *Borden Chemicals and Plastics Operating LP v. Bridgeline Gas Marketing, LLC*,[20] the Bankruptcy Court established this principle to conclude that payments made by the plaintiff prior to filing for Chapter 11 protection qualified as forward contracts under the Bankruptcy Code and were thus protected from claims by a trustee. Borden had made prepayments for natural gas it received a month later. Borden's agent sought return of those payments during

---

14. *See* Chapter 4, *supra*, for a complete discussion of regulatory impact.

15. TRADING AND CAPITAL-MARKETS ACTIVITIES MANUAL, §4310.1.

16. *See* Section I.B., *supra*.

17. *The Economic Purpose of Futures Markets and How They Work*, Commodity Futures Trading Commission Web site, http://www.cftc.gov/educationcenter/economicpurpose.html.

18. CFTC v. Zelener, 2003 U.S. Dist. LEXIS 17660, *8 (N.D. Ill. 2003).

19. *Id.* at *9.

20. 336 B.R. 214 (Bkrtcy.D.Del 2006).

a statutory period prior to the bankruptcy filing. Bridgeline, the gas supply company, argued that the payments were protected by the Bankruptcy Code because they were settlement payments pursuant to forward contracts.[21] The court acknowledged a distinguishing feature of forward contracts: "the part[y is] expect[ed] to make actual delivery."[22] Because the agreement between Borden and Bridgeline contemplated actual delivery of gas, the court concluded that the agreement constituted a forward agreement. Thus, the court held that the forward payments received by Bridgeline were protected from any of Borden's bankruptcy claims.

B. Futures

Futures contracts are essentially exchange-traded forward contracts with standardized terms.[23] Like a forward contract, "[a] futures contract is an agreement between parties for the future delivery of a commodity at a price agreed upon today."[24] However, a futures contract's "principal purpose is to transfer price risk rather than ownership of the underlying commodity."[25] Thus, while a futures contract will specify the terms of delivery pursuant to contract maturity, actual delivery of the underlying commodity uncommon, as futures trading "generally involves mechanisms that permit the parties to avoid delivery, either by cash settlement or entering into an offsetting transaction."[26] Futures contracts are required by law to trade on federally licensed contract markets that are regulated by the Commodity Futures Trading Commission (CFTC).[27]

1. **Reduction of Counterparty Risk** Two unique features reduce counterparty risk in futures transactions:

(1) Futures require a performance bond, that is, a "good faith" margin deposit as collateral for the transaction;

(2) Futures are marked-to-market on a daily basis with an exchange of cash flow between member firms reflecting the net market movements of aggregated positions.

---

21. *Id.* at 216–17 (citing 11 U.S.C. §546(e)).

22. *Id.* at 218 (quoting Williams v. Morgan Stanley Capital Group Inc., 294 F.3d 737, 741 (5th Cir. 2002) (internal citations omitted)).

23. TRADING AND CAPITAL-MARKETS ACTIVITIES MANUAL, §4320.1.

24. CFTC v. Zelener, 2003 U.S. Dist. LEXIS 17660, *8 (N. D. Ill. 2003).

25. *Id.*

26. *Id.*

27. TRADING AND CAPITAL-MARKETS ACTIVITIES MANUAL, §4320.1. *See* Chapter 4, Sec. II *supra* for a complete discussion of CFTC jurisdiction and regulation.

2. Suitability as Hedging Instruments Futures possess several characteristics that make them more suitable than forwards for hedging purposes, and less suitable for merchandising purposes.[28]

(1) Many types of commodities and other assets are suitable for futures contracts. Historically, the underlying assets for futures contracts were agricultural commodities, but now they include nonagricultural commodities such as metals, and other financial instruments such as foreign currencies.

(2) The terms of the contract are standardized by the exchange in which the future is traded and not by the contract participants. Standardization increases liquidity because many participants can trade the same financial instrument.

(3) The exchange or marketplace for futures acts as a clearinghouse—it "acts as the buyer to all sellers and the seller to all buyers." Participants may "offset" their positions—sell back any positions they bought or vice versa, without actually having to deliver or take delivery of the underlying commodity.

(4) Participants are not required to put up the entire value of a futures contract; rather, the exchange typically requires only a margin, or fraction of the total value of the contract.

C. Distinction between Forwards and Futures

Forwards and futures are both noncash contractual instruments that enable market participants to both manage risk and enhance yield. In a forward contract, two counterparties "agree to exchange a specified amount of a designated product for a specified price on a specified future date or dates."[29] The terms of forward contracts are individually negotiated and are customized according to the counterparties' specific needs.[30] Forward contracts are not readily tradable on a formalized market platform. Futures contracts serve the same purpose as forwards; however, their terms are standardized and they are traded on organized exchanges.[31]

The main differences between futures and forwards are:

(1) Futures trade on "open outcry" exchanges, either electronic or physical, such as the Chicago Mercantile Exchange, the Chicago Board of Trade, or the New York Mercantile Exchange, or via electronic trading systems that match buyers and sellers such as EUREX.

(2) Futures contract specifications are standardized by the exchange

---

28. *The Economic Purpose of Futures Markets and How They Work*, Commodity Futures Trading Commission Web site, http://www.cftc.gov/educationcenter/economicpurpose.html.

29. TRADING AND CAPITAL-MARKETS ACTIVITIES MANUAL, §4310.1.

30. *Id.*

31. *Id.*, §4320.1.

(3) Obligations under a futures contract may be readily extinguished by entering into an offsetting transaction.

The distinction between a forward and futures contract is significant because
a futures contract is regulated by the CFTC. The uncertainty over whether a
contract is a forward or a future introduces "legal risk." Legal risk can impact
the efficacy of a hedge if regulatory issues impede the smooth operation of a
transaction.

Differentiating between a forward contract and a futures contract is not
always easy. The Commodity Exchange Act (CEA) does not expressly define a
"futures contract" but instead distinguishes "transactions involving contracts of
sale of a commodity for future delivery."[32] It, therefore, may not always be clear
if the CFTC has regulatory reach into a transaction.[33]

D. Foreign Exchange Forwards and Futures

Foreign exchange futures are derivative contracts traded on an exchange where
the delivery of underlying currency is the subject matter of the contract. Foreign
exchange futures contracts are traded in the United States on the International
Money Market of the Chicago Mercantile Exchange as well as on various overseas exchanges, including the London International Financial Futures Exchange
and the Singapore International Monetary Exchange.[34] For futures contracts, the
exchange on which the contract is traded determines margin requirements.

In an over-the-counter (OTC) foreign exchange (FX) forward agreement, two
parties agree to exchange a notional amount of capital in one currency valued in
a different currency at a designated exchange rate on a specified future date. The
exchange rate specified in an FX forward or future normally differs from the spot
exchange rate. The divergence in rates typically reflects interest rate differentials
between the countries of the two currencies that are being exchanged. If the
forward or future rate for a currency is higher than the current spot rate, the currency is said to be trading at a *premium*.[35] If the forward or future rate is lower
than the current spot rate, the currency is said to be trading at a *discount*.[36]

As with spot transactions, forward and futures contracts enable investors
to manage risk and speculate. However, while spot transactions require the
commitment of capital to convert one currency into the other at the prevailing
exchange rate, forwards and futures generally require little or no capital until
maturity when the contract is settled and the underlying notional amount of
capital is exchanged at the specified rate. Counterparties in forward contracts

---

32. 7 U.S.C. §2(a)(1)(A).
33. 7 U.S.C. §§2(a)(1)(A), 6(a)(1).
34. TRADING AND CAPITAL-MARKETS ACTIVITIES MANUAL, §4320.1.
35. TRADING AND CAPITAL-MARKETS ACTIVITIES MANUAL, §4305.1.
36. *Id.*

may require initial margin collateral to be placed in an account to secure the transaction. Additional maintenance margin collateral may need to be deposited in the account if the spot rate moves significantly against one of the counterparties. For forwards, the margin requirement is a negotiated term specified in a formalized contractual agreement governing the counterparties' derivatives transactions called the Credit Support Annex of an International Swaps and Derivatives Association (ISDA) Master Agreement. Normally the amount of collateral required for a forward or futures contract is small relative to the size of the notional amount of capital specified in the contract. Thus, unlike spot transactions, forward and futures contracts give the counterparties a substantial amount of financial leverage, enabling speculation on changes in the value of large amounts of currency with very little commitment of capital.

E. Options

Options differ from forward and futures derivatives in that they provide unilateral price protection.

> Options transfer the right but not the obligation to buy or sell an underlying asset, instrument, or index on or before the option's exercise date at a specified price (the *strike price*). A *call option* gives the option purchaser the right but not the obligation to purchase a specific quantity of the underlying asset (from the call option seller) on or before the option's exercise date at the strike price. Conversely, a *put option* gives the option purchaser the right but not the obligation to sell a specific quantity of the underlying asset (to the put option seller) on or before the option's exercise date at the strike price.[37]

> Although options contemplate a future transaction in an underlying, "in practice settlement is generally effectuated by a cash payment representing the difference between the market price and the strike price."[38] Indeed, in some circumstances an actual transaction in the underlying is impracticable or impossible. For example, an option on an underlying index

>> does not contemplate the purchase or sale of an ownership interest in a pool of securities. It is simply a bet on the future value of the index. If at the expiration date the index is above the value stated in the option contract, the holder of a call option has the contractual right to receive the difference. If at the expiration date the index is below the value stated in the option contract, the holder of a put option has the contractual right to receive the difference.[39]

> The price paid by the buyer of an option is referred to as premium. This premium is a dynamic measure of the factors that affect the option's value.[40]

---

37. TRADING AND CAPITAL-MARKETS ACTIVITIES MANUAL, §4330.1.
38. Dow Jones & Co. v. Int'l Sec. Exch., Inc., 451 F.3d 295, 298 (2d Cir. 2006).
39. *Id.* at 301 n. 6.
40. TRADING AND CAPITAL-MARKETS ACTIVITIES MANUAL, §4330.1.

Options are priced using the Black-Scholes formula, a complex mathematical equation which values the option according to the price and volatility of the underlying security, the option strike price, the time until expiration, and the risk-free interest rate for the duration of time until maturity of the option.[41] The value of an option rises as volatility increases and as the price of the underlying security approaches the strike price.[42]

Options allow counterparties to hedge or speculate on an asset's price movement using very little capital (i.e., a high degree of leverage). However, options also allow the buyer to substantially limit downside risk. Because options accord the right—not the obligation—to buy or sell, the owner of the option has no market risk beyond the premium that has been paid to purchase the option. The seller of the option receives the premium in exchange for taking on exposure to the underlying security. The seller may hedge out this exposure by accumulating a position in the underlying security that offsets its obligation under the option contract. The size of the position that the seller must assume to compensate for its obligation varies with the option's *delta*, or the sensitivity of the price of the option to the price of the underlying instrument. While options might serve the purposes of hedging risk or enhancing yield as do other derivatives, they also offer the compelling advantage of enabling the buyer to pay a fee (the premium) to entirely cut off all downside risk by shifting it to the seller.

Although options are not considered securities, the SEC is authorized to regulate the public trading of put and call options for securities and indexes.[43] In *Board of Trade of the City of Chicago v. SEC*,[44] the Seventh Circuit observed that futures and options were "competing financial instruments often used for hedging."[45] The court examined whether a group of market participants (hereinafter "Group") were in fact a clearing agency that must register with SEC. The Group served as a clearinghouse for trading options on government securities. The court found the Group was an "exchange" for purposes of the SEC because the Group "(1) for a price based on transactions executed, it (2) [brought] together buyers and sellers of (3) fungible instruments (or standardized options), (4) clear[ed] the transactions thus executed and (5) disseminat[ed] price and other trading information, and also: (6) admit[ed] and (7) discipline[d] members; and establishe[d] trading rules for (8) members and (9) customers."[46] Thus, although options are not securities, they can be regulated by the SEC if employed by an exchange.

---

41. *Id.*
42. *See* Chapter 15, *infra*, for a complete discussion of option pricing.
43. 15 U.S.C. §77b(a)(1).
44. 883 F.2d 525 (7th Cir. 1989).
45. *Id.* at 526.
46. *Id.* at 534.

F. Swaps

A swap is an OTC derivatives contract in which two parties agree to exchange "cash flows" on a "notional amount" over a period of time in the future. The parties exchange cash flows pursuant to an agreed-upon payment schedule, made up of one or more payment dates throughout the life of the contract. Cash flows are computed by applying the agreed-upon formula for each party's respective "leg" (set of payments) of the swap to a "notional amount" (an a underlying sum of capital which does not itself change hands).

1. **Characteristics of Swaps** Most swaps have the following characteristics:

(1) Credit risk exposure similar to that of forward transactions (swaps, like forwards, are privately negotiated),

(2) A beginning valuation date, intermediate swap interest exchange dates, and a final termination date;

(3) Extreme flexibility allowing them to be crafted to meet the specific needs of the counterparties.[47]

The Bank for International Settlements estimated that at the end of December, 2006, then-outstanding OTC derivatives contracts combined for a notional amount of over $415 trillion. Interest rate swaps made up over half of this amount, totaling more than $229 trillion. The next highest swap contract, credit default swaps, came in at almost $29 trillion, followed by foreign exchange, commodity, and then equity swaps.

Privately negotiated agreements for the exchange of large sums of money require careful and extensive contracting over many terms and provisions. Because parties tend to enter into numerous swap transactions over the course of a business relationship, parties commonly enter into swaps pursuant to a "master agreement." The master agreement sets out the general terms and conditions that will govern the parties' relationship, including common representations, covenants, and operating provisions. The parties then memorialize the economic terms of individual transactions in supplements to the master agreement known as "Confirmations." The International Swaps and Derivatives Association, a financial trade association made up of institutions that deal in OTC derivatives, created the standardized contract (the "ISDA Master Agreement") most often used to govern OTC derivatives transactions.

2. **The ISDA Master Agreement** The ISDA Master Agreement allows parties entering into a swap relationship to document all of their derivatives transactions under a single agreement. Indeed, it specifies that each party enters into individual transactions in reliance on the fact that all such transactions, combined with the Master Agreement, form a single agreement. Thus, while the

---

47. *See* also Chapter 10, *infra,* for discussion of different types of swaps.

ISDA Master Agreement provides convenience, its most important function is to provide economic certainty.

The ISDA Master Agreement provides convenience by reducing transaction costs. The Master Agreement serves as an industry-standard contract available for off-the-shelf use by counterparties. Further, ISDA provides definitional booklets that may be incorporated into any given transaction. For example, parties entering into an interest rate swap might reference the "2006 ISDA Definitions" in their Confirmation. Such definitions would include various floating rate indices as well as the mechanical operating provisions for establishing fixed and floating payment amounts. Such incorporated definitions and operating provisions reduce the transaction costs of entering into any given transaction.

Specific provisions of the Master Agreement are also aimed at reducing transaction costs. For example, the Master Agreement specifies that payments due each party under a single transaction in the same currency are to be "netted." Thus, instead of each party paying the other what is due under its respective leg of the swap, balances are calculated and only the difference changes hands. This netting feature both increases efficiency and diminishes settlement risk. Further, if the parties enter into numerous different swap transactions that are both in the same currency and on the same payment schedule, the ISDA Master Agreement provides the option of netting across all such transactions. If desired, the parties may simply state this intention in individual confirmations.

The ISDA Master Agreement's most important function is to provide economic certainty. Specifically, it provides for close-out netting in the event of a party default. Should a party default, the agreement provides that the nondefaulting party may elect to designate an early termination date, effective across all outstanding transactions. After such a designation, all outstanding transactions between the parties are terminated and their values are calculated and netted to arrive at a single amount owed to one party. This provides significant protection for the nondefaulting party; had the default been caused by a party entering bankruptcy, the nondefaulting party could find itself liable for a significant sum of money to a defaulting party's representative in insolvency, with the countervailing sum transformed into a mere claim as an unsecured creditor.

G. Credit Derivatives

One of the seminal events of the 2008 economic crisis was the federal bailout and subsequent government investment in AIG. The implosion at AIG stemmed in large part from its sale of credit derivatives to counterparties. Theses credit derivatives "insured" corporate credit and required significant payments to counterparties when a subject credit worsened or defaulted. Because neither counterparty to these contracts needed to have any exposure to the underlying subject credit, AIG was able to "write protection" for many times the value of the outstanding credit of the subject companies themselves.

Credit derivatives are "off-balance-sheet arrangements that allow one party (the beneficiary) to transfer credit risk of a reference asset—which the beneficiary may or may not own—to another party (the guarantor)."[48] Credit derivatives were used by banks to shift their overall credit-risk exposure through contingent payments based on events of default and the periodic exchange of payments or the payment of a premium.[49] There are two major categories of credit derivatives: a credit default swap (CDS), a private contract in which private parties bet on the probability of a debt issuer defaulting; and a collateralized debt obligation (CDO), an asset pool consisting of numerous debt obligations held by a special purpose entity (SPE) whose interests are divided and resold into different "tranches" based on differences in credit quality of the assets in the pool.[50]

Because of their private transaction nature, credit derivatives are generally unregulated and governed only by the standardized agreements promulgated by the International Swaps and Derivatives Association (the ISDA).[51] The Federal Reserve, however, still retains some regulatory power over credit derivatives that a member bank may enter into by monitoring the bank's capital adequacy, safety and soundness. For example, the Federal Reserve may promulgate guidelines governing the amount and types of CDOs that can be counted toward a member bank's minimum capital adequacy requirement.[52] As the government has become more involved in AIG, the regulatory reach into this market place has seen a de facto increase.

---

48. TRADING AND CAPITAL-MARKETS ACTIVITIES MANUAL §2110.1.

49. *Id.*

50. Frank Partnoy & David A. Skeel, Jr., *Ninth Annual Corporate Law Symposium: Debt as a Lever of Control: The Promise and Perils of Credit Derivatives*, 75 U. CIN. L. REV. 1019, 1021–22 (2007).

51. *Id.* at 1036–37.

52. TRADING AND CAPITAL-MARKETS ACTIVITIES MANUAL §2110.1.

10. TYPES OF SWAPS

As discussed in the previous chapter, a swap is a bilateral OTC derivatives contract in which two parties agree to exchange "cash flows" on a "notional amount" over a period of time. The notional amount is a reference amount upon which the payment formula is based. The parties exchange cash flows pursuant to an agreed-upon payment schedule, made up of one or more payment dates throughout the life of the contract. Cash flows are computed by applying the agreed-upon formula relating to each parties' respective "leg" (set of payments) of the swap to a "notional amount" (a hypothetical underlying value which does not necessarily itself change hands). The simplest swap is the "plain vanilla" interest rate swap, in which counterparties exchange fixed rate risk for floating rate risk.

I. "PLAIN VANILLA" INTEREST RATE SWAPS

The "plain vanilla" interest rate swap is described in *K3C Inc. v. Bank of America*:[1]

> An interest rate swap is a transaction by which a borrower can hedge against the risk of interest rate fluctuations. The borrower and another party agree to exchange cash flows over a period of time. Most commonly, one party exchanges fixed rate payments for floating rate payments based on an underlying index such as LIBOR (London Inter Bank Offer Rate). This effectively converts the party's floating rate loan to a fixed rate loan. Thus, if the interest rate on a borrower's adjustable or floating rate loan rises, the increase in interest owed is offset by payments received through the interest rate swap.[2]

---

1. 204 Fed. Appx. 455 (5th Cir. 2006) (Unpublished).
2. *Id.* at 458.

For example, consider a company, MIERACO, Inc., which issues a 5-year bond at a rate of 6 percent per year. A bond purchaser/investor will receive $6,000 per year on an investment of $100,000. Consider a second company, RONITCO, LLC, which issues a $100,000 bond to investors at a rate of 200 basis points over the London Interbank Offered Rate (LIBOR) (a floating rate bond). RONITCO's bond purchasers will earn a return that will float relative to LIBOR. So if LIBOR is at 2%, RONITCO will pay its bondholder $4,000 per year on a $100,000 investment if LIBOR remains unchanged, and more or less as LIBOR rises or falls.

If RONITCO's CEO, Eve Temimah, feels that interest rates might go up, thus adversely impacting RONITCO's liability to its bondholders (since RONITCO's liabilities float relative to LIBOR), RONITCO could enter into a plain vanilla swap with MIERACO, whereby RONITCO would pay MIERACO a fixed rate of 6% in return for a floating rate of 200 over LIBOR on a notional value of $100,000.

RONITCO and MIERACO have effectively swapped places. RONITCO swaps its floating rate obligation to bondholders for a fixed rate obligation to MIERACO and will receive a fixed rate to subsequently pay out from RONITCO; both MIERCO and RONITCO will use the income stream from the swap to pay its obligations to its bondholders.

The cost to each party to enter into the transaction will be dictated by market conditions. In other words, if companies with credit ratings identical to that of MIERACO and RONITCO could access capital in the market by either issuing fixed rate bonds at 6% or floating rate bonds at LIBOR plus 200 basis points, the cost to each party for entering into the transaction will be zero. If the choice to similarly situated companies is to issue bonds at 200 over LIBOR or a fixed rate of 5% for an identical duration, the floating leg of the transaction must pay for the privilege of earning 6% from its counterparty. The swap will fluctuate in value as market conditions change.

The plain vanilla swap contract meets the functional definition of a derivative in that it shifts interest rate risk from one counterparty to the other (fixed for floating rate risk). Both counterparties now have undertaken the counterparty risk that the contra party will be unwilling or unable to meet its obligation under the terms of the swap when the obligations ripen. Note that no principal is exchanged between the counterparties and the notional value is merely a reference amount used to calculate each party's obligations under the swap agreement. Also, consider that either of the counterparties could have entered into this agreement whether or not they had a related obligation to bondholders.

The basic structure of the plain vanilla swap can be used as a template for swaps across a number of asset classes. For example, assume that the counterparties exchange cash flows whereby the counterparty obliged to pay the floating leg of the swap pays based upon a formula tied to the relative performance of a basket of stocks of a specified notional amount. The fixed payer will pay a fixed rate of interest on the same notional value. While the structure is similar to the plain vanilla swap, this swap is considered an "equity swap" because the underlying item upon which the payment stream is based is a basic of stocks. If the same principle were applied to a notional amount of oil it, would be an energy swap. The structure of the plain vanilla swap can be used with any commodity, and allows a counterparty who has a floating-rate financial risk to swap that risk for a fixed-rate risk as long as she can find a willing counterparty. While the structure of a fixed-for-floating-rate swap can be used to hedge a broad array of financial risks, the structures of the contracts may be layered in a number of financial transactions.

For example, in *Thrifty Oil Co. v. Bank of America*,[3] a Thrifty subsidiary was seeking fixed-rate financing. Bank of America provided a floating-rate loan of $45 million. At the same time, it provided swaps totaling $45 million in notional amount whereby it paid the Thrifty subsidiary a floating interest rate in exchange for the fixed-rate payment the Thrifty subsidiary ultimately sought out. The swaps followed an amortization schedule similar to the payment schedule of the floating-rate loan and terminated on the same date as the term loan's maturity. The result was effectively a fixed-rate loan, plus some "basis risk" (the floating interest rate paid by the subsidiary on the term loan was based on the Federal Funds Rate whereas the floating interest received via the swaps was based on LIBOR).[4] Regardless, this result was the most economical means for the subsidiary to acquire the fixed-rate financing it sought. The Ninth Circuit Court of Appeals noted that

> the close resemblance between this arrangement and fixed-rate financing merely confirms that the borrower has successfully exploited the flexibility of a derivative interest rate swap to achieve a specific financial objective. No matter how tightly the borrower integrates the swap with its loan, the payments made under the swap cannot represent interest.[5]

II. CURRENCY SWAPS

Currency swap agreements are mechanisms for hedging foreign exchange (FX) risk and taking on exposure to a currency over a set interval of time. A foreign exchange swap is a simultaneous purchase and sale of an amount of foreign currency for two different value dates.[6] The parties to the swap contract to pay and

---

3. 322 F.3d 1039 (9th Cir. 2002).
4. *Id.* at 1044–45, 1045 n. 7.
5. *Id.* at 1049.
6. TRADING AND CAPITAL-MARKETS ACTIVITIES MANUAL, §4305.1.

receive the same amount of currency on the specified dates.[7] The counterparties agree to exchange two currencies at a particular rate on one date (the "near date") and to reverse payments, almost always at a different rate, on a specified subsequent date (the "far date").[8] The value dates may be any two future dates. Unlike forwards and futures, the buy and sell components of the swap are recorded as a single transaction with the same counterparty.[9] The swap allows each party to use a currency for a period of time in exchange for another currency that is not needed during that time.[10] Institutions use foreign exchange swaps as efficient mechanisms to invest or hedge temporary idle currency balances.[11]

A variation on a foreign exchange swap is a foreign currency swap. In a currency swap, counterparties exchange equal initial principal amounts of two currencies at the spot rate, exchange a stream of fixed or floating interest rate payments in their swapped currencies for the agreed duration of the swap, and then re-exchange the principal amount at maturity at the initial spot exchange rate.[12] The initial exchange of principal may be omitted and a "difference check" may be paid by one party to the other to cover the net obligation instead of actually exchanging periodic interest payments.[13] Foreign exchange swaps and foreign currency swaps are used for a variety of purposes, including shifting the currency of an asset, accommodating outright forward transactions, bridging gaps in the maturity structure of outstanding spot and forward contracts, and hedging or speculating on interest rates in different countries.[14] Like forwards and futures, foreign currency swaps can be structured to offer the benefit of significant financial leverage, since there is often no exchange of underlying principal. In contrast, foreign exchange swaps do entail a shift of principal between two currencies for the duration of the contract. Swaps are most useful and efficient for entities that wish to lock in both sides of the FX transaction.

III. CREDIT-DEFAULT SWAPS

Credit derivatives are off-balance-sheet financial instruments that permit one party (the beneficiary) to transfer the credit risk of a reference asset, which it typically owns, to another party (the guarantor) without actually selling the

---

7. *Id.*

8. Federal Reserve Bank of New York, *All About the FX Market*, 40, http://www.newyorkfed.org/education/addpub/usfxm/.

9. TRADING AND CAPITAL-MARKETS ACTIVITIES MANUAL, §4305.1.

10. *Id.*

11. *Id.*

12. *All About the FX Market*, p. 44.

13. *Id.*

14. *Id.*; *see also* TRADING AND CAPITAL-MARKETS ACTIVITIES MANUAL, §4305.1.

asset."[15] A credit derivative is a "contract which transfers credit risk from a protection buyer to a credit protection seller."[16] Protection buyers "can use credit derivatives to manage particular market exposures and return-on-investment," whereas protection sellers "generally use credit derivatives to earn income and diversify their own investment portfolios."[17]

A. Purpose and Function

The courts have defined a credit-default swap as a "bilateral financial contract in which 'a protection buyer makes periodic payments to . . . the protection seller, in return for a contingent payment if a predefined credit event occurs in the reference credit,' i.e., the obligation on which the contract is written."[18] The main purpose of credit-default swaps is to allow financial institutions, investors, and other market participants the opportunity to isolate and transfer specific credit risk from one party to another at a predetermined cost.

While CDS agreements are often compared to insurance contracts, they are not insurance contracts.[19] As pointed out by the International Swaps and Derivatives Association (ISDA), a trade group representing large financial institutions and other derivatives players, "there is no requirement that the protection buyer own the asset on which it is buying protection or that it suffer any loss."[20] The notional value covered by the agreement does not need to bear any relationship to the notional value held by the protection buyer.[21] Parties are free to use credit-default swaps as vehicles of speculation. If the predefined redit event occurs in the reference credit as per the agreement, during the period outlined, then the protection seller must fulfill his obligations under the agreement.

The majority of credit-default swap protection buyers use the agreements to hedge specific risks. In these cases, the credit risk being hedged could be identical to the credit risk of the asset the protection buyer has in possession. Alternatively, many sophisticated parties hedge risks that are "reasonably correlated with the performance" of the reference entity, "so that . . . the [protection buyer] may seek to isolate and hedge country risk written on some portion of the

---

15. TRADING AND CAPITAL-MARKETS ACTIVITIES MANUAL, §4350.1.

16. Eternity Global Master Fund Ltd. v. Morgan Guaranty Trust Co., 375 F.3d 168, 172 (2d Cir. 2004).

17. *Id.*

18. Eternity Global Master Fund Ltd. v. Morgan Guaranty Trust Co. of NY, 375 F.3d 168, 172, n. 6 (2d. Cir., 2004), quoting Joyce A. Frost, *Credit Risk Management from a Corporate Perspective,* in HANDBOOK OF CREDIT DERIVATIVES 90 (1999).

19. AON Financial Products v. Societe Generale, 476 F.3d 90, 96 (2d. Cir., 2007), citing brief of *amicus curiae* Int'l Swaps and Derivatives Ass'n, Inc. (ISDA), at 7.

20. *Amicus curiae* brief of Int'l Swaps and Derivatives Ass'n, Inc. (ISDA) in AON Financial Products v. Societe Generale, 476 F.3d 90 (2d. Cir., 2007).

21. *Id.*

sovereign's outstanding debt."[22] For example, a hedge fund that owns a significant amount of securities in an emerging country may seek to hedge the political risk in the country by entering into a credit-default swap with a counterparty using the Sovereign as the Reference Entity. The hedge fund may have determined that there is a correlation between the credit risk of the securities and the credit risk of the Sovereign. In this example, the hedge fund (protection buyer) would be assuming "the risk of how well-correlated the two defaults will be. That correlation of default is the most important credit risk management issue associated" with credit-default swaps.[23] Other inherent risks of the agreement are counterparty risk and legal risks, discussed below.

B. ISDA Master Agreement

The International Swaps and Derivatives Association has helped standardize the credit-default swap market to improve efficiency and reduce transaction costs.[24] This standardization has helped the market for default swaps expand at a rapid pace. Credit-default swaps are documented in three parts: (1) the standard "ISDA Master Agreement," (2) the negotiated "Schedules" (which outline alterations to the standard ISDA agreement, and (3) the "Confirmations (which document specific elements of the transaction including defining the "precise risk" each party wishes to transfer).[25] The standard ISDA agreement contains standard terms that govern the CDS market, including the "legal and credit relationship between the counterparties . . . representations and warranties, events of default and termination, covenants and choice of law."[26]

C. Importance of Clearly Defined Terms

A credit-default swap must specifically and clearly articulate the exact protection being sought or sold; consequently, the "credit event" and "reference entity" must be unambiguously defined. If the credit event or reference entity is incorrectly defined or described in the Schedule and Confirmation associated with the ISDA agreement, the "protection buyer" may not receive the desired and expected protection, or the "protection seller" could unexpectedly be liable for large sums of money. When sophisticated parties enter into credit-default swap agreements, courts will examine and enforce the specific language in the agreement, applying the traditional precepts of contract law, and will not consider extrinsic

---

22. Eternity Global, 375 F.3d at 172.

23. ISDA *amicus curiae* brief, *supra* note 21.

24. PARTNOY, FRANK AND DAVID SKEEL, THE PROMISE AND PERILS OF CREDIT DERIVATIVES, at 8, (University of Pennsylvania Law School, Year 2006), Paper 125, http://lsr.nellco.org/upenn/wps/papers/125.

25. ISDA *amicus curiae* brief, *supra* note 21, at 8–9.

26. Id.

evidence, surrounding circumstances, or industry customs, unless the terms are ambiguous.[27]

1. Credit Event The *Eternity Global*[28] case highlights the need to precisely define and articulate what constitutes a "credit event." In this case, Eternity purchased a series of Argentinean bonds and sought to hedge their credit risk to the Republic of Argentina by purchasing credit protection from Morgan Guaranty Trust Company of New York ("Morgan") for a specified time period, beginning in October 2001. The protection was designed using a series of credit-default swaps that listed the Republic of Argentina as the reference entity. Under the agreement Eternity paid Morgan a fixed fee; in exchange, upon the occurrence of a "credit event," Morgan would be required to purchase the bonds from Eternity for par value. The confirmation list agreed to by the parties listed categories of credit events based on certain Argentine obligations including repudiation, moratorium, or restructuring.[29] The transactions can be summarized below:

CDS EXAMPLE 1: Complex Financial Transaction
Credit-default Swap b/w Eternity Global and Morgan Guaranty

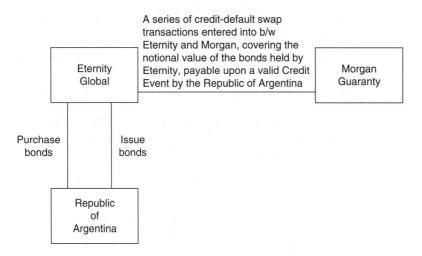

FIGURE **10.1** EXAMPLE OF CREDIT-DEFAULT SWAP

---

27. Eternity Global Master Fund Ltd. v. Morgan Guaranty Trust Co. of NY, 375 F.3d 168, 177 (2d. Cir., 2004).

28. *Id.* at 168.

29. *See* Eternity Global Master Fund Limited v. Morgan Guaranty Trust Co. of New York, 2002 WL 31426310 (S.D.N.Y.) (not reported in F.Supp.2d) at 3–4.

On November 1, 2001, the Argentinean President announced a voluntary exchange program for the bonds held by Eternity, involving exchanging the current bonds they held for newly issued secured bonds that carried a lower interest rate and a longer period maturity. While this program was "voluntary," Eternity viewed it as a coerced exchange, because if they did not exchange the bonds, they would be left with illiquid bonds that were subordinate to the newly issued bonds. In addition, Eternity viewed the newly issued bonds less favorably than the initial bonds they had purchased prior to the announcement. The market reacted by selling off the Argentinean bonds. As a result, Eternity claimed the "voluntary" exchange represented a restructuring under the credit-default swap with Morgan, and thus, a valid credit event, entitling them to exchange the bonds for their notional par value. However, Morgan claimed that since the exchange was "voluntary," there was no restructuring of the bond, and therefore, no credit event.[30]

In this case, the court analyzed whether the voluntary debt exchange program taken by Argentina in 2001 constituted a credit event that would trigger the credit-default swap agreement. To assess ambiguity in a disputed credit-default swap, the court outlined a four step method:[31]

(1) The courts will first look at the express terms and language in the credit-default swap agreement.

(2) If an ambiguity remains, the courts will then look at the ISDA "Master Swap Agreement."

(3) The court will also look at the version of the ISDA definitions that were "incorporated into the disputed contracts."

(4) Lastly, if the ambiguity has not been clarified, the court may look at extrinsic evidence including the "background 'customs, practices, and usages' of the credit derivatives trade."

---

30. According to the ISDA Agreement: "'Restructuring' means that, with respect to one or more Obligations, including as a result of an Obligation Exchange . . . any one or more of the following events occurs . . . :

    (i) a reduction in the rate or amount of interest payable or the amount of scheduled interest accruals;

    (ii) a reduction in the amount or principal or premium payable at maturity or at scheduled redemption dates;

    (iii) a postponement or other deferral of a date or dates for either: (A) the payment or accrual of interest or (B) the payment of principal or premium;

    (iv) a change in the ranking in priority of payment of any Obligation causing the subordination of such Obligation; or

    (v) any change in the currency or composition of any payment of interest or principal."

See Eternity Global Master Fund Limited v. Morgan Guaranty Trust Co. of New York, 2002 WL 31426310 (S.D.N.Y.) (not reported in F.Supp.2d) at 3–4.

31. Eternity Global, 375 F.3d at 177.

If the agreement is clear on its face, and no ambiguity exists, then the contract will be "enforced according to the plain meaning of its terms."[32] In this case, the court upheld Eternity's breach of contract claim after determining that sufficient ambiguity existed as to whether a voluntary debt exchange constituted a credit event under the credit-default swap.

2. **Reference Entity** The paramount case illustrating the importance of "reference entity" clarification is *Aon Financial Products, Inc. v. Societe Generale*.[33] In this case, a series of complex credit transactions stemming from a simple loan agreement led to years of litigation and a loss of approximately $10 million for a sophisticated financial institution (Aon Corporation), not to mention countless legal bills.

The case stemmed from a basic loan agreement, in which Bear Stearns International Limited (BSIL) agreed to lend Escobel Land, Inc. (Escobel) $9,307,000 to finance the construction of a condominium complex in the Philippines. In conjunction with the loan, BSIL sought and received a surety bond from the Government Service Insurance System (GSIS) that guaranteed the repayment of Escobel's $10 million obligation in the event Escobel defaulted on the loan. While GSIS is statutorily backed by the Republic of the Philippines (under Philippine law) and is considered a government agent, it is its own individual and separate entity (a point of major conflict throughout the litigation).

While the surety bond decreased BSIL's counterparty default risk, it sought to further limit its exposure to the loan agreement by entering into a credit-default swap agreement with Aon Financial Products, Inc. (AFP), whose payment was guaranteed by Aon Corporation (together with AFP, AON).[34] This credit-default swap covered the notional value of the $10 million loan. Under this agreement, AON promised to pay BSIL $10 million, plus out of pocket expenses in the event that GSIS failed to make payment under the surety bond for "whatever reason or cause," and waived all defenses, in exchange for consideration totaling $425,000 from BSIL.

The agreement was covered by New York State law based on a choice of law provision and comprised three documents: (1) an ISDA Master Agreement listing AFP and BSIL as parties, (2) a Schedule elaborating on certain aspects of the Master Agreement, and (3) a Confirmation letter from AFP to BSIL setting forth the specific terms and conditions of the transaction.[35] AON, uncomfortable with its exposure to $10 million in liability, sought to reduce its risk by, in turn,

---

32. *Id.*

33. 476 F.3d 90 (2d Cir. 2007).

34. Throughout the rest of this discussion, AFP and AON will be referred to as one party, despite the fact that they are two entities, because they retain the same liability and exposure in the litigation, are affiliate entities, and treating them as one does not detract or affect the description of the case.

35. Subsequently BSIL assigned its rights under all of these agreements to Ursa Minor (another institution) who subsequently assigned its rights to Bankers Trust (as part of a larger complex packaged deal).

entering into a credit-default swap with Societe Generale (SG). This credit-swap agreement did not make reference to or incorporate the credit-swap agreement between BSIL and AON. The transactions are illustrated in the exhibit below:

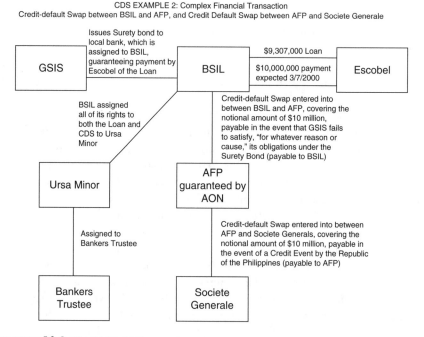

CDS EXAMPLE 2: Complex Financial Transaction
Credit-default Swap between BSIL and AFP, and Credit Default Swap between AFP and Societe Generale

FIGURE 10.2 COMPLEX CREDIT-DEFAULT SWAP

While the BSIL/AON credit-default swap agreement listed GSIS as the reference entity, the AON/SG credit-default swap listed the Republic of the Philippines as its reference entity. It is unclear whether AON sought to completely hedge its risk and believed that a credit event by GSIS equated to a credit event by the Republic of the Philippines (as a result of the surety bond), or whether it simply wanted to hedge the specific portion of its risk dealing with transacting business in the Philippines and therefore intended there to be this difference. As discussed earlier, one of the benefits of credit-default swaps is that a party may hedge or speculate on specifically tailored risks. In retrospect, this difference was crucial throughout the litigation.

When it came time to pay back its loan, Escobel defaulted. What historically would have been an isolated loss for the lender instead set off a chain of events set in motion by the above complex financial arrangements and agreements. First, a letter of demand was sent to GSIS. GSIS categorically denied liability under the surety bond, alleging that the assignment to BSIL was not valid and that the individuals who approved and drafted the surety bond lacked the authority to do so. BSIL (or now Bankers Trustee in its place) then sent a notice of a credit event and demand to AON under its credit-swap agreement. AON claimed that it also did not have to pay because the credit-swap agreement was premised on there being a valid surety bond, and if no such surety bond existed, AON was not liable. Despite making this argument, AON informed Societe Generale of the situation, and made them aware that they might be liable for the $10 million.

The first suit brought as a result of this complex transaction[36] sought to determine whether AON was liable under its credit-default swap agreement with BSIL (which was subsequently transferred to Ursa Minor Ltd.). The court interpreted the agreement on its face because the language was clear and unambiguous. The court held that AON had an obligation to pay under the credit-default swap "irrespective of the [Surety] Bond's potential invalidity or unenforceability with respect to GSIS."[37] The reference entity in this swap-agreement was GSIS, and one of the credit events under the agreement was a failure to pay. As long as GSIS failed to pay, AON was liable. AON had explicitly waived all of its defenses in the agreement and was liable to pay as long as Escobel and GSIS did not pay "'for whatever reason or cause' including where the underlying obligation was illegal or invalid."[38] The court examined the specific language in the agreement and interpreted the language in a matter in which an ordinary businessperson would interpret it. On appeal, the appellate court determined that the credit-default swap contained "a clear waiver of defenses concerning the invalidity, illegality, or unenforceability of the transaction.[39]

Found liable for the $10 million, AON sought to collect under its credit-default swap agreement with Societe Generale. AON claimed that it was straightforward: if AON was liable to BSIL for the $10 million, then Societe Generale was liable to AON for the $10 million. However, in the BSIL-AON credit-default swap, the reference entity was GSIS, but in the AON-SG credit-default swap the reference entity was the Republic of the Philippines. Either AON misinterpreted its protection, or sought to get out of liability via a combination of good lawyering, a lack of judicial precedent in credit-default swaps, and/or an inexperienced (in credit-default swaps) judiciary.[40] Their gamble almost paid off.

---

36. Ursa Minor Ltd. v. Aon Financial Products, Inc., 2000 WL 1010278 (S.D.N.Y., 2000) (not reported in F.Supp. 2d).

37. *Id.* at *7.

38. *Id.*

39. Ursa Minor Limited v. Aon Financial Products, 7 Fed.Appx. 129, 131 (2d Cir. 2001) (ruling by Summary Order).

40. It is likely that the business people at AON intentionally set the swaps up the way they were because they believed that their protection was heavily correlated with the protection they received, but at a cheaper price (They received $425,000 for the protection they provided BSIL, but paid only $300,000 for their protection from Societe Generale). In their minds, GSIS would not default or refuse to pay unless the Republic of Philippines

The district court believed that "the clear intent of the parties was that Societe Generale would guarantee payment to AON . . . on the condition that they become liable to BSIL upon the occurrence of a 'Credit Event.'"[41] One such credit event under the agreement was a "Sovereign Event." The primary issue the court dealt with was whether or not the refusal by GSIS, and subsequently, the Republic of Philippines, to repay the loan constituted a Sovereign Event. Was the repayment of the loan an obligation of the Republic of the Philippines under the credit-default agreement? Here, the court looked at evidence outside of the direct words in the contract (outside the "four corners of the contract") and determined that although the Republic of the Philippines was not a signatory to the surety bond or any of the underlying agreements, it was nonetheless a guarantor of its agent GSIS's obligation under Philippine law.[42] As a result, the Court held that a credit event occurred and Societe Generale's "refusal to honor its obligations to pay [AON] makes it the defaulting party owing indemnification" in the amount of $10 million plus interest and legal expenses.[43]

If AON meant to receive 100 percent protection from their exposure to the credit-default swap with BSIL, then they should (and likely would have) used the same reference entity in their credit-default swap with Societe Generale. Unlike the district court, the appellate court saw a clear distinction between the two credit-swap agreements.[44] In fact, the Second Circuit determined that the first credit-swap agreement should not be looked at in conjunction with this subsequent credit-default swap agreement because they are two separate agreements, made by two different sets of parties, neither of which incorporated the other. The only similarity is that AON is a party in both agreements. Credit-default swaps are bilateral contracts and only incorporate terms, agreements, or other factors that are explicitly referenced in the document.

The International Swaps and Derivative Association, which is responsible for the standardization of CDS agreements, emphasized the need for clarity and uniform standardized interpretations of the basic terms and elements of the CDS. ISDA felt strongly that the ruling by the district court was incorrect and was afraid that the ruling would "threaten the legal certainty inherent in standard ISDA documentation, by reaching outside the [Societe Generale] CDS to a separate contract not involving [Societe Generale]."[45] ISDA felt compelled to

---

also defaulted. They also likely believed the government would back the debts of GSIS. They were wrong and it cost them $10 million.

41. Aon Financial Products v. Societe Generale, 2005 WL 427535 (S.D.N.Y. 2005) (not reported in F. Supp.) at *1.

42. *Id.* at *5.

43. *Id.* at *6.

44. *See* Aon Financial Products v. Societe Generale, 476 F.3d 90 (2d. Cir., 2007).

45. *Amicus curiae* brief of Int'l Swaps and Derivatives Ass'n, Inc. (ISDA) in AON Financial Products v. Societe Generale, 476 F.3d 90 (2d. Cir., 2007).

send its first ever *amicus curiae* to the Second Circuit, presenting detailed information about how the credit-default swap market operates while highlighting its belief that the district court decision would jeopardize the clarity and expansion of this market in the future. ISDA argued that if the district court's finding was left intact, "it would have a chilling effect on the financial markets and would eliminate a significant means by which banks, financial institutions and corporations diversify their risks."[46]

The Second Circuit clearly took the opinion of ISDA very seriously. In its ruling, it overturned the district court while often quoting ISDA's *amicus curiae*. The Second Circuit determined that there was "no reason to assume that the risk transferred to [AON] was precisely the risk that it transferred or sought to transfer to" Societe Generale. "GSIS is not the Republic of the Philippines; its obligations are not the Republic of the Philippines' obligations; and failure by GSIS to make a payment on its obligations is not the equivalent to the failure of the Republic of the Philippines to make a payment on its obligations."[47] To determine what constitutes a credit event, the court will look first to the language of the contract. If it is unambiguous, the court is required to give effect to the contract as written. The terms of each credit-default swap independently define the risk being transferred.

D. Other Issues

Timetables and deadlines in credit-default swaps are inflexible and enforced accordingly.[48] CDS agreements are governed under a fixed timetable.[49] For example, if a credit event occurs one day after the agreement expires, the event will not be covered by the CDS. Settlement of a CDS can be accomplished via physical settlement (delivery by protection buyer to protection seller of bonds in exchange for par value from protection seller) or cash settlement (delivery by protection seller to protection buyer of the net cash between par value and the current market value).[50]

E. Regulatory Action

In testimony before the House Committee on Agriculture on November 20, 2008, Erik Sirri, the Director of the Division of Trading and Markets of the U.S.

---

46. *Id.*

47. Aon Financial Products v. Societe Generale, 476 F.3d 90, 99–101. The court also pointed out that AON paid Societe Generale nearly $100,000 less than the amount that BSIL paid AON for protection (which is more than 20% less).

48. *See* Deutsch Bank AG v. AMBAC, 2006 WL 1867497 (S.D.N.Y., 2006) (not reported in F.Supp.).

49. *Id.*

50. YERES, DAVID, AN OVERVIEW OF THE USES OF AND ISSUES SURROUNDING CREDIT DERIVATIVES, (Practising Law Institute, PLI Order No. 10870, February 26–27, 2007), by Clifford Chance US LLP (2003), 536.

Securities and Exchange Commission, described the credit-default swap market and the regulators' interest in it as follows:

> The current credit-default swap (CDS) market operates solely on a bilateral, over-the-counter basis and has grown to many times the size of the market for the underlying credit instruments. In light of the problems involving AIG, Lehman, Fannie, Freddie, and others, attention has focused on the systemic risks posed by CDS. The ability of protection sellers (such as AIG and Lehman) to meet their CDS obligations has raised questions about the potentially destabilizing effects of the CDS market on other markets. Also, the deterioration of credit markets generally has increased the likelihood of CDS payouts, thus prompting protection buyers to seek additional margin from protection sellers. These margin calls have strained protection sellers' balance sheets and may be forcing asset sales that contribute to downward pressure on the cash securities markets.
>
> In addition to the risks that CDS pose systemically to financial stability, CDS also present the risk of manipulation. Like all financial instruments, there is the risk that CDS are used for manipulative purposes, and there is a risk of fraud in the CDS market.
>
> The SEC has a great interest in the CDS market because of its impact on the securities markets and the Commission's responsibility to maintain fair, orderly, and efficient securities markets. These markets are directly affected by CDS due to the interrelationship between the CDS market and the securities that compose the capital structure of the underlying issuers on which the protection is written. In addition, we have seen CDS spreads move in tandem with falling stock prices, a correlation that suggests that activities in the OTC CDS market may in fact be spilling over into the cash securities markets.
>
> OTC market participants generally structure their activities in CDS to comply with the CFMA's swap exclusion from the Securities Act and the Exchange Act. These CDS are "security-based swap agreements" under the CFMA, which means that the SEC currently has limited authority to enforce antifraud prohibitions under the federal securities laws, including prohibitions against insider trading. If CDS were standardized as a result of centralized clearing or exchange trading or other changes in the market, and no longer subject to individual negotiation, the "swap exclusion" from the securities laws under the CFMA would be unavailable.[51]

On November 14, 2008, The President's Working Group on Financial Markets (PWG) announced a series of initiatives to strengthen oversight and the

---

51. Erik Sirri, (testimony concerning credit-default swaps before the House Committee on Agriculture, November 20, 2008), http://www.sec.gov/news/testimony/ts112008ers.htm.

infrastructure of the over-the-counter derivatives market.[52] The initiatives announced include the development of credit-default swap central counterparties, and the establishment of a Memorandum of Understanding among the Federal Reserve Board of Governors, the Securities and Exchange Commission, and the Commodity Futures Trading Commission regarding credit-default swap central counterparties. In its press release, the Treasury described steps towards central clearing of credit-default swaps as a means of reducing the systemic risk associated with counterparty credit exposures. At the prompting of the PWG, several potential central counterparty credit providers have developed an approach to clearing credit-default swaps.

By clearing and settling CDS contracts submitted by participants in the central counterparty (CCP), the CCP could substitute itself as the purchaser to the CDS seller and the seller to the CDS buyer. This novation process by a CCP would mean that the two counterparties to a CDS would no longer be exposed to each others' credit risk. A single, well-managed, regulated CCP could vastly simplify the containment of the failure of a major market participant. In addition, the CCP could net positions in similar instruments, thereby reducing the risk of collateral flows.

Moreover, a CCP could further reduce risk through carefully regulated uniform margining and other robust risk controls over its exposures to its participants, including specific controls on market-wide concentrations that cannot be implemented effectively when counterparty risk management is uncoordinated. A CCP also could aid in preventing the failure of a single market participant from destabilizing other market participants and, ultimately, the broader financial system.

A CCP also could help ensure that eligible trades are cleared and settled in a timely manner, thereby reducing the operational risks associated with significant volumes of unconfirmed and failed trades. It may also help to reduce the negative effects of misinformation and rumors that can occur during high volume periods, for example when one market participant is rumored to "not be taking the name" or not trading with another market participant because of concerns about its financial condition and taking on incremental credit risk exposure to the counterparty. Finally, a CCP could be a source of records regarding CDS transactions, including the identity of each party that engaged in one or more CDS transactions. Of course, to the extent that participation in a CCP is voluntary, its value as a device to prevent and detect manipulation and other fraud and abuse in the CDS market may be limited.[53]

---

52. Press Release HP-1272, *PWG Announces Initiatives to Strengthen OTC Derivatives Oversight and Infrastructure*, (November 14, 2008), http://www.treas.gov/press/releases/hp1272.htm.

53. *See* Sirri testimony, *supra* note 52.

The importance of financial instruments and their ability to shift risk throughout the capital markets has necessitated increased involvement by the regulatory authorities in previously untouched markets. Increased regulation is designed as a means of shoring up capital market trading systems to prevent systemic risk.

11. REGULATION OF DERIVATIVES

I. DERIVATIVES REGULATION

As we have discussed in the previous two chapters, derivatives are financial instruments, the value of which is derived from the value of an underlying asset. There are four categories of derivatives: forwards, futures, options, and swaps.[1] Depending on the structure of a derivative, it may be subject to regulation by one of the three regulatory agencies: the SEC, the CFTC, and the Federal Reserve. Sometimes the jurisdiction is overlapping.[2] Although new derivatives regulation is in the works, understanding the current regulatory structure will be vital to appreciating the developing initiatives as new regulators emerge and old regulators evolve.

II. THE COMMODITY FUTURES TRADING COMMISSION (CFTC)

A. Jurisdiction

The Commodity Exchange Act of 1936 (CEA)[3] set forth the first federal regulatory framework for futures trading in agricultural commodities.[4] In 1974 Congress passed the Commodity Futures Trading Commission Act,[5] overhauling the CEA and establishing the Commodity Futures Trading Commission (CFTC), an independent agency with powers greater than those of its predecessor agency, the Commodity Exchange Authority. While the Commodity Exchange Authority regulated only agricultural commodities enumerated in the Commodity Exchange Act, the 1974 act granted the CFTC exclusive jurisdiction over futures trading in all commodities.[6] The agency's mandate has been renewed and expanded several times since then, extensively by the Commodity Futures Modernization Act of 2000 (the "CFMA of 2000"),[7] and most recently by the CFTC Reauthorization Act of 2008.[8]

---

1. Derivatives are discussed in detail in Chapter 9, *infra*.
2. *See* Appendix B, *infra*, for a summary of regulatory jurisdiction over derivatives.
3. Ch. 545, 49 Stat. 1491 (1936) (current version at 7 U.S.C. §1 et seq.).
4. CFTC, *Futures Regulation before the Creation of the CFTC*, available at http://www.cftc.gov/aboutthecftc/historyofthecftc/history_precftc.html.
5. Pub. Law No. 93-463, 88 Stat. 1389 (1974).
6. *See* "About the CFTC" at http://www.cftc.gov/aboutthecftc/index.htm.
7. Pub. Law No. 106-554, 114 Stat. 2763 (Dec. 21, 2000).
8. Food, Conservation, and Energy Act of 2008, Pub. Law No. 110-246 (2008).

III. REGULATORY BACKGROUND

Federal regulation of futures trading in the United States began as early as the 1880s, when the first futures exchanges were founded. Futures were designed to serve as an alternative to forward transactions. As discussed, forwards are financial contracts in which two counterparties agree to exchange a specified amount of a designated product for a specified price on a specified future date or dates. Forwards differ from futures in that their terms are not standardized and they are not traded on organized exchanges. Because they are individually negotiated between counterparties, forwards can be customized to meet the specific needs of the contracting parties.[9] The risks associated with the use of forwards are generally those associated with OTC derivatives contracts, the most significant being counterparty credit risk.[10] While structurally similar to a forward transaction, the exchange and clearing mechanism of futures transaction virtually eliminated counterparty risk.[11]

In 1921, Congress enacted the Future Trading Act, imposing a tax on grain futures trades made independent of an exchange designated by the Secretary of Agriculture. However, the Supreme Court found the Future Trading Act to be an improper exercise of the federal taxing authority.[12] Congress quickly tried again with the Grain Futures Act, which was upheld under the commerce power of the Constitution,[13] and with it the self-policing of exchanges was codified into law.

A. Commodity Exchange Act (CEA) of 1936

In 1936 Congress expanded the Grain Futures Act and changed the name to the Commodity Exchange Act (CEA),[14] extending federal regulation to a list of enumerated commodities that included cotton, rice, mill feeds, butter, eggs, Irish potatoes, and grains. The CEA added provisions prohibiting fraud by parties to a futures contract and authorizing a Commodity Exchange Commission to limit speculative trading and require registration of futures merchants and brokers. Futures commission merchants were required to segregate customer funds that were deposited for purposes of margin; fictitious and fraudulent transactions such as wash sales and accommodation trades were prohibited; all commodity option trading was banned (until 1981). The regulatory power of CEA did not extend to require exchanges to set their own speculative position limits.

---

9. *Trading and Capital-Markets Activities Manual*, §4310.1 (Board of Governors of the Federal Reserve System).

10. *See* Sec. I.B., *supra*.

11. *See* Chapter 10 for a complete description of forwards and futures and their distinctions.

12. Hill v. Wallace, 259 U.S. 44 (1922).

13. Chicago Board of Trade v. Olsen, 262 U.S. 1 (1923).

14. 7 U.S.C. §1 et seq.

Further amendments to the CEA added a number of commodities under the ambit of its regulatory power, imposed federal limits on speculative positions, and instituted minimum net financial requirements for futures commission merchants. The CEA was overhauled in 2000 by the Commodity Futures Modernization Act of 2000 (CFMA).[15] In addition to CFTC enforcement actions, the Supreme Court has interpreted the Commodity Exchange Act to include an implied right of action for private parties, permitting parties harmed for violations of the act to bring private suits for damages.[16]

B. Commodity Futures Modernization Act (CFMA) of 2000

The stated goals of CFMA include:

1. streamlining and eliminating unnecessary regulations of commodity futures exchanges and other entities registered under the CEA;
2. transforming the role of the CFTC to oversight of the futures markets;
3. providing a statutory and regulatory framework for allowing the trading of securities futures; and
4. clarifying the regulatory jurisdiction of the CFTC.[17]

The further purposes of the CFMA are to serve the public interest in liquid, fair, and secure trading facilities through a system of self-regulation, to prevent price manipulation or any other disruptions of the market integrity, to protect against systemic risk and fraud, and to promote innovation and fair competition. Following adoption of the CFMA, the CFTC adopted new rules for derivatives-clearing organizations. It also undertook internal restructuring to ensure better adaptation of CFMA.[18]

The CFTC was vested with the regulation of commodities contracts. Section 1a of the Commodity Exchange Act (the "CEA") defines "commodity" as a number of agricultural product[19] "and all other goods and articles, exception onions . . . , and all services, rights, and interests in which contracts for future delivery are presently or in the future dealt in."[20] The CEA gives the CFTC exclusive jurisdiction of "transactions involving contracts of sale of a commodity for future delivery, traded or executed on a contract market designated or derivatives

---

15. Pub. Law No. 106-554, 114 Stat. 2763, Appendix E (Dec. 21, 2000).

16. Merrill Lynch, Pierce, Fenner & Smith v. Curran, 456 U.S. 353 (1982).

17. Pub. Law No. 106-554, 114 Stat. 2763, Appendix E, Sec. 2.

18. *See* Sec. III.C, *infra*.

19. Those agricultural products include "wheat, cotton, rice, corn, oats, barley, rye, flaxseed, grain sorghums, mill feeds, butter, eggs, *Solanum tuberosum* (Irish potatoes), wool, wool tops, fats and oils (including lard, tallow, cottonseed oil, peanut oil, soybean oil, and all other fats and oils), cottonseed meal, cottonseed, peanuts, soybeans, soybean meal, livestock, livestock products, and frozen concentrated orange juice."

20. 7 U.S.C. §1a(4).

transaction . . . exchange, or market."[21] "Contract of sale" broadly includes "sale, agreement of sale, and agreements to sell."[22]

C. Jurisdictional Disputes

An issue emerged when the market saw the creation of new derivative products with securities as underlying assets. Despite the broad jurisdiction-granting language in the CEA, the CFTC faced challenges from the SEC regarding jurisdiction over security derivatives. In 1982, a basic jurisdictional agreement, commonly known as the "Shad-Johnson Accord," was reached between the CFTC and the SEC on the regulatory responsibility of each agency for a variety of financial instruments, in particular stock index futures.[23] The agreement established jurisdictional boundaries for the CFTC and the SEC: the accord prohibited futures contracts on individual stocks and narrow-based stock indexes. Instead, the agreement authorized the SEC to regulate options on individual securities and gave the CFTC the authority to regulate futures contracts on broad-based stock indexes and individual government securities and options on such future contracts.[24]

D. The Commodity Futures Modernization Act

The jurisdictional framework under the Shad-Johnson Accord remained in effect until the enactment of the Commodity Futures Modernization Act of 2000 (CFMA).[25] The CFMA provided a new jurisdictional framework by making significant changes in derivatives regulations. First of all, the CFMA solved the long time dispute over securities-related futures contracts by granting overlapping jurisdiction to both the CFTC and the SEC of securities futures. The CFMA also mandated a timeframe for the two agencies to establish trading rules for such products.[26]

Additionally, the CFMA created a three-tiered system, under which there are exchanges, less-regulated organized markets, and unregulated derivative

21. *Id.* §2(a)(1)(A): ("The Commission shall have exclusive jurisdiction, . . . , with respect to accounts, agreements (including any transaction which is of the character of, or is commonly known to the trade as, an "'option,'" "'privilege,'" "'indemnity,'" "'bid,'" "'offer,'" "'put,'" "'call,'" "'advance guaranty,'" or "'decline guaranty'"), and transactions involving contracts of sale of a commodity for future delivery, traded or executed on a contract market designated or derivatives transaction execution facility registered . . .").

22. *Id.* §1a(7).

23. The Shad-Johnson Jurisdictional Accord, Pub. Law No. 97-3033, 96 Stat. 1409 (Oct. 13, 1982) (codified in scattered sections of 15 U.S.C.).

24. Thomas Lee Hazen, *Disparate Regulatory Schemes for Parallel Activities: Securities Regulation, Derivative Regulation, Gambling, and Insurance*, 24 ANN. REV. BANKING & FIN. L. 375, 389 (2005).

25. Pub. Law No. 106-554, 114 Stat. 2763 (Dec. 21, 2000).

26. C.F.M.A. §202(a)(5), (which amends 15 U.S.C. §78f(g)(5)).

markets. Under the new CFMA regime, exchanges (denominated "contract markets" by the act) will be designated to trade all commodities, except for special requirements for securities futures. The CFMA also allows trading of certain commodities and derivatives on certain derivatives transaction execution facilities (DTEFs), which are subject to fewer regulatory requirements than designated contract markets are.[27] In addition to contract markets and DTEFs, the CFMA creates a new category of market known as an exempt board of trades (XBOT), in which trading is limited to eligible contract participants and contracts not susceptible to manipulation or having no cash market. An XBOT is prohibited from trading securities futures. The CEA, other than the antifraud provisions, does not apply to XBOTs.

E. Exclusions

Outside the three-tiered system, parties to a derivative product may still choose to conduct the transactions privately on a bilateral basis. The CFMA provides that the CFTC does not have jurisdiction over bilateral transactions involving either excluded commodities or exempted commodities.[28]

Excluded commodities. The CEA as amended by the CFMA provides that "eligible contract participants"[29] may engage in bilateral transactions involving "excluded commodities" by trading manually[30] or trading on an electronic trading facility.[31] If the parties choose to trade through an electronic trading facility, the transaction must be done on a principal-to-principal basis.[32] The definition of "excluded commodities" is very broad.[33]

Exempted Commodities. Similarly, the CEA as amended by the CFMA provides that "eligible contract participants" may engage in bilateral transactions involving "exempted commodities" by trading manually[34] or trading on an electronic trading facility.[35] An exempted commodity is defined as any commodity that is not an excluded commodity or an agricultural commodity.[36] Therefore it covers

---

27. 7 U.S.C. §7a(b)(3).
28. 7 U.S.C .§2(d)–(g).
29. 7 U.S.C. §1a(12).
30. 7 U.S.C. §2(d)(1)(B).
31. 7 U.S.C. §2(d)(2)(C).
32. 7 U.S.C. §2(d)(2)(A). However, it is still possible to operate a "futures dealership" in excluded commodities because the CFTC stated that the principal-to-principal requirement is satisfied even if a single party undertakes to act as universal counterparty to other transactions. *See* Thomas Lee Hazen, *The Law of Securities Regulation* §1.02[2][A], which (citing *A New Regulatory Framework for Multilateral Transaction Execution Facilities,* [2000–01] Transfer Binder Comm. Fu. Law Rep. (CCH) 28,413 (CFTC Dec.13, 2000)).
33. 7 U.S.C. §1a(13).
34. 7 U.S.C. §2(h)(1).
35. 7 U.S.C. §2(h)(3).
36. 7 U.S.C. §1a(14).

all other assets such as crude oil, gold, construction material, and various economic measures not eligible for excluded status under the section 2(d) of the CEA.

These exemptions give the market participants in derivatives products a great deal of flexibility in structuring their transactions to avoid the regulation of the CFTC. Any participant constructing such a transaction should be fully aware of these exemptions. The gaps created by CEA regulatory authority have been addressed in *The Treasury's Blueprint*.[37] In its recommendations, the Treasury describes the ideal of a synthesis of the need for coordination of the CFTC and the SEC:

> Globalization and the increasing need to present a unified regulatory front on futures and securities regulation in the international policy arena also encourage a merger. Two separate agencies handling futures and securities inhibit the ability of the United States to negotiate with foreign regulators and harmonize international regulatory standards. Perhaps the most significant difference in approach is with respect to the concept of mutual recognition, whereby financial intermediaries registered or supervised in a foreign jurisdiction are permitted access to U.S. markets without registering in the United States, a concept embraced by the CFTC in the 1980s and a concept currently being considered by the SEC.[38]

F. Forwards

Forward contracts are financial contracts in which two counterparties agree to exchange a specified amount of a designated product for a specified price on a specified future date or dates.[39] Although the CEA gives the CFTC exclusive jurisdiction over "transactions involving contracts of sale of a commodity for future delivery" on exchanges,[40] the statute provides that "future delivery does not include any sale of any cash commodity for deferred shipment or delivery" (commonly known as "cash forward" contracts).[41] Therefore, cash forward

---

37. The Department of the Treasury, *Blueprint for a Modernized Financial Regulatory Structure* (March 2008). *See* notes 1–2 and accompanying text, *supra*.

38. *Id.* at 109.

39. Trading and Capital-Markets Activities Manual §4310.1 (Board of Governors of the Federal Reserve System).

40. 7 U.S.C. §2(a)(1)(A) ("The Commission shall have exclusive jurisdiction, . . . , with respect to accounts, agreements (including any transaction which is of the character of, or is commonly known to the trade as, an "option," "privilege," "indemnity," "bid," "offer," "put," "call," "advance guaranty," or "decline guaranty"), and transactions involving contracts of sale of a commodity for future delivery, traded or executed on a contract market designated or derivatives transaction execution facility registered . . .").

41. 7 U.S.C. §1a(19).

contracts are not within the regulatory purview of the CEA and are allowed to be traded off-exchange or over the counter.[42]

G. Options

An option contract refers to the right, but not the obligation, to buy or sell an underlying asset, instrument, or index on or before the exercise date at a given price.[43] Pursuant to the Futures Trading Act of 1986, the trading of options on domestic agricultural commodities and other physicals is subject to the jurisdiction of the CFTC.[44] The CFTC also has the power to regulate foreign options.[45] On the other hand, the SEC is authorized to regulate the public trading of put and call options for securities and indexes, because those options are also considered as securities.[46]

H. Futures

A futures contract is an obligation to buy or sell a specified quantity of an underlying asset at a specified price at a specified time in the future.[47] The CFTC has jurisdiction over futures on commodities, but there has been a great deal of contention regarding futures contracts on individual stocks and securities indexes.

The jurisdiction of the CFTC over futures on exempt securities[48] (e.g., U.S. Treasury securities) and broad stock indexes has long been permitted.[49] Until the CFMA of 2000, however, the Shad-Johnson Accord[50] prohibited futures contracts on individual stocks and narrow-based stock indexes. However, those financial products had been effectively traded as "synthetic security futures." Synthetic security futures refer to a complex series of options trades through which a single stock futures contract can be created synthetically[51]—for example, by buying a call option on a single stock and selling a put option on the same stock.

---

42. *See* Willa E. Gibson, *Are Swap Agreements Securities or Futures? The Inadequacies of Applying the Traditional Regulatory Approach to OTC Derivatives Transactions*, 24 J. CORP. L. 379 (1999).

43. TRADING AND CAPITAL MARKETS ACTIVITIES MANUAL §4330.1.

44. 52 Fed. Reg. 777.

45. 17 C.F.R. §30.

46. 15 U.S.C. §77b(a)(1).

47. National Futures Association, *Glossary of Futures Terms*, 13.

48. Under §3(a) of the Securities Act of 1933 or §3(a)(12) of the Securities Exchange Act of 1934.

49. McDermott, Will & Emery LLP, *Congress Makes Changes to the Regulation of Futures and Derivatives Transactions*, McDermott Newsletters (Jan. 2001), available at http://www.mwe.com/index.cfm/fuseaction/publications.nldetail/object_id/eab1d60e-c2ce-47dc-beb4-2d6b54759878.cfm.

50. *See* Sec. II.B., *supra*.

51. *See* U.S. General Accounting Office, *Report to Congressional Requesters, Issues Related to the Shad-Johnson Jurisdictional Accord* at 9–10 (Apr. 2000).

In this way, options on single stocks could be used to replicate futures on single stocks which were prohibited before the CFMA. Synthetic security futures incur twice the transactional costs but effectively avoid regulation under the accord. Because the CFMA now permits nonsynthetic security futures to be traded, there is now no need for investors to conduct such complex and expensive transactions.[52]

As one of its significant changes, the CFMA of 2000 now allows the trading of futures contracts on narrow-based securities indexes as well as future contracts on individual securities. The Act defines a security futures contract as "a contract of sale for future delivery of a single security or of a narrow-based security index, including any interest therein or based on the value thereof, except an exempted security under . . . the Securities Exchange Act of 1934."[53] The act further provides that a narrow-based security index is one that meets the following criteria:

1. It has nine or fewer component securities;
2. a component security comprises more than 30% of the index's weighting;
3. the five highest-weighted component securities in the aggregate comprise more than 60% of the index's weighting; or
4. in which the lowest weighted component securities comprising, in the aggregate, 25% of the index's weighting have an aggregate dollar value of average daily trading volume of less than $50,000,000 (or in the case of an index with 15 or more component securities, $30,000,000), except that if there are two or more securities with equal weighting that could be included in the calculation of the lowest weighted component securities comprising, in the aggregate, 25% of the index's weighting, such securities shall be ranked from lowest to highest dollar value of average daily trading volume and shall be included in the calculation based on their ranking starting with the lowest ranked security.[54]

Security futures (including futures on narrow-based securities indexes) are coregulated by the CFTC and the SEC and are subject to standards and requirements found in both the federal securities and commodity laws. Therefore, security futures can be traded either on a national securities exchange registered with the SEC or a commodities market registered with the CFTC.[55] However, any commodities market or security exchange where security futures are traded must be cross-registered with the SEC and the CFTC, respectively.[56]

---

52. David B. Esau, *COMMENT: Joint Regulation of Single Stock Futures: Cause or Result of Regulatory Arbitrage and Interagency Turf Wars?*, 51 CATH. U.L. REV. 917, 925 (2002).

53. 7 U.S.C. §1a(31).

54. 7 U.S.C. §1a(25).

55. *See* Thomas Lee Hazen, *Derivatives Regulation* §1.18[8][C] (2004).

56. *Id.* §1.18[8][C].

Futures on broad-based security indexes, however, are regulated by the CFTC, and the SEC no longer must concur in their approval.[57] The CEA provides a safe harbor which protects an index from being characterized as a narrow based index if (1) it has at least nine component securities; (2) no component security comprises more than 30 percent of the index's weighting; and (3) each component security is (a) registered pursuant to the Securities Exchange Act of 1934; (b) one of 750 securities with the largest market capitalization; and (c) one of 675 securities with the largest dollar value of average daily trading volume.[58]

I. Regulatory Distinctions between Forwards and Futures[59]

The distinction between a forward contract and a futures contract[60] becomes a deciding factor in determining whether a derivative product will be subject to CFTC regulation. Courts have struggled to develop a clear-cut definition or list of elements distinguishing forwards and futures. The CEA governs transactions involving contracts for the purchase or sale of a commodity for "future delivery," except "any sale of any cash commodity for deferred shipment or delivery."[61] The key words defining the scope of the CEA's authority are: *for future delivery*. Thus, whether or not the agreement in question contemplates *actual future delivery* determines whether it is subject to regulation under the CEA.

In practice, it is frequently difficult to tell whether a particular agreement contemplates actual delivery or whether it is a mechanism for price specula-tion.[62] Courts of appeal confronted with the issue have historically applied a totality of the circumstances approach to determine whether a contract is a futures contract and thus subject to regulation by the CFTC under the CEA. In *CFTC v. Co Petro Marketing Group, Inc.*,[63] the Ninth Circuit adopted a multi-factor approach which looked at the totality of circumstances surrounding the transaction. In *Co Petro*, a gasoline broker entered into "agency agreements" with customers, under which the customers would purchase a specified quantity and type of fuel at a fixed price for future delivery at an agreed future date and pay a deposit based upon a fixed percentage of the purchase price. The broker

---

57. 7 U.S.C. §2(a)(1)(C).

58. 7 U.S.C. §1a(31).

59. *See* Chapter 10 for more on the distinctions between forwards and futures.

60. "Futures contracts are exchange-traded agreements for delivery of a specified amount and quality of a particular product at a specified price on a specified date. Futures contracts are essentially exchange-traded forward contracts with standardized terms." *Trading and Capital-Markets Activities Manual* §4320.1.

61. 7 U.S.C. §1a(19). *See* Lachmund v. ADM Investor Servs., 191 F.3d 777, 785–86 (7th Cir. 1999).

62. *See* CFTC v. Zelener, 387 F.3d 624, 625 (7th Cir. 2004) (Ripple, C.J., dissenting from the denial of rehearing en banc).

63. 680 F.2d 573 (9th Cir. 1982).

did not require its customers to take delivery of the fuel; rather, the broker would sell the fuel for the customers and refund (or deduct from the deposit, if the difference results in a loss) the difference between the previously agreed price and the actual sale price. The gasoline broker argued that the CFTC lacked the jurisdiction over those transactions because they were "cash forward" contracts. The court, however, held that those agency agreements were futures contracts based on the overall surrounding circumstances, such as the uniformity in the basic units of volume and relevant dates and the fact that the customers used those standardized agency agreements to participate in offsetting and liquidating transactions.

In *Nagel v. ADM Investor Services, Inc.*,[64] the Seventh Circuit held that the totality of the circumstances approach dictated that an agreement is a forward contract when (1) the contract specifies individualized terms such as place of delivery and quantity, such that the contract is not fungible with other contracts for the sale of the commodity, except for cases in which the seller promises to offset the contract; (2) parties to the contract are industry participants contracting in the commodity rather than non-industry speculators trading for the contract's price; and (3) delivery cannot be deferred indefinitely.[65]

Later in *CFTC v. Zelener*,[66] the U.S. District Court for the Northern District of Illinois questioned the totality of circumstances approach and instead focused on the "technical meanings" of the statutory language and forms of the transactions. In that case, the customers entered into contracts with defendant companies with regard to the delivery of foreign currencies at a given price within 48 hours. The contracts, however, contained rollover provisions to allow the customers to constantly roll over their position instead of taking the actual delivery of the foreign currency after 48 hours. Once the customers wanted to exit those transactions, their positions were simply canceled out by selling foreign currencies back to the defendant companies and their loss/gain would be calculated accordingly. The court looked at the contracts to find that the defendant companies did not have the obligations to buy back the foreign currencies and could choose to execute delivery to the customers. Based on the rationale that the contracts were technically forward contracts, the court held that the fact that the customers' contracts contained rollover provisions and that the gain or loss was magnified over a longer period did not turn the transactions into future contracts. The *Zelener* majority opinion has been criticized as a marked departure from the traditional "totality of the circumstances approach" that courts had previously used to determine whether a transaction constituted a forward

---

64. 217 F.3d 436 (7th Cir.2000).
65. *Id.* at 441.
66. 373 F.3d 861 (7th Cir.), rehearing denied *en banc*, 387 F.3d 624 (7th Cir. 2004).

or futures contract.[67] A dissent to the Court's refusal to reconsider the case *en banc* described the traditional approach:

> when the following circumstances are present, a contract will be deemed a forward contract: (1) the contract specifies individualized terms such as place of delivery and quantity, so that the contract is not fungible with other contracts for the sale of the commodity, except for cases in which the seller promises to offset the contract; (2) parties to the contract are industry participants contracting in the commodity rather than non-industry speculators trading for the contract's price; (3) delivery cannot be deferred indefinitely.[68]

"If one or more of these features is missing, the contract may or may not be a futures contract."[69] It seems that the approaches differ in that the recent approach looks for indicia of a futures contract, that is, whether the derivatives contract itself has become like an asset, whereas the traditional approach assumed a futures contract absent a showing the contract to indeed be a forward or spot transaction.

In *CFTC v. Intertrade Forex, Inc.,*[70] the Magistrate District of Florida found that Intertrade traded illegal "off-exchange futures contracts" because the financial instruments had the characteristics indicative of futures contracts. Intertrade offered to buy and trade Forex options contracts through its Web site on behalf of Intertrade's retail customers. The contracts bore the hallmarks of futures contracts because they represented contracts for future delivery of foreign currencies, the prices were established at contract initiation, were settled in order to avoid delivery. The court found that the contracts were illegally traded because Intertrade was not a regulated entity.

In *CFTC v. National Investment Consultants, Inc.,*[71] the Northern District of California found that defendants illegally marketed and traded futures contracts regulated by the CEA. The defendants marketed "standardized contracts for the purchase or sale of commodities for future delivery at prices [established at initiation], and could be fulfilled through . . . means to avoid delivery."[72] The court held that violations of the CEA occur when (1) such transactions are not conducted on a regulated board of trade; (2) such transactions are not conducted through a contract market; and (3) such transactions are not recorded in a writing that complies with the CEA.[73] Thus, defendants engaged in the sale and trade of illegal futures contracts.

---

67. CFTC v. Zelener, 387 F.3d 624, 626–27 (Ripple, C.J., dissenting from the denial of rehearing *en banc*).

68. CFTC v. Zelener, 387 F.3d 624, 626 (7th Cir. 2004) (Judge Ripple, Dissenting).

69. *Id.*

70. 2005 WL 332816 (M.D.Fla. 2005).

71. 2006 WL 2548564 (N.D.Cal. Sept. 1, 2006).

72. *Id.* at *4.

73. *Id.* at *5.

Since the passage of the CFMA of 2000, the CEA explicitly excludes over-the-counter derivative transactions, including forward contracts or off-exchange future contracts, between two eligible contract participants regarding excluded commodities (financial instruments) and exempted commodities (crude oil, gold, etc.).[74] The CFMA of 2000, however, preserved the distinction between agricultural commodities and all other kinds of commodities. Therefore, it is important to note that for agricultural commodities, the distinction between a forward contract and a future contract still matters. Anyone structuring a derivative product on agricultural commodities should be aware such a distinction exists, taking into consideration the various tests that courts have adopted.

J. Swaps

A swap contract (or a swap agreement) generally refers to a derivative transaction between two parties, in which payments or rates are exchanged over a specified period and according to specified conditions.[75] The CEA incorporates the definition of a swap agreement from the bankruptcy code.[76]

As a result of the 1992 amendment to the CEA, the CFTC was given the authority to exempt "classes of swap agreements that are not part of a fungible class of agreements that are standardized as to their material economic terms, to the extent that such agreements may be regarded as subject to [the Act]."[77] In 1993, the CFTC adopted 17 C.F.R. 35, known as Part 35, which provides safe-haven exemptions from the CEA's exchange trading requirements for certain swap transactions[78] and allows the CFTC to grant additional exemptions on a case-by-case basis.[79] The swap agreements on the exempted list include any agreement which is:

a rate swap agreement, basis swap, forward rate agreement, commodity swap, interest rate option, forward foreign exchange agreement, rate cap agreement, rate floor agreement, rate collar agreement, currency swap agreement, cross-currency rate swap agreement, currency option, any other similar agreement (including any option to enter into any of the foregoing), any combination of the foregoing, or a master agreement for any of the foregoing.[80]

Part 35 limits the exempted swap transactions to certain institutional investors, corporations meeting certain criteria, government entities, broker-dealers

---

74. *See* Sec. II.D., *supra*.
75. BLACK'S. LAW. DICTIONARY 1488 (Bryan A. Garner ed., 8th ed., 2004).
76. *See* 11 U.S.C. §101(53B).
77. 7 U.S.C. §6(c)(5)(B).
78. 17 C.F.R. §35.1(b)(1).
79. 17 C.F.R. §35.2.
80. 17 C.F.R. §35.1(b)(1)(i)–(ii).

and high net worth persons.[81] In addition to the limitation on eligible swap participants,[82] the regulations impose three additional conditions:

1. The swap agreement is not part of a fungible class of agreements that are standardized as to their material economic terms;
2. The creditworthiness of any party having an actual or potential obligation under the swap agreement would be a material consideration in entering into or determining the terms of the swap agreement, including pricing, cost, or credit enhancement terms of the swap agreement; and
3. The swap agreement is not entered into and traded on or through a multilateral transaction execution facility.[83]

After the CFMA, the CFTC has no jurisdiction over bilateral swap contracts entered into by eligible contract participants regarding a commodity other than an agricultural commodity.[84] Therefore, if a swap contract can be structured as between eligible contract participants, it is exempted from the CFTC's regulation.

The SEC does not have jurisdiction over non–security-based swap agreements,[85] but the SEC has limited authority to regulate security-based swap agreements. Security-based swap agreements are excluded from the definition of security[86] but are still subject to the anti-fraud provisions in the securities law.[87] Therefore, the SEC's authority is limited to insider trading, fraud, and market manipulation regarding security-based swap agreements.[88]

---

81. 17 C.F.R. §35.1(b)(2).

82. 17 C.F.R. §35.2 (a).

83. 17 C.F.R. §35.2 (b)–(d).
The CFTC issued a detailed policy statement on swaps in 1989 and recognized "a non-exclusive safe harbor for transactions satisfying the requirements set forth herein." The CFTC relied on multiple rationales for exempting swaps from regulation. *See* CFTC Policy Statement Concerning Swap Transactions, 54 Fed. Reg. 30,694 (July 21, 1989). Some commentators argue that market participants should still look at the 1989 policy statement to determine whether a swap transaction is exempt or not. *See* Frank Partnoy, *The Shifting Contours of Global Derivatives Regulation*, 22 U. PA. J. INT'L ECON. L. 421, 438–39 (2001).

84. 7 U.S.C. §2(g).

85. *See* 15 U.S.C. §§77b-1(a), 78c-1(a) (excluding "non–security-based swap agreements" from the definition of "security").

86. 15 U.S.C. §77b-1(b)(1), 78c-1(b)(1) (excluding "security-based swap agreements" from the definition of "security").

87. 15 U.S.C. §77q(a), 78j(b), (providing that it is unlawful "to use or employ, in connection with the purchase or sale of any security registered on a national securities exchange or any security not so registered, or any *securities-based swap agreement* . . . , any manipulative or deceptive device or contrivance in contravention of such rules and regulations as the Commission may prescribe as necessary or appropriate in the public interest or for the protection of investors").

88. Hazen, *Derivatives Regulation* at §1.02[2][E].

The CEA provides that the CFTC shall not have any jurisdiction over "covered swap agreements" offered, entered into, or provided by a bank.[89] A covered swap agreement is defined as a swap agreement on a commodity other than an agricultural commodity entered into between eligible contract participants manually or through an electronic trading facility. However, the Federal Reserve, along with other banking regulators, has the jurisdiction to monitor swap agreements entered into by member banks in order to detect any unsafe and unsound practices.

K. Hybrid Instruments

There are certain derivative products that may have characteristics shared by traditional financial products such as securities or bank notes. Under the CFMA, hybrid instruments that are predominantly securities or banking products are completely excluded from all CEA requirements. A hybrid instrument is defined by the CFMA as a security or banking product with a payment indexed to a commodity value or rate or providing for delivery of a commodity.[90] The CFMA sets forth a fairly straightforward predominance test that is not difficult to apply. A hybrid instrument will be considered predominantly a securities or banking product, as applicable, if the following applies:

1. The issuer of the hybrid instrument receives payment in full of the purchase price of the hybrid instrument, substantially contemporaneously with delivery of the hybrid instrument;
2. the purchaser or holder of the hybrid instrument is not required to make any payment to the issuer in addition to the purchase price paid during the life of the hybrid instrument or at maturity;
3. the issuer of the hybrid instrument is not subject by the terms of the instrument to mark-to-market margin requirements; and
4. the hybrid instrument is not marketed as a futures contract or option on a futures contract subject to the CEA.[91]

Those hybrid instruments, however, may still fall under the regulatory jurisdiction of various other agencies, such as the SEC or the Federal Reserve, depending on the nature of such hybrid instruments.

L. Foreign Exchange Products

Trading in foreign exchange instruments has posed a complex set of regulatory issues. Prior to 1974, regulation under the CEA was restricted to agricultural

---

89. 7 U.S.C. §27e.
90. 7 U.S.C. §1a(24).
91. 7 U.S.C. §§2(f)(2), 27a, 27b.

contracts.[92] Foreign exchange contracts were not subject to CEA regulation. The post-1974 reformed version of the CEA vested the CFTC with limited antifraud and antimanipulation jurisdiction over off-exchange (OTC) foreign currency futures and options transactions offered to or entered into with retail customers.[93] Under the CFMA, only certain regulated entities may be counterparties to off-exchange currency trades with retail customers. These regulated entities include registered futures commission merchants (FCMs) and certain affiliates. All other off-exchange futures and options transactions with U.S. retail customers are unlawful unless transacted on or subject to the rules of a regulated exchange.[94]

1. **The Treasury Amendment** The issue of whether and how foreign exchange transactions should be regulated pursuant to the CEA has been hotly debated. The 1974 Commodity Futures Trading Commission Act incorporated a provision (dubbed the Treasury Amendment) mandating that transactions in foreign currency would not be regulated under the CEA unless they involved contracts for *future delivery on a board of trade*.[95] The Treasury Amendment was intended to protect individuals and small traders involved in foreign exchange transactions.[96] As such, the CFTC interpreted the Amendment to authorize it to regulate all foreign exchange transactions *except* those between banks and other sophisticated, informed institutions.[97]

In the following years, the implications of the Treasury Amendment for CFTC regulation of foreign exchange contracts were litigated in a number of prominent cases. In the 1993 case *CFTC v. Standard Forex*,[98] the U.S. District Court for the Eastern District of New York evaluated whether Standard Forex's foreign exchange trading contracts were subject to regulation under the CFTC. Standard Forex characterized its offerings as spot or forward contracts; however, the contracts were standardized, had no performance date, and were always offset by the customer.[99] The court held that Standard's foreign exchange offerings were de facto futures contracts and thus subject to CFTC regulation.[100] The court also concluded that the "board of trade" language of the Treasury Amendment authorized the CFTC to regulate formal platforms created for private, unsophisticated

---

92. CFTC, "About the CFTC," available at http://www.cftc.gov/aboutthecftc/historyofthecftc/history_1970s.html.

93. NFA, *Forex Transactions: A Regulatory Guide*, p. 1, available at http://www.nfa.futures.org/compliance/publications/forexRegGuide.pdf.

94. *Id.*

95. TRADING AND CAPITAL-MARKETS ACTIVITIES MANUAL, 191.

96. *Id.*

97. *Id.*

98. 1993 WL 809966 (E.D.N.Y.).

99. *Id.* at *4–*5.

100. *Id.* at *20.

investors to trade currencies, such as Standard Forex's trading operation.[101] However, in a subsequent case, *CFTC v. Frankwell Bullion*,[102] the Ninth Circuit Court of Appeals interpreted "board of trade" more narrowly, holding that only currency transactions consummated on organized exchanges should be regulated by the CFTC. In practice, it is often extremely difficult to distinguish between organized exchanges and informal, OTC trading platforms. As the *Standard Forex* case demonstrates, there is no bright line distinction between forwards and futures contracts.[103]

2. CFTC Reauthorization On June 18, 2008, Congress enacted The CFTC Reauthorization Act of 2008 as Title XIII of the Food, Conservation, and Energy Act of 2008.[104] The CFTC Reauthorization Act of 2008 (The Act) amends the Commodity Exchange Act and provides, in part, for:

- the reauthorization of the CFTC through fiscal year 2013;
- CFTC jurisdiction retail over-the-counter foreign currency transactions;
- CFTC's oversight authority with respect to any "significant price discovery contract" listed on an electronic trading facility;
- increased penalties for market manipulation and related activities.

The CFTC Reauthorization Act of 2008 strengthens CFTC oversight powers concerning foreign exchange transactions by clarifying the CFTC's authority over retail currency trading in direct response to the *Zelener* line of cases. Specifically, the Act provides that:

> . . . [T]he Commission shall have jurisdiction over, an agreement, contract, or transaction in foreign currency that—is a contract of sale of a commodity for future delivery (or an option on such a contract) or an option . . . and . . . is offered to, or entered into with, a person . . . that is not an eligible contract participant, unless the counterparty, or the person offering to be the counterparty, of the person is—. . . a financial institution; . . . a broker or dealer . . . or an associated person of a broker or dealer.[105]

IV. REGULATORY AGENCIES

A. Commodity Futures Trading Commission (CFTC)

The Commodity Futures Trading Commission (CFTC) was created in 1974 as an independent federal agency with the mandate to regulate commodity futures

---

101. *Id.*

102. 99 F.3d 299 (9th Cir. 1996).

103. *See also* Section IV.D., *supra*, for a discussion of the distinction between forwards and futures.

104. Food, Conservation, and Energy Act of 2008, Pub. Law No. 110-246 (2008).

105. CFTC Reauthorization Act of 2008. 7 USC 1 Sec. 13101.

and option markets in the United States. CFTC was given exclusive jurisdiction over futures trading in all commodities and some options on such contracts.[106] The same legislation authorized the creation of "registered futures associations," giving the futures industry the opportunity to create a nationwide self-regulatory organization.

1. Role of the CFTC Today, "the CFTC's mission is to protect market users and the public from fraud, manipulation, and abusive practices related to the sale of commodity and financial futures and options, and to foster open, competitive, and financially sound futures and option markets."[107] Providing government oversight for the entire industry, the CFTC delegates responsibility for regulation of futures trading among self-regulatory organizations such as the National Futures Association (NFA) and various exchanges.

The CFTC also oversees the activities of firms and individuals who act as intermediaries between customers and markets. These include: futures commission merchants (FCMs) and introducing brokers (IBs), who are required to register with the NFA; commodity pool operators (CPOs) and commodity trading advisors (CTAs), who are not required to register with the NFA but who are still subject to disclosure requirements; principals and employees of these firms; and floor brokers and floor traders.

2. Structure The CFTC consists of a maximum of five Commissioners appointed by the President, with the advice and consent of the Senate, to serve staggered five-year terms. The President designates one of the Commissioners to serve as Chairman. No more than three Commissioners at any one time may be from the same political party.[108] The Organization chart attached as Appendix C shows the current structure of the CFTC and the four main divisions within the organization:

1. **The Division of Clearing and Intermediary Oversight** oversees market intermediaries, including derivatives-clearing organizations, financial integrity of registrants, customer fund protection, stock index margin, sales practice reviews, foreign market access by intermediaries, and National Futures Association activities related to intermediaries.

2. **The Division of Market Oversight** is responsible for fostering markets that accurately reflect the forces of supply and demand for the underlying commodity and are free of abusive trading activity, oversees trade execution facilities, and performs market surveillance, market compliance, and market and product review functions.

3. **The Division of Enforcement** investigates and prosecutes alleged violations of the Commodity Exchange Act and Commission regulations.

---

106. *See* Pub. Law No. 93-463, 88 Stat. 1389.

107. *See* "About the CFTC," http://www.cftc.gov/aboutthecftc/index.htm.

108. *See* "About the CFTC," http://www.cftc.gov/aboutthecftc/commissioners/index.htm.

Violations may involve commodity futures or option trading on United States futures exchanges or the improper marketing and sales of commodity futures products to the general public.

4. **The Office of the Chief Economist** provides economic support and advice to the Commission, conducts research on policy issues facing the agency, and provides education and training for Commission staff.[109]

3. Disciplinary Action When the CFTC takes action, it publishes lists of sanctions.[110] The Proceedings Bulletin includes information about the Commission's administrative and injunctive enforcement actions and its statutory disqualification-from-registration proceedings. It lists individuals and firms charged with violations of the Commodity Exchange Act and CFTC rules, and those that the Commission claims are statutorily disqualified from registration. If charges are dismissed or no sanctions were imposed, the matter is not included in the Bulletin unless it is on appeal. The lists of Reparations Sanctions in Effect provides information about firms or individuals who have violated the Commodity Exchange Act or the Commission's regulations and have not paid awards made through the Commission's Reparations Program, resulting in the suspension of the registrations of these individuals or firms. The Administrative Sanctions in Effect List contains the registration and trading sanctions currently in effect as a result of administrative enforcement or statutory disqualification proceedings.

B. National Futures Association (NFA)

In 1981, the CFTC granted registration to the National Futures Association as a self-regulatory futures association and approved its articles, bylaws, and rules. The NFA is an industry-wide organization for the members of the futures industry. Membership is mandatory and currently stands at more than 4,200 firms and 55,000 associates. The NFA regulates every firm or individual who conducts futures trading business with public customers.[111]

1. Regulatory Activities The NFA performs several regulatory activities:

1. Auditing and conducting surveillance of members to enforce compliance with NFA financial requirements;
2. Establishing and enforcing rules and standards for customer protection;
3. Conducting arbitration of futures-related disputes;
4. Performing screening to determine fitness to become or remain an NFA Member.

The NFA has the authority to take disciplinary actions against firms or individuals for violating its rules. Action may take the form of a formal complaint or a

---

109. *Id.*
110. Available at http://www.cftc.gov/customerprotection/disciplinaryhistory/index.htm.
111. *See* "Who We Are," http://www.nfa.futures.org/aboutnfa/indexAbout.asp.

warning letter, and penalties can include censure, reprimand, suspension, expulsion, prohibition from future association with any NFA member, and fines. The NFA also develops and enforces its own rules in a variety of areas including advertising practices, telephone solicitation, risk and fee disclosure, and minimum capital requirements.

2. Mandatory Registration As authorized under Section 17 of the Commodity Exchange Act,[112] NFA performs registration functions previously performed by the CFTC. Section 17 expressly permits NFA to have rules resulting in mandatory membership. With limited exceptions, all persons and organizations that intend to do business as futures professionals must register under the CEA; in addition, all individuals and firms that wish to conduct futures-related business with the public must apply for NFA Membership or Associate status.[113] Mandatory membership is the cornerstone of NFA's regulatory structure, and effective industry-wide self-regulation is not possible without it. NFA Bylaw 1101 very clearly prohibits the conduct of customer business with non-NFA Members.[114]

3. Governance NFA's 25-member Board of Directors consists of representatives of every category of membership. These representatives, elected by their peers, are joined by representatives from United States futures exchanges and nonindustry Board members to form a governing body that is responsible for interpreting the mission of the organization, developing policy, and ensuring a sound financial structure.[115]

V. EXCHANGES

A. Historical Background

Before there was a Commodity Futures Trading Commission or a National Futures Association, farmers came together with buyers to conduct financial transactions. Initially these transactions involved immediate delivery of a physical product, or "spot" delivery. Trading required visual and verbal interaction, necessitating physical locations and limited access to prevent overcrowding and to ensure that simultaneous participation by all participants was possible. Over time, the participants and transactions at these meeting places grew in size and complexity, creating the need for regulation. In order to insure fairness, many of these meeting places evolved into self-regulating exchanges.

---

112. *See* 7 U.S.C. §21.

113. *See Who Has to Register,* http://www.nfa.futures.org/registration/who_has_to_register.asp.

114. *See NFA Membership,* http://www.nfa.futures.org/registration/nfa_membership.asp.

115. *See Who We Are,* http://www.nfa.futures.org/aboutnfa/indexAbout.asp.

B. Types of Exchanges

1. **Membership Associations** The traditional model for an exchange is a locally organized and owned membership association. The members control management, trading, and key decision-making of a member-owned exchange. The exchange is run for the exclusive benefit of the members; membership is often limited and exclusive. For open outcry exchanges, where trading is conducted in a physical location such as a trading pit by verbally calling out offers, bids, and acceptances, trading rights have traditionally conferred ownership of a seat or seats on the exchange. The exchanges are typically funded through membership fees and are often nonprofit. The New York Mercantile Exchange (NYMEX) was initially such a member-owned exchange. While the individual rules of exchanges vary, each exchange typically publishes a rulebook outlining key information such as its structure, it functions, and the terms of the futures contracts traded on the exchange.

The Rulebook for the Chicago Board of Trade (CBOT), for example, lists the powers and duties of its Board of Directors.[116] Key responsibilities include action "in a judicial capacity in the conduct of hearings with respect to any charges proffered against members and, after such hearings, determine what disciplinary action, if any, should be taken by the Exchange with respect to those charges." CBOT also determines the commodities traded, which members may trade those commodities, the delivery months, hours of trading, and the days of the contract month on which delivery may be made. Perhaps the most impressive of these powers are the options available related to the declaration of emergencies. If the Board determines that an emergency situation exists that is likely to disrupt "the free and orderly market in a commodity" or threaten the financial integrity or the normal functioning of the Exchange it may:

- terminate trading;
- limit trading to liquidation of contracts only;
- order liquidation of all or a portion of a member's proprietary and/or customers' accounts;
- order liquidation of positions of which the holder is unable or unwilling to make or take delivery;
- confine trading to a specific price range;
- modify the trading days or hours;
- alter conditions of delivery;
- fix the settlement price at which contracts are to be liquidated;
- require additional performance bonds to be deposited with the Clearing House.

---

116. CHICAGO BOARD OF TRADE RULEBOOK, http://www.cbot.com/cbot/pub/page/0,3181,931,00.html.

2. Demutualized Exchanges The availability of automated trading has changed these traditional trading circumstances dramatically. Access can be unconstrained and need not be limited by location. Wide availability of this technology has contributed to increasing competition between exchanges. One example of a modern exchange structure is the demutualized exchange, the ownership of which is typically conferred via shares. This model often utilizes an independent decision-making body and functions similarly to a corporate entity. Demutualized exchanges generally lend themselves to electronic trading and earn the majority of their profits from transaction fees.

In recent years, many exchanges have shifted ownership away from a member-based structure to a demutualized model. This process usually involves a complete change of the internal structure of the exchange. The transition from a member-based to a demutualized exchange reduces the control of some intermediaries (floor traders and brokers), expands direct trading access, and may make activities such as licensing agreements and alliances with other exchanges more attractive. Demutualization is often seen as a precursor to public listing, although it may be undertaken to move toward electronic trading, to promote cross-border alliances, or both. Demutualized exchanges can vary significantly in character. The New York Mercantile Exchange (NYMEX) demutualized in 2000, dividing ownership between 816 NYMEX division seats and 772 New York Commodities Exchange (COMEX) division seats. The Intercontinental Exchange (ICE), on the other hand, was owned prior to its initial public offering by only seven shareholders, most of whom were large corporate entities, including both hydrocarbon companies and financial institutions.

3. Public Exchanges Another possible structure is a fully public exchange. The New York Stock Exchange and ICE are examples. Public listing allows an exchange to change the incentive structure for decision making to one that reflects shareholder interests, rather than the interests of individual members. Listing also allows an exchange to release and realize any underlying value of the exchange while opening ownership, and therefore decision making, to the wider investment community.

C. Electronic Communications Networks (ECNs)

In recent years, Electronic Communications Network (ECN)s have emerged. ECNs are nonexchange computer networks created to facilitate trading of financial products, primarily equities (stocks) and currencies. The ECN is essentially an electronic broking platform and is usually initiated and supported by a small number of high volume liquidity providers. In commodity markets they are typically used to match buyers and sellers in over-the-counter (OTC) transactions. Examples include platforms run by large brokers such as ICAP (Internet Content Adaptation Protocol) and Spectron who marry their voice broker network to a proprietary electronic quoting system for transacting OTC trades. ECNs are not typically used to trade futures; however Bloomberg Tradebook is attempting to offer execution services of futures and options through their vast distribution network.

D. Markets Created by the CFMA

The passage of the Commodity Futures Modernization Act in 2000 lead to the adoption by the CFTC of new rules for the various types of exchanges (with different levels of regulatory oversight), including designated contract markets, derivatives transaction execution facilities, exempt boards of trade, and exempt commercial markets. The CFMA created a three-tiered system, under which there are exchanges, less regulated organized markets, and unregulated derivative markets.[117]

1. Designated Contract Markets Designated Contract Markets (DCMs) are boards of trade (or exchanges) that operate under the regulatory oversight of the CFTC.[118] DCMs are most like traditional futures exchanges, which may allow access to their facilities by all types of traders, including retail customers. DCMs may list for trading futures or option contracts based on any underlying commodity, index or instrument. CFTC regulations detail the procedures and requirements for operating as a board of trade (or exchange).[119]

2. Derivatives Transaction Execution Facilities Derivatives transaction execution facilities (DTEFs) are trading facilities that limit access primarily to institutional or otherwise eligible traders or limit the products traded. DTEFs, therefore, are able to operate under a lower level of regulation than DCMs. There are two types of DTEF markets: regular DTEFs (or eligible participant DTEFs) and commercial DTEFs (or eligible commercial entity DTEFs).[120]

3. Derivatives Clearing Organizations A derivatives clearing organization (DCO) is a clearinghouse, clearing association, clearing corporation, or similar entity that enables each party to an agreement, contract, or transaction to substitute, through novation or otherwise, the credit of the DCO for the credit of the parties; arranges or provides, on a multilateral basis, for the settlement or netting of obligations; or otherwise provides clearing services or arrangements that mutualize or transfer credit risk among participants. To obtain and maintain registration, a DCO must comply with the DCO core principles.[121]

4. Exempt Boards of Trade In addition to contract markets and DTEFs, the CFMA created a new category of market known as an exempt boards of trade (EBOTs), in which trading is limited to eligible contract participants and contracts not susceptible to manipulation or having no cash market.[122] An EBOT

---

117. 7 U.S.C. §7a(b)(3).
118. 7 U.S.C. §7.
119. 17 C.F.R. Part 38.
120. 7 U.S.C. §7a.
121. *See* 7 U.S.C. §7a-1.
122. *See* 7 U.S.C. §7a-3.

is prohibited from trading securities futures. The CEA, other than with respect to the antifraud provisions, does not apply to EBOTs.

E. Regulatory Jurisdiction

The regulatory authority of the CFTC is further distributed to the exchanges. The exchange responsible for enforcement of a transaction will be largely dependent on the commodity that is traded. While a person could certainly buy agricultural products on a variety of exchanges, the contract that is traded is a proprietary instrument of a particular exchange. In the United States most, but not all, futures contracts that relate to energy are traded on the New York Mercantile Exchange. Many agricultural products are traded on the Chicago Board of Trade.

VI. CURRENT AND EMERGING ISSUES

A. Efforts to Restructure Regulatory Entities

In the wake of the financial crisis, there has been a great deal of speculation as to who would be an appropriate OTC derivatives market regulator. The SEC and the CFTC are coordinating discussions on regulatory authority but no conclusion has been reached as regulators await Congressional initiative. There has been some discussion of restructuring the CFTC. The CFTC is relatively small, with fewer than 500 employees in total and a limited budget. It is also the only financial regulator not funded through fees. In 2007, the U.S. Office of Management and Budget recommended that the CFTC fund its activities through a new "transaction fee" to shift the regulator's cost from the general taxpayer to the primary beneficiaries of CFTC's oversight. Budget is not the only concern faced by the CFTC; there has been talk that much of the regulatory oversight functions of the CFTC are duplicative of other agencies.[123] These criticisms are not new. In fact, it has been suggested that the CFTC and the SEC be combined, although debate on this possibility has continued for over twenty years.[124] The Treasury Department has recently reiterated this recommendation,[125] but there is no clear indication that Congress intends to make such a change any time soon. There are, of course, political considerations regarding the impact on farming states of a combination of the CFTC and the SEC. It should be noted that under the current bifurcated structure the CFTC is responsible to the Congressional Agriculture Committee whereas the SEC reports to the House Committee on Financial Services.

---

123. *See* discussion of Amaranth case, Appendix A, *infra*.

124. Nash, Nathaniel C., *Single Financial Regulator Backed,* (NEW YORK TIMES, February 6, 1988).

125. *See* The Department of the Treasury, *Blueprint for a Modernized Financial Regulatory Structure,* 107 (March 2008), http://www.treas.gov/press/releases/reports/Blueprint.pdf.

B. Foreign Boards of Trade

In 1996, the CFTC issued a no-action letter to an off-shore exchange, the Deutsche Terminborse (predecessor to Eurex), permitting it to place computer terminals in the U.S. offices of its members for trading of futures and options contracts.[126] In 2006 public hearings on the topic were held that considered the advisability of developing threshold criteria that might be used to define whether a board of trade was located outside the United States and thereby eligible for issuance of a no-action letter.[127] This hearing led to the issuance by the CFTC of a Statement of Policy affirming the use of the no-action process for foreign boards of trade (FBOTs) providing direct access for U.S. persons to their electronic trading systems.[128] The CFTC contends that the Statement of Policy "will ensure the consistent treatment of requests and the application of an appropriate degree of review, while maintaining the ability to respond flexibly to the individual factual circumstances raised by particular requests by FBOTs to provide direct access to their trading systems." In spite of this, no clear standards exist for determining when a no-action letter will be issued.

APPENDIX A

CASE STUDY: *CFTC v. AMARANTH ADVISORS, LLC*

Clearly distinguishing the role of the CFTC, particularly as it relates to self-regulatory organizations, can be difficult. The regulatory authority of the CFTC and other federal agencies may overlap. In 1983, the reauthorization of the CEA, among other things, codified the Shad-Johnson Accord (later revised under the CFMA of 2000),[129] clarifying the division of responsibilities between the Securities Exchange Commission and the CFTC, and ultimately giving the CFTC jurisdiction over broad-based stock index futures. However, the trading of other commodities may be regulated by other federal agencies as well as the CFTC, which can create confusion. The following case study provides a recent example of the complexities that can (and did) arise in an enforcement action brought by the CFTC against a trader of natural gas futures, where the Federal Energy Regulatory Commission (FERC) also brought suit.

---

126. CFTC Interpretive Letter No. 96-28 (February 29, 1996).

127. *See* 71 FR 30665, May 30, 2006; corrected at 71 FR 32059, June 2, 2006 and request for comment. *See* 71 FR 34070, June 13, 2006.

128. U.S. Commodity Futures Trading Commission Issues Statement of Policy on Direct Access to Foreign Boards of Trade, CFTC Press Release 5252-06, (October 31, 2006), http://www.cftc.gov/newsroom/generalpressreleases/2006/pr5252-06.html.

129. The Shad-Johnson Jurisdictional Accord, Pub. Law No. 97-3033, 96 Stat. 1409 (Oct. 13, 1982), codified in scattered sections of 15 U.S.C.

In 2007 the CFTC charged the hedge fund Amaranth Advisors, L.L.C., and its former head natural gas trader, Brian Hunter, with attempting to manipulate the price of natural gas futures, a violation under the Commodity Exchange Act, and making false statements to the NYMEX. The following day, FERC issued an order to show cause in the same matter.

The CFTC complaint alleges that the defendants intentionally and unlawfully attempted to manipulate the price of natural gas futures contracts on the NYMEX on two days in 2006, specifically, February 24, 2006 and April 26, 2006, the last days of trading ("expiry days") for the March 2006 and May 2006 (respectively) NYMEX natural gas futures contract. The value or "settlement price" of each NYMEX natural gas futures contract is calculated based on the volume-weighted average of trades executed from 2:00–2:30 p.m. (the "closing range") on the expiry day of such contracts. CFTC contends that the defendants acquired more than 3,000 NYMEX natural gas futures contracts in advance of the closing range, which they sold during the closing range. The CFTC also alleges that Amaranth held large natural gas swaps positions, on the Intercontinental Exchange (ICE). The settlement price of the ICE swaps is based on the NYMEX natural gas futures settlement price determined by trading done during the closing range on expiry day. The Complaint alleges that Amaranth intended to lower the prices of the NYMEX natural gas futures contracts to benefit its larger swaps positions on ICE.

OPINION[130]

On July 25, 2007, the Commodity Futures Trading Commission (the "CFTC") brought this action against Amaranth Advisers, LLC and others (collectively, "Amaranth"), alleging price manipulation with respect to natural gas futures contracts and seeking injunctive relief and civil penalties. The very next day, July 26, 2007, the Federal Energy Regulatory Commission ("FERC") commenced an administrative enforcement proceeding against Amaranth, based essentially on the same transactions, for civil penalties and the disgorgement of profits. Hence, Amaranth is being pursued by two federal regulatory agencies in two separate proceedings in two different jurisdictions, based on the same alleged conduct.

Amaranth moves for a preliminary injunction to enjoin FERC—which is not a party to the instant lawsuit—from proceeding with its administrative action pending the outcome of this case. Amaranth contends that because this suit was filed by the CFTC, which has primary, if not exclusive, jurisdiction over the natural gas futures contracts market, the FERC administrative proceeding should be

---

130. Excerpted from the opinion of Judge Chin in the United States District Court, Southern District of New York, in CFTC v. Amaranth Advisors, LLC., 2007 Civ. 06682 (DC) (S.D.N.Y, Nov. 1, 2007).

stayed to avoid inconsistent outcomes and to relieve Amaranth of the burden of defending itself in two different proceedings. Although I agree that it would be prudent for FERC to defer to this lawsuit, for the reasons that follow, I decline to order FERC to stay its administrative action. Amaranth's motion for a preliminary injunction is denied.

A. Facts

1. **Federal Regulation of Natural Gas** Two federal agencies regulate the trading of natural gas. The CFTC is responsible for overseeing commodity futures markets, including the natural gas futures market, under the Commodity Exchange Act, 7 U.S.C. §1 et seq. (the "CEA"). FERC regulates the interstate transmission of electricity, natural gas, and oil pursuant to the Natural Gas Act, 15 U.S.C. §717 et seq. (the "NGA").

In 2005, Congress enacted the Energy Policy Act, Pub. Law No. 109-58, 119 Stat. 594 (codified as amended in scattered sections of U.S.C.; "EPAct 2005"), which "broadened FERC's authority over natural gas commodity markets to include, among other things, more authority to police natural gas markets, punish manipulation, and impose greater penalties for other types of violations." *U.S. Gov't Accountability Office, Report to the Permanent Subcomm. on Investigations, Comm. on Homeland Security and Governmental Affairs, Roles of Federal and State Regulators in Overseeing Prices*, GAO-06-968, at 2 (Sept.2006) (citing EPAct 2005) (FERC Ex. 5). Recognizing that their jurisdictions may overlap, Congress required the CFTC and FERC to enter into a memorandum of understanding ("MOU"), "relating to information sharing, which shall include, among other things, provisions ensuring that information requests to markets within the respective jurisdiction of each agency are properly coordinated to minimize duplicative information requests" (15 U.S.C. §717t-2(c)(1)).

On October 12, 2005, the CFTC and FERC entered into a MOU, which acknowledged FERC's exclusive jurisdiction over the transportation and certain interstate sales of natural gas, and the CFTC's exclusive jurisdiction over accounts, agreements, and transactions involving futures contracts. At the same time, recognizing that their oversight and enforcement activities might overlap, the agencies agreed to "coordinate on a regular basis oversight, investigative, and enforcement activities of mutual interest" by sharing information. (MOU at 3) (FERC Ex. 3).

Also pursuant to EPAct 2005, FERC promulgated Rule 1c.1, known as the Anti-Manipulation Rule. The Rule prohibits "any entity, directly or indirectly, in connection with the purchase or sale of natural gas," from engaging in deception or fraud. 18 C.F.R. §1c.1 (2007).

B. Prior Proceedings

1. **This Lawsuit** After a year-long investigation, the CFTC commenced this action on July 25, 2007, alleging that Amaranth and Hunter attempted to manip-

ulate the prices of natural gas futures contracts for March 2006 and May 2006 during the last half hour that those contracts traded on NYMEX. (CFTC Mem. 1). The CFTC's complaint also alleged that Amaranth violated section 9(a)(4) of the CEA by making false statements to NYMEX regarding the May 2006 trades in question. (*Id.*). The CFTC seeks to enjoin defendants from trading commodity interests and from engaging in business activities related to commodity interest trading, as well as civil penalties not exceeding $130,000 for each violation of the CEA. (FERC Mem. 17).

On August 16, 2007, Amaranth moved in this case for a preliminary injunction enjoining FERC from pursuing administrative action against defendants until final resolution of the instant lawsuit. Although FERC is not a party in this action, it has appeared and submitted arguments, orally and in writing, opposing the motion.

*****

In this case, Judge Chin denied Amaranth's motion, but indicated that "Amaranth's concern in having to defend itself in two separate actions for the violations of two Acts based on the same underlying conduct" was "understandable." He concluded his remarks by urging the CFTC and FERC to coordinate their efforts in the two proceedings.[131]

APPENDIX B

CASE STUDY: *CFTC v. Zelener*

In *CFTC v. Zelener*,[132] the Seventh Circuit found that certain foreign currency transactions were spot transactions rather than futures contracts, and thus outside of the CFTC jurisdiction. The case involved foreign currency speculative transactions. It appears that in direct response to the *Zelener* case, Congress passed the provisions of the CFTC Reauthorization Act of 2008, regulating retail foreign exchange contracts.

The *Zelener* Court began its analysis by noting that forwards rolled forward indefinitely were not futures contracts, as established by *Nagel v. ADM Investor Services, Inc.*[133] Furthermore, the CEA defines a futures contract as a contract for future delivery, but excludes from the definition of future delivery any sale of any

---

131. *See* case study of Amaranth Advisors in Chapter 13, *infra*, for further discussion of the substantive issues involved.

132. 373 F.3d 861 (7th Cir. 2004).

133. 217 F.3d 436 (7th Cir. 2000); rollover of grain sales do not turn them into futures.

cash commodity for deferred shipment or delivery, that is, any forward contract.[134] The Court traced several cases to establish a test based on the presence of the following circumstances, indicating whether a contract could be deemed a forward:

1. The contract specifies idiosyncratic terms regarding place of delivery, quantity, or other terms, and so is not fungible with other contracts for the sale of the commodity, as securities are fungible. But there is an exception for the case in which the seller of the contract promises to sell another contract against which the buyer can offset the first contract, which creates a futures contract.[135]

2. The contract is between industry participants, such as farmers and grain merchants, rather than arbitrageurs and other speculators who are interested in transacting in contracts rather than in the actual commodities.

3. Delivery cannot be deferred forever, because the contract requires the farmer to pay an additional charge every time he rolls the hedge.

As long as all three features are present, the contract is a forward; however, if one or more of the factors are absent, the contract may or may not be a futures contract. Applying the factors, the Court reached the conclusion that the foreign exchange transactions were spot and not future contracts and thus outside the regulatory power of CFTC.

The decision provoked numerous proposals to grant CFTC antifraud authority over retail foreign exchange "futures look-alike" contracts, and thus specifically override the *Zelener* decision. The proposed language, however, would apply only to certain retail foreign currency transactions—futures and "futures look-alike" contracts as were involved in the *Zelener* case. Legitimate spot transactions (such as the purchase of foreign currency at a currency exchange) are not included within the jurisdiction of the CFTC.

---

134. 7 U.S.C. §1a(11).

135. *See* In re Bybee, 945 F.2d 309, 313 (9th Cir. 1991); In re Co. Petro Marketing Group, Inc., 680 F.2d 566 (9th Cir. 1982).

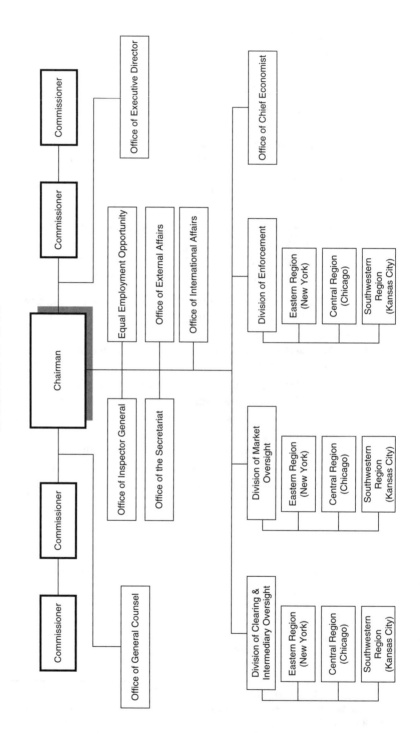

12. FIDUCIARY OBLIGATION TO MANAGE RISK

I. CONTROLLING RISK[1]

The recent headlines publicize the dangers inherent in capital market trading activities. The credit crunch roiling the financial markets, and the breakneck speed at which Bear Stearns and AIG went from major financial firms to illiquidity, demonstrate the state of readiness required by corporate fiduciaries in managing capital market trading activities and investments. When markets behave in unpredictable ways, corporate fiduciaries may be held responsible to stakeholders (i.e., shareholders, regulators, and unit holders) for not taking steps to control or manage risk. Derivatives and mortgage-related losses have heightened the awareness of directors, senior managers, regulators, customers, and shareholders to the potential risks associated with inefficient risk management and due diligence practices.

Effective risk management can reduce the risks associated with financial instruments trading. Directors and officers use operational risk management techniques to define their roles and responsibilities. They apply best practices to monitor and control trading of financial instruments.

Regulators and shareholders use operational risk techniques to describe prudent behavior and to encourage the implementation of sound risk management strategies. This chapter is an overview of the risks to directors and officers arising out of capital markets trading in derivatives and other financial instruments. It describes operational risk management in the context of financial risk management and capital market trading activities, and summarizes the responsibilities of directors and officers. It offers directors and officers solutions to mitigate exposure to loss.

A. Directors' and Officers' Duty to Manage Risk

Directors and officers have a duty to participate in risk management. Internal protocols and procedures are a subset of operational risk management. When there is a breakdown in internal controls, directors and officers will be held accountable for operational failures contributing to trading losses.

The Bank for International Settlements (BIS), an international organization fostering international monetary and financial cooperation that serves as a bank for central banks, issued recommendations for the supervision of operational risk management practices by central banks. In *Sound Practices for the Management*

---

1. The steps necessary to manage enterprise risk are not new and were not born of the crisis of 2008. Indeed, in 2000 the Chubb Insurance company, a leading U.S. director and officer liability insurer, in conjunction with the Risk and Derivatives Consulting Board, Inc., published *Market Volatility and the Rogue Trader: A Handbook for Directors, Officers and Risk Managers.* While almost a decade old, the principles identified in that work are relevant in a post-2008 world and have been included in part here, with permission.

and Supervision of Operational Risk,[2] the BIS outlines a set of principles that provide a framework for the effective management and supervision of operational risk, for use by banks and supervisory authorities when evaluating operational risk management policies and practices. When evaluating operational risk management standards at banks, the BIS advances ten principles:

Developing an Appropriate Risk Management Environment

Principle 1: The board of directors should be aware of the major aspects of the bank's operational risks as a distinct risk category that should be managed, and it should approve and periodically review the bank's operational risk management framework. The framework should provide a firm-wide definition of operational risk and lay down the principles of how operational risk is to be identified, assessed, monitored, and controlled/mitigated.

Principle 2: The board of directors should ensure that the bank's operational risk management framework is subject to effective and comprehensive internal audit by operationally independent, appropriately trained and competent staff. The internal audit function should not be directly responsible for operational risk management.

Principle 3: Senior management should have responsibility for implementing the operational risk management framework approved by the board of directors. The framework should be consistently implemented throughout the whole banking organization, and all levels of staff should understand their responsibilities with respect to operational risk management. Senior management should also have responsibility for developing policies, processes and procedures for managing operational risk in all of the bank's material products, activities, processes and systems.

Risk Management: Identification, Assessment, Monitoring, and Mitigation/Control

Principle 4: Banks should identify and assess the operational risk inherent in all material products, activities, processes and systems. Banks should also ensure that before new products, activities, processes and systems are introduced or undertaken, the operational risk inherent in them is subject to adequate assessment procedures.

Principle 5: Banks should implement a process to regularly monitor operational risk profiles and material exposures to losses. There should be regular reporting of pertinent information to senior management and the board of directors that supports the proactive management of operational risk.

Principle 6: Banks should have policies, processes and procedures to control and/or mitigate material operational risks. Banks should periodically review their risk limitation and control strategies and should adjust their

---

2. Basel Committee on Banking Supervision, February 2003, http://www.bis.org/publ/bcbs96.htm.

operational risk profile accordingly using appropriate strategies, in light of their overall risk appetite and profile.

Principle 7: Banks should have in place contingency and business continuity plans to ensure their ability to operate on an ongoing basis and limit losses in the event of severe business disruption.

Role of Supervisors

Principle 8: Banking supervisors should require that all banks, regardless of size, have an effective framework in place to identify, assess, monitor and control/mitigate material operational risks as part of an overall approach to risk management.

Principle 9: Supervisors should conduct, directly or indirectly, regular independent evaluation of a bank's policies, procedures and practices related to operational risks. Supervisors should ensure that there are appropriate mechanisms in place which allow them to remain apprised of developments at banks.

Role of Disclosure

Principle 10: Banks should make sufficient public disclosure to allow market participants to assess their approach to operational risk management.[3]

While the Basel Committee addresses operational risk in the context of financial institutions, the principles approach can be utilized by nonfinancial enterprises in managing operational risk.

1. Risk Management for Financial and Nonfinancial Institutions As a result of the passage of the Sarbanes-Oxley Act,[4] corporate directors and officers of all financial and nonfinancial domestic, publicly traded corporations must attest to the efficacy of a company's internal controls. Specifically,

> under [Section] 404 [of Sarbanes-Oxley], a company's annual report must contain 'an internal control report' which states that management is not only responsible for the establishment and maintenance of financial reporting controls and procedure, but is further charged with assessing the effectiveness of those controls and procedures over the prior year.[5]

By requiring management to sign-off on the effectiveness of the company's internal financial controls and by mandating attestation by independent auditors

---

3. *Id.*

4. Pub.Law No. 107-204, 116 Stat. 745, enacted July 30, 2002, amending various sections of the Securities Act of 1933, the Securities Exchange Act of 1934, and the Investment Advisers Act of 1940.

5. Thomas O. Gorman and Heather J. Stewart, *Is There a New Sheriff in Corporateville? The Obligations of Directors, Officers, Accountants, and Lawyers After Sarbanes-Oxley of 2002,* 56 ADMIN. L. REV. 135, 153–154 (Winter 2004).

of those controls,[6] compliance with Section 404 is necessarily a burdensome undertaking in both terms of time and expense.[7]

The corporate officer or director who attests to the efficacy of the internal controls may find himself personally liable under the federal securities laws. In *In re Scottish Re Group Securities Litigation*,[8] a class action was brought by shareholders of Scottish Re alleging, among other things, that the officers of Scottish Re violated federal securities laws in connection with the company's accounting for deferred tax assets in its financial statements, and its certification of the adequacy of the company's internal controls. The District Court denied the officers' motion to dismiss the Sarbanes-Oxley claim against them, finding that there were sufficient facts alleged to support the claim that they violated the securities laws by providing false Sarbanes-Oxley certifications in connection with the company's Forms 10-K and Forms 10-Q filings. These certifications stated that to the best of their knowledge, each Form "does not contain any untrue statement of a material fact or omit to state a material fact necessary to make the statements made, in light of the circumstances under which such statements were made, not misleading."

Furthermore, under Section 404, every report filed under Section 13(a)[9] or Section 15(d)[10] of the Exchange Act must include a not only a proclamation that management is responsible for establishing and maintaining the controls and procedures of financial reporting, but also the independent auditors' assessment of the performance of those controls for the previous year.[11] Section 404 gives rise to *personal* liability under the securities laws to directors and officers who sign Forms 10-K and 10-Q. Accordingly, the section is distasteful to corporate officers, because it holds them personally accountable and liable for the proper function of the company's internal controls and may force the officers to disclose embarrassing assessments by independent auditors. Indeed, Section 404 is a significant concern to any company, foreign or domestic, that lists its stock on the American exchanges and to its officers who are personally liable for the efficacy of the controls to which they have attested.[12] In attesting to the establishment and maintenance of financial reporting controls and procedure,

---

6. Robert Schroeder, *Paulson Calls for Some Sarbanes-Oxley Changes*, THOMSON FINANCIAL NEWS, (Nov. 20, 2006).

7. Floyd Norris, *Watching America: Will It Listen to Foreigners, or Do as It Pleases?* N.Y. TIMES, (Jan. 28, 2005).

8. 2007 WL 3256660 (S.D.N.Y. Nov. 2, 2007).

9. 15 U.S.C. §78m(a).

10. 15 U.S.C. §78o(d).

11. Gorman and Stewart, *supra* note 4, at 157.

12. Clyde Stoltenberg, Kathleen A. Lacey, Barbara Crutchfield George, and Michael Cuthbert, *A Comparative Analysis of Post-Sarbanes-Oxley Corporate Governance Developments in the US and European Union: The Impact of Tensions Created by Extraterritorial Application of Section 404*, 53 AM. J. COMP. L. 457 (Spring 2005).

management must, de facto, demonstrate knowledge of the financial risks to the enterprise.

B. Financial Risk

Financial or "market" risks are those that stem from economic uncertainty and volatility. Financial risks include unpredictable movements in interest rates, exchange rates, asset valuation, and stock and commodity prices. The risk of market movements in individual financial instruments or complex portfolios can be a function of one, several, or all these risk factors. The relationship between a particular derivative and a corresponding market risk can be quite complex. The market risks arising from positions with options, either explicit or embedded in other instruments, can be especially difficult. There are complex formulae designed to quantify the risks associated with derivatives. The process of adequately measuring, monitoring, and controlling these market risks is called "operational risk management."

There are several types of market risks. They include:

Delivery risk, which is the risk that a counterparty will not deliver the physical commodity, or, that when it is delivered it will be of an unsuitable grade.

Swing risk, which reflects day-to-day volume and price volatility that can result from production variation or flexible customer needs contracts.

Curve risk, which relates to the relationship of spot prices to future or forward delivery prices.

Directors must understand and be able to control the management of unique financial risks affecting their business and trading activities.[13]

C. Quantifying Financial Risk

Companies use "Value at Risk" measurements to calculate normal market risks over a defined period of time. By using Value at Risk analyses in conjunction with stress tests, directors and senior managers can assess the impact of financial risks on the enterprise and its trading operation.

1. **Value at Risk** Value at Risk (VAR) is a widely used method of calculating a firm's risk across all its financial activities. VAR takes the market value of a firm's positions and then estimates what the firm's market exposure is to those positions. The estimates are based on probabilities of market moves, using historical data. VAR can compute a firm's maximum market exposure with a high degree of accuracy. However VAR cannot compute the exposure to extreme market conditions. Fluctuations in price and the underlying market conditions that drive price are described in terms of volatility risk.

---

13. *See also* Sec. II.B, *infra,* for a discussion of other types of market risk.

2. Volatility Risk Volatility risk reflects the speed at which asset prices fluctuate. The more rapidly prices change, the more volatile an asset is said to be. Financial risk managers factor volatility variables into complex VAR formulas to predict price ranges of a derivative portfolio. Volatility analysis is based on statistical data. Since past performance is not necessarily an indication of the future, volatility analyses, while interesting, are not necessarily predictive.

3. Stress Testing Stress testing is used to test the effects of extreme conditions on a portfolio of financial instruments. Such testing estimates what effects a series of adverse conditions might have on financial positions and pricing models.

Stress testing can take two forms.

1. Asking questions and plugging in variables that existed during times of market crises;
2. Asking questions about what it would take for a portfolio to decline by a certain percent.

Stress testing affords management the opportunity to deal with new risks, before the moment of crisis reveals them. Risk managers can use stress testing as a means of independently verifying model data and mark-to-market pricing assumptions.

The Obama Administration uses stress testing as a means of determining the viability of financial institutions receiving government assistance. To protect taxpayers, to ensure that every dollar is directed toward lending and economic revitalization, the Financial Stability Plan will implement a comprehensive approach to analyzing bank risks:

> A Comprehensive Stress Test: A Forward Looking Assessment of What Banks Need to Keep Lending Even Through a Severe Economic Downturn
>
> Today, uncertainty about the real value of distressed assets and the ability of borrowers to repay loans as well as uncertainty as to whether some financial institutions have the capital required to weather a continued decline in the economy have caused both a dramatic slowdown in lending and a decline in the confidence required for the private sector to make much needed equity investments in our major financial institutions.[14]

Pricing models incorporated into stress tests are based on variables and assumptions that must be consistently tested and verified for accuracy. The financial markets are changing at an incredibly rapid pace. Never before in history have markets moved with such rapidity and with such a degree of volatility as they do today. On April 24, 2009 the Federal Reserve released a white paper intended to assist analysts and other interested members of the public in

---

14. http://www.FinancialStability.gov/docs/fact-sheet.pdf.

understanding the results of the Supervisory Capital Assessment Program or "stress tests" applied to bank holding companies:[15]

> Most U.S. banking organizations currently have capital levels well in excess of the amounts required to be well capitalized. However, losses associated with the deepening recession and financial market turmoil have substantially reduced the capital of some banks. Lower overall levels of capital—especially common equity—along with the uncertain economic environment have eroded public confidence in the amount and quality of capital held by some firms, which is impairing the ability of the banking system overall to perform its critical role of credit intermediation. Given the heightened uncertainty around the future course of the U.S. economy and potential losses in the banking system, supervisors believe it prudent for large bank holding companies (BHCs) to hold additional capital to provide a buffer against higher losses than generally expected, and still remain sufficiently capitalized at over the next two years and able to lend to creditworthy borrowers should such losses materialize. The purpose of the Supervisory Capital Assessment Program (SCAP), which is being conducted by the supervisory agencies, is to assess the size of these capital needs.
>
> The SCAP is a forward-looking exercise designed to estimate losses, revenues, and reserve needs for BHCs in 2009 and 2010 under two macroeconomic scenarios, including one that is more adverse than expected. Should the assessment indicate the need for a BHC to raise capital or improve the quality of its capital to better withstand losses that could occur under more stressful-than-expected conditions, supervisors will expect that firm to augment its capital to create a buffer. This buffer would be drawn down over time if losses were to occur. In evaluating the SCAP results, it is important to recognize that the assessment is a "what if" exercise intended to help supervisors gauge the extent of additional capital needs across a range of potential economic outcomes. A need for additional capital or a change in composition of capital to build a buffer under an economic scenario that is more adverse than expected is not a measure of the current solvency or viability of the firm.[16]

The risk that a market situation could undermine a basic assumption contained in a pricing model is a grave concern for risk managers and regulators. Therefore, in the corporate context, portfolio testing must be conducted frequently, and pricing models must be updated to reflect new market conditions. By understanding the nature of the capital markets, directors can understand

---

15. *See* Federal Reserve Press Release dated April 24, 2009 available at http://www.federalreserve.gov/newsevents/press/bcreg/20090424a.htm.

16. For the specific criterion used, see *The Supervisory Capital Assessment Program: Design and Implementation April 24, 2009* available in the Appendix.

how to manage portfolio risks by updating pricing models in a timely and responsible manner.

D. Portfolio Dynamics

Risk must be measured and managed comprehensively. That is, the focus should be on the dynamics of the portfolio rather than on specific instruments, which can ignore the interplay among various instruments. Past crises have, in part, reflected a failure by some institutions to recognize and limit concentrations of risk within their portfolios, which would have been revealed if the portfolio had been stress tested and analyzed in a more comprehensive manner.

In considering the risks across a portfolio of various financial instruments, including leveraged derivatives transactions, risk managers must consider the accumulated credit risks inherent in those transactions. The risks of counterparty failure must be managed in the same comprehensive manner as the financial risks inherent to the portfolio.

II. OPERATIONAL RISK MANAGEMENT

Operational risk is the risk of loss resulting from inadequate or failed internal processes, people, and systems, or from external events. Where a corporation is involved in financial transactions, it is incumbent upon its corporate leadership to manage the operational risks that attach to the use of complex financial instruments. The primary goal of operational risk management is to manage the enterprise's trading, position taking, credit extension, and operational activities in a timely manner.

Operational risk management provides a means for investment fiduciaries to monitor the investment of assets which have been entrusted to them. By clearly defining risk tolerance, implementing monitoring techniques, and designing effective reporting structures, directors can reduce their potential liability. Operational risk management allows directors to oversee front line traders and salesmen.

Holistic risk management involves setting the strategic direction of the enterprise and setting the company's risk tolerance levels for each of these classes of risk. The operational risk to any trading operation is extremely high. Operational risk is not limited to traditional "back office" activities, but also encompasses front line managerial decisions as to trading lines, credit limits, and liquidity parameters.

The risks of operational failure in enterprises that conduct significant trading activities has been demonstrated by some of the headline cases of losses attributed to rogue traders or tracking inadequacies. The risks associated with human misfeasance and malfeasance can expose the corporation and its executives to liability. The goal of operational risk management is to shield the enterprise, its directors, and executives from losses and liability by developing and implementing a flexible and prudent risk management system.

A. Directors' and Officers' Understanding of Financial Instruments

The complexity of financial transactions, whether they are effectuated through special purpose entities or through stand-alone transactions, requires in-depth understanding by those who use those financial instruments. In the corporate context, directors, officers, and risk managers are required not only to understand the complex nature of risk and financial instruments used to control or take advantage of those risks, but also to understand the steps that can be taken to manage the risks that arise from the use of specific financial instruments.

Officers and directors can be held liable for failing to understand the nature of financial instruments, and for failing to oversee those they have put in charge of managing those instruments. In *Brane v. Roth*,[17] an Indiana court held directors of a grain co-op liable when the co-op lost money as a result of an unhedged grain position. The directors had relied on an accountant who suggested hedging the company's market exposure to grain. The directors hired a "manager" to implement a hedging strategy, but neglected to oversee the manager or his implementation of the hedging strategy. The manager, inexperienced in hedging, hedged only a small percentage of the co-op's total grain exposure; $20,000 of grain sales was hedged although the company had over $7,000,000 of potential exposure. As a result, the co-op suffered a substantial loss on the unhedged position.

The directors were held liable for the loss. The court reasoned that the directors breached their duty to their shareholders by hiring a manager inexperienced in hedging, failing to maintain reasonable supervision over him, and failing to acquire knowledge of the basic fundamentals of hedging to be able to properly supervise the manager.

As *Brane* demonstrates, directors and officers need to acquire sufficient knowledge regarding financial instruments to make informed decisions about risk management. Once informed, directors and officers can fulfill their fiduciary duties by implementing protocols and procedures to manage enterprise risks.

B. Risk Policy

The first step in managing operational risk is to formulate an enterprise-wide risk policy. This risk policy should be a comprehensive summary of the will of the board with regard to capital market trading activities and risk management. It will describe, among other things, acceptable investments, position limits, procedures, reporting structures, credit and liquidity rules, and settlement guidelines.

---

17. 590 N.E. 2d. 587 (Ind. App. 1992).

There are several categories of risk that the board should address in its risk policy statement. These include, but are not limited to:

- *Operational Risk* relates to how the transaction is recorded and monitored. The risk policy statement should describe the reporting structure of front office, back office, and compliance personnel. The board should require sufficient information to monitor firm-wide trading activities. The definition of operational risk includes legal risk, which is the risk of loss resulting from failure to comply with laws and contractual obligations. It also includes the exposure to litigation from all aspects of an institution's activities. The definition does not include strategic or reputational risks,[18] although operational risk can affect reputational risk.[19]
- *Financial Risk* relates to risks of price movements in commodity and financial markets. The risk policy statement might include specific "Value at Risk" calculations to describe the board's risk tolerance.
- *Credit Risk* relates to an analysis of whether a counterparty will fulfill its contractual obligations to the enterprise. Credit or counterparty risk may result from overexposure to a single counterparty or customer across all the enterprise's financial activities (not limited to derivatives trading). The risk policy statement should include specific directives for analyzing the creditworthiness of counterparties. Directors must set exposure limits for each major counterparty.
- *Legal Risk* relates to whether a counterparty will be required by law to honor its contractual obligations (questions of authority, ultra vires, legality, etc.). The risk policy statement might list certain required documentation.
- *Liquidity Risk* relates to the ability of the enterprise to liquidate positions when the need arises. The risk policy statement might limit transactions to markets that meet specific liquidity criterion.
- *Settlement Risk* relates to the timing of the exchange of assets under the terms of a contract. The counterparty paying out the asset is exposed to the extent that a counterparty has not remitted the contra asset or consideration as agreed. The risk policy statement might require "netting agreements" between the enterprise and its counterparties which allow the enterprise to aggregate liabilities and obligations across the spectrum of their financial activities.
- *Delivery Risk* is the risk that a counterparty will not deliver the physical commodity, or, that when it is delivered it will be of an unsuitable grade.

---

18. *Supervisory Guidance on Operational Risk Advanced Measurement Approaches for Regulatory Capital* OCC Release 2003-53c at 5 (July 2, 2003).

19. *See* Section I.F., *supra*.

C. Reporting Lines and Audit Techniques

Qualitatively, effective operational risk management requires designing reporting lines and audit techniques to help the board maintain control over trading activities, sales practices, and money management. The goal of operational risk management is to put in place procedures that prevent anyone from exceeding the board's mandate for acceptable risk. The board can adopt several techniques to accomplish this by:

- drafting a specific risk policy statement that describes, in a quantitative and qualitative way, the board's risk tolerance levels;
- requiring employees to abide by a code of ethical conduct;
- requiring qualitative reports on a regular basis;
- designing reporting structures and compensation incentives that are consistent with the board's risk policy
- empowering certain directors to share primary responsibility for setting risk management policies and overseeing firm-wide compliance with the risk policy statement. The risk of noncompliance with the standards set by the board can be limited by implementing an effective risk management program.

Critically important to managing operational risk throughout the enterprise is to establish management information systems that are transparent enough to allow managers to monitor all corporate activities with regards to the use of financial instruments. These information systems must capture all trades, including new products and innovations. Because of the high-speed nature of financial innovation, there may be some lag time before tracking systems are able to monitor their use. The board should be aware of this technology limitation and might require a daily exception report for new products. The primary goals of management information systems are to:

1. prevent traders from concealing trades;
2. prevent traders from falsely recording trades;
3. prevent traders from intentionally manipulating pricing data and/or pricing models;
4. track and monitor on a daily exception basis any violations by traders of delegated authority levels.

D. Empowering Board Members

Boards should consider establishing a Risk Management Committee (RMC), whose specific charge is the active management of risk on an enterprise-wide basis. The RMC will provide the board with a forum for open discussions about risk issues and risk policy. This committee will work with other board and senior management committees such as the "Market Risk Committee," and the "Credit Risk Committee" to develop a holistic approach to managing the risks associated with a portfolio of derivatives and financial instruments. The RMC will have primary responsibility for adopting standards and procedures for dealing with specific risk management tasks.

An alternative to establishing a specific risk management committee is for the board to charge the Finance Committee or the Audit Committee with the risk management function. Since a comprehensive approach to managing risks requires multiple risk disciplines, businesses, and support units, the Finance Committee may be the most appropriate committee for handling enterprise-wide risk management issues.

The committee reporting to the board on risk issues should have an agenda that addresses:

- credit exposure,
- significant financial commitments,
- capital adequacy,
- new opportunities,
- implementation of enterprise policies,
- any risk management issues,
- education and lectures on derivatives and risk management.

The Audit Committee of the board will bear primary responsibility for ensuring that board risk policies are implemented and adhered to throughout the firm.

E. Reporting Structures

In the operational risk management context, the key to a successful reporting structure is the complete segregation of front office and back office duties and responsibilities. Traders must be prevented from having access to the systems that might allow them to manipulate trade information, price data, or pricing models. By separating front office trading from back office settlement functions, senior management can prevent traders from hiding trades or exceeding acceptable risk parameters.

The ideal framework or organizational structure for overseeing capital market trading activities requires three distinct operating groups:

- The *Front Office*'s primary role is making trading decisions, putting on trading positions, and originating transactions. While the Front Office is primarily responsible for implementing trading strategies, it is required to comply with the board's risk policy.
- The *Back Office*'s primary role is supporting the transactions initiated by the traders, and insuring that all trades are recorded for administrative and oversight purposes. The Back Office is responsible for accounting and reconciliation of all transaction flows.
- The *Compliance Group*'s primary role is monitoring the trades initiated by the Front Office. The Compliance Group is responsible for independently pricing transactions, monitoring portfolios, reviewing trading strategies,

and generally reporting to senior management on the Front Office's level of compliance with enterprise risk policy.

Each of these operating groups should report independently to senior management. The information collected from these groups will form the contents of the board reports. A "chief risk officer" should prepare and present this information to the appropriate board members.

These three independent groups should be in place at all locations where derivatives and or financial products are traded. This is particularly true for remote locations far removed from the home office or principal trading location. While the Internet and technology have made management information systems a vital tool of effective operational risk management, it is difficult, at best, to manage trading risks in a remote location far removed from the home office.

F. Information Flow

Senior managers need to be kept informed about firm-wide risk and capital market trading activities. Unlike other types of operational risk, capital market trading activities place intense time pressure on the board of directors. The risk to the enterprise from financial products representing huge notional values which may, overnight, become illiquid or impossible to hedge must be constantly monitored by the board and its risk managers. Because many financial instruments contain derivative components, which may be highly leveraged, and because some financial instruments can become illiquid overnight, they can jeopardize the financial stability of the enterprise.

Directors must be kept informed, on a real time basis, if a position threatens the enterprise. Because of the time sensitive nature of derivatives trading, information flow is critical for directors and officers whose companies engage in "real time" management information reporting.

Information needs to be summarized for the board in a timely and consistent manner. The board should require frequent updates and reports on how their risk policies are being implemented throughout the enterprise. In doing so, the board can better insulate itself and the enterprise from shareholder liability when trading losses affects the financial health of the enterprise.

1. **Daily Exception Report** When a position is large enough to have a material effect on the enterprise, the board should be provided with real-time information in a more consistent manner. Daily reports which describe the firm's trading activities should be presented to the board. These reports should be designed to help directors understand the current activity in the trading operation. There should be an enterprise liaison that is available if a director has any questions, and the production of these reports should not preclude any ad hoc information flow or inquiry. Generally, board reports should include:

- a list of current positions;
- a plain English description of the goals that the positions are trying to achieve (e.g., enhancing yield or hedge);

- a description of the economic effects of current positions;
- specific names of traders, their market performance, and current positions;
- a plain English analysis of the firm's current risk profile;
- a description of what market factors could affect current positions;
- an explanation of any market disruptions;
- an explanation of how a particular market headline will affect the enterprise;
- mark-to-market valuation of current positions;
- an explanation of any exceptions, limit breaches, or violations of risk tolerance policies.

2. Red Flags In analyzing reports to the board, directors should look for unusual trading activities identified by the firm's senior risk managers. Unusual trading activities include:

- large and highly concentrated positions;
- increased volatility;
- excessive activity by one trader or group of traders;
- trades that do not settle on time (i.e., "fails");
- excessive trading with one counterparty;
- unusual wire transfer activity;
- trading strategies that are inconsistent with the board's risk policy;
- large losses;
- large profits;
- excessive growth in profits or losses from any product (old or new) or any trading desk (i.e., emerging markets or equity derivatives).

G. Ethical Concerns

1. Compensation Firm-wide compensation should be based on furthering the board's goals, and not only on a trader's profitability. Where trading serves as a firm profit center, compensation is often directly linked to a trader's success or failure. There are inherent risks to directors where firms grant incentives to traders that can cause them to value profits above all. Therefore, this direct link needs to be tempered by the board's risk appetite to discourage unethical behavior. Secretary Geithner's reaction to compensation at AIG highlights the dangers of compensation encouraging inappropriate risk-taking:

> I share the anger and frustration of the American people, not just about the compensation practices at AIG and in other parts of our financial system, but that our system permitted a scale of risk-taking that has caused grave damage to the fortunes of all Americans.[20]

---

20. The prepared testimony of Treasury Secretary Tim Geithner on American International Group at a hearing of the House Financial Services Committee, March 24, 2009.

The Secretary illucidate this sentiment in subsequent testimony:

> Innovation and complexity overwhelmed the checks and balances in the system. Compensation practices rewarded short-term profits over long-term return.[21]

A means of achieving a balance between risk policies and trading activities is to adjust compensation formulas to reflect the risk taken to achieve a particular result. This risk-adjusted approach will help deter traders from taking overly risky positions.

By the same token, compliance personnel should not restrict the front office personnel to such an extent that they are unable to trade. In general, enterprise-wide compensation should be flexible and based on:

- contribution to the overall profitability of the firm, and
- efforts to work within the risk parameters set by the board.

2. Code of Conduct The conduct of an enterprise and its employees must mirror the level of the integrity of its managers or leaders. Compensation policy is only one means of achieving ethical behavior in capital market trading activities. The key to a successful risk management program is a corporate culture reflecting the attitudes and dispositions of the board. The board of directors and senior managers set the tone or culture of the institution. Management must convey the message of ethical values and integrity to the employees of the company. These issues cannot be compromised. Management has to demonstrate, through its actions and its communications, that it is committed to high ethical standards.

The board should distribute, and employees should confirm receiving, a code of conduct describing enterprise risk policy. This code should describe an employee's responsibility to the firm and to its shareholders. Employees should sign an acknowledgment that they will abide by firm-wide risk policies. By anchoring risk policy in ethical goals, directors demonstrate business ethics that may be echoed throughout the firm. By creating a sense of a high standard of leadership among the firm's employees, directors can feel more comfortable that they are being provided with timely, material, and accurate information.

3. Free Flow of Information Ethical leadership encourages employees to support the board's efforts to manage operational risk. Employee-initiated communications are an important part of the risk management process. When the board creates a sense of integrity throughout the enterprise, employees will be more willing to provide ad hoc information about positions, events, and market risks. This information reflects what the staff feels the board should know, and are offered without the board requesting them. A free flow of

---

21. March 26, 2009, tg-71 Treasury Secretary Tim Geithner Written Testimony House Financial Services Committee Hearing.

information to the board is the goal of ethics in operational risk management. It will generally happen when employees feel a sense of commitment to the board's values and risk policies.

H. Flexibility

Within broad parameters, risk policy must evolve and develop while the board remains flexible and responsive to change. In a constantly changing world, no system of control and review can remain valid for all time in all circumstances. Needs will change as available technologies do. Whatever review system is adopted, it must be regularly assessed and changed as the organization's risk management needs change.

Care must be taken during regular reviews of the control systems. Tracking systems should be modernized as changes occur in the marketplace. It becomes increasingly apparent that new business techniques and continuing aspects of deregulation make new review procedures essential. New business lines will often evolve very quickly and old business lines will diminish in importance. It is certain that business will be conducted over new geographic areas, as electronic commerce and the Internet render the traditional geographic restrictions on a business's market increasingly irrelevant. This dynamic environment requires regular refinement of a firm's risk management strategy.

III. EXECUTIVE PROTECTION

Directors can take specific steps to protect themselves and their firm from operational risks. In managing these risks, directors have an obligation to understand and participate in the risk management process to reduce their potential liability when losses occur. Directors do not need to become number crunchers, but their legal obligations to make informed decisions will require them to understand how risk management and derivatives transactions work. The board should require all directors and officers to be informed of the company's risk exposure and of the effects adverse market and interest rate conditions may have on the company's financial risk profile. Directors may reduce their personal financial exposure by monitoring risks, seeking information, educating themselves, disclosing trading risks to shareholders, and seeking insurance to cover derivatives-related losses.

A. Responsibility for Risk Management

Directors and officers can delegate their functional responsibility for risk management, but they cannot delegate their ultimate legal liability. Corporate fiduciaries can rely on experts, but must become fully informed before they make important decisions. The business judgment rule protects a director when an informed business decision proves unsuccessful, as directors are generally not held liable for making the wrong decision. It is unsettled whether the business judgment rule protects directors who fail to take any action.

Ignorance is not a defense available to directors and officers. A clear-cut information and reporting trail provides an evidentiary trail that the directors and officers are informed when they rely on the advice of experts and senior managers. It is therefore vitally important to create a clear-cut reporting chain of material and relevant information from senior management to the board.

B. Business Judgment Rule

Directors need information before they can make decisions regarding risk management. The business judgment rule is a legal presumption that, in making a business decision, the directors of a corporation acted on an informed basis, in good faith, and in honest belief that the action taken was in the best interests of the company. The business judgment rule allows directors to make decisions without a court second guessing their judgment. This presumption, however, will not protect directors who fail to become informed before they make a decision.[22]

C. Education at Financial Institutions

Education is a key focus of operational risk management, and it may play a key role in the relationship of regulators to financial institutions. By encouraging education in the area of operational risk management, bank supervisors can encourage effective risk management in the derivatives marketplace without directly regulating derivatives market participants.

Education is a means of analyzing successful protocols, procedures, and best practices. This analysis can help improve operational risk management and encourage the implementation of successful risk management techniques for financial institutions and capital market participants.

D. Disclosure under Sarbanes-Oxley Act

1. **Disclosures in MD&A** Public companies must adequately disclose their capital markets trading activity. Section 401(a) of the Sarbanes-Oxley Act[23] amended the Securities Exchange Act of 1934, adding Section 13(j), which directed amendments to the SEC rules to require disclosure of off-balance sheet transactions. A registrant is now required to provide an explanation of its off-balance sheet arrangements in a separately captioned subsection of the registrant's required disclosure documents entitled "Management's Discussion and Analysis" (MD&A).

The SEC has long recognized the need for a narrative explanation of financial statements and accompanying footnotes and has developed MD&A over the

---

22. *See* Brane v. Roth, 590 N.E. 2d. 587 (Ind. App. 1992), discussed in Sec. II.A, *supra*.

23. Pub. Law No. 107-204 §401(a), codified at 15 U.S.C. §78m(j).

years to fulfill this need. The disclosures in the MD&A are necessary to increase the transparency of a company's financial performance and provide investors with the disclosure necessary to evaluate a company and make informed investment decisions. The MD&A provides an opportunity to give investors a clear understanding of what the financial statements show and do not show and also provides an opportunity to alert investors to the important trends and risks that have shaped the past or are reasonably likely to shape the future. Events, variables, uncertainties, and other corporate events that would not otherwise be required to be disclosed under the Generally Accepted Accounting Principles (GAAP) are required to be disclosed by the MD&A rules, such as (1) information necessary to an understanding of the registrant's financial condition, changes in financial condition, and results of operations; (2) any known trends, demands, commitments, events or uncertainties that will result in, or that are reasonably likely to result in, the registrant's liquidity increasing or decreasing in any material way; (3) the registrant's internal and external sources of liquidity and any material unused sources of liquid assets; (4) the registrant's material commitments for capital expenditures as of the end of the latest fiscal period; (5) any known material trends, favorable or unfavorable, in the registrant's capital resources, including any expected material changes in the mix and relative cost of capital resources, considering changes between debt, equity, and any off-balance sheet financing arrangements; (6) any unusual or infrequent events or transactions or any significant economic changes that materially affected the amount of reported income from continuing operations and, in each case, the extent to which the income was so affected; (7) significant components of revenues or expenses that should, in the company's judgment, be described in order to understand the registrant's results of operations; (8) known trends or uncertainties that have had, or that the registrant reasonably expects will have, a material favorable or unfavorable impact on net sales or revenues or income from continuing operations; (9) matters that will have an impact on future operations and have not had an impact in the past; and (10) matters that have had an impact on reported operations and are not expected to have an impact upon future operations.[24]

The SEC intentionally rendered the MD&A rules so that they would be

flexible [in order] to avoid boilerplate discussions. Therefore, while only one item in [the] current MD&A rules specifically identifies off-balance sheet arrangements, the other requirements clearly require disclosure of off-balance sheet arrangements if necessary to an understanding of a registrant's financial condition, changes in financial condition and results of operations.[25]

---

24. Regulation S-K, Item 303(a). Codified at 17 C.F.R. 229.303(a).
25. SEC Release Nos. 33-8144, 34-46767, (November 4, 2002).

The disclosure threshold is "reasonably likely" to have a material current or future effect. It is not necessary to disclose "if the likelihood of either the occurrence of an event implicating an off-balance sheet arrangement, or the materiality of its effect, is remote."[26]

2. Off-Balance Sheet Transactions An "Off-Balance Sheet Transaction" is defined as any transaction, agreement or other contractual arrangement to which an entity that is not consolidated with the registrant is a party, under which the registrant, whether or not a party to the arrangement, has, or in the future may have: (1) any obligation under a direct or indirect guarantee or similar arrangement, including guarantees that may be a source of potential risk to a registrant's future liquidity, capital resources, and results of operations, regardless of whether or not they are recorded as liabilities; (2) contracts that contingently require the guarantor to make payments to the guaranteed party based on changes in an "underlying" (i.e., a derivative); (3) a retained or contingent interest in assets transferred to an unconsolidated entity or similar arrangement; (4) derivatives, to the extent that the fair value thereof is not fully reflected as a liability or asset in the financial statements (as the impact of such derivatives is often not transparent to investors because those derivative instruments are classified as equity and subsequent changes in the fair market value may not be periodically recognized in the financial statements); or (5) any obligation or liability, including a contingent obligation or liability, to the extent that it is not fully reflected in the financial statements, which includes a contingent obligation, arising out of a material variable interest held by the registrant in an unconsolidated entity, where such entity provides financing, liquidity, market risk, or credit risk support to, or engages in leasing, hedging or research and development services with, the registrant.[27] The Sarbanes-Oxley Act refers to off balance sheet transactions that "may" have a material future effect on the registrant. Accordingly, the supporting SEC rules require that the disclosure is required where the likelihood is higher than remote that a future event will occur implicating an off-balance sheet arrangement or that a future event will have a material effect on such an arrangement.

---

26. *Id.*
27. *Id.*

13. LITIGATION ISSUES

A variety of litigation issues may arise in the context of financial instruments and derivatives transactions. These issues can involve violations of federal securities laws, failure to follow the rules set down by self-regulated organizations, common law theories such as fraud and negligence, and violations of state securities laws. A single derivative transaction can give rise to more than one of these causes of action.

I. FEDERAL SECURITIES LAWS

A. Securities Exchange Act of 1934 Rule 10b-5 Claim
The principal federal laws regulating securities transactions are the Securities Act of 1933 (the "Securities Act")[1] and the Securities Exchange Act of 1934 (the "Exchange Act").[2] Rule 10b-5,[3] promulgated pursuant to authority granted under the Exchange Act, is the principal antifraud rule of the Securities and Exchange Commission (SEC). It prohibits deceptive conduct and misstatements and

---

1. 15 U.S.C. §77a *et seq.*
2. 15 U.S.C. §78a *et seq.*
3. 17 C.F.R. §240.10b-5.

omissions of material fact by any person in connection with the purchase or sale of a security. Although it does not explicitly allow for a private right of action, the Supreme Court has held that an implied private right of action exists for Rule 10b-5 violations.[4]

For a plaintiff to establish a Rule 10b-5 violation, all of the following elements must be proven:

1. a misstatement or omission, or other fraudulent device;
2. a purchase or sale of a security in connection with the fraud;
3. scienter by the defendant;
4. materiality of the misstated or omitted fact;
5. justifiable reliance by the plaintiff; and
6. damage resulting from the misstatement, omission, or fraudulent device.[5]

In the derivatives context, then, it will be vital for a plaintiff to demonstrate that a particular derivatives transaction is, indeed, a security.[6] The definition of security is "sufficiently broad to encompass virtually any instrument that might be sold as an investment."[7] The definition of security is quite broad because it was adopted to restore investors' confidence in the financial markets; it includes not only the typical instruments that fall within the ordinary concept of a security but also any uncommon and irregular instruments.[8] The securities laws cannot be avoided by calling a security by a term that is not listed in the statute because "Congress' purpose in enacting the securities laws was to regulate investments, in whatever form they are made and by whatever name they are called."[9] However, "it is also important to bear in mind that Congress, in enacting the securities laws, did not intend to provide a federal remedy for all common law fraud."[10] Rule 10b-5 actions are most often based on a suitability claim.[11]

1. Churning In addition to the prohibition against recommending unsuitable investments, brokers are also restricted from churning a customer's account.[12]

---

4. Herman & MacLean v. Huddleston, 459 U.S. 375, 380 (1983).

5. Platsis v. E.F. Hutton & Co., 946 F.2d 38, 40 (6th Cir. 1991).

6. *See* Chapter 4, Section I.B, *supra*, for a complete discussion of this issue.

7. SEC v. Infinity Group Co. 212 F.3d 180, 186 (3d Cir. 2000), quoting Reves v. Ernst & Young, 494 U.S. 56, 61 (1990).

8. Marine Bank v. Weaver, 455 U.S. 551, 555 (1982).

9. Reves v. Ernst & Young, 494 U.S. 56, 61 (1990).

10. Rivanna Trawlers Unlimited v. Thompson Trawlers, Inc., 840 F.2d 236, 241 (4th Cir. 1988); *see also* Marine Bank v. Weaver, 455 U.S. 551, 556 (1982), which states that Congress did not "intend to provide a broad federal remedy for all fraud").

11. *See* Chapter 14, *infra*, for a complete discussion of suitability.

12. The National Association of Securities Dealers (NASD) has identified excessive trading activity as a violation of a broker's responsibility of fair dealing. NASD Rule 2310, NASD Manual (CCH) 4261 (2000) [hereinafter NASD Rule 2310] at Rule IM-2310-2(b)(2) (2002).

Churning is excessive trading in an account, done not to affect the investor's trading strategy but to generate brokers' commissions. Churning is often referenced as "quantitative unsuitability," and requires proof that the broker controlled the account.[13] Therefore, excessive trading alone is not enough to establish churning without proof of control.

Churning does not require that a transaction be done with the authorization of a customer. In *Caiola v. Citibank, N.A.*,[14] the plaintiff, Louis S. Caiola, brought federal securities fraud and state law claims against the defendant bank arising from extensive physical and synthetic investments; the court held that Citibank had indeed engaged in "churning" despite a lack of authorization to engage in the securities transactions which were done on behalf of Caiola without his authorization.

Caiola had an extensive relationship with Citibank. Caiola and Citibank entered into numerous derivatives transactions derived from Phillip Morris stock. In the context of these transactions, Caiola relied on Citibank to synthetically create economic exposure to Phillip Morris stock using derivatives (for instance by structuring equity swaps and options). Caiola specifically did not want to own the actual securities that were traded on exchanges and relied on Citibank to hedge its risk using "delta hedging" strategies, thereby not fully recreating synthetic positions in the physical market.[15] In engaging in off-exchange transactions, Caiola hoped to eliminate the "footprints" that are left on exchanges when transactions are recorded on-exchange. Furthermore, by synthetically creating positions, Caiola hoped not to move markets when buying or selling large amounts of Phillip Morris stock and options.

Despite the fact that Caiola did not authorize Citibank to engage in physical transactions, Citibank went ahead and purchased the underlying securities of Phillip Morris stock and options on exchange rather than creating economic exposure synthetically. Although the transactions in the physical securities were unauthorized (in that Citibank was only authorized to create risk for Caiola synthetically while hedging its own risk by delta hedging), this lack of authorization with regards to the specific physical transactions did not deprive Caiola of standing to assert that Citibank had violated Rule 10b-5.

> Indeed, it is well-settled that claims under Rule 10b-5 arise when brokers purchase or sell securities on their clients' behalf without specific authorization. For example, a claim for unauthorized trading, which occurs when a broker intentionally places trades without obtaining the customer's approval,

---

13. In re Howard, 2000 WL 1736882 (N.A.S.D.R.), at *6 (Nov. 16, 2000) (Nat'l Adjudicatory Council); In re Bruff, Exchange Act Release No. 34-40583, 68 SEC Docket 562, 565 (SEC Oct. 21, 1998), which states that "excessive trading is itself a form of unsuitability").

14. 295 F.3d 312 (2d Cir. 2002).

15. *See* Chapter 15, *infra*, for a discussion of delta hedging.

historically has been well-established under Rule 10b-5. . . . By definition, a broker who is liable for making unauthorized trades makes them without the customer's authorization. Churning claims, which depend on a broker's liability for excessive trading, also have been recognized under Rule 10b-5.[16]

2. Investor Partially at Fault The Supreme Court has held that an investor partially at fault is not necessarily barred from recovery in a Rule 10b-5 claim.[17] A private action for damages in these circumstances may be barred on the grounds of the plaintiff's own culpability only where (1) the plaintiff's misconduct is at least substantially equal to that of the defendant; and (2) "preclusion of suit would not significantly interfere with the effective enforcement of the securities laws and protection of the investing public."[18] The court noted that "implied private actions provide 'a most effective weapon in the enforcement' of the securities laws and are 'a necessary supplement to Commission action.'"[19]

B. Securities Act of 1933

One alternative to bringing a claim under Rule10b-5 is to bring such a claim under section 12(2) of the Federal Securities Act of 1933.

Any person who—

. . . .

(2) offers or sells a security . . . by means of a prospectus or oral communication, which includes an untrue statement of a material fact or omits to state a material fact necessary in order to make the statements, in light of the circumstances under which they were made, not misleading (the purchaser not knowing of such untruth or omission), and who shall not sustain the burden of proof that he did not know, and in the exercise of reasonable care could not have known, of such untrust or omission, shall be liable to the person purchasing such security from him.[20]

The benefit of using section 12(2) is that scienter, i.e., the intent to deceive, is not required to violate this section.[21] Without the scienter requirement, it is

---

16. Caiola, 295 F.3d 312, 323–324 (citations omitted).

17. Bateman Eichler, Hill Richards, Inc. v. Berner, 472 U.S. 299 (1985).

18. *Id.* at 310–11.

19. *Id.* at 310, quoting J. I. Case Co. v. Borak, 377 U. S. 426, 432 (1964). *See also* Norman S. Poser, *Liability of Broker-Dealers for Unsuitable Recommendations to Institutional Investors*, 2001 B.Y.U.L. REV. 1493, 1549 (2001).

20. 15 U.S.C. §77l.

21. *See, e.g.,* O'Connor v. R.F. Lafferty Co., 965 F. 2d 893, 899 (10th Cir. 1992); MidAmerica Fed. Sav. & Loan Ass'n v. Shearson, 886 F.2d 1249, 1256 (10th Cir. 1989); "It is a firmly entrenched principle of 12(2) that the 'availability elsewhere of truthful

much easier to prevail in such actions. All that is required is proof that the broker made unsuitable recommendations.

II. COMMON LAW THEORIES

Common law theories of liability in actions related to derivatives transactions involve situations in which a counterparty investment bank has made a recommendation to a customer and that transaction has resulted in a loss. Common law theories typically used in derivatives actions include breach of fiduciary duty, common law fraud, negligence, and the shingle theory. These theories of liability are the backbone for state actions (as opposed to federal actions, where Rule 10b-5 serves as the typical impetus for a claim). Often, common law theories are added to a Rule 10b-5 claim against a defendant. The plaintiff will claim that a defendant owed some special duty to its counterparty. In presenting the facts of the case, the plaintiff will attempt to demonstrate the defendant was in a superior position of knowledge and that the plaintiff relied on the defendant. The complaint in *Gibson Greeting Cards v. Bankers Trust*[22] is illustrative of many of these common law theories.

In 1994, following a series of interest rate increases by the Federal Reserve, a number of clients sued their counterparty investment banks for losses related to derivatives transactions. One of those plaintiffs, Gibson Greeting Cards, sued Bankers Trust for losses associated with a series of derivatives transaction. The facts that Gibson presented in its complaint[23] demonstrate a disparity of knowledge and experience with regards to these transactions. In addition, Gibson sought to demonstrate that a "special relationship" existed between itself and Bankers Trust that required a greater duty than one between two arm's-length counterparties. The tone of the following selection of the complaint demonstrates the tenor of the facts that a derivatives plaintiff might present:

> Gibson has had a banking relationship with Bankers Trust dating back to when Gibson first became a publicly traded company in 1983. What began as a traditional commercial banking relationship developed over the years into a close and multifaceted business relationship. Bankers Trust became and remains the lead bank and agent for Gibson's primary source of working capital, a $210 million revolving credit agreement. In addition, Bankers Trust advised Gibson on various merger and acquisition opportunities and solicited

---

information cannot excuse untruths or misleading omissions' by the seller." *See also* Sanders v. John Nuveen & Co., Inc., 619 F.2d 1222, 1229 (7th Cir. 1980).

22. Civ. No. 1-94-620 (S.D. Ohio 1994).

23. Gibson Greetings, Inc. v. Bankers Trust Company, Civil Action Complaint Filed U.S. District Court Southern District of Ohio, Western Division, Civ. No. 1-94-620 (Oct. 11, 1994).

Gibson's participation in transactions and joint ventures in which Bankers Trust was also to be a principal. As the result of serving as Gibson's advisor and principal source of working capital borrowings, Bankers Trust came to occupy a position of the highest trust and confidence with Gibson. Officers and agents from Bankers Trust's Chicago and New York offices made numerous visits to Gibson's, offices in Cincinnati. They were given extensive access to Gibson management personnel and to Gibson's confidential financial and operating information, including financial management philosophies and risk tolerances. Bankers Trust became well aware that Gibson is a conservatively managed company with relatively little debt. Bankers Trust had a long history of knowing that Gibson did not engage in speculative financial investments or transactions but instead maintained a conservative financial investment and planning philosophy intended to protect the Company's assets and to assure that financing for its manufacturing and marketing activities would be available at all times.[24]

Disputes over derivatives are governed under the terms of the contract. In *Gibson Greeting Cards v. Bankers Trust,* disputes arose when Gibson lost money. The ISDA Master Agreement[25] was used to document the transactions; notwithstanding the terms of the ISDA agreement, which provide for numerous counterparty protections in the event of a dispute, several causes of action may be prosecuted with regards to derivatives transactions. The tort theories, usually based on an asymmetry of information, generally fall under one of the following claims:

- Breach of Fiduciary Duty,
- Negligent Misrepresentation, and
- Fraud and Fraudulent Concealment.

The contracts claims included in derivatives-related litigation also focus on the asymmetry of information and include:

- Implied contractual duty of disclosure,
- Mutual Mistake,
- Unilateral Mistake, and
- Duress.

The complaint and answer in *Gibson Greeting Cards v. Bankers Trust* demonstrate the nature of interest rate swaps and the claims that may be brought when a loss occurs as a result of asymmetrical information. It is interesting to note the differing perspectives as to the nature of the relationship of the counterparties to the transactions. In the complaint, Gibson describes Bankers Trust as

---

24. *Id.* at 3.
25. *See* Chapter 10, Sec. III.B, *supra.*

their partner and advisor. Bankers Trust, in its answer to Gibson's complaint, describes their relationship as one conducted at arm's length as counterparties with no fiduciary duty attached:

> Bankers Trust has been one of Gibson's many bank lenders since 1983; . . . prior to September 30, 1994, Bankers Trust was the Agent Bank for the group of eleven banks who provided Gibson with a $210 million revolving credit facility by agreements dated as of August 2, 1993; . . . Gibson has employed investment banking firms to act as financial advisor to Gibson in connection with merger and acquisition opportunities, but has not retained Bankers Trust for that purpose; . . . Bankers Trust contacted Gibson to see if Gibson might be interested in investing in some transactions in which Bankers Trust might also invest, but . . . Gibson declined to do so, and . . . Bankers Trust was not acting as a financial advisor to Gibson in any such instance; . . . Bankers Trust's transactions with Gibson have always been arm's-length commercial transactions between sophisticated enterprises. . . . Employees of Bankers Trust and employees of BT Securities visited Gibson's offices in Cincinnati from time to time (although mostly for purposes unrelated to the transactions that are the subject of the Complaint); . . . Bankers Trust and BT securities were given access only to such information about Gibson as was appropriate in light of the credit extended by Bankers Trust and the arm's length commercial relationships between Bankers Trust, BT securities and Gibson. . . . Gibson solicited proposals in the fall of 1991 regarding a potential interest rate swap in which Gibson wished to engage. . . . Clients such as Gibson enter into derivatives contracts to serve many different objectives of their own choosing, based on their own assessments of what future interest rate movements, currency exchange movements or other market movements might be . . . Bankers Trust does not act as a financial advisor to Bankers Trust's counterparties.[26]

Bankers Trust is quite clear in presenting itself as an arm's-length counterparty in derivatives transactions. In fact, Bankers Trust describes itself as one of Gibson's many bankers and not an advisor at all.

Shortly after the suit was filed, Gibson and Bankers Trust reached an out-of-court settlement, which ended Gibson's exposure to losses of as much as $27.5 million. According to company officials, Gibson paid Banker's Trust $6.18 million, part of which would come from the $3.4 million Bankers Trust paid to Gibson in earnings on earlier derivative contracts.[27]

---

26. Gibson Greetings, Inc. v. Bankers Trust Company, Civil Action Answer Filed U.S. District Court Southern District of Ohio, Western Division, Civ. No. 1-94-620 (Oct. 11, 1994).

27. *See* http://www.fundinguniverse.com/company-histories/Gibson-Greetings-Inc-Company-History.html.

A. Breach of Fiduciary Duty

Although various States interpret relationships between brokers and their customers differently, there is a general consensus among states that a broker has a duty not to recommend unsuitable investment options for the customer.[28] The leading case in this area is *Twomey v. Mitchum.*[29] In *Twomey*, the court held that "the relationship between broker and principal is fiduciary in nature and imposes on the broker the duty of acting in the highest good faith toward the principal. . . . The duties of the broker, being fiduciary in character, must be exercised with the utmost good faith and integrity."[30]

This duty was defined more narrowly in *Banca Cremi, S.A. v. Alex. Brown & Sons, Inc.,*[31] where the court refused to find a fiduciary duty owed to the customer by the defendant brokerage firm because the defendants conducted their business at arm's length in a principal-to-principal relationship. The lack of formal relationship between the parties made the court unwilling to find a fiduciary duty. In *Procter & Gamble Co. v. Bankers Trust Co.,*[32] the court reasoned:

> No fiduciary relationship exists . . . [where] the two parties were acting and contracting at arm's length. Moreover, courts have rejected the proposition that a fiduciary relationship can arise between parties to a business relationship.[33]

More recently, in *Lehman Bros. Commercial Corp. v. Minmetals International Non-Ferrous Metals Trading Co.,*[34] the court also concluded that "[a] fiduciary duty does not arise in the normal course of an arm's-length business transaction."

In *De Kwiatkowski v. Bear Stearns & Co.,*[35] the Second Circuit held that a broker must undertake a specific role to trigger a duty to volunteer advice and warnings between transactions. Absent negligence in performing transaction execution, liability cannot rest on a broker's failure to give ongoing market advice that it had no duty to give. The Court held that although a broker has no general, ongoing duties to a customer holding a nondiscretionary account, in certain "special circumstances" an ongoing duty can arise. Special circumstances may arise, for example, when a broker takes advantage of an unsophisticated or incapacitated

---

28. *See* Norman S. Poser, *Liability of Broker-Dealers for Unsuitable Recommendations to Institutional Investors*, 2001 B.Y.U.L. REV. 1493, 1496 (2001).
29. 69 Cal. Rptr. 222 (Cal. Dist. Ct. App. 1968).
30. *Id.* at 236 (quoting Abrams v. Bendat, 331 P.2d 657, 661 (Cal. Dist. Ct. App. 1958)); *see also* Roger W. Reinsch, J. Bradley Reich, and Nauzer Balsara, *Trust Your Broker?: Suitability, Modern Portfolio Theory, and Expert Witnesses*, 17 ST. THOMAS L. REV. 173, 180 (2004).
31. 132 F.3d 1017 (4th Cir.1997).
32. 925 F. Supp. 1270 (S.D. Ohio 1996).
33. *Id.* at 1289 (quoting Beneficial Commerce Corp. v. Murray Glick Datsun, Inc., 601 F. Supp. 770, 772 (S.D.N.Y. 1985)).
34. 179 F. Supp. 2d 118, 150 (S.D.N.Y. 2000).
35. 306 F.3d 1293 (2nd Cir. 2002).

customer or when a customer is so unsophisticated or incapacitated that the broker is deemed to have de facto control over the account.

Henryk de Kwiatkowski made and lost hundreds of millions of dollars betting on the United States dollar by trading in currency futures. Kwiatkowski traded on a governmental scale: at one point, his positions accounted for 30 percent of the total open interest in certain currencies on the Chicago Mercantile Exchange. After netting over $200 million in the first trading weeks, Kwiatkowski's fortunes turned; between late December 1994 and mid-January 1995, Kwiatkowski suffered single-day losses of $112 million, $98 million, and $70 million. He continued losing money through the winter. Having lost tens of millions over the preceding several days, Kwiatkowski liquidated all his positions starting on Sunday, March 5, 1995, and finishing the next day. In all, Kwiatkowski had suffered net losses of $215 million.

In June, 1996, Kwiatkowski sued the brokerage firm (and related entities) that had executed his trade orders, Bear, Stearns & Co., Inc., Bear, Stearns Securities Corporation, and Bear Stearns Forex Inc. (collectively, "Bear Stearns" or "Bear"), as well as his individual broker, Albert Sabini, alleging (*inter alia*) common law negligence and breach of fiduciary duty. At trial, Kwiatkowski contended that Bear and Sabini failed adequately to warn him of risks, failed to keep him apprised of certain market forecasts, and gave him negligent advice concerning the timing of his trades.

The Court recognized that size alone does not make a client "special" in terms of additional obligations required by the broker. In fact, the size of an account might demonstrate the relative sophistication and experience of the client. A client like de Kwiatkowski is "the very opposite of the naive and vulnerable client who is protected by 'special circumstances.'"[36] The court held that no special circumstances exist between a broker and its customer absent evidence to the contrary:

> A broker ordinarily has no duty to monitor a nondiscretionary account, or to give advice to such a customer on an ongoing basis. The broker's duties ordinarily end after each transaction is done, and thus do not include a duty to offer unsolicited information, advice, or warnings concerning the customer's investments. A nondiscretionary customer by definition keeps control over the account and has full responsibility for trading decisions. On a transaction-by-transaction basis, the broker owes duties of diligence and competence in executing the client's trade orders, and is obliged to give honest and complete information when recommending a purchase or sale. The client may enjoy the broker's advice and recommendations with respect to a given trade, but has no legal claim on the broker's ongoing attention.[37]

---

36. *Id.* at 1309.

37. *Id.* at 1302, citing Press v. Chem. Inv. Servs. Corp., 166 F.3d 529, 536 (2d Cir. 1999), which states that broker's fiduciary duty is limited to the "narrow task of

The giving of advice triggers no ongoing duty to do so.[38]

Under agency law, there is a well-established duty of an agent to provide material information to the principal that is relevant to the agency relationship.[39] A broker is generally considered to be an agent of its customer and is therefore often a defendant in such cases. However, a common defense by a broker in a lawsuit is that the broker was a "specific" agent for as opposed to a "general" agent of the customer. "A general agent is one authorized to conduct a series of transactions," whereas a special agent is only "authorized to conduct a single transaction, or a series of transactions" that do not entail continuity of service.[40] A general agency endures continuously until terminated, whereas a special agency relationship is presumed to start and stop with each unrelated

---

consummating the transaction requested;" Independent Order of Foresters v. Donaldson, Lufkin & Jenrette, Inc., 157 F.3d 933, 940-41 (2d Cir. 1998), in a nondiscretionary account, "the broker's duties are quite limited," including the duty to obtain client's authorization before making trades and to execute requested trades; Schenck v. Bear, Stearns & Co., 484 F. Supp. 937, 947 (S.D.N.Y. 1979), which notes that the "scope of affairs entrusted to a broker is generally limited to the completion of a transaction"; Robinson v. Merrill Lynch, Pierce, Fenner & Smith, Inc., 337 F. Supp. 107, 111 (N.D. Ala. 1971), which states: "The relationship of agent and principal only existed between [broker and nondiscretionary customer] when an order to buy or sell was placed, and terminated when the transaction was complete."; Leib v. Merrill Lynch, Pierce, Fenner & Smith, Inc., 461 F. Supp. 951, 952–54 (E.D. Mich. 1978), which says the same, drawing a distinction between discretionary and nondiscretionary accounts; accord Paine, Webber, Jackson & Curtis, Inc. v. Adams, 718 P.2d 508, 516–17 (Colo. 1986), which observes the same distinction, and holds that existence of broad fiduciary duty depends on whether the broker has "practical control" of customer's account.

38. Id., Caravan Mobile Home Sales, Inc. v. Lehman Bros. Kuhn Loeb, Inc., 769 F.2d 561, 567 (9th Cir. 1985), in which a securities broker had no duty to provide customer with information about stock after purchase was complete; Leib, 461 F. Supp. at 953, which states that a broker has no duty to keep nondiscretionary customer abreast of "financial information which may affect his customer's portfolio or to inform his customer of developments which could influence his investments"; Robinson, 337 F. Supp. at 112: "The broker has no duty to relay news of political, economic, weather or price changes to his principal, absent an express contract to furnish such information."; Puckett v. Rufenacht, Bromagen & Hertz, Inc., 587 So.2d 273, 280 (Miss. 1991) states: "If a broker were under a duty to inform all of its customers of every fact which might bear upon any security held by the customer, the broker simply could not physically perform such a duty."; Walston & Co. v. Miller, 410 P.2d 658, 661 (Ariz. 1966) states: "Any continuing duty to furnish all price information and information of all facts likely to affect the market price would be so burdensome as to be unreasonable."

39. See Frederick Mark Gedicks, *Suitability Claims and Purchases of Unrecommended Securities: An Agency Theory of Broker-Dealer Liability*, 37 ARIZ. ST. L.J. 535, 574–75 (2005).

40. Cheryl Goss Weiss, *A Review of the Historic Foundations of Broker-Dealer Liability for Breach of Fiduciary Duty*, 23 J. CORP. L. 65, 72 (1997); *see also id.* at 576–77.

transaction.[41] Therefore, if a broker is a specific agent to a customer, the broker has a strong defense that he or she did not owe a duty to the customer if the transaction at issue was not the specific transaction on which the broker assisted the client.

B. Common Law Fraud

Dealers may have a duty to disclose material information regarding risks associated with derivatives trades. Failure to disclose such information can constitute fraud.[42] In order to establish a common law fraud claim, every element of fraud must be proven, including reasonable reliance, which is often the most difficult to prove.[43] Currently, common law fraud claims can be included with unsuitability claims, but the area of law has not yet been separately developed. As a result, common law fraud claims are often included as a factor of claims brought under Rule 10b-5.[44]

C. Shingle Theory

Under the "shingle theory," identifying oneself as a broker or dealer in securities is held to implicitly represent that such person will deal fairly and equitably with a customer. Under this theory, one who poses as a broker or dealer cannot recommend unsuitable transactions for the customer even if that person is not actually a broker or dealer. The basis for the theory is statutory (pursuant to the Exchange Act's requirement that a broker/dealer may not solicit securities transactions unless he is a member of a "registered securities association" or a registered "national securities exchange)[45] and is reinforced by the common law doctrine of "holding out."[46] The "holding out" doctrine provides that one who represents himself as possessing expert knowledge and skill is held to the higher standard of care consistent with the representation.[47]

---

41. *Id.* at 67; *see also* Gedicks, *supra* note 39, 37 ARIZ. ST. L.J. 535, 576–77.

42. *See* Procter & Gamble Co. v. Bankers Trust Co., 925 F. Supp. 1270 (S.D. Ohio 1996).

43. *See* Norman S. Poser, *Liability of Broker-Dealers for Unsuitable Recommendations to Institutional Investors*, 2001 B.Y.U.L. REV. 1493, 1540–42; *see also* Reinsch, Reich and Balsara, *supra* note 30, 17 ST. THOMAS L. REV. 173, 182.

44. *See* Clark v. John Lamula Investors, Inc., 583 F.2d 594 (2d Cir. 1978); Matthew J. Benson, *Online Investing and the Suitability Obligations of Brokers and Broker-Dealers*, 34 SUFFOLK U. L. REV. 395 (2001); *see also* Reinsch, Reich and Balsara, *supra* note 30, 17 ST. THOMAS L. REV. 173, 182.

45. Broker-dealers who are members of a registered national exchange but not a registered national securities association are authorized to effect or solicit "transactions solely on that exchange." 15 U.S.C. §78o(b)(1)(B).

46. *See* Gedicks, *supra* note 39, 37 ARIZ. ST. L.J. 535, 558–59.

47. *Id.*

D. Tort Theory

For plaintiffs attempting to assert a negligence claim against a broker, tort principles support the use of the industry's professional standards to establish a standard of care. The Second Restatement of Torts requires individuals to exercise the degree of care and skill "normally possessed by members of that profession or trade in good standing in similar communities."[48] However, the rule does not apply when an individual represents that he has greater or lesser skill or knowledge. Therefore, if a plaintiff can prove a broker failed to meet the standard in the industry, the plaintiff might have a strong negligence claim if he can prove the remaining elements of negligence (duty, breach, causation, damages).

E. Contract Theory

One important aspect of contract law in derivatives transactions is the unenforceability of contractual waiver, merger, no-reliance, and other clauses restricting rights and remedies under the securities laws. Congress voided these contractual waivers under the securities laws because of their concern that the investor protection goals of the Acts would be easily frustrated by such provisions, especially when directed toward unsophisticated investors. Another often litigated issue arises when a customer and broker enter into a contractual agreement and the customer trades irrationally. This may demonstrate that the customer has an addictive personality and perhaps lacks the requisite mental capacity to enter into contracts.[49] Some courts have held that a broker has a duty to know the mental competence of his customers and take action in such situations.[50]

III. STATE BLUE SKY LAWS

In addition to the federal securities laws, states have their own securities laws. These are referred to as "Blue Sky Laws." State laws differ, but one common thread among them is that where the customer places her trust and confidence in the broker, the broker owes the customer a fiduciary duty, and making an unsuitable recommendation may be a breach of this duty.[51]

---

48. RESTATEMENT (SECOND) OF TORTS §299A (1965).

49. Barbara Black, *Economic Suicide: The Collision of Ethics and Risk In Securities Law*, 64 U. PITT. L. REV. 483, 493 (2003).

50. *See id.*, citing Beckstrom v. Parnell, 730 So. 2d 942 (La. App. 1998). In *Beckstrom*, the court emphasized the full service broker's knowledge of his customer's incapacity in finding the broker liable for failing to warn the customer of the unsuitable transaction (but did not suggest that the broker could not follow the customer's instructions if he had been warned).

51. *See* Norman S. Poser, *Liability of Broker-Dealers for Unsuitable Recommendations to Institutional Investors*, 2001 B.Y.U.L. REV. 1493, 1496; *see also* NORMAN S. POSER, BROKER-DEALER LAW AND REGULATION 2.02 (3d ed. 2000).

However, this does not mean that states agree that every broker-customer relationship is fiduciary in nature. For example, in New York, the broker-customer relationship is considered to be a fiduciary one, but the broker's fiduciary obligation is limited to the matters entrusted to the broker by the customer.[52] On the other hand, Massachusetts courts state that a "simple stockbroker-customer relationship" is a business relationship unless the customer has given the broker discretionary authority to trade the account and the broker has consented to such authority.[53] Therefore, depending on the facts and jurisdiction of the case, a plaintiff in a derivatives action may sue based on the federal security laws and under the state laws as well.

IV. LITIGATION ISSUES REGARDING SPECIFIC DERIVATIVES

A. Options

Pursuant to the Futures Trading Act of 1986, the trading of options on domestic agricultural commodities and other physicals is subject to the jurisdiction of the CFTC.[54] On the other hand, the SEC is authorized to regulate the public trading of put and call options for securities and indexes because those options are also considered as securities.[55]

The federal securities laws have also been held to apply to over-the counter (OTC) cash settled option agreements.[56] The Second Circuit concluded that the plaintiff sufficiently pleaded fraud in connection with the purchase or sale of securities under Rule 10b-5.[57] Noncompliance in executing such transactions could be a basis for a finding of liability against a broker.

As stated earlier, the FTPA allows certain transactions to be exempted from CFTC regulation.[58] The Supreme Court addressed this issue in *Dunn v. Commodity Futures Trading Commission*.[59] In *Dunn*, the CFTC alleged that Dunn and others violated the antifraud provisions of the CFTC by soliciting investments, including options, to buy or sell foreign currencies in the OTC market or off-exchange rather than through a board of trade or regulated exchange.

---

52. Conway v. Icahn & Co., 16 F.3d 504, 510 (2d Cir. 1994): "The relationship between a stockbroker and its customer is that of principal and agent and is fiduciary in nature, according to New York law."

53. Brine v. Paine, Webber, Jackson & Curtis, Inc., 745 F.2d 100, 103 (1st Cir. 1984).

54. 52 Fed. Reg. 777.

55. 15 U.S.C. §77b(a)(1).

56. Caiola v. Citibank, N.A., 295 F.3d 312, 333 (2d Cir. 2002): "The parties dispute whether cash-settled over-the-counter options on the value of a security are covered by section 10(b). We hold that they are."

57. *Id.*

58. Futures Trading Practices Act of 1992, Pub. Law No. 102-546, 106 Stat. 3590.

59. 519 U.S. 465 (1997).

The CFTC argued that an option in foreign currency is not a transaction "in" foreign currency but rather a contract right to engage in such a transaction at a future date, bringing it within the jurisdiction of the CFTC. The Supreme Court sided with Dunn, finding that foreign currency options are "transactions in future currency" within the meaning of the statute[60] and therefore exempt from the CFTC's jurisdiction. This was a significant holding, as it means that brokers handling these OTC foreign currency options are exempt from CFTC liability because the transactions are deemed outside the scope of CFTC regulation. As described in Chapter 11, The CFTC Reauthorization Act of 2008 (The Act) amends the Commodity Exchange Act addressing the jurisdictional issues of the Dunn case and provides, in part, for CFTC jurisdiction retail over-the-counter foreign currency transactions; The CFTC Reauthorization Act of 2008 clarifies the CFTC's authority over retail currency:

> . . . [T]he Commission shall have jurisdiction over, an agreement, contract, or transaction in foreign currency that—is a contract of sale of a commodity for future delivery (or an option on such a contract) or an option . . . and . . . is offered to, or entered into with, a person . . . that is not an eligible contract participant, unless the counterparty, or the person offering to be the counterparty, of the person is—. . . a financial institution; . . . a broker or dealer . . . or an associated person of a broker or dealer.

1. **Risk Disclosure** A broker is required to provide a risk disclosure statement to the customer and obtain the customer's signature acknowledging receipt of the statement.[61] Many courts have considered mere delivery of the risk disclosure statements sufficient as long as the broker did not tell the customer to disregard the warning.[62] However, the Sixth Circuit took a different approach in 2007. In *Nashery v. Carnegie Trading Group, LTD.*,[63] plaintiffs contended that the defendant broker misrepresented the reliability of his investment strategy for commodity options. They claimed that they relied to their detriment on the misrepresentations, and these misrepresentations drove them to invest with defendants. Although the Sixth Circuit held for the defendant, the court imposed

---

60. 7 U.S.C. §2(ii).

61. CFTC Regulation of Domestic Exchange-Traded Commodity Options Transactions, 17 C.F.R. §33.7 (2002). CFTC Rules generally require the customer's signature before opening the account. *See* 17 C.F.R. §1.55(a)(1)(ii) (2002).

62. *See* Purdy v. CFTC, 968 F.2d 510 (5th Cir. 1992); Hill v. Bache Halsey Stuart Shields, Inc., 790 F.2d 817, 824 (10th Cir. 1986) (commodities futures); Clayton Brokerage Co. v. CFTC, 794 F.2d 573 (11th Cir. 1986). But *see* Crook v. Shearson Loeb Rhoades, Inc., 591 F. Supp. 40, 44 (N.D. Ind. 1983), which ruled that even if customer received the risk disclosure statement, he would not have understood commodities futures trading. *See also* Black, *supra* note 49, 64 U. PITT. L. REV. 483, 498.

63. 2007 U.S. App. LEXIS 15677 (6th Cir. 2007).

a "facts and circumstances" test to determine broker liability under the CEA. The court held:

> The mere presentation of a risk disclosure statement does not relieve a broker of any obligation under the Commodity Exchange Act, 7 U.S.C.S. §§1–25, to disclose all material information about risk to customers. The extent of disclosure necessary to provide full information about risk will vary depending on the facts and circumstances of trading as well as on the nature of the relationship between the broker and customer.[64]

The question remains whether brokers have a duty to warn customers about risks involved in investing in a specific option contract. Although the traditional view limits broker's duties to customers for nondiscretionary accounts, some courts have imposed a duty on brokers to warn customers about certain risky investments. In *Quick & Reilly, Inc. v. Walker*,[65] the jury found the broker liable on a negligence theory, apparently for the broker's failure to warn the customer of the risks in options trading. In *Gochnauer v. A.G. Edwards & Co.*,[66] the customers had an account with the broker, with conservative investment objectives on record. The broker advised and assisted them in establishing a speculative options trading account without properly informing them of the risks. The court held that the broker should have warned the customers of the risks.

In *CFTC v. Millennium Trading Group, Inc.*,[67] the court held that if a customer seeks to hold a broker liable for the solicitation of fraud in the context of options trading, the plaintiff must prove the following elements: (1) there was a misrepresentation, misleading statement, or deceptive omission by the defendant; (2) the defendant acted with scienter; and (3) the misrepresentation was material. Defendant brokers solicited members of the general public to open accounts to trade off exchange foreign currency futures contracts (FOREX futures) and options on foreign currency. The brokers profited on the transactions while the customers lost money. The court found the defendants liable for solicitation of fraud by failing to disclose material facts. Some of the facts considered were: (1) the likelihood that a customer would realize large profits from trading the options; (2) the risk involved in trading the options; (3) the defendants' poor track record for trading the options on behalf of customers; and (4) the commissions customers were to be charged. Furthermore, the defendants

---

64. *Id.* at *7.

65. 930 F.2d 29 (9th Cir. 1991) (unreported decision), reported in full at 1991 U.S. App. LEXIS 5472; *see also* Black, *supra* note 49, 64 U. PITT. L. REV. 483, 500–501.

66. Gochnauer v. A.G. Edwards & Co., 810 F.2d 1042, 1044 (11th Cir. 1987); *see also* Black, *supra* note 49, 64 U. PITT. L. REV. 483, 500–501.

67. CFTC v. Millennium Trading Group, Inc., 2007 U.S. Dist. LEXIS 65784, *15–*16 (D. Mich. 2007).

misappropriated at least one customer's funds and engaged in unauthorized trading in customer accounts to earn further commissions and fees.[68]

B. Swaps

Legal risk arises from the possibility that a swap contract will be unenforceable or not legally binding on the counterparty. Litigation may arise from a lack of adequate legal documentation for the transaction; therefore, it is important to ensure that the documents are properly prepared for the contemplated transaction.

Korea Life Insurance Co. v. Morgan Guaranty Trust Co.[69] illustrates several of the litigation issues associated with swap or options agreements. Plaintiff, a foreign insurer and an investment bank, entered into a series of complicated swap agreements in January 1997 with defendant trust company. The effect of the transactions was that plaintiff sold a put option to defendant on the baht (Thai) currency. Plaintiff entered into this agreement in order to circumvent Korean laws which did not allow it, as a life insurance company, to invest in currencies in this way. Plaintiff incurred the risk that the baht could depreciate significantly against the dollar. However, the agreement allowed for plaintiff to terminate the transaction at fair market value if it gave the defendants two business days notice. By July 1997, the value of the baht had deteriorated significantly and plaintiff notified defendants it wanted to unwind the transactions. Defendants were concerned about unwinding at that time because of market liquidity problems and did not unwind the transaction until 23 days before maturity, which was the following January. Defendants demanded payment for the entire amount. Plaintiff then asserted legal claims including negligent misrepresentation, illegality, breach of contract, unjust enrichment, commercial frustration, and impracticability. The court addressed each of these claims.

The court found that, in order for a negligent misrepresentation claim to be successful, a plaintiff has to prove that:

1. the defendant had a duty, as a result of a special relationship, to give correct information;
2. the defendant made a false representation that it should have known was incorrect;
3. the information supplied in the representation was known by the defendant to be desired by the plaintiffs for a serious purpose;
4. the plaintiffs intended to rely and act upon that representation; and
5. the plaintiffs reasonably relied on it to their detriment.[70]

In this case, Korea Life alleged that Morgan Guaranty misrepresented the nature of the transaction and the stability of the baht and that it relied on those

---

68. *Id.* at *6.
69. 269 F. Supp. 2d 424 (D.N.Y. 2003).
70. *Id.* at 436.

misrepresentations when entering the transaction. However, the court did not find sufficient evidence to support Korea Life's assertion here and dismissed the claim. The court stated, "[I]t cannot be said that [plaintiff] did not understand the nature of the transaction; both its Equity Department and the International Department did analyses of the transaction, and fairly identified the risks involved."[71]

Korea Life's next claim was that a security agreement that was part of the transactions was illegal under Korean law. Although the agreement may have been illegal under Korean law, the court held that the effect of illegality upon a contractual relationship is determined, not by Korean law, but by the law of the jurisdiction which is selected under conflicts analysis.[72] The transaction was legal under New York law (the jurisdiction which was selected between the parties) and the court subsequently dismissed the illegality claim.

Korea Life's next claim, breach of contract, was based on the assertion that there was a right to unwind the transaction if it gave Morgan Guaranty two business days notice. The defendant claimed no duty to unwind existed because that responsibility was not in both swap agreements. Korea Life argued that the agreements should be read as one integrated set of transactions and part of the same bargain, which would lead to the conclusion that the duty to unwind was part of the agreement. The court, applying the general rules of contract construction in the context of swap transactions, agreed and held that Korea Life was entitled to summary judgment on the issue of whether the Morgan Guaranty had to unwind the transaction.[73]

Korea Life also brought claims for unjust enrichment, commercial frustration, and impracticability, but failed in this case on all three.[74] The unjust enrichment claim failed because the court found a valid and enforceable written contract governing the subject matter in dispute. Furthermore, the claim was based on the baht depreciation, a known risk to the parties. The court held that "a claim for unjust enrichment cannot be premised on a known risk."[75] As to the commercial frustration and impracticability claims, the court held that "claims based on theories of commercial frustration and impracticability also must fail. The potential devaluation of the Thai baht was a risk of the deal, and not a ground of rescission."[76]

C. Forward Contracts
While similar to futures contracts (discussed below), forwards contracts are excluded from the regulatory jurisdiction of the CFTC because they are privately

---

71. *Id.*
72. *Id.* at 440.
73. *Id.* at 446.
74. *Id.* at 447.
75. *Id.*
76. *Id.*

negotiated bilateral contracts that are not conducted on an organized market-place or exchange. The reason for the exclusion is that the CEA's regulatory scheme was not intended to apply to private commercial merchandising transactions involving the deferred delivery of a commodity.[77] The foreign exchange forward market is also excluded from CFTC's jurisdiction pursuant to the treasury amendment, which Congress enacted to insure that off-exchange market transactions in foreign currency would not be subject to CFTC's regulatory jurisdiction.[78]

The critical issue involved in most forward contract litigation is whether the contract at issue was indeed a forward, and not subject to CFTC regulation, or was rather a futures contract, which is subject to CFTC regulation.[79] The answer determines who may enter into such a contract and where trading may occur.

This was the principal issue in *CFTC v. Zelener*,[80] where the court concluded that speculative transactions in foreign currency were not contracts of sale of a commodity for future delivery regulated by the CFTC. The court reasoned that the transactions were not futures contracts because, among other reasons, "the customer buys foreign currency immediately rather than as of a defined future date, and because the deals lack standard terms."[81] Forward contracts must therefore be carefully drafted to avoid being categorized as futures agreements which are subject to CFTC regulation.

D. Futures Contracts

As explained in *Zelener*, if contracts are construed by a court to be forwards as opposed to futures, the transaction is exempt from CFTC regulation. On the other hand, if the contracts are futures, the CFTC can bring a variety of claims, as illustrated in *CFTC v. International Financial Services*.[82] In that case, defendant broker's arrangements with the clearinghouse allegedly ensured in most cases that customers would lose their money to those entities. The defendant argued that the transactions at issue were not "futures," and the CFTC therefore did not have jurisdiction. The court established two elements for classifying contracts as futures.

First, futures contracts are contracts for the purchase or sale of a commodity for delivery in the future at a price that is established at the time the contract is initiated. Second, the ability to offset the obligation to purchase by selling the

---

77. *See* Willa E. Gibson , *Investors, Look Before You Leap: The Suitability Doctrine Is Not Suitable for OTC Derivatives Dealers*, 29 Loy. U. Chi. L.J. 527, 563 (1998).

78. *Id.*

79. *See also* Chapter 9, Sec. III.C., *supra*, for a discussion of the distinction between forwards and futures.

80. 373 F.3d 861, 863 (7th Cir. 2004).

81. *Id.* at 864.

82. 323 F. Supp. 2d 482 (D.N.Y. 2004).

contract, or to offset the obligation to deliver by buying a contract, is essential, since investors rarely take delivery against the contracts. The lack of an expectation that delivery of the physical commodity will be made is an important factor indicating the presence of a futures contract.[83]

In applying these elements to the facts, the court concluded that the transactions at issue were indeed futures. The basis for this conclusion was multifaceted. First, there was an agreement between the parties for the sale of foreign currencies in the future for agreed upon prices at the time of the initiation of the contract. Second, there was an offset in lieu of delivery of the underlying currencies. Third, the contracts called for the purchase or sale of standardized amounts of foreign currencies. Fourth, the customers were required to pay an initial margin and then to fortify their accounts when losses decreased their balances below a certain level. Finally, the customers intended to speculate on the intervening price changes without having to acquire the underlying commodity. Although defendants argued that the lack of a specific future date must mean that the contracts are not futures, the court stated that a "date is not always specified thus allowing some futures contracts to be of indefinite duration."[84]

Once the court determined the contracts were futures, it then turned to analyzing the different claims under the CEA and potential liability. These claims included illegal off-exchange trades, solicitation fraud, and unauthorized trades.

With regard to the illegal off-exchange trades claims, the CEA prohibits commodities futures transactions not "conducted on or subject to the rules of a board of trade which has been designated or registered by the Commission as a contract market or derivatives transaction execution facility for such commodit[ies]."[85] The court sided with the CFTC and noted that the foreign currency futures contracts were never registered with the commission and therefore were illegal under the CEA.[86]

To establish a violation of the CEA antifraud provisions,[87] the CFTC had to prove "(1) the making of a misrepresentation, misleading statement, or a deceptive omission; (2) scienter; and (3) materiality."[88] The court found that the

---

83. *Id.* at 494.

84. *Id.* at 498.

85. 7 U.S.C. §6(a)(1); *see* CFTC v. Noble Metals Int'l, Inc., 67 F.3d 766, 772 (9th Cir. 1995).

86. 323 F. Supp. 2d 482, 499.

87. 7 U.S.C. §6b(a) makes it unlawful for any person, in or connection with any order to make, or the making of, any contract of sale of any commodity for future delivery, made, or to be made, for or on behalf of any other person . . . (i) to cheat or defraud or attempt to cheat or defraud such other person; . . . (iii) willfully to deceive or attempt to deceive such other person.

88. 323 F. Supp. 2d 482, 499, citing CFTC v. R.J. Fitzgerald & Co., 310 F.3d 1321, 1328 (11th Cir. 2002); *see also* CFTC v. AVCO Financial Corp., 28 F. Supp. 2d 104, 115 (S.D.N.Y. 1998), *aff'd in relevant part sub nom.* CFTC v. Vartuli, 228 F.3d 94, 101 (2d Cir. 2000).

CFTC met this burden, and held that defendants violated the antifraud provisions. The court concluded that defendants "systematically misled financially unsophisticated clients, often immigrants with poor language skills, into investing large sums of money in transactions virtually guaranteed, if not actually intended, to fail, thereby enriching [the Defendants]."[89]

The defendants argued that certain risks disclosed in writing established that misstatements could not have been material and could not have been properly relied upon by plaintiffs as required by the CEA's antifraud provisions. The standard for determining materiality for a misstatement is whether there is substantial likelihood that a reasonable investor would consider it important in making an investment decision.[90] The court found that the misstatement was material because it failed to disclose the possibility of significant losses. The court did not have to consider whether the customers relied on the defendants because "where, as here, the CFTC, an administrative agency, brings an enforcement action, reliance is not a necessary element of a violation under the CEA."[91] In the context of the CEA, scienter also may be shown by proof of recklessness. The court easily found the required scienter and upheld the CFTC's fraud claim.

Unauthorized trading constitutes a violation of the CEA when an associated person executes trades without the customer's permission or contrary to the customer's trading instructions.[92] The court granted the CFTC's summary judgment on the claim that defendants participated in unauthorized trading on behalf of its clients. The evidence established that defendants pressured the clients to "engage in numerous trades at highly unfavorable price quotes, which differed dramatically from those shown on a streaming Reuters feed and which made it virtually impossible for customers to profit."[93] The defendants unsuccessfully argued that they had a special power of attorney which enabled them to partake in these transactions, but the court held that defendants were not authorized to engage in trades that the defendants knew would generate unfair commissions. Furthermore, the evidence proved that any transaction would be made only with the clients' approval, which did not happen. These facts were sufficient to grant the summary judgment motion in favor of the CFTC.

If the defendant company is held liable under the CEA, as was the case with *International Financial Services,* a key question is whether the individual

89. *Id.*

90. *Id.* at 500; *see also* Saxe v. E.F. Hutton & Co., 789 F.2d 105, 111 (2d Cir. 1986).

91. *Id.* at 502; *see also* Slusser v. CFTC, 210 F.3d 783, 785–86 (7th Cir. 2000); *see also* CFTC v. Rosenberg, 85 F. Supp. 2d 424, 446–47 (D.N.J. 1998): "Customer reliance need not be proven in an enforcement action alleging fraud."

92. 7 U.S.C. §6b(a)(iv); *see also* Crothers v. Commodity Futures Trading Comm'n, 33 F.3d 405, 409 (4th Cir. 1994); Haltmier v. CFTC, 554 F.2d 556, 560 (2d Cir. 1977).

93. 323 F. Supp. 2d 482, 503.

defendants can be held personally liable in the event that the defendant company defaults. The CEA provides:

> Any person who, directly or indirectly, controls any person who has violated any provision of this chapter or any of the rules, regulations, or orders issued pursuant to this chapter may be held liable for such violation in any action brought by the Commission to the same extent as such controlled person. In such action, the Commission has the burden of proving that the controlling person did not act in good faith or knowingly induced, directly or indirectly, the act or acts constituting the violation.[94]

In *International Financial Services,* the two defendants in question were Robinson and Lai. Robinson was the "President and Chief Executive Officer [ ], ran daily activities, supervised its employees, handled customer complaints, enjoyed general signatory authority over checking accounts held for [Defendant], reviewed customer accounts regularly, and knew that [ ] it [was] virtually impossible for customers to profit."[95] The court found that Robinson was therefore subject to "control person" liability.

Lai hired Robinson to run the company and sat on the company's board of directors, in which capacity he advised Robinson with respect to the "basic objectives" and "tone of the company."[96] The court found ample evidence to hold him subject to control person liability because, "Lai was a shareholder and director of the [Defendant Company], enjoyed substantial authority to control activities, had actual or constructive knowledge of its violations, and at a minimum, refrained from taking steps to forestall those violations, if not actually masterminded and encouraged them."[97] Given both defendants' significant roles, they were held personally liable.

V. ARBITRATION

Typically, customer disputes with brokers are resolved in arbitration. The standard resolution forum is sponsored by the SROs within the securities industry. Although it may seem logical for brokers to have a significant duty to protect its customers from risky investments, case law supports imposing only a duty to warn a customer about the risks of a specific investment.[98] Arbitrators have elected not to impose a more stringent duty o n brokers to prevent their customers from committing what some refer to as "economic suicide."[99]

---

94. 7 U.S.C. §13c(b).
95. 323 F. Supp. 2d 482, 505.
96. *Id.* at 507.
97. *Id.*
98. Black, *supra* note 49, 64 U. Pitt. L. Rev. 483, 524.
99. *Id.*

14. SUITABILITY

I. THE SUITABILITY DOCTRINE

The doctrine of suitability imposes a general obligation on investment professionals to ensure that the transactions they recommend are suitable for their clients. The doctrine has its origins in the investor protection provisions of the federal securities laws and thus has evolved principally as a tool to protect retail investors.[1] Concepts of suitability have been used, however, to prosecute claims against banks that created and sold derivatives instruments to institutional customers.[2] Sustained by the perception that derivatives are more complex and less

---

1. *See, e.g.,* Norman S. Poser, *Liability of Broker-Dealers for Unsuitable Recommendations to Institutional Investors,* 2001 B.Y.L.U. Rev. 1493 (2001); Andrew M. Pardieck, *Kegs, Crude, and Commodities Law: On Why It Is Time to Reexamine the Suitability Doctrine,* 7 Nev. L.J. 301 (2007).

2. *See* Proctor & Gamble Co. v. Bankers Trust Co., 925 F. Supp. 1270 (S.D. Ohio 1996); Gibson Greetings, Inc. v. Bankers Trust Co., Civ. No. 1-94-620 (S.D. Ohio 1994); In re County of Orange v. Fuji Securities, Inc., 31 F. Supp. 2d 768 (C.D. Cal. 1998).

understood by market participants than other more traditional financial instruments, the attorneys, and their clients, enjoyed some measure of success.[3]

A. Basis of the Suitability Doctrine

The concept of "suitability" is used by plaintiffs in cases in which the transaction involves a security and the plaintiff asserts that the transaction was not conducted at arm's length. The suitability doctrine requires that the broker must have a reasonable basis for believing the recommendation to have been suitable for the customer, in light of the customer's financial condition and understanding of the investment and its risks. The Government Securities Act of 1993, which amended the Exchange Act, is the impetus for the suitability rule. There are two requirements for a successful suitability claim under Rule 10b-5 under the Exchange Act.

First, a plaintiff must establish that the defendant acted with scienter. It must be proven that "there was a material misrepresentation or omission and that this misrepresentation or omission was made with scienter," defined as "with intent to deceive, manipulate, or defraud."[4] Many jurisdictions have relaxed this scienter requirement and now only require reckless disregard for the truth. However, plaintiffs have a significant obstacle to overcome, as successfully proving this element of a Rule 10b-5 suitability claim remains very difficult.

The second requirement is that a plaintiff must demonstrate that he or she reasonably relied on the defendant's advice to invest. In determining whether such reliance exists, the most important factor to consider is the level of plaintiff's sophistication as an investor. Other factors considered by courts include: the investor's access to relevant information when making purchase decisions; discretionary versus nondiscretionary account status; the extent of a fiduciary relationship between the investor and the broker; the possibility of fraud; and the generality or specificity of the misrepresentations.[5]

---

3. The above cases involved losses sustained by supposedly sophisticated corporate clients, institutions, and municipalities. The plaintiffs' attorneys charged lack of suitability and failure to disclose the risks of derivatives trading. The cases all resulted in settlements.

4. *See* Clark v. John Lamula Investors, Inc., 583 F.2d 594, 600 (2d Cir. 1978), which cites Ernst & Ernst v. Hochfelder, 425 U.S. 185 (1976) for the proposition that scienter is required; Brown v. E.F. Hutton Group, Inc., 991 F.2d 1020 (2d Cir. 1993).

5. *See* Banca Cremi v. Brown, 955 F. Supp. 499, 511 (D. Md. 1997), *aff'd*, 132 F.3d 1017 (4th Cir. 1997), which notes that the level of an institutional investor's sophistication and expertise is significant and highly dispositive in determining whether the investor justifiably relied on the misrepresentations of the derivatives dealer; *see also* Platsis v. E.F. Hutton & Co., 642 F. Supp. 1277, 1299 (W.D. Mich. 1986) , *aff'd*, 829 F.2d 13 (6th Cir. 1987), which holds that investor sophistication is dispositive.

Whether reliance is "reasonable" depends primarily upon the level of sophistication of the investor.[6] When an investor's sophistication is high, the chance of that investor reasonably relying on the broker is lower and makes a suitability claim harder to prove. This is because the doctrine of suitability is designed to protect unsophisticated investors from making investments which they did not fully understand. However, courts have held that an investor's sophistication alone is not enough to bar an unsuitability claim. The Third Circuit has concluded:

> Even sophisticated investors deserve the protection of the securities laws, including protection from intentionally or recklessly fraudulent conduct by securities salesmen: a salesman cannot deliberately ignore that which he has a duty to know and recklessly state facts about matters of which he is ignorant. . . . The fact that his customers may be sophisticated and knowledgeable does not warrant a less stringent standard.[7]

The Second Circuit's view is similar:

> A sophisticated investor is not barred [from] reliance upon the honesty of those with whom he deals in the absence of knowledge that the trust is misplaced. Integrity is still the mainstay of commerce and makes it possible for an almost limitless number of transactions to take place without resort to the courts.[8]

The suitability obligation derives from a number of sources, including the rules of industry self-regulatory organizations (SROs), the antifraud provisions of the federal securities laws, and common law fiduciary duty. Each of these sources is considered below. Although violations of SRO suitability rules may subject industry members to disciplinary sanctions, the rules do not provide a private cause of action for customers. They may, however, be considered in arbitrations/lawsuits alleging negligence or breach of fiduciary duty on the part of members, as evidence of the standards of conduct that should be applied to those members.[9] In instances where an investment professional acts as principal (as in most transactions in the OTC market) the professional will not be considered a fiduciary of the customer, and any suitability claim based on a breach of such a duty will not survive. Furthermore, most courts hold that industry professionals acting as agents for customers do not owe a duty to determine suitability,

---

6. *See, e.g.,* Renner v. Chase Manhattan Bank, N.A., No. 03-7319, 2004 U.S. App. LEXIS 144 (2d Cir. 2004); *see also* Emergent Capital Inv. Mgmt., LLC v. Stonepath Group, Inc., 343 F.3d 189 (2d Cir. 2003).

7. AES Corp. v. Dow Chem. Co., 325 F.3d 174, 182 (3d Cir. 2003).

8. Hanly v. SEC, 415 F.2d 589, 596 (2d Cir. 1969); *see also* Lehigh Valley Trust Co. v. Central National Bank, 409 F.2d 989, 992 (5th Cir. 1969).

9. The SROs in both the securities and futures industries maintain arbitration forums for the resolution of customer disputes. Mandatory arbitration clauses are now contained in most customer agreements.

unless the customer's account is discretionary, or some other "special circumstances" apply to the relationship.

B. Special Circumstances

The case of *De Kwiatkowski v. Bear, Stearns & Co., Inc.*,[10] examines when "special circumstances" apply and when they do not. Henryk de Kwiatkowski was a Polish native who survived World War II and went on to forge an extraordinarily successful career in Canada and the United States. A wealthy entrepreneur and founder of an international aircraft leasing business, Kwiatkowski had a background in trading to hedge the risks associated with his company's foreign currency transactions, as well as considerable experience speculating on the dollar for profit.

Over a two-week period in late 1994, Kwiatkowski purchased, through his futures account at Bear, Stearns & Co. ("Bear"), a basket of 65,000 futures contracts, all long on the dollar and shorting the yen, the pound, the Swiss franc and the German mark. The position had a notional value of $6.5 billion and, at one point, amounted to 30% of the Chicago Mercantile Exchange's total open interest in certain of the currencies.[11] After netting over $200 million in the first trading weeks, Kwiatkowski's fortunes turned. Between late December 1994 and mid-January 1995, he suffered single-day losses of $112 million, $98 million, and $70 million. He continued losing money throughout the winter. Having lost tens of millions of dollars over the preceding days, Kwiatkowski liquidated all his positions in early March 1995. In all, Kwiatkowski suffered net losses of $215 million.

Kwiatkowski brought suit against Bear, contending, among other issues, that Bear had breached a duty owed him by failing adequately to advise him about the unique risks posed by the size of his futures position, failing to provide him with market forecasts that were pessimistic about the dollar, and by relying on disclosure forms dating from the opening of his account some years previously rather than undertaking new risk and suitability analyses.[12]

The Second Circuit held that absent "special circumstances" involving unsophisticated or incapacitated customers, or an otherwise than at arm's-length

---

10. 306 F.3d 1293 (2nd Cir. 2002).

11. All of the trades were initially executed on the Chicago Mercantile Exchange ("CME"). Later, Kwiatkowski moved half of the contracts to the OTC market, where, he was advised, he could trade with less visibility and liquidate with a lesser likelihood of impacting the market.

12. Kwiatkowski's account was nondiscretionary and he had made declarations and signed risk-disclosure statements upon opening his account in 1991. These disclosures provided that commodity futures trading was "highly risky" and a "highly speculative activity," that futures were "purchased on small margins and . . . subject to sharp price movements," and that Kwiatkowski should "carefully consider whether such [futures] trading [was] suitable for [him]."

relationship with the customer, a broker ordinarily has no duty to monitor a nondiscretionary account or to give advice to such a customer on an ongoing basis. In this regard, Kwiatkowski was the very opposite of the naive and vulnerable client the "special circumstances" rule was designed to protect. He may have been a "special customer" by reason of his vast wealth, his trading experience, his business sophistication and his gluttonous appetite for risk, but these were factors that weighed strongly against, and not at all in favor of, heightened duties on the part of the broker.

Kwiatkowski had contended that in the course of dealing, Bear voluntarily undertook additional duties to furnish information and advice on which he came to rely and that his trading losses were caused or enlarged by the failure of Bear to properly perform those duties. The Court found, however, that the advisory services that Bear advertised and provided to Kwiatkowski were wholly consistent with his status as a nondiscretionary customer. Kwiatkowski had bargained for the expertise of the firm's Private Client Services Group, but he simultaneously signed account agreements making clear that he was solely responsible for his own investments. It was thus obviously contemplated that Kwiatkowski would receive a great deal of advice from Bear's analysts and economists and that the giving of such advice would not alter the nondiscretionary nature of the account. The court did enumerate exceptions to the rule, however, including instances involving a violation of a federal or industry rule concerning risk disclosure upon the opening of an account.

Kwiatkowski had also argued that negligence on the part of Bear was evidenced by industry practice and internal Bear rules indicating that the firm should have provided more than it did in the way of risk warnings and account monitoring. Kwiatkowski alluded to the NYSE's Know-Your-Customer rule[13] and its requirement that brokers "use due diligence to learn the essential facts relative to every customer, *every order*, every cash or margin account" (emphasis added).[14]

The Second Circuit expressly stated, however, that "deviation from industry or internal standards for monitoring risk and suitability does not necessarily amount to the breach of a duty."[15] The court held that it made no sense, as a policy matter, to discourage the adoption of higher standards than the law required by treating them as predicates for liability. Noncompliance with such standards could only be considered as evidence of a failure to exercise due care where a separately identifiable duty of care was owed and a breach of that duty was alleged by other circumstances.

---

13. *See* Sec. II.B.2., *infra.*

14. Although not applicable to commodities brokers, Kwiatkowski's broker at Bear had testified that in practice the firm adhered to the rule in the commodities context.

15. 306 F.3d at 1311.

II. EQUITIES AND EQUITY DERIVATIVES

A. FINRA and Self-Regulated Organizations (SROs)

In the securities markets, recommendations that brokers make to investors are governed by the suitability rules of industry SROs, subject to oversight by the Securities and Exchange Commission (SEC). SROs are nongovernmental organizations that create and enforce industry regulations and standards. Historically, the National Association of Securities Dealers (NASD) promulgated rules applying to over-the-counter trading in securities and options on securities,[16] while the national securities exchanges, including the New York Stock Exchange (NYSE), imposed rules governing transactions executed on those exchanges. In July 2007, the NASD and the member regulation, enforcement, and arbitration functions of the NYSE were consolidated into a new SRO, the Financial Industry Regulatory Authority (FINRA).[17] FINRA describes its oversight role as follows:

> The Financial Industry Regulatory Authority (FINRA), is the largest non-governmental regulator for all securities firms doing business in the United States. All told, FINRA oversees nearly 5,000 brokerage firms, about 173,000 branch offices and approximately 656,000 registered securities representatives . . . FINRA is dedicated to investor protection and market integrity through effective and efficient regulation and complementary compliance and technology-based services. . . . FINRA touches virtually every aspect of the securities business—from registering and educating industry participants to examining securities firms; writing rules; enforcing those rules and the federal securities laws; informing and educating the investing public; providing trade reporting and other industry utilities; and administering the largest dispute resolution forum for investors and registered firms. It also performs market regulation under contract for The NASDAQ Stock Market, the American Stock Exchange, the International Securities Exchange and the Chicago Climate Exchange.[18]

FINRA has promulgated a consolidated rulebook and a generally applicable suitability rule. The pertinent NASD and NYSE rules continue to govern the recommendations of the respective member organizations under FINRA. FINRA describes the synthesis of NASD and NYSE rules as follows:

> The FINRA Rule book consolidates the rules promulgated by the NASD and the New York Stock Exchange. FINRA is establishing a consolidated FINRA

---

16. The term "security" as defined in the Securities Act of 1933 and the Securities Exchange Act of 1934 ("the Exchange Act") includes "any put, call, straddle, option or privilege on any security . . . or group or index of securities."

17. FINRA is also responsible, by contract, for regulating the Nasdaq Stock Market, the American Stock Exchange, and the International Securities Exchange.

18. http://www.finra.org/AboutFINRA/index.htm.

rulebook that will consist solely of FINRA Rules. Until the completion of the rulebook consolidation process, the FINRA rulebook includes NASD Rules and Incorporated NYSE Rules (together referred to as the 'Transitional Rulebook'), in addition to the new consolidated FINRA Rules. As the new FINRA Rules are approved and become effective, the rules in the Transitional Rulebook that address the same subject matter of regulation will be eliminated. When the consolidated rulebook is completed, the Transitional Rulebook will have been eliminated in its entirety.

While the NASD Rules generally apply to all FINRA members, the Incorporated NYSE Rules apply only to those members of FINRA that are also members of NYSE. FINRA Rules apply to all members, unless such rules have a more limited application by their terms.[19]

B. SRO Rules

The federal system of securities regulation relies to a great extent upon self-regulation by various segments of the securities markets. The SROs establish principles designed to protect investors and market participants by outlining codes of behavior and best practice principles. Self-regulation in the securities industry preceded both state and federal regulation, and today all of the exchanges in operation (e.g., the stock exchanges, options exchanges, and exchanges that trade security futures products) effectively perform self-regulatory functions. With the enactment of the securities laws and the creation of the SEC, federal regulation was laid on top of the system of regulation already in place in the markets.[20]

In general, SROs have broad authority to impose governance standards, set rules, and undertake enforcement and disciplinary proceedings with respect to their members.[21] However, the activities of the SROs are subject to SEC oversight. For example, the SEC must approve SRO rulemakings prior to their being enacted, and the SEC may in some instances require that the SROs establish specific rules. In addition, most market participants must be members of the SRO for their segment of the securities market.

SROs generally require broker-dealers to recommend only those investments that are suitable for the investor.[22] These requirements are aimed at protecting customers from inappropriate sales practices. If a broker-dealer has control over a customer's account, the broker-dealer is required to obtain information from the investor, including the investor's investment objectives and finances. Based

---

19. http://www.finra.org/Industry/Regulation/FINRARules/index.htm.

20. *The Department of the Treasury Blueprint for a Modernized Financial Regulatory Structure*, (Department of the Treasury, March 2008).

21. *Id.*

22. *See* Willa E. Gibson , *Investors, Look Before You Leap: The Suitability Doctrine Is Not Suitable for OTC Derivatives Dealers*, 29 LOY. U. CHI. L.J. 527, 546–47 (1998).

on that information, the broker-dealer decides whether the investor is suited for the transactions he or she contemplates.[23] Each SRO has its own rules for enforcing the suitability requirement.

1. The NASD Suitability Rule The NASD, the precursor to FINRA, adopted a suitability requirement for addressing problems between stockbrokers and customers. NASD Rule 2310 states in part:

> In recommending to a customer the purchase, sale or exchange of any security, a member shall have reasonable grounds for believing that the recommendation is suitable for such customer upon the basis of the facts, if any, disclosed by such customer as to his other security holdings and as to his financial situation and needs.[24]

The suitability rule is a cornerstone of the "fair dealing" philosophy espoused by FINRA and the industry participants. The rule is intended to promote ethical sales practices and high standards of professional conduct among members.[25] Members' responsibilities include having a reasonable basis for recommending a particular security or strategy (the "reasonable basis" suitability obligation), as well as having reasonable grounds for believing that the recommendation is suitable for the customer to whom it is made (the "customer-specific" suitability obligation).

Rule 2310 applies, by its terms, to recommendations made to both individual and institutional customers, although its requirements are more prescriptive with respect to individual customers.[26] The NASD conceded that the manner in which a member fulfills his suitability obligation to an institutional customer will vary depending on the nature of the customer and the specific transaction.[27] Thus, the member must determine the suitability of a recommended transaction *unless* he is satisfied that the institutional customer is independently capable of evaluating investment risk in general, and the recommended product in particular.[28]

Although a FINRA suitability rule violation subjects a broker-dealer to possible disciplinary action, most courts do not recognize an implied private right of

---

23. *Id.*

24. NASD Rule 2310, NASD Manual (CCH) 4261 (1998) [hereinafter NASD Manual].

25. NASD Interpretive Memo 2310-2.

26. Part (b) of the rule obliges a member to make reasonable efforts to obtain information about an individual customer's financial and tax status, investment objectives, and any other information used or considered to be reasonable by the member for the purpose of making recommendations to such customer. The information must be obtained before the member commences trading in the account.

27. NASD Interpretive Memo 2310-3. While the Interpretive Memo is instructive in this regard, it is not a rule and thus functions only as a guideline to members.

28. *Id.*

action.[29] However, violations of Rule 2310 can still assist plaintiffs in proving negligence or breach of fiduciary duty.[30] Rule 2310 applies only to recommendations, so if a broker sells a nonrecommended security to a customer, the broker will not violate the rule. There are differing views as to what constitutes a recommendation for the purposes of this rule, and a violation will depend on the particular facts of the case.

Rule 2310 differs from Rule 10b-5 under the Exchange Act in that there is no scienter requirement by the broker for a Rule 2310 violation; however, like Rule 10b-5, Rule 2310 applies to both institutional investors and individuals. However, Rule 2310 applies in a more limited fashion to institutional investors on the rationale that such investors do not need as much protection. Neither the CFTC nor the National Futures Association (NFA) has adopted a rule that corresponds to NASD Rule 2310. Therefore, commodities futures and commodities options brokers are not required to have a reasonable belief that a recommendation is suitable for the customer.

NASD Rule 2110 requires that members observe high standards of commercial honor and just and equitable principles of trade in the conduct of business.[31] According to the NASD, the rule imposes fundamental responsibility for fair dealing in all relationships with customers. "Sales efforts must therefore be undertaken only on a basis that can be judged as being within the ethical standards of the [NASD's] Rules, with particular emphasis on the requirement to deal fairly with the public."[32]

An additional level of scrutiny is mandated for both options and futures trading in securities and applies equally to individual and institutional customers. NASD Rule 2860 prohibits a member from recommending an option contract to a customer unless the member has reasonable grounds for believing, after reasonable inquiry, that the recommended transaction is "not unsuitable" for the customer, and that the customer has such knowledge and experience in financial matters that he may reasonably be expected to be capable of evaluating the risks of the recommended transaction, and is financially able to bear the risks of the recommended position in the option contract. NASD Rule 2865

---

29. *See* Jablon v. Dean Witter & Co., 614 F.2d 677 (9th Cir. 1980), which states there is no implied private right of action for violation of an SRO rule. *But see* Buttrey v. Merrill, Lynch, Pierce, Fenner & Smith, Inc., 410 F.2d 135, 142 (7th Cir. 1969), in which the private right of action for violation of an SRO rule may be implied if the defendant's conduct was tantamount to fraud.

30. Miley v. Oppenheimer & Co., 637 F.2d 318, 333 (5th Cir. 1981); *see also* Norman S. Poser, *Liability of Broker-Dealers for Unsuitable Recommendations to Institutional Investors,* 2001 B.Y.U.L. REV. 1493, 1531–32 (2001).

31. NASD Conduct Rule 2110, NASD MANUAL (CCH) 4111 (1998).

32. *Fair Dealing with Customers,* NASD MANUAL, Rule IM-2310-2.

places analogous obligations on members with respect to recommendations regarding transactions or strategies for trading security futures.

As a matter of practice, a brokerage firm's compliance manual will detail the specific guidelines that members must follow for qualifying accounts to trade particular products, and for supervising those accounts thereafter. An issue may arise as to whether these procedures are adequate to carry out the requirements of the above rules.

2. NYSE Know-Your-Customer Rule Prior to the formation of FINRA, the New York Stock Exchange ("NYSE"), in its role as an SRO, imposed a "know your customer" rule on brokers. NYSE Rule 405 requires its member firms "to use due diligence to learn the essential facts relative to every customer [and] every order."[33] However, application of this rule has been limited by courts. Rule 405 violations in disciplinary proceedings have been charged only when the customer's information was not recorded accurately, so that the firm was unable to "know the customer."[34]

Rule 405 provides that:

> Every member organization is required through a principal executive or a person or persons designated under the provisions of Rule 342(b)(1) [¶2342] to
>
> (1) Use due diligence to learn the essential facts relative to every customer, every order, every cash or margin account accepted or carried by such organization and every person holding power of attorney over any account accepted or carried by such organization.[35]

Rule 405 is currently regarded as protecting investors from being induced to purchase securities whose risks they cannot undertake.[36] The rule applies to both institutional and individual accounts, and to transactions either initiated by a customer or recommended by a broker.[37]

In addition, the NYSE has an express suitability rule that applies to recommendations of option contracts. Like its NASD counterpart, NYSE Rule 723 requires that a member recommending the purchase or sale of an option contract

---

33. NYSE Rule 405, 2 N.Y.S.E. GUIDE (CCH) 4057 [hereinafter NYSE GUIDE]; *see also* G. Thomas Fleming III & Usman S. Mohammed, *NYSE Rule 405, the "Know Your Customer" Rule: Current Application and Limitations*, SEC. ARB. COMMENTATOR at 1, (Mar. 2002); *see also* Barbara Black, *Economic Suicide: The Collision of Ethics and Risk in Securities Law*, 64 U. PITT. L. REV. 483, 493–94 (2003).

34. *See* In re Silberman, NYSE Disc. Action 01-229, 2001 NYSE Disc. Action LEXIS 165 (Dec. 19, 2001).

35. FINRA manual Rule 405 available at http://finra.complinet.com/en/display/display_main.html?rbid=2403&element_id=6932.

36. *See* Norman S. Poser, *Liability of Broker-Dealers for Unsuitable Recommendations to Institutional Investors*, 2001 B.Y.U.L. REV. 1493, 1536 (2001).

37. *Id.*

have a reasonable belief that the customer possesses the requisite understanding and ability to bear the risks of the options transaction.

C. The Antifraud Provisions of the Federal Securities Laws—Unsuitability as a Basis for a Section 10b Cause of Action

The SEC will itself pursue an unsuitability claim under Section 10b of the Exchange Act if it considers the conduct of the broker so egregious as to amount to a fraud perpetrated on the customer.[38] Section 10b of the Exchange Act and Rule 10b-5 promulgated thereunder make it unlawful for any person, directly or indirectly, in connection with the purchase or sale of any security to (1) employ any device, scheme, or artifice to defraud; (2) make any untrue statement or omission of a material fact; or (3) engage in any act, practice, or course of business which operates or would operate as a fraud or deceit upon any person. Although not enumerated therein, private claimants also have an implied right of action under Section 10b.

Unsuitability claims are analyzed either as "misrepresentation/omission" cases under Rule10b-5(b), or "fraudulent conduct" cases under Rules10b-5(a) and (c).[39] An unsuitability claim based on a misrepresentation/omission theory is considered a subset of an ordinary misrepresentation or omission claim brought under Section 10b.[40] In order to prevail, the SEC will be required to prove: (1) that the securities purchased were unsuited to the customer's needs; (2) that the broker knew or reasonably believed that the securities were unsuitable; (3) that the broker recommended or purchased the unsuitable securities anyway; and (4) that, with scienter, the broker made material misrepresentations or failed

---

38. The Second Circuit was the first to hold that a broker's recommendation of unsuitable securities could amount to a violation of Section 10b of the Exchange Act and Rule 10b-5 promulgated thereunder. Clark v. John Lamula Investors, Inc., 583 F. 2d 594 (2nd Cir. 1978). The SEC may initiate either federal district court proceedings, or an administrative proceeding under the provisions of the Exchange Act. The forum selected will generally depend upon the seriousness of the broker's conduct and the nature of the relief sought.

39. O'Connor v. R.F. Lafferty & Co., 965 F. 2d 893, 897 (10th Cir. 1992): "Some courts examining a 10(b), Rule 10b-5 unsuitability claim have analyzed it simply as a misrepresentation or failure to disclose a material fact. . . . In such a case, the broker has omitted telling the investor the recommendation is unsuitable for the investor's interests. The court may then use traditional laws concerning omission to examine the claim. . . . In contrast, [the plaintiff] asserts an unsuitability claim based on fraud by conduct. She does not assert [that the broker] omitted to tell her the stocks he purchased were unsuitable for her investment needs. Rather, she claims that his purchase of the stocks for her account acted as a fraud upon her."

40. Brown v. E.F. Hutton Group Inc., 991 F. 2d 1020, 1031 (2nd Cir. 1993).

to disclose material information relating to the suitability of the securities.[41] A private claimant must prove a fifth element: justifiable detrimental reliance.[42]

Institutional investors, in particular, face difficulties establishing claims both under the misrepresentation/omission theory of liability and the fraudulent conduct theory of liability. Under the misrepresentation/omission premise, justifiable reliance on the alleged misstatements or omissions of the broker must be proven. The courts have considered various factors to be relevant in determining justifiable reliance in such cases, including the sophistication and expertise of the claimant in financial and securities matters, the existence of long-standing business or personal relationships, access to relevant information, the existence of a fiduciary relationship, and concealment of, and opportunity to detect, the fraud.[43] The sophistication of the investor is often the critical element in determining whether the investor is entitled to relief under Section 10b. If a commercial entity is considered sophisticated with regard to, for example, its business expertise, or its employment of experienced financial personnel for the purpose of assessing financial investments or strategies, the court will not find reliance placed by the entity on a broker's misstatements to be justified.

In *Banca Cremi, S.A., v. Alex. Brown & Sons, Inc.*,[44] a Mexican bank filed suit against a Maryland securities brokerage firm alleging, *inter alia*, a Section 10b/ Rule 10b-5 violation after the bank suffered losses on a number of collateralized mortgage obligations (CMOs) when the market in CMOs collapsed in 1994.[45] The bank claimed that the brokers had violated the Exchange Act by making material misstatements and omissions regarding the CMOs sold to the bank, and by selling the bank investments which it knew to be unsuitable.

The Fourth Circuit affirmed the district court's finding that the bank was a sophisticated investor capable of investigating the investment risk. It took into account both the bank's employees—hired for their business expertise—and the access that the bank had to a wealth of information regarding CMOs, which illustrated that while the investments were potentially very profitable, they were also highly risky.[46] In any action for fraud, reliance on false statements needs to

---

41. In the Matter of Dale E. Frey, 2003 SEC LEXIS 306 (February 5, 2003).

42. Brown v. E.F. Hutton Group Inc., 991 F. 2d 1020, 1031 (2nd Cir. 1993).

43. *See, e.g.*, Banca Cremi, S.A., v. Alex. Brown & Sons, Inc., 132 F. 3d 1017, 1028 (4th Cir. 1997).

44. 132 F. 3d 1017, 1028 (4th Cir. 1997).

45. The Bank had invested in "inverse floater" CMOs which earned interest at rates that moved inversely to specified floating index rates. The inverse floaters thus earned high returns whilst interest rates declined or remain constant, but would lose substantial value if interest rates increased. The market for CMOs collapsed in 1994 when the Federal Reserve Board increased short-term interest rates by a total of 2.5% over a nine-month period. CMO holders flooded the market and CMO liquidity dried up.

46. In finding that the bank was sophisticated, the court referred to the factors specifically promulgated by the NASD to measure the sophistication of institutional investors,

be accompanied by a right to rely. Here, the bank lost its right to rely by its own recklessness. It continued to purchase CMOs after it had sufficient information, given its sophistication, to be well apprised of the risks it faced in investing in CMOs. Given that the bank was aware of the risks involved, it was not justified in relying on the broker's alleged omissions and misstatements.

Establishing an unsuitability claim under the lesser-litigated fraudulent conduct theory requires proof that the broker recommended or, in the case of a discretionary account, purchased unsuitable securities with an intent to defraud or with reckless disregard for the customer's interests, *and* that the broker exercised control over the customer's account.[47] This latter element would be a "substantial, if not insuperable" obstacle for an institutional investor to overcome in establishing a suitability claim.[48]

A firm may face liability under the control person provisions of the Exchange Act if it fails to properly supervise the conduct of its members with respect to their suitability obligations under the securities laws.[49]

III. COMMODITIES-BASED DERIVATIVES/FINANCIAL FUTURES AND OPTIONS

A. CFTC Disclosure Rules

Options on securities are regulated by the SEC, but futures and commodity options (including options on futures) are not subject to SEC regulation. They are, however, regulated by the Commodity Futures Trading Commission (CFTC).[50] The commodities futures markets generally are regulated by the CFTC pursuant to the Commodity Exchange Act (CEA).[51] The Commodity Futures Modernization Act of 2000 (the CFMA)[52] created a three-part regulation system consisting of exchanges, less regulated organized markets, and unregulated derivatives markets.

---

i.e., the "institutional investor's 'capability to evaluate investment risk independently, and the extent to which the [investor] is exercising independent judgment'" and concluded that it was "clear that the Bank would also qualify as a highly sophisticated institutional investor under the NASD standards." Banca Cremi, 132 F. 3d at 1029.

47. O'Connor v. R.F. Lafferty & Co., 965 F. 2d 893, 898 (10th Cir. 1992).

48. Norman S. Poser, *Liability of Broker-Dealers for Unsuitable Recommendations to Institutional Investors*, 2001 B.Y.L.U. Rev. 1493, 1552 (2001).

49. Exchange Act §20; 15 U.S.C. §78t.

50. *See generally* Chapter 4, *supra*, for a discussion of SEC and CFTC jurisdiction.

51. 7 U.S.C. §1 et seq.

52. Pub. Law No. 106-554, 114 Stat. 2763 (Dec. 21, 2000).

The CFTC does not have a suitability rule.[53] Its proxy is a mandatory disclosure rule[54] that precludes the opening of a futures account until a customer has been furnished with a risk disclosure statement setting out the risks involved in futures trading, and has signed an acknowledgement that he understands and is willing to undertake those risks. The effect of the disclosure statement is to place upon the customer the onus to consider whether futures trading is suitable for him in light of his circumstances and financial resources.[55]

The CFMA permits over-the-counter, and essentially unregulated, transactions between qualified market participants and no longer grants the CFTC responsibility for reviewing the economics underlying publicly-traded derivatives.[56] The CFTC does not have direct supervisory authority with respect to the self-regulatory practices of derivatives participants.[57] It also does not impose a suitability requirement on futures professionals, but instead requires futures commission merchants (FCMs) opening accounts to provide their customers with risk disclosure statements.[58] The Futures Trading Practices Act of 1992 ("FTPA") amended the CEA to provide the CFTC with authority to grant exemptions from the CEA for any transaction that meets certain criteria.[59]

The risk disclosure statements signed by clients of FCMs when opening an account inform the customer that trading futures is risky and that one should "carefully consider whether such trading is suitable . . . in light of your circumstances and financial resources."[60] Therefore, instead of putting the onus on the professional to determine an investment's suitability, it appears that the customer is the one who is responsible for determining whether the investment is advisable. The CEA does not require brokers to determine if a transaction is suitable for a customer, and brokers may recommend commodities futures trading without making any determination as to its suitability.[61] However, courts can

---

53. *See* Andrew M. Pardieck, *Kegs, Crude, and Commodities Law: On Why It Is Time to Reexamine the Suitability Doctrine,* 7 NEV. L.J. 301 (2007), for the history of the CFTC's proposed but ultimately not adopted suitability rule.

54. CFTC Reg. 1.55.

55. *Id.* The CFTC regulations provide specific language for use in risk disclosure documentation, although risk disclosure statements approved by SROs may be used in lieu thereof if they provide for the same amount of disclosure.

56. *See* THOMAS LEE HAZEN, DERIVATIVES REGULATION §2.02 (2004).

57. Thomas Lee Hazen, *Disparate Regulatory Schemes for Parallel Activities: Securities Regulation, Derivative Regulation, Gambling, and Insurance,* 24 ANN. REV. BANKING & FIN. L. 375, 394 (2005).

58. Willa E. Gibson , *Investors, Look Before You Leap: The Suitability Doctrine Is Not Suitable for OTC Derivatives Dealers,* 29 LOY. U. CHI. L.J. 527, 561 (1998).

59. Futures Trading Practices Act of 1992, Pub. Law No. 102-546, 106 Stat. 3590.

60. *Id; see* Customer Protection Rules, 43 Fed. Reg. at 31,886, 31,888.

61. Barbara Black, *Economic Suicide: The Collision of Ethics and Risk in Securities Law,* 64 U. PITT. L. REV. 483, 493 (2003).

consider the totality of the circumstances in order to determine whether the FCM acted properly. In *United States CFTC v. Calvary Currencies,*[62] the court said:

> The U.S. Commodity Futures Trading Commission regulates "transactions." In order to determine the nature of a transaction, it is often necessary to look beyond the written contract. In order to gain the fullest understanding possible of the parties' agreement and their purpose, courts often must consider the course of dealings between the parties and the totality of the business relationship. It is appropriate, then, to look to both the client agreement and the subsequent currency trades to determine the nature of the transaction.[63]

Furthermore, an affirmative misrepresentation of suitability would constitute fraud, assuming scienter and reliance.[64] However, this still falls short in comparison to the SEC's hard line approach, which implements intense oversight of the securities exchanges.

B. National Futures Association

The National Futures Association (NFA) is the self-regulatory organization for the commodities market. Although it does not impose a suitability requirement like the NASD, the NFA has a "know-your-customer" rule which requires the futures commission merchant to obtain information about a customer before opening an account.[65] An affirmative misrepresentation of suitability will constitute fraud, assuming scienter and reliance.[66]

Although the CFTC has argued that a blanket disclosure highlighting the risks involved in all futures trading is comparable if not preferable protection to a suitability analysis, the distinction reflects the philosophy of the futures industry that futures trading is intended for sophisticated investors that have the capability of assessing whether futures products are appropriate for them.[67]

---

62. 473 F. Supp. 2d 453 (D. Md. 2006).

63. *Id.* at 63–64.

64. *Id.*

65. *See* Willa E. Gibson , *Investors, Look Before You Leap: The Suitability Doctrine Is Not Suitable for OTC Derivatives Dealers,* 29 Loy. U. Chi. L.J. 527, 560-61 (1998); *see also* Conrad G. Bahlke, *"Suitability" and "Appropriateness" of Derivative Instruments,* in Derivatives: Avoiding Risk and Managing Litigation, at 29, 44 (1996); (PLI Corp. Law & Practice Course Handbook Series No. B-931, 1996).

66. *See* Black, *supra* note 61, 64 U. Pitt. L. Rev. 483, 493.

67. *See, e.g.,* speech of CFTC General Counsel, C. Robert Paul, before the Subcommittee on Risk Management, Research, and Specialty Crops of the House of Representatives Committee on Agriculture 106th Congress, 2nd Session, available at http://commdocs. house.gov/committees/ag. Mr. Paul also acknowledged that the Know-Your-Customer rule administered by the NFA buttresses the risk disclosure requirements of the CFTC rules. Note, however, that the NFA rule requires futures commission merchants (FCMs) and introducing brokers to ascertain detailed information about their futures customers

C. CEA Antifraud Provision

The CFTC made clear in its 1986 decision in *Phacelli v. ContiCommodity Services, Inc.*,[68] that a futures professional does not violate the antifraud provision of the CEA (Section 4b) merely because he fails to determine whether a customer is suitable for futures trading. Subsequent CFTC and federal court decisions have consistently followed this view, holding that no legal duty to recommend only suitable futures transactions arises under Section 4b of the CEA.[69] The CFTC will, however, find fraud where there is a failure on the part of the futures professional to disclose the risks involved in futures trading. Again, such decisions tend to involve clearly unsuitable and unsophisticated investors.[70]

D. Municipal Securities Rulemaking Board

The Municipal Securities Rulemaking board (MSRB) is the SRO established by the SEC under the Exchange Act to regulate the activities of dealers in municipal securities.[71] It has a suitability rule similar to the NASD rule and places an affirmative duty of inquiry on the dealer with respect to recommendations to noninstitutional accounts.[72] Furthermore, a dealer is required to make a suitability determination before recommending a municipal security transaction to any account, including an institutional account.

IV. SWAPS

As discussed in chapter 4, regulatory relief for over-the-counter (OTC) swap transactions was codified by Congress in the CFMA. Such regulatory relief extends to derivatives products traded by "eligible contract participants," including corporations, trusts, and individuals that meet minimum net worth/assets requirements, and regulated financial institutions, investment companies, broker-dealers, and FCMs. Thus, while the statutory exemption reflects the concept of sophistication on the part of the end user counterparty (and the concomitant notion that sophisticated market participants can and should be

---

who are individuals, including their age, occupation, net worth and trading experience, as a way of gauging what their risk tolerance might be.

68. No. 80-385-80-704, 1986 WL 68447 (Sept. 5, 1986).

69. *See, e.g.*, Dyer v. Merrill Lynch, Pierce, Fenner & Smith, Inc., 928 F.2d 238 (7th Cir. 1991).

70. *See* Andrew M. Pardieck, *Kegs, Crude, and Commodities Law: On Why It Is Time to Reexamine the Suitability Doctrine*, 7 NEV. L.J. 301 (2007), for an analysis of CFTC engagement in suitability determinations "under the rubric of disclosure."

71. *See* 15 U.S.C. 78o-4.

72. Sec. Rulemaking Bd., MSRB Rule G-19, MSRB MANUAL (CCH) P 3591.

expected to bear the burden of protecting themselves),[73] it also reflects the fact that the dealer counterparty is nevertheless subject to some form of federal regulatory oversight.

The national banks, which are the leading players in the OTC market, are regulated by the Office of the Comptroller of the Currency (OCC), overseen by the Federal Reserve. Charged with ensuring the safety and soundness of the national banking system, the OCC views suitability less as a consumer protection issue and more as a credit risk or reputational risk issue for the bank. Thus, while it does not impose a legal obligation on banks to recommend only suitable transactions, it operates on the premise that banks engaging in derivative transactions that are inappropriate for the customer or that the customer does not understand generate greater potential for customer default, litigation, and damage to the bank's reputation.[74]

To diminish these risks, sound risk management principles require that the bank determine whether derivative transactions are appropriate for customers.[75] To ensure customer appropriateness, banks should understand the nature of the counterparty's business and the purpose of its derivative activities. A bank should not recommend transactions that it knows, or has reason to believe, are inappropriate for customers. Similarly, if the bank believes that a customer does not understand the risks of a derivative transaction, the bank should consider refraining from the transaction. Should the customer wish to proceed, prudence dictates that the bank document its analysis of the transaction and any risk disclosure information provided to the customer. Maintaining such documentation will protect the bank in event that the transaction is put in issue.

V. MORTGAGE-BACKED SECURITIES AND THE SUBPRIME CREDIT CRISIS

The recent collapse of the mortgage-backed securities market may be a source of future litigation, as banks created instruments which, due to subsequent events in the real estate market, turned out to be unsuitable for investors with lower risk appetites. In 2007 and 2008 the high levels of delinquencies, defaults, and foreclosures among subprime borrowers led to the undoing of broad capital markets, the shockwaves of which have been felt throughout the global economy. The rise in real estate prices over the last ten years was enhanced, in large part, by low interest rates facilitating the purchase of homes and investment properties. This increased real estate activity, and easy access to funding, allowed

---

73. *See Over-the-Counter Derivatives Markets and the Commodity Exchange Act*, REPORT OF THE PRESIDENT'S WORKING GROUP ON FINANCIAL MARKETS, (November 1999).

74. RISK MANAGEMENT OF FINANCIAL DERIVATIVES, COMPTROLLER'S HANDBOOK (January 1997).

75. *Id.*

borrowers to access equity contained in their homes and speculators to make investments in property that would never have been possible without the availability of cheap money.

Banks lend money for, among other things, the funding of long-term purchases, such as a home, or to refinance those same purchases. In the years leading up to the mortgage melt down, banks aggressively pumped capital into the economy, taking advantage of spreads between the rates at which banks borrow, and the mortgage rates they charge their customers. Cash was readily available to banks to lend to their customers due to the fact that, once these loans were created, the loans were resold in the form of "mortgage-backed securities."

The risks associated with the purchase of structured instruments such as mortgage-backed securities have been the subject of concern for many years as lower interest rates encouraged investors to seek out higher yields by taking on additional risk. In May 2002, the Office of the Comptroller of the Currency issued a caution alerting national banks to the potential risks of yield chasing, that is, assuming higher levels of credit, interest rate, and liquidity risk in order to boost investment returns.[76] The OCC warned of the need for banks to maintain prudent risk management practices to control such risks. In particular, the OCC advised that banks should conduct appropriate due diligence in advance of purchasing structurally complex asset-backed securities, including simulating the impact of such purchases on capital and earnings under a variety of default scenarios. In addition, the OCC urged banks to supplement credit ratings from the rating agencies with internal credit analyses when assuming exposure to low investment grade securities.

In the OCC's warning against "chasing yield," there was no reference with specificity to mortgage-backed securities. During the past year, however, many banks and their affiliates have sustained significant losses arising out of mortgage-backed securities, as rising interest rates and falling real estate prices have led to increased defaults among subprime borrowers. Banks that held mortgage backed-securities in their proprietary accounts have been hurt by declining prices. In addition, banks are coming under increased scrutiny for their role in selling mortgage-backed securities to investors.

Mortgage-backed securities (MBSs) comprise debt securities issued in the market by entities called CDOs (collateralized debt obligations), created for the purpose of buying mortgage loans from originating banks or mortgage companies, repackaging the accompanying credit risk and selling that risk to investors. The allotted securities generally consist of a number of different debt tranches, the credit rating of which decreases as the yield increases, and an equity tranche. *The Trading and Capital-Markets Activities Manual*, published by the Board of

---

76. OCC Circular, May 2002.

Governors of the Federal Reserve System, describes residential mortgage-backed securities as follows:[77]

A mortgage loan is a loan which is secured by the collateral of a specified real estate property. The real estate pledged with a mortgage can be divided into two categories: residential and nonresidential. Residential properties include houses, condominiums, cooperatives, and apartments. Residential real estate can be further subdivided into single-family (one- to four-family) and multi-family (apartment buildings in which more than four families reside). Nonresidential property includes commercial and farm properties. Common types of mortgages which have been securitized include traditional fixed-rate, level-payment mortgages, graduated-payment mortgages, adjustable-rate mortgages (ARMs), and balloon mortgages.

Mortgage-backed securities (MBS) are products that use pools of mortgages as collateral for the issuance of securities. Although these securities have been collateralized using many types of mortgages, most are collateralized by one- to four-family residential properties. MBS can be broadly classified into four basic categories:

- mortgage-backed bonds;
- pass-through securities;
- collateralized mortgage obligations and real estate mortgage investment conduits; and
- stripped mortgage-backed securities.

A. Mortgage-Backed Bonds

Mortgage-backed bonds are corporate bonds which are general obligations of the issuer. These bonds are credit enhanced through the pledging of specific mortgages as collateral. Mortgage-backed bonds involve no sale or conveyance of ownership of the mortgages acting as collateral.

B. Pass-Through Securities

A mortgage-backed, pass-through security provides its owner with a pro rata share in underlying mortgages. The mortgages are typically placed in a trust, and certificates of ownership are sold to investors. Issuers of pass-through instruments primarily act as a conduit for the investors by collecting and proportionally distributing monthly cash flows generated by homeowners making payments on their home mortgage loans. The pass-through certificate represents a sale of assets to the investor, thus removing the assets from the balance sheet of the issuer.

---

77. TRADING AND CAPITAL-MARKETS ACTIVITIES MANUAL, §4110.1 (Board of Governors of the Federal Reserve System).

C. Collateralized Mortgage Obligations and Real Estate Mortgage Investment Conduits

Collateralized mortgage obligations (CMOs) and real estate mortgage investment conduits (REMICs) securities represent ownership interests in specified cash flows arising from underlying pools of mortgages or mortgage securities. CMOs and REMICs involve the creation, by the issuer, of a single-purpose entity designed to hold mortgage collateral and funnel payments of principal and interest from borrowers to investors. Unlike pass-through securities, however, which entail a pro rata share of ownership of all underlying mortgage cash flows, CMOs and REMICs convey ownership only of cash flows assigned to specific classes based on established principal distribution rules.[78]

The risks associated with mortgage-backed securities include "prepayment risk," the option is the homeowner's right to prepay a mortgage any time, at par. The prepayment option makes mortgage securities different from other fixed-income securities, as the timing of mortgage principal repayments is uncertain.[79] While the risk of default on the mortgages supporting various mortgage-backed securities was not of primary concern, as banks issued mortgage-backed securities backed by weaker mortgage pools, previously unrealized risk seeped into the market for these securities. The weaker mortgage pools supported instruments with higher yields as the mortgagee was paying higher rates. Investors who purchased these securities did so to chase higher yields to combat a declining interest rate environment. The potential for litigation involving the various stakeholders in the subprime mortgage market collapse is significant, ranging from claims regarding alleged negligent mismanagement of investment portfolios by fund managers, to claims relating to the lending practices of banks and mortgage originators. Included in the mix is the likelihood of claims challenging the suitability of mortgage-backed securities as an investment class for a range of investors.

APPENDIX A

NASD RULE 2310 RECOMMENDATIONS TO CUSTOMERS (SUITABILITY)

(a) In recommending to a customer the purchase, sale or exchange of any security, a member shall have reasonable grounds for believing that the recommendation is suitable for such customer upon the basis of the facts, if any, disclosed by such customer as to his other security holdings and as to his financial situation and needs.

---

78. *Id.*
79. *Id.*

(b) Prior to the execution of a transaction recommended to a non-institutional customer, other than transactions with customers where investments are limited to money market mutual funds, a member shall make reasonable efforts to obtain information concerning:

(1) the customer's financial status;

(2) the customer's tax status;

(3) the customer's investment objectives; and

(4) such other information used or considered to be reasonable by such member or registered representative in making recommendations to the customer.

(c) For purposes of this Rule, the term "non-institutional customer" shall mean a customer that does not qualify as an "institutional account" under Rule 3110(c)(4).

NASD RULE 2860(19) OPTIONS—SUITABILITY

(A) No member or person associated with a member shall recommend to any customer any transaction for the purchase or sale (writing) of an option contract unless such member or person associated therewith has reasonable grounds to believe upon the basis of information furnished by such customer after reasonable inquiry by the member or person associated therewith concerning the customer's investment objectives, financial situation and needs, and any other information known by such member or associated person, that the recommended transaction is not unsuitable for such customer.

(B) No member or person associated with a member shall recommend to a customer an opening transaction in any option contract unless the person making the recommendation has a reasonable basis for believing, at the time of making the recommendation, that the customer has such knowledge and experience in financial matters that he may reasonably be expected to be capable of evaluating the risks of the recommended transaction, and is financially able to bear the risks of the recommended position in the option contract.

NASD RULE 2865(19) SECURITIES FUTURES—SUITABILITY

(A) No member or person associated with a member shall recommend to any customer any transaction or trading strategy for the purchase or sale of a security future unless such member or person associated with the member has reasonable grounds to believe upon the basis of information furnished by the customer after reasonable inquiry by the member or person associated with the member concerning the customer's investment objectives, financial situation and needs, and any other information known by the member or associated person, that the recommended transaction or trading strategy is not unsuitable for the customer.

(B) No member or person associated with a member shall recommend to a customer a transaction in any security future unless the person making the recommendation has a reasonable basis for believing, at the time of making the recommendation, that the customer has such knowledge and experience in financial matters that the customer may reasonably be expected to be capable of evaluating the risks of the recommended transaction, and is financially able to bear the risks of the recommended position in the security future.

NYSE RULE 405–DILIGENCE AS TO ACCOUNTS

Every member organization is required through a general partner, a principal executive officer or a person or persons designated under the provisions of Rule 342(b)(1) to

(1) Use due diligence to learn the essential facts relative to every customer, every order, every cash or margin account accepted or carried by such organization and every person holding power of attorney over any account accepted or carried by such organization.

NYSE RULE 723—OPTIONS—SUITABILITY

No member organization or member, allied member or employee of such member organization shall recommend to a customer an opening transaction in any option contract unless the person making the recommendation has a reasonable basis for believing, at the time of making the recommendation, that the customer has such knowledge and experience in financial matters that he may reasonably be expected to be capable of evaluating the risks of the recommended transaction, and is financially able to bear the risks of the recommended position in the option contract.

SECTION 10 OF THE SECURITIES EXCHANGE ACT 1934

It shall be unlawful for any person, directly or indirectly, by the use of any means or instrumentality of interstate commerce or of the mails, or of any facility of any national securities exchange

- To effect a short sale, or to use or employ any stop-loss order in connection with the purchase or sale, of any security registered on a national securities exchange, in contravention of such rules and regulations as the Commission may prescribe as necessary or appropriate in the public interest or for the protection of investors.

- Paragraph (1) of this subsection shall not apply to security futures products.
- To use or employ, in connection with the purchase or sale of any security registered on a national securities exchange or any security not so registered, or any securities-based swap agreement (as defined in section 206B of the Gramm-Leach-Bliley Act), any manipulative or deceptive device or contrivance in contravention of such rules and regulations as the Commission may prescribe as necessary or appropriate in the public interest or for the protection of investors.

Rules promulgated under subsection (b) that prohibit fraud, manipulation, or insider trading (but not rules imposing or specifying reporting or recordkeeping requirements, procedures, or standards as prophylactic measures against fraud, manipulation, or insider trading), and judicial precedents decided under subsection (b) and rules promulgated thereunder that prohibit fraud, manipulation, or insider trading, shall apply to security-based swap agreements (as defined in section 206B of the Gramm-Leach-Bliley Act) to the same extent as they apply to securities. Judicial precedents decided under section 17(a) of the Securities Act of 1933 and sections 9, 15, 16, 20, and 21A of this title, and judicial precedents decided under applicable rules promulgated under such sections, shall apply to security-based swap agreements (as defined in section 206B of the Gramm-Leach-Bliley Act) to the same extent as they apply to securities.

RULE 10B-5 EMPLOYMENT OF MANIPULATIVE AND DECEPTIVE DEVICES

It shall be unlawful for any person, directly or indirectly, by the use of any means or instrumentality of interstate commerce, or of the mails or of any facility of any national securities exchange,

- To employ any device, scheme, or artifice to defraud,
- To make any untrue statement of a material fact or to omit to state a material fact necessary in order to make the statements made, in the light of the circumstances under which they were made, not misleading, or
- To engage in any act, practice, or course of business which operates or would operate as a fraud or deceit upon any person, in connection with the purchase or sale of any security.

SECTION 4B OF THE COMMODITY EXCHANGE ACT (AS AMENDED)

(a) Unlawful Actions- It shall be unlawful—
(1) for any person, in or in connection with any order to make, or the making of, any contract of sale of any commodity in interstate commerce

or for future delivery that is made, or to be made, on or subject to the rules of a designated contract market, for or on behalf of any other person; or

(2) for any person, in or in connection with any order to make, or the making of, any contract of sale of any commodity for future delivery, or other agreement, contract, or transaction subject to paragraphs (1) and (2) of section 5a(g), that is made, or to be made, for or on behalf of, or with, any other person, other than on or subject to the rules of a designated contract market—

(A) to cheat or defraud or attempt to cheat or defraud such other person;

(B) willfully to make or cause to be made to such other person any false report or statement or willfully to enter or cause to be entered for such other person any false record;

(C) willfully to deceive or attempt to deceive such other person by any means whatsoever in regard to any order or contract or the disposition or execution of any order or contract, or in regard to any act of agency performed, with respect to any order or contract for or, in the case of paragraph (2), with such other person; or

(D)(i) to bucket an order if such order is either represented by such person as an order to be executed, or is required to be executed, on or subject to the rules of a designated contract market; or

(ii) to fill an order by offset against the order or orders of any other person, or willfully and knowingly and without the prior consent of such other person to become the buyer in respect to any selling order of such other person, or become the seller in respect to any buying order of such other person, if such order is either represented by such person as an order to be executed, or is required to be executed, on or subject to the rules of a designated contract market unless such order is executed in accordance with the rules of the designated contract market.

(b) Clarification- Subsection (a)(2) shall not obligate any person, in or in connection with a transaction in a contract of sale of a commodity for future delivery, or other agreement, contract or transaction subject to paragraphs (1) and (2) of section 5a(g), with another person, to disclose to such other person nonpublic information that may be material to the market price, rate or level of such commodity or transaction, except as necessary to make any statement made to such other person in or in connection with such transaction, not misleading in any material respect.

15. OPTIONS

I. CHARACTERISTICS OF OPTIONS

An option is categorized as a derivative because it derives its value from another underlying asset, instrument, or index. Options "transfer the right but not the obligation to buy or sell the underlying asset, instrument or index on or before the option's exercise date at a specified price (the strike price)."[1] A contract that gives a purchaser such a right is inherently an option even if it called something else. For example, if a consumer agrees to purchase a specified amount of home heating oil at a specified price in six months, that contract is a forward contract. If the contract allows the purchaser to buy oil after the six month period (at the same price) at the consumer's discretion, that part of the contract is an option contract. A transaction's name is not dispositive as to its economic reality. How a contract works economically is determinative of whether it is, indeed, an option or rather some other derivative.

---

1. TRADING AND CAPITAL-MARKETS ACTIVITIES MANUAL §4330.1 (Board of Governors of the Federal Reserve System).

Options generally have six characteristics.[2]

Underlying security. "An option is directly linked to and its value is derived from a specific security, asset, or reference rate."[3]

Strike price. It contains a strike price or an exercise price, which is the price for which an option contract permits its owner to buy or sell the underlying instrument.

Expiration date. Options contain an expiration date; they are wasting assets in that they are only good for a prespecified period of time and cannot be exercised after the expiration date.

Long or short position. Every option has a long and short position; the buyer is said to have a long option position while the seller is said to have a short option position.

American or European. An option purchaser may have the right to purchase the underlying asset at any time between the date the option is purchased and the date of the option expiration (American option) or the right to purchase the underlying asset only on a specified date (European option). Because of the greater flexibility in an American option, it typically will have a greater premium. The majority of listed options traded on American exchanges are American options.

Premium. Every option has a premium, which is the price paid for the option. There are two major factors that determine an option's premium, time value and intrinsic value. "The intrinsic value of an option is the difference between the actual value of [an underlying asset] and the exercise price of the option. Thus if ABC stock is trading at $50 per share, and the exercise price of the option is $40 per share, then the intrinsic value of the option is $10. The time value of an option 'refers to whatever value the option has in addition to its intrinsic value.' The time value 'reflects the expectation that, prior to expiration, the price of [the underlying asset] will increase by an amount that would enable an investor to sell or exercise the option at a profit.'"[4]

II. HOW OPTIONS WORK

Options are contracts which give the purchaser a right to buy or sell an underlying asset at a specified price at some time in the future. The important element of options is that the purchaser has the *right*, but not an *obligation*, to purchase or

---

2. *Id.*
3. *Id.*
4. Custom Chrome, Inc. v. Commissioner, 217 F.3d 1117, 1125 (9th Cir. 2000).

sell the underlying asset. This differs from other derivatives where both parties may be obligated to settle the transaction.

A. Calls and Puts

An option that confers the right to purchase an underlying asset at specified price, at or by a specific date is referred to as a *call option* and an option to sell an underlying asset is referred to as a *put option*. A call option is said to be in the money if when the price of the underlying asset exceeds the strike price. A put option is in the money when the price of the asset is less than the exercise price.

In every option contract there is an option writer, or person selling the option, and an option purchaser. It is important to distinguish between writing and purchasing an option because they have very different risks, profiles, and obligations. A call option gives the buyer (who pays a premium for this right) the right to purchase the underlying asset. The option contract will specify the strike price at which the asset can be purchased at or prior to the option's maturity date. Buyers may choose not to exercise this right if the market conditions are not favorable. A put option gives the buyer the right to sell an underlying asset at a specific strike price at or prior to the option's maturity date.

An option gives the purchaser the right to buy or sell an asset at a specified price. The price at which the option purchaser may exercise the right is referred to as the *strike price*. In return for the right, the option purchaser will pay to the option writer a fee which is referred to as a *premium*.

I. **Call Option** The value of a call option is directly correlated to the value of the underlying asset. As the share price of the underlying asset increases, so does the intrinsic value component of the option contract. The relationship of the price of the underlying item to the price of the option is called the option's "delta." When a call option is very far "out of the money"—that is to say, when the value of the underlying asset is far below the strike price of the option—the relationship of asset price movement to option price movement may be de minimus.

The potential profitability of a call option is unlimited because, in theory, the value of the underlying asset can increase infinitely. While a call option has infinite potential gain, the maximum amount a purchaser of a call option can lose is the premium paid for the option. An option writer is obligated to deliver the underlying asset when the option purchaser exercises the option. Just as an

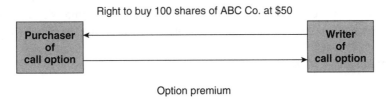

Right to buy 100 shares of ABC Co. at $50

| Purchaser of call option | Writer of call option |

Option premium

FIGURE 15.1

option purchaser has unlimited potential gain, the option writer has exposure to unlimited loss. If the share price rises to $10,000 for example, the option writer who has committed to selling the item for $100 would still be required to deliver the shares. In return for writing the option, the option seller receives a premium, similar in concept to an insurance premium, in which the option seller is analogous to an insurance underwriter. The price of the option premium is dependent on components of the Black-Scholes model and on market value.

2. Put Option A put option gives the option purchaser the right to sell an asset at a specified price at some point in time. With regard to a put option, the value of the option has an inverse relationship to the value of the underlying asset. While the value of call option can increase infinitely, the value of a put option is limited because the share price can only fall to zero.

Put options obligate the option writer to sell to the purchaser the underlying asset at the agreed upon price. Unlike the call option, the put option has limited exposure because the underlying asset cannot go below zero in value.

CASE STUDY: *LEVY V. BESSEMER TRUST*

Levy v. Bessemer Trust Company[5] demonstrates the structure of simple options, option collar strategies, and the risks involved in adequately failing to utilize the options market.

FACTS

David Levy signed an investment management agreement and opened an investment management account with Bessemer Trust (BTC). Levy was enticed to enter into this arrangement because of BTC's representations to him that they were experts in providing financial services and investment advice to high net worth individuals. Levy had received 257,000 shares of Corning stock that could not be sold for one year. At the time that Levy received the shares the Corning stock was at 31 3/8 per share and was worth approximately $8 million. BTC agreed to monitor and manage the shares and to notify him as to any action that should be taken with regard to the shares. Levy specifically informed BTC that he wanted to ensure that the shares were protected against possible downward movement in the price of the shares during the period during which he was prohibited from selling the shares. In response, BTC notified Levy that there was no possible way to obtain immediate protection against downward price movement in light of the restrictive nature of the shares.

---

5. 1997 U.S. Dist. LEXIS 11056 (S.D.N.Y. 1997).

Levy was subsequently advised by a broker at Paine Webber that there were various hedging strategies available to persons who held restrictive shares of a company that could afford downward price protection. Levy specifically learned that he could protect the shares by entering into a transaction known in the industry as a "European Options Collar." In a European Options Collar transaction, Levy's shares could be protected by simultaneously purchasing a European put option and selling a European call option that could only be exercised on a certain date after the end of the period during which Levy was prohibited from selling his shares. This would hedge his risk, because the purchase of the European put option would guarantee a floor price for the shares on the day of the exercise and the sale of the European call option would set a ceiling on the price of the shares that would exceed the current market price. The call option would also produce income to cover the purchase price of the put option.

Upon learning of this transaction, Levy called BTC and informed them of this transaction. BTC replied by saying that they had never heard of this transaction. Levy then closed his account with BTC and purchased the abovementioned European Option Collar through Merrill Lynch. At the time that Levy first directed BTC to protect his shares against downward price movement, Corning shares had risen in excess of $37 per share. At that time, Levy learned that he could have entered into a European Options Collar by purchasing a European put option at $33.33 and simultaneously selling a European call option at $44. This would have insured that the value of the shares would never have been less than $33.33 per share. At the time that Levy arranged a European options collar through Merrill Lynch, the price of Corning shares had declined to 27 3/4 from its previous high of 37 3/8. Levy was able to hedge his shares with a downside protection of $24.75 with a possible upside value of $31.90. With this arrangement, the maximum possible value of the shares was now less than the floor on their value would have been had BTC arranged this transaction when Levy had first inquired about it.

THEORIES OF LIABILITY IN *LEVY*

Levy filed a lawsuit against BTC claiming negligence, gross negligence, breach of a fiduciary duty, negligent misrepresentation, breach of duty to supervise, breach of contract, and fraud. The court found that all of these claims had merit except the breach of contract claim.

Negligence. The court found that there were sufficient allegations to establish proximate cause for the damages that Levy sustained in the form of a decreased maximum share value. The court also found that BTC's unawareness regarding a strategy of which Merrill Lynch was aware and about which Levy repeatedly inquired may be sufficient to amount to recklessness.

Negligent misrepresentation. Levy claimed that BTC's misrepresentation regarding its expertise in asset management and investment advice, as well as its misrepresentation that no mechanism existed to protect the shares against downward price movement, induced him to keep his account with BTC. The court found merit in Levy's claim that this misrepresentation caused him to forego purchasing a European Collar Option at a time when the value of his Corning shares was higher than it was when he ultimately purchased the option, causing a loss in the value of the shares due to BTC's misrepresentation.

Breach of fiduciary duty. The court found (1) that BTC did have a fiduciary duty to Levy, (2) that despite repeated inquiries, BTC gave Levy erroneous investment information in breach of that fiduciary duty, (3) that BTC made misrepresentations to induce Levy to maintain his account with BTC and forego other investment advisors, and (4) that if BTC had given Levy the correct information when he first inquired about downside protection of his Corning shares, he would have taken appropriate action which would have increased the value of his shares.

Breach of duty to supervise. The court found that Levy had sufficiently alleged that BTC failed to supervise the account and maintain a proper system of supervision and control to prevent the account representative from giving erroneous advice. This erroneous advice caused Levy to (1) forego investment options that he expressly desired at a time when such an option would have increased the value of his shares and (2) belatedly take advantage of the European Option Collar which resulted in a decrease in the value of the shares.

Breach of contract. The court found that Levy failed to allege this claim because he failed to specify whether the representations that BTC made were part of a contract, what the terms of the agreement were, and which provisions were breached.

Fraud. The court found that the fraud claim had merit in that Levy had alleged that BTC knowingly made false statements about its services and expertise to induce Levy to retain BTC and that Levy relied upon these misrepresentations in retaining BTC.

III. THE BLACK-SCHOLES MODEL AND OPTION PRICING

The Black-Scholes model was developed in 1973 by Fisher Black, Robert Merton, and Myron Scholes as a relatively simple method for traders, portfolio managers, and arbitrageurs to determine the theoretical value of an option.[6] Prior to the Black-Scholes model, there was no standard method for pricing options.

---

6. Fischer Black and Myron Scholes. *The Pricing of Options and Corporate Liabilities,* 81 J. POL. ECON. 637 (1973).

The development of this model paved the way for the growth of the derivative market. The fact that the Black-Scholes model can quantify risk makes it an invaluable resource in determining the value of an option for those wishing to use an option for either hedging or speculative purposes.

A. Assumptions

The significance of the Black-Scholes model is that it can take information regarding an option, use it to calculate the volatility of an option, and, based upon the results of this calculation, determine what the option is worth. In this model the following assumptions are made: "(1) that the variance of return on the common stock is constant over the life of the option contract and known by market participants; (2) that the short term interest rate is known and constant throughout the life of the contract and that this rate is the borrowing and lending rate for market participants; (3) that the option holder is completely protected against distributions that affect the price of the common stock; and (4) that over a finite time interval, the returns on a common stock are normally distributed. Given these assumptions, the value of an option contract is only a function of the common stock price and time."[7] With these assumptions, "a model was established for determining the equilibrium value of an option."[8]

B. Required Data

The mathematical formula developed by Black, Merton, and Scholes is fairly simple in that it requires five pieces of information:

(1) The strike price;
(2) the amount of time remaining to expiration of the option;
(3) the current price of the underlying asset;
(4) the risk-free interest rate; and
(5) the volatility.

Items 1 through 4 are easily observed and can be obtained from a wide variety of market vendors. Item 5, the option volatility, requires an estimation of the future volatility of the underlying asset. Of course, the future volatility of an underlying asset can never be known for certain. This is one of the limitations of the Black-Scholes' equation; it assumes that future volatility is known.

C. Volatility

1. **Types of Volatility** When referring to options, there are four types of volatility that are most commonly discussed: future volatility (discussed above),

---

7. Fischer Black and Myron Scholes, *The Valuation of Option Contracts and a Test of Market Efficiency*, 27 J. FINANCE 399, 400 (May 1972).
    8. *Id.* at 416.

historical volatility, forecast volatility, and implied volatility.[9] Historical volatility measures how the price of the underlying asset has moved in the past. For example, ABC Co. stock is trading at $100. A look at the historical pricing over the past year reveals that the stock price has traded as low as $80 and as high as $120. This indicates that the historical volatility of ABC Co. is 20%. The forecast volatility is what is perceived to be the volatility, in the future, based on the historical volatility and other market factors. Finally, there is the implied volatility. This is the volatility that is being perceived in the market, which is reflected in the selling price of the option.

The impact of volatility on the value of an option as quantified by the Black-Scholes model will depend in part upon the intrinsic value of the option. The intrinsic value of an option will depend upon the value of the option versus the current value of its underlying asset. For example, a $50.00 call option will have an intrinsic value of $10.00 when the underlying stock is trading at $60.00. It stands to reason that the greater the intrinsic value the lower the effects on the Black-Scholes model; as intrinsic value increases and other factors such as the closeness in time to the option's expiration date are taken into account, the likelihood decreases that the option will fall out of the money barring significant volatility. This brings the discussion full circle by demonstrating the need for a determination of volatility, as well as why the Black-Scholes model is a groundbreaking formula for ascertaining the value of an option.

The element of volatility captured by the Black-Scholes model, when factored into the value of an option, makes the valuation more reliable. This has resulted in significant growth in the use of options since the introduction of the model. Other option models have arisen since the Black-Scholes model came on the scene in 1973, but it remains the foundation for the other models that have followed. The Black-Scholes model has been one of the major reasons for the proliferation of option and derivatives trading during the last thirty years.

2. Measures of Volatility "Given the complexity of the market risk arising from options, and the different models of option valuation, a set of terms has evolved in the market and in academic literature that now serves as common language for discussing options risk."[10]

Delta measures the rate of change in the option price relative to the change in the price of the underlying asset,[11] and is an output of the Black-Scholes model described earlier. Delta is measured between 0 and 1.00; however, when referring to delta, the market expresses delta without a decimal point (e.g., delta of 50). If an option has a delta of zero, that means that a movement in the price of the underlying asset will have very little impact on the price of the option. An option with a delta of 100 will move up or down in concert with the movement

---

9. *See* SHELDON NATENBERG, OPTION VOLATILITY & PRICING, 68–73 (1994).

10. TRADING AND CAPITAL-MARKETS ACTIVITIES MANUAL, §4330.1.

11. *Id.*

in the price of the underlying asset. For each one-point move in the underlying asset, the option price will also move one dollar in the same direction.

Gamma measures the sensitivity of the delta to movements in the asset price.[12] If an option has a gamma of five, that means that for each one point movement in the underlying asset, the delta will move five points.[13] Gamma is an important tool for managing risk. A large gamma position means that the trader is exposed to a high degree of risk, because the trader's directional risk can rapidly shift. A low gamma position means that the trader will be less exposed to risk, because the delta will be less sensitive to changes in the market. Understanding the gamma will also help determine the rate at which a trader would need to adjust his position in order to maintain a delta neutral position.

Theta measures the option's value relative to change in the time left until expiration.[14] As time to expiration declines, so does the option value. Options have what is referred to as intrinsic value and time value.[15]

Intrinsic value = Share price—Exercise price

Time value = Call option price—Intrinsic value

As the option gets closer to expiration, the time value of the option will decrease.

Vega measures the sensitivity of the option value to changes in the market's expectations for the volatility of the underlying instrument (the implied volatility).[16] As discussed earlier, the value of an option increases as the volatility increases.

Rho measures the sensitivity of the option price relative to changes in the short-term interest rate.[17]

An estimation of the delta of an instrument can be used to determine the appropriate hedge ratio for an unhedged position in that instrument. The existence of gamma risk means that the use of delta hedging[18] techniques is less effective against large changes in the price of the underlying instrument. "While a delta-hedged short position is protected against small changes in the price of the underlying asset, large price changes in either direction will produce losses (though of a smaller magnitude than would have occurred had the price moved against a naked written option)."[19]

---

12. *Id.*

13. Natenberg, *supra,* at 105.

14. TRADING AND CAPITAL-MARKETS ACTIVITIES MANUAL, §4330.1.

15. *See generally* GUY COHEN, OPTIONS MADE EASY, 164–167, 2005.

16. TRADING AND CAPITAL-MARKETS ACTIVITIES MANUAL §4330.1.

17. *Id.*

18. *See infra* Section IV.

19. TRADING AND CAPITAL-MARKETS ACTIVITIES MANUAL §4330.1.

D. Authority of Black-Scholes Model

Courts consider the Black-Scholes model to be an authoritative measure of proof of the value of options and have allowed it as evidence in various cases as a model accepted by modern finance theory for the valuation of options. In *Mathias v. Jacobs*, [20] the court accepted the Black-Scholes model as evidence of the value of the options at issue, reiterating that this model is accepted by modern finance as a method for valuing options and describing the essential components of the model: "(1) the price on the date of the valuation; (2) the exercise price at which the option holder can purchase the stock; (3) the amount of time over which the option will be valid and outstanding; (4) the volatility of the underlying stock; and (5) the risk-free rate of interest rates at the time the option is being valued."[21] In *Seinfeld v. Bartz*,[22] the court also accepted the Black-Scholes model as evidence of the value of the options at issue, calling the Black-Scholes model "reliable" for this purpose and describing this model as one which, in order to determine the value an option, "relies on values such as the volatility of the underlying stock, the risk free rate of interest, the expiration date of the option, the dividends on the underlying stock, the exercise price of the option, and the market price of the underlying stock."[23] As demonstrated by these two examples, the courts consider the Black-Scholes model to be an essential piece of evidence in helping the court determine the value of options.

IV. DELTA HEDGING

Delta hedging refers to the process of minimizing market exposure of a position or a portfolio. A delta neutral hedge refers to having a position that has an unbiased view or that is not exposed to fluctuations in the market in the short term. If someone has positive delta, that means he or she is taking the position that the market will increase. If someone has negative delta, it means he or she is taking the position that the market will decrease.

The case of *Caiola v. Citibank*[24] demonstrates how delta hedging is used to manage risk. Louis Caiola regularly traded millions of shares and options on Philip Morris. Because of the size of his transactions, Citibank recommended that Caiola expose himself to Phillip Morris risk using over-the-counter and synthetic transactions to recreate the positions he would hold if he acquired the positions on the exchange. In this way, the process of acquiring a position would not affect the exchange prices of the stocks and options.

---

20. 238 F. Supp. 2d 556 (S.D.N.Y. 2004).
21. *Id.* at 574 n 12.
22. 322 F.3d 693 (9th Cir. 2003).
23. *Id.* at 696.
24. 295 F. 3d 312 (2nd. Cir. 2002)

A synthetic transaction is typically a contractual agreement between two counterparties, usually an investor and a bank, that seeks to economically replicate the ownership and physical trading of shares and options. The counterparties establish synthetic positions in shares or options, the values of which are pegged to the market prices of the related physical shares or options. The aggregate market values of the shares or options that underlie the synthetic trades are referred to as "notional" values and are treated as interest-bearing loans to the investor. As Citibank explained to Caiola, synthetic trading offers significant advantages to investors who heavily concentrated on large positions of a single stock by reducing the risks associated with large-volume trading. Synthetic trading alleviates the necessity of posting large amounts of margin capital and ensures that positions can be established and unwound quickly. Synthetic trading also offers a solution to the "footprint" problem by permitting the purchase of large volumes of options in stocks without affecting their price.[25]

Caiola agreed to engage in synthetic trading; it was understood that Citibank would hedge its market risk in being the counterparty to his transactions by engaging in delta hedging. Delta hedging required Citibank to calculate its net exposure to Phillip Morris shares based on its contra position to Caiola and then purchase or sell a position on an exchange that would neutralize that risk. For example, if Citibank sold an over-the-counter call option on 100 shares of Phillip Morris stock to Caiola and that option had a delta of 10 (i.e., for every dollar move in the stock the option would fluctuate in value by 10 cents) Citibank would buy 10 shares of Citibank stock on the exchange in order to hedge its position. While the transaction in the option would not be recorded on the exchange, the smaller hedge would be. As the delta of the option changed, Citibank would sell shares of Phillip Morris or add to its position. Because the delta of a position is constantly changing, a delta hedge is also refereed to as "dynamic hedge."

At some point, however, contrary to its representations and unbeknownst to Caiola, Citibank secretly stopped delta hedging and transformed Caiola's synthetic portfolio into a physical one by executing massive trades in the physical markets that mirrored Caiola's synthetic transactions. These transactions, Caiola alleged, exposed him to the risks that synthetic trading was intended to avoid. Caiola brought federal securities fraud and state law claims against Citibank arising from extensive physical and synthetic investments. The District Court dismissed Caiola's complaint, but the Second Circuit reversed, holding that Caiola sufficiently alleged both purchases and sales of securities and material misrepresentations for purposes of Rule 10b-5.

A. Contracts that are Economically Options

A transaction or series of interconnected transactions may economically be options even if not described as such. The economic reality of a transaction, not

---

25. *Id.* at 315–316.

its name, determines whether a transaction is an option. The transaction at the heart of *Korea Life Insurance Co. v. Morgan Guaranty Trust*[26] is illustrative of this point. In *Korea Life,* a number of contracts were entered into which in aggregate comprised the economics of an option, in particular, a put option on the Thai baht currency. This case involved contracts in foreign currencies with no specific reference to options.

Morgan Guaranty, a commercial bank, set up a special purpose entity, Frome Company Limited, which then issued one year notes to European investors raising $25 million. These notes were guaranteed by Morgan, which promised the investors repayment with interest at the London Interbank Offered Rate (LIBOR). Frome then gave this $25 million to Morning Glory, a limited liability investment company created by Korea Life as its special purpose entity specifically to engage in the transactions at issue, in exchange for 2.5 million of Morning Glory's common shares. Morning Glory then purchased a one-year certificate of deposit issued by Korea Exchange Bank (KEB), maturing in one year and paying interest at 6.05%, and paid a fee of $70,000 to KEB. One year later, at maturity, Morning Glory was entitled to receive $26,512,500 in principal and interest on the certificate of deposit issued by KEB, and obligated to redeem its shares that it had issued to Frome by paying Morgan Guaranty either (a) $24,187,500, which is 96.75% of the $25 million Frome had contributed, or (b) depending upon the conditions relating to the rise and fall of the Thai baht in relation to the Japanese yen, they agreed to discount the $25 million, plus or minus the product of two inter-related formulae quantifying those currency relationships.

If the yen and the baht both depreciated, Morning Glory would be obligated to pay a "Baht Payment Amount" to KEB, and KEB would be obligated to pay the same amount to Morgan. At the same time, Morgan would be obligated to pay KEB and KEB to pay Morning Glory a "Yen Payment Amount" serving as a hedge to Morning Glory's risks. Thus, if the baht and the yen both depreciated at the historical rate of five-to-one, Morning Glory would owe money to KEB, and KEB to Morgan, but any amount owed would be cancelled out by the amount Morgan owed to KEB, and KEB to Morning Glory. If the yen were to appreciate, no payment obligation would be due from either party to the other, but if the baht were to appreciate, Morgan would have to pay KEB and KEB in turn would have to pay Morning Glory an amount proportional to the baht's appreciation. There would be no hedge if the baht depreciated and the yen remained stable against the dollar or appreciated. Despite this, Morning Glory's obligation to pay KEB and KEB's obligation to pay Morgan was absolute. In order to guard against the contingency that the yen remained stable or appreciated while the baht depreciated,

---

26. 269 F. Supp. 2d 424 (S.D.N.Y. 2003).

the Morning Glory/KEB Agreement gave Morning Glory the right to demand that its position be unwound upon two days written notice.

The transaction and agreements involving the Thai baht are the economic equivalent of Morgan Stanley buying a put option from Korea Life. The economic reality of this transaction is hidden in a convoluted series of transactions. The transaction was set up so that Korea Life sold to Morgan a put option through special purpose entities. Morning Glory/Korea Life would receive a $1.4 million premium (the difference between the amounts that Morning Glory would receive at maturity, $26,512,500, minus the $24,187,500 that they would have to pay to Morgan if the ratio of the baht to the yen stayed within the historical 5 to 1 ratio). In return they would accept the risk that if the baht did not stay within its historical ratio norms with the yen they could end up paying, based upon the formulae listed above, up to five times the change in the ratio from the historical norm, which in this case could be up to $125 million.

These transactions reflect the elements of a put option/currency swap. Korea Life accepted a premium and assumed the downside risk of the change in price of an underlying asset based upon an agreed to formula, which in this case was the Thai baht in relation to its historical ratio to the Japanese yen.

Although the transactions described in the case are not described as options, they economically function as options. Korea Life had unlimited exposure when the Thai baht went down in value relative to the yen, and collected a fee for entering into the transaction by collecting interest on $25,000,000 using Frome's capital. Since the unlimited upside exposure inured to Morgan's benefit, the transactions are structurally similar to Morgan buying a put option from Korea Life through various special purpose entities.

B. OTC vs. Exchange-Traded Options

Options can be traded over-the-counter (OTC) or on organized exchanges. An over-the-counter option is a bilateral option contract that is entered into by two parties away from an exchange. The terms such as strike, settlement date, and quantity of underlier are subject to negotiation by the counterparties. In an OTC option, the counterparties deal directly with each other, and the option writer has an obligation to deliver the underlying asset directly to the option's purchaser. In addition to option risk, counterparties to an OTC option are taking on counterparty credit risk, which refers to the ability of the counterparty to meet its obligations under the option contract.

With an exchange traded option, terms such as the strike price and the expiration date are specified by the exchange on which the option is trading. Option exchanges provide liquidity to the marketplace by creating a location where buyers and sellers can come to purchase standardized products that do not require negotiating terms.

C. Regulation of Options

Options that are traded on an organized exchange are regulated by the Commodity Futures Trading Commission (CFTC)[27] and the Securities and Exchange Commission (SEC).[28] Although both of these federal agencies had rights to a claim of jurisdiction over the regulation of options, disputes over these claims between these agencies increased as the number of options and the volume of trades involving options increased. This tension resulted in a number of resolutions to help clearly define the role of each agency in the regulation of options.[29] This generally led to the CFTC regulation of options on futures not involving securities, while the regulation of options that involved securities was left to the SEC. The Commodity Futures Modernization Act of 2000 (CFMA) drew new jurisdictional lines, redefined certain terms and altered the levels of regulation of futures options. This has resulted in a three-tiered layer of regulation.[30] In addition, recent court cases have affirmed the CFTC's jurisdiction over options involving foreign currencies,[31] off-exchange foreign currency transactions,[32] and transactions involving contracts of sale of a commodity for future delivery.[33]

Although the CFMA has further clarified the role of the CFTC and the SEC in the regulation of options, this is not likely to be the last word on this issue in light of the fact that the option market will continue to grow in complexity and volume in the future.

V. OPTION STRATEGIES

Options can be employed with stocks and other options to create various option strategies.

A. Synthetic Call

A synthetic call is created when a trader buys an underlying stock and buys a put as well. The risk profile of a synthetic call is very similar to that of a straight call. The trader is long in the stock and at the same time, through purchase of a put, has hedged the position against a drop in the share price.

B. Covered Call

A covered-call strategy is one where the trader buys the underlying stock and sells a call. The writer of an option (i.e., the seller of a call), has not a choice but rather an obligation to deliver the shares at the agreed upon price.

---

27. *See* Chapter 4, Sec. II.A., *supra*.
28. *See* Chapter 4, Sec. I.A., *supra*.
29. *See* Chapter 4, Sec. II.B., *supra*.
30. *See* Chapter 4, Sec. II.C., *supra*.
31. CFTC v. Premium Income Corporation, 2007 U.S. Dist. Lexis 11430.
32. CFTC v. Madison FOREX International, LLC, 2006 U.S. Dist. Lexis 96294.
33. CFTC v. Matthew Reed, 481 F. Supp. 2d 1190 (2007).

C. Collar

A collar is an option strategy where a trader buys the stock, buys a put, and sells a call. In this strategy the profit range has been locked in. If the share price goes above the strike price of the call, the option will be exercised. If the share price goes below the strike price of the put, the put will be exercised. If the put is sold the loss is limited to the amount paid for the put less the premium received for the call.

There are many option strategies that can be combined in sophisticated and complex ways to create a myriad of other derivative instruments. As demonstrated in the Korea Life case, the first step in understanding a particular transaction is to identify who bears the risk and what are the limitations on that risk. Within that analysis will be a determination of the economic realities and consequence of the agreement at hand. Whether structured within swap agreements or as part of debt securities, the basic components of the option can be analyzed and priced applying models such as the Black-Scholes formula.

16. STRUCTURES

I. CREATION OF STRUCTURES

As discussed in the previous chapter, options can be used to enhance yield by taking on specific limited or uncapped risk. They can also be structured within other securities. The appeal of the reward of entering into a particular derivatives transaction may provide incentives to a purchaser to participate in a transaction that might not have been appealing without the derivative feature. For example, if a bond obligation includes a provision allowing the issuer to repurchase the bond on or by a date certain, at a fixed price, it has built into its structure a "call option." The issuer has purchased the option from the investor and in return pays a premium in the form of a higher interest rate. The issuer may not have issued the security without the flexibility provided by the option, and the investor may not have purchased the bond without the added premium paid to him for selling the option. By incorporating derivative components into debt instruments, issuers can access capital from investors who might have specific financial goals that go beyond a credit-related yield or a defined and fixed return on capital.

Debt instruments can be structured so that interest to investors is contingent on some variable other than the credit of the issuer and the agreed upon interest rate. For example, a mortgage-backed bond is an obligation that has been linked to the pledge of specific mortgages as collateral; interest is paid based on the payment stream derived from underlying mortgages. Similarly, a note might be structured so interest payments are linked to the increasing value of an underlying asset or index. In that such a structure effects the payment obligation of the issuer, it has within it an embedded derivative. Structured notes are specifically tailored securities that contain both elements of debt instruments and derivative instruments.[1] They are often referred to as "hybrid" securities. Most structured

---

1. KAREN MCCANN AND JOSEPH CILIA, STRUCTURED NOTES, at 2, (Federal Reserve Bank of Chicago, Financial Markets Unit, November 1994).

notes contain "embedded options." These options can be embedded to enhance the note's yield, or to decrease the cost of funding for the issuer.[2]

Structured notes provide an efficient means of shifting risk. By isolating and assuming specific risks, market participants that ordinarily could not provide an investment vehicle to meet the needs of an investor or provide capital for a company might be able to make an investment when that investment contains built-in derivative components.

Structured notes allow the parties to hedge or speculate in specifically identifiable risks, tailored to meet the particular needs of the parties involved. Because these instruments contain derivative components, it may be difficult to price these securities. The embedding of a derivative into a structured note requires a Black-Scholes[3] analysis to determine appropriate pricing. For example, if a structured note pays interest contingent on an index such as LIBOR remaining in a particular range, the note might be deconstructed into its component parts: that is, the debt obligation and the option collar[4] on LIBOR inherently contained in the range contingency of the issuer's obligation.

While structured note may have a unique market risk resulting from its derivative components, the attendant credit risk remain unchanged. Credit risk is a measure of the issuer's ability to meet its obligations under the terms of the note. If, for example, a structured note is issued by a triple A rated ("AAA") issuer (e.g., a government sponsored entity such as Fannie Mae or Freddie Mac), the ability of the issuer to pay under the terms of its obligation may be of minimal concern. However, the market risk of the derivative component of the issue is not factored into the rating of the underlying security. Therefore, the investor must apprehend the market risk of the structure in addition to the credit risk of the issuer.[5]

II. HISTORICAL EXAMPLE: ERLANGER "COTTON" BONDS

While structured notes and their pricing may seem like the purview of rocket scientist and financial innovators, they have actually been around for quite some time. For examples, during the Civil War, the Confederate States of America (hereinafter, the "Confederacy" or "South"), desperately in need of financing to compete effectively with the Union's well-financed military, needed a creative financial solution to raise money. The southern states, unlike their brethren in

---

2. *Id.*
3. *See* Chapter 15, Sec. III, *supra.*
4. *See* Chapter 15, Sec. V.C., *supra.*
5. McCann and Cilia, *supra* note 1, at 2.

the North, lacked an industrial economy. Their only true asset was cotton, and that asset became increasingly difficult to convert into currency, because the South refused to sell it to the North and southern ports were faced with a naval blockade limiting the South's ability to trade with Europe. To address this difficulty, the Confederacy dispatched James Slidell to France to negotiate a loan with European investors.[6]

The European investors were extremely wary about investing money in the Confederacy for multiple reasons. First, the South had no track record as a government and therefore no credit history of repaying debt. In fact, their elected president "openly advocated the repudiation of state debts while a member of the U.S. Senate."[7] The current Civil War placed an enormous risk of default on the bonds. If the Confederacy were to lose the war, as many expected, there would be little chance the bonds would be honored by the Union. The Confederacy also faced enormous inflation on its currency, creating a large currency risk, as well as an inconsistent revenue stream.[8] These risks and uncertainties, as well as others, created a massive credit risk premium to secure financing. Normally this massive risk premium would be prohibitive for (widespread) debt financing, but the South had one extremely valuable asset: cotton. As a result of the war, the price of cotton skyrocketed.

The bankers of the time used cotton to create a structured note that allowed the South to find financing. The bankers created a specifically tailored note for European investors that consisted of a twenty-year security that paid seven percent interest annually (payable semiannually).[9] To eliminate currency exposure, the interest and principal on the note were payable in British sterling or French francs.[10] In order to provide value to the bond, and thus reduce the interest rate paid by the South, the note was convertible into cotton on demand for six pence per pound. At the time, cotton was selling for 24 pence in Liverpool, England, an amount 400 percent higher than the convertible rate. This was the equivalent of the Confederacy selling a deep "in-the-money" call (derivative) to purchase cotton.[11] The risk premium was born by the

---

6. WEIDENMIER, MARC, COMRADES IN BONDS: THE SUBSIDIZED SALE OF CONFEDERATE WAR DEBT TO BRITISH LEADERS, at 5, (Claremont McKenna College, February 2003), http://www.stanford.edu/group/sshi/Conferences/2002-2003/Debt2003/weidenmier.pdf.

7. *Id.* at 4.

8. Barto Arnold *et al.*, *The Erlanger Cotton Loan*, The Denbigh Project, http://nautarch.tamu.edu/projects/denbigh/erlanger.htm.

9. *See* Weidenmier, *supra* note 6, at 5.

10. *Id.*

11. The catch was that the cotton would be delivered in the Confederacy, and thus one would have to run the blockade to retrieve the cotton, or wait until the war was over, when the bond would be redeemable for cotton for six months following the war. However,

discounted option premium built into the note. Below is an illustration of this transaction:

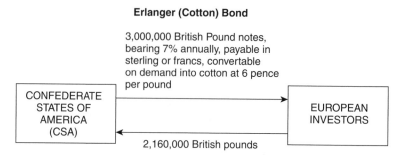

Erlanger (Cotton) Bond

3,000,000 British Pound notes, bearing 7% annually, payable in sterling or francs, convertable on demand into cotton at 6 pence per pound

CONFEDERATE STATES OF AMERICA (CSA)

EUROPEAN INVESTORS

2,160,000 British pounds

FIGURE 16.1

While the interest rate on the bond appeared to be reasonable for the Confederacy, a deeper look into this structured note will illustrate why the effective obligations of the Confederacy were far greater than a seven percent yield would suggest. First, the conversion of the note into cotton at six pence per pound represented a deep "in-the-money" call option sold by the Confederacy to the European investors. Secondly, the note contained a sinking-fund provision, requiring the Confederacy to pay back a portion of the principal on the note. This was a benefit that added value to the investors. Third, the note contained a currency swap feature that transferred all of the currency risk to the Confederacy. Lastly, the notes were sold at a discount of 90 percent of face value.[12]

Overall, the effective interest rate the Confederacy was paying to its European note holders was much higher than the seven percent on the face of the note. The seven percent, as well as the discounted face value of the notes, represented the netted rate after factoring the above derivatives and features against the default risk (which could not be shifted).[13] This debt instrument was specifically tailored through the use of derivatives to enable this structured note to satisfy the goals of both sides. In this example, the market risk of cotton price fluctuation served as a support to the Confederacy's financial obligations. The credit risk of the South being unable to meet its obligations, however, was a separate and distinct consideration from the financial implications of the attendant transaction but was compensated for with a deeply discounted premium paid by investors for the built-in cotton option.

---

this assumed a risk that the Confederacy would remain intact, or that the Union would honor the Confederacy's debts if peace were reached.

12. Barto, *supra* note 8.

13. The default risk includes political risk. In addition, the Confederacy believed that if enough European investors purchased Confederacy debt, it would cause them to pressure their governments in favor of the Confederacy. This may have affected the price of the bonds as well.

III. MODERN EXAMPLE: THE ORANGE COUNTY STRUCTURED NOTE

While the Confederate-structured notes used embedded options to affect the yield of notes issued by a party with high credit risk, structured notes today are often used to enhance the yield of notes with little or no credit risk. However, while the credit risk of these triple A rated ("AAA") entities is extremely low, other risks, such as interest rate risk, market risk, and liquidity risk are often unsuspectingly high.[14]

Beginning in 1991, low interest rates encouraged the Treasurer of Orange County, California, to seek high-yielding securities. The Treasurer used reverse repurchase transactions ("repos")[15] to take advantage of the low interest rates and to add extreme leverage to the portfolio, and then used the proceeds from these repo transactions to purchase structured notes from government-sponsored entities such as the Federal National Mortgage Association ("Fannie Mae"), which contained high yields due to their structure with little or no credit risk.[16] "The repo market allows investors to finance short-term positions."[17] The Federal Reserve's *Trading and Capital-Markets Activities Manual* describes repos as follows:

> A repurchase agreement (repo) involves the sale of a security to a counter-party with an agreement to repurchase it at a fixed price on an established future date. At initiation of the transaction, the buyer pays the principal amount to the seller, and the security is transferred to the possession of the buyer. At expiration of the repo, the principal amount is returned to the initial buyer (or lender) and possession of the security reverts to the initial seller (or borrower). Importantly, the security serves as collateral against the obligation of the borrower and does not actually become the property of the lender. . . .
>
> In a repurchase agreement, a bank borrows funds when it "sells" the security and commits to "repurchase" it in the future. In a reverse repurchase agreement, the bank lends funds when it "buys" the security and commits to "resell" it in the future. A reverse repo is sometimes termed a resale agreement or a security purchased under agreement to resell (SPAR). The terms "repo" and "reverse repo" thus describe the same transaction, but from the perspective of each counterparty.[18]

An examination of the securities purchased by Orange County and how they used repos to fund these transactions illustrates how these complex financial

---

14. McCann and Cilia, *supra* note 1, at 2.

15. *See* Chapter 8, Sec. III.A.1, for a discussion of repos.

16. Norris, Floyd, *Market Place; In Orange County, Strategies Sour*, THE NEW YORK TIMES, (Dec. 5, 1994), http://query.nytimes.com/gst/fullpage.html?res=9506E3DC1739F936A3 5751C1A962958260.

17. *See* TRADING AND CAPITAL-MARKETS ACTIVITIES MANUAL §4215.1 at page 2.

18. *Id.* at §4015.1.

instruments are structured and highlights the associated risks of these types of instruments.[19]

Orange County purchased a structure known as an inverse interest only (I/O) floater.[20] Under this structure, the yield of the note will vary inversely with changes in the reference rate. The purchaser of an inverse floating note is taking a position that interest rates will remain low or move lower.[21] The purchaser of this instrument uses this instrument to speculate on the direction interest rates are heading by earning a higher rate of interest as long as interest rates stay low.

Orange County purchased inverse I/O floaters and was thereby speculating on interest rates remaining low. Orange County leveraged its positions using reverse repo transactions by "selling" the securities on a short-term basis with a promise to repurchase them and using the proceeds to purchase more securities.[22] Leveraging the portfolio in this way greatly increased the stakes for this structured note position and compounded the problem as interest rates increased.[23]

The inverse I/O floater bonds structured for Orange County paid a 7 percent annualized interest rate for the first three months, and then paid a rate of 10 percent minus the three-month LIBOR rate.[24] There was a step-up feature in the note that kicked in two years later, which raised the formula to 11.25 percent minus LIBOR.[25] While this step-up appeared to benefit Orange County, Fannie Mae retained a call option which allowed them to repurchase the notes at par value upon step-up. This way, if Fannie Mae thought it was paying too high a rate, it could buy the notes back. Below is an illustration of this transaction:

Inverse I/O Floating-Rate Note (5-year note)

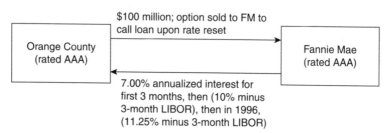

FIGURE 16.2

---

19. *See* Chapter 8, Section III.A.2., for further discussion of this case.

20. *See* TRADING AND CAPITAL-MARKETS ACTIVITIES MANUAL §4040.1.

21. *Id.*

22. A reverse repo is a transaction in which a counterparty buys a security and commits to resell it in the future. *See* TRADING AND CAPITAL-MARKETS ACTIVITIES MANUAL §4015.1.

23. *See* Norris, *supra* note 18.

24. *Id.*

25. *Id.*

When Orange County purchased these notes, the three-month LIBOR and three month treasury notes were both yielding around 3.25 percent.[26] As a result, a yield of 7 percent for Orange County was a superior yield at that time, especially considering the notes came from a GSE that had an AAA credit rating. If the formula kicked in immediately, the notes would have yielded 6.75 percent, which still would have been a superior rate. Orange County was funding these purchases by rolling over reverse repo transactions every three to six months, which initially allowed them to borrow at about 3.31 percent.[27] Initially, by borrowing at 3.31 percent and receiving 7.00 percent, the County earned a sizeable profit. Although this transaction seemed like a sure thing in the short term, it contained enormous risk. In particular, if rates moved higher, the County would be hit on both sides of the transaction: the yield that it would have to pay to finance the transaction through repo agreements would go up, and, simultaneously, the yield on the inverse I/O floater notes it purchased would go down, squeezing the County's profit at a rapid rate.

This is exactly what occurred. Over the course of 1994, three month LIBOR went from 3.25 percent on February 1 to 6.5 percent on December 30.[28] As a result, in less than a year, the yield on these structured notes went from 7 percent to 3.5 percent, while the borrowing costs on the repo transactions used to finance the structured notes skyrocketed to about 6 percent.[29] Orange County's easy profit rapidly deteriorated into massive losses. Because the money used to fund these notes was borrowed and highly leveraged, the county's losses were magnified, and eventually resulted in the bankruptcy of the AAA rated county.

IV. RISKS INVOLVED

The Orange County case highlights the enormous risks inherent in certain structured notes. While the credit risk in these types of transactions can be almost non-existent, as it was in this case where the issuers were AAA rated government-sponsored entities, other types of risk exist.

A. Interest Rate Risk

The obvious risk associated with the structured note entered into by Orange County was interest rate risk. The yield in the repo transaction and the yield in the structured note transaction both depended on interest rates remaining low. Any investor entering into a structured note agreement must evaluate the

---

26. Three-month historic treasury note rates found at http://research.stlouisfed.org/fred2/data/TB3MS.txt; LIBOR rates found at "Historic LIBOR Rates," British Banker's Association, online at http://www.bba.org.uk/bba/jsp/polopoly.jsp?d=141&a=627.

27. See Norris, supra note 18.

28. See supra, note 26.

29. Id.

expected results at various changes in interest rates (or changes in their structured note specific reference entity).

B. Liquidity Risk

The second risk Orange County faced was liquidity risk. The original note was tailored specifically for the two initial parties: Fannie Mae and Orange County. These specific notes are not prevalent and do not trade on a daily basis. In order to undo this transaction, Orange County would have had to find a buyer or would have had to enter into a mirror image of the same transaction. At the time Orange County would be looking for a buyer, the note would be trading at a below-market interest rate. Therefore, no rational investor would buy the note unless it was sold for less than its par value, further increasing the county's losses. If Orange County instead chose to enter into the mirror image transaction, it would face a similar problem in that any rational counterparty would require a reduction in face value to enter the transaction. In addition, the County would face additional transaction costs.

C. Reinvestment Risk

A third risk assumed by Orange County in this example was reinvestment risk. The note contained an option for Fannie Mae to repay the loan and end the transaction for par value. Fannie Mae would do this only if the interest rates remained low. If Fannie Mae did end the transaction, Orange County might have had difficulty finding other high yielding securities without taking on additional risk, especially in a climate of low interest rates. Considering that Orange County used leveraged and borrowed money to fund these transactions, even a few days between investments could cost the County considerably. Anyone investing in structured notes must be fully aware of all inherent risks involved in these instruments.

D. OCC Warning

During the low interest period in 1993 and early 1994, various financial institutions and sophisticated market participants (like Orange County) entered into these types of structured note transactions to enhance yield above the prevailing low market interest rates. As rates unexpectedly moved higher in 1994, these market participants lost a considerable amount of money on their assets because they failed to grasp their risk exposure. From the end of 2001 until 2004, prevailing interest rates remained below two percent, and even hovered around one percent, a historically low level. As rates moved lower, and many market participants refinanced their debts, bank yields rapidly declined. Once again, banks, with little memory of 1994, sought out higher yielding securities, turning to structured note investments.

 To remind financial institutions about the levels of risk these transactions could entail, the Office of the Comptroller of the Currency (OCC) issued a bulletin on May 22, 2002, to all national bank CEOs and all federal branches and agencies in regard to risky "yield-chasing" strategies that were once again returning to the markets.[30] While these financial institutions are (generally) run by some of the most sophisticated and educated market players, it was important for these banks to be reminded of the most basic of financial tenets, "there is no 'free lunch.' To obtain higher yields, banks must take more credit risk, interest rate risk, liquidity risk, or combinations thereof."[31] The OCC specifically highlighted the risks in structured note products:

In 1993, many banks acquired large volumes of structured notes, focusing on the excellent credit quality of agency issuers and high yields, but overlooking the complex structures, embedded options and resultant price sensitivity. . . . When interest rates increased sharply in 1994, many of these investment portfolios suffered severe depreciation. . . . Such structures [specifically "long maturities" with "short non-call periods"] often leave a bank vulnerable to interest rate movements in either direction" [because even if rates fall, then the issuer is likely to exercise their option and call the note][32]

Considering the numerous regulatory agencies that have issued warnings, guidance, and increased standards on national and local banks,[33] bank executives

---

30. *Unsafe and Unsound Investment Portfolio Practices: Supplemental Guidance*, (OCC Bulletin, Office of the Comptroller, 2002) OCC CB LEXIS 27.

31. *Id.* at 3.

32. *Id.* at 10.

33. The OCC was not the first regulator to warn banks. In fact, the Securities and Exchange Commission (SEC) warned money fund managers on June 30 that certain structured notes were not appropriate investments, including both inverse floating notes and range notes, and advised the managers to exit their positions. The OCC originally warned banks and purchasers of structured notes on July 14, 1994, when they issued Advisory Letter AL 94-2. In this letter, the OCC defined six types of common structures and pronounced structure notes to be "inappropriate investments for most national banks." Other regulators followed suit. On August 5, 1994, the Federal Reserve issued SR letter 94-45, entitled "Supervisory Policies Relating to Structured Notes." This letter highlighted valuable uses of structured notes, including the ability to hedge particular risks, but emphasized the "importance of bank management's ability to . . . understand and manage the risks associated with structured notes." The Office of Thrift Supervision (OTS) also weighed in by issuing Thrift Bulletin 65 on August 16, 1994. The OTS emphasized the importance of modeling different interest rate scenarios to determine what would result if interest rates moved quickly one way or the other. Lastly, the Federal Deposit Insurance Corporation (FDIC) enhanced their supervision and regulatory approach to structured notes. As the insurer of $100,000 per account in each FDIC insured bank, the FDIC had a tremendous amount at stake in ensuring that banks employ appropriate risk management. In late 1994, the FDIC instituted a policy requiring examiners of state-chartered banks that are not members of the Federal Reserve System, to classify as "substandard" "structured notes that could experience loss of principal."

and money fund managers may now have an affirmative and explicit duty to their clients, stockholders, and depositors to possess a detailed understanding of how the security they are purchasing is structured, and at the very least, run through a model to estimate how the security will perform under different scenarios, including various interest rates, default rates, and combinations thereof. The manager must confirm that the client understands the associated risks (credit risk, market risk, interest rate risk, liquidity risk, reinvestment risk) of the investment, and must ensure that the client evaluates those risks on a regular basis along with the suitability of the securities for the client's portfolio.

V. RANGE NOTES

Range notes are types of structured bonds that normally pay two separate yields, depending on whether the reference entity (usually a rate index) is within or outside of a certain range. The reference entity is predominately an index linked to interest rates, but it could also be linked to currency exchange rates, commodity values, and equity indexes.[34] The purchaser of a range note is often paid a higher-than-normal rate of interest if the reference rate remains within the range specified and is often paid less interest or no interest at all if the reference rate falls or rises outside of the range. It makes no difference whether the rate moves up or down; the only factor is by how much. For example, if the reference entity is LIBOR, the note may pay the investor eight percent interest as long as three-month LIBOR remains between four and six percent, but if it is below four or above six then the note might not pay any interest at all.

The risk of the transaction varies tremendously depending on how wide the range is, and this is usually incorporated into the value of the difference between the two assigned yields. If the reference range is narrower, there will likely be a greater spread between the two separate yields, and if the range is wide, there will likely be a narrower spread between the two separate yields. Another factor includes how close the present reference rate is to each boundary of the designed range. The two parties can design the note to accrue interest by assessing the yield at designed times. In practice, parties usually choose to accrue interest daily, quarterly, semi-annually, or annually, or even over the entire life span of the note.[35] The yield can be assessed based upon the closing price of the index on a specific date, or it can be averaged out over the period. Given the disparity between the two yields received, it is extremely difficult to predict or anticipate the value of such an investment. This leads to a high degree of price

---

All "mark-to-market" losses must be classified as a "loss" by the examiners. *See* KAREN MCCANN AND JOSEPH CILIA, STRUCTURED NOTES, at 3–4, (Federal Reserve Bank of Chicago, Financial Markets Unit, November 1994).

34. *Id.* at 2.

35. *Id.*

risk. In addition, range notes contain the same risks evident in structured notes in general, including primarily interest rate risk, liquidity risk, and reinvestment risk.

Range notes have options built into them that allow the investor to benefit so long as an index stays within a certain range. In *Proctor & Gamble v. Bankers Trust*[36] a similar structure was created using a swap and is described as follows:

> In late January 1994, P&G and BT negotiated a second swap, known as the "DM swap," based on the value [**12] of the German Deutschemark. The Confirmation for this swap is dated February 14, 1994. For the first year, BT was to pay P&G a floating interest rate plus 233 basis points. P&G was to pay the same floating rate plus 133 basis points; P&G thus received a 1% premium for the first year, the effective [*1277] dates being January 16, 1994 through January 16, 1995. On January 16, 1995, P&G was to add a spread to its payments to BT if the four-year DM swap rate ever traded below 4.05% or above 6.01% at any time between January 16, 1994, and January 16, 1995. If the DM swap rate stayed within that band of interest rates, the spread was zero. If the DM swap rate broke that band, the spread would be set on January 16, 1995, using the following formula:

> Spread = 10 * [4-year DM swap rate—4.50%]

The leverage factor in this swap was shown in the formula as ten.[37]

In the Proctor & Gamble SWAP, so long as the four-year DM swap rate stayed within a specified range (i.e., between 4.05% and 6.01%), Proctor & Gamble would receive 1% of the notional value of the agreement. If the DM swap traded outside of that range, additional payment would need to be made. This structure is similar to a range note, where payments are contingent on an index remaining in a specified range for payments to continue.

Structuring securities can be accomplished by incorporating derivatives structures in which payments are contingent on a specified contingency. By understanding the function and utility of various financial instruments, investors and issuers can access capital using innovative financial solutions to accomplish specific goals. The capital markets play an essential role in the world economy, providing a means for individuals and institutions to access capital, shift risk, and enhance return on their investments. Financial instruments allow market participants to manage risk by shifting unwanted risk to a counterparty who might be more willing or able to manage or capitalize on that risk. It is by understanding the economic needs and the instruments filling those needs that capital market participants, attorneys, and end users might facilitate capital access and risk transference to accomplish fiscal goals.

---

36. Procter & Gamble Co. v. Bankers Trust Co., 925 F. Supp. 1270, 1276 (S.D. Ohio 1996).

37. *Id.* at 1276.

APPENDIX: THE SUPERVISORY CAPITAL ASSESSMENT PROGRAM
Design and Implementation

April 24, 2009

Board of Governors of the Federal Reserve System

Table of Contents

I. INTRODUCTION AND EXECUTIVE SUMMARY

Most U.S. banking organizations currently have capital levels well in excess of the amounts required to be well capitalized. However, losses associated with the deepening recession and financial market turmoil have substantially reduced the capital of some banks. Lower overall levels of capital—especially common equity—along with the uncertain economic environment have eroded public confidence in the amount and quality of capital held by some firms, which is impairing the ability of the banking system overall to perform its critical role of credit intermediation. Given the heightened uncertainty around the future course of the U.S. economy and potential losses in the banking system, supervisors believe it prudent for large bank holding companies (BHCs) to hold additional capital to provide a buffer against higher losses than generally expected, and still remain sufficiently capitalized at over the next two years and able to lend to creditworthy borrowers should such losses materialize. The purpose of the Supervisory Capital Assessment Program (SCAP), which is being conducted by the supervisory agencies, is to assess the size of these capital needs.

The SCAP is a forward-looking exercise designed to estimate losses, revenues, and reserve needs for BHCs in 2009 and 2010 under two macroeconomic scenarios, including one that is more adverse than expected. Should the assessment indicate the need for a BHC to raise capital or improve the quality of its capital to better withstand losses that could occur under more stressful-than-expected conditions, supervisors will expect that firm to augment its capital to create a buffer. This buffer would be drawn down over time if losses were to occur. In evaluating the SCAP results, it is important to recognize that the assessment is a "what if" exercise intended to help supervisors gauge the extent of additional capital needs across a range of potential economic outcomes. A need for additional capital or a change in composition of capital to build a buffer under an economic scenario that is more adverse than expected is not a measure of the current solvency or viability of the firm.

This paper describes the SCAP process conducted by the federal bank regulatory agencies (the agencies) from Feb. 25, 2009 through late April of 2009.[1] All domestic BHCs with year-end 2008 assets exceeding $100 billion were required to participate in the SCAP as part of the ongoing supervisory process. These 19 firms collectively hold two-thirds of the assets and more than one-half of the loans in the U.S. banking system, and support a very significant portion of the credit intermediation done by the banking sector. The firms were asked to project their credit losses and revenues for the two years 2009 and 2010, including the level of reserves that would be needed at the end of 2010 to cover expected

---

1. The federal bank regulatory agencies that participated in the SCAP are the Board of Governors of the Federal Reserve System, the Federal Reserve Banks, the Federal Deposit Insurance Corporation, and the Office of the Comptroller of the Currency.

losses in 2011, under two alternative economic scenarios. The *baseline scenario* reflected the consensus expectation in February 2009 among professional forecasters on the depth and duration of the recession, while the *more adverse scenario* was designed to characterize a recession that is longer and more severe than the consensus expectation. The firms were also asked to provide supporting documentation for their projected losses and resources, including information on projected income and expenses by major category, domestic and international portfolio characteristics, forecast methods, and important assumptions.

The SCAP process was extensive. In early March, firms submitted their projections to the agencies, which included significant amounts of detailed data. Supervisory teams, organized by specific asset classes, revenues, and reserves, evaluated the substance and quality of the initial submissions and, where appropriate, requested additional data or evaluation of the sensitivity of projections to alternative assumptions. The supervisors also developed independent benchmarks based on firm-specific portfolio characteristics against which they evaluated the appropriateness of the firms' projections for losses and resources that would be available to absorb losses. Results for each firm also were evaluated to assess the sensitivity of the firm to changes in the economy based on projections under the baseline and the more adverse scenarios. The evaluations drew on the expertise of more than 150 senior supervisors, on-site examiners, analysts, and economists from the agencies. Senior supervisory officials made the determination of the necessary capital buffer for each BHC.

While the SCAP is conceptually similar to stress tests that firms undertake as part of their ongoing risk management, the objective of this program was to conduct a comprehensive and consistent assessment simultaneously across the 19 largest BHCs using a common set of macroeconomic scenarios, and a common forward-looking conceptual framework. This framework allowed supervisors to apply a consistent and systematic approach across the group to evaluate the projected loss and resource estimates submitted by the firms. The extensive information on the characteristics of loan, trading, and securities portfolios and modeling methods provided by these institutions allowed supervisors to conduct a cross-firm analysis and assess the projections. In addition, the SCAP is considerably more comprehensive than stress tests that focus on individual business lines, because it simultaneously incorporates all of the major assets and the revenue sources of each of the firms.

As discussed in the interagency statement released on February 10, the SCAP may result in a determination that a BHC may need to augment its capital base to establish a buffer. This capital buffer should position the largest BHCs to continue to play their critical role as intermediaries, even in a more challenging economic environment. The United States Treasury has committed to make capital available to eligible BHCs through the Capital Assistance Program as described in the Term Sheet released on February 25. In addition, BHCs can also apply to Treasury to exchange their existing Capital Purchase Program preferred stock to help meet their buffer requirement.

Section II describes the program design of the SCAP and Section III provides detail on how the assessment of losses and revenues were conducted, and how the capital need was calculated.

II. PROGRAM DESIGN

This section provides a discussion of the SCAP framework, a general description of the process, the guidance given to BHCs, and the projections that the participating BHCs were asked to make.

II. A. Discussion of SCAP Analytical Framework

The SCAP process involves the projection of losses on loans, assets held in investment portfolios, and trading-related exposures, as well as the firm's capacity to absorb losses in order to determine a sufficient capital level to support lending under a worse-than-expected macroeconomic scenario. The traditional role of capital, especially common equity, is to absorb unexpected losses and thus to protect depositors and other creditors. Given the heightened uncertainty about the economy and potential losses in the banking system, and the potential in the current environment for adverse economic outcomes to be magnified through the banking system, supervisors believe it prudent for large BHCs to hold substantial capital to absorb losses should the economic downturn be longer and deeper than now anticipated. The SCAP was designed to assess these capital needs as part of the ongoing supervisory process. The program is consistent with current regulatory capital guidelines, which require BHCs to hold capital commensurate with their risks, and to generally hold a dominant share of their regulatory capital in the form of common equity.

The SCAP was designed under the assumption that the institutions continue to operate under the regulatory and accounting frameworks existing as of December 31, 2008 and considering the effect of significant changes that have or are expected to occur during the next two years.[2] Loans held in portfolio subject to accrual accounting are carried at amortized cost, net of an allowance for loan losses. The use of accrual accounting for these assets is based on BHCs' intent and ability to hold these loans to maturity, which reflects, in part, a combination of more stable deposit funding and information advantages about the quality of the loans they underwrite. The economic value of loans in the accrual book is reduced through the loan loss reserving process when repayment becomes doubtful, but is not reduced for fluctuations in market prices, which may be

---

2. Significant changes in accounting considered included the recently issued Financial Accounting Standards Boards Financial Staff Position FAS 115-2 and FAS 124-2, *Recognition and Presentation of Other-Than-Temporary Impairments* that is effective in 2009 and expected changes to consolidation accounting that will be effective in 2010.

driven by market liquidity considerations, if those factors do not affect the ultimate likelihood of repayment. The adherence of SCAP to current practices is important because the majority of assets at most of the BHCs participating in the SCAP are loans that are booked on an accrual basis. As a result of the loss recognition framework for assets in the accrual loan book, the results of this exercise are not comparable with those that would evaluate such assets on a mark-to-market basis.

The SCAP analysis is forward looking, but over a limited time horizon. Losses and resources are projected over a two-year period (2009 to 2010) and include an assessment of the sufficiency of loan loss reserves expected at the end of 2010, which captures expected losses in 2011. This choice of horizon reflects a tradeoff between capturing the full extent of losses that might be incurred on assets that were originated when underwriting standards were more lax in 2006 and 2007 and a reasonable ability to project with some degree of confidence the losses and resources at more distant future points. Given the profile of the consensus baseline outlook for the macro economy and the alternative more adverse scenario that includes a return to positive real GDP growth within the two years, this horizon seems likely to capture a large portion of losses from positions held as of the end of 2008.

While this approach likely captures the bulk of the losses that might be realized on these assets, it is important to note that it does not include the substantial losses that have already been taken. That is, forward-looking losses in the SCAP are not "lifetime" losses which occur from origination to the life-end of the assets, but they do represent a substantial addition to those losses that have already been realized and, as noted above, when combined with losses already taken, are likely to represent a substantial share of the losses associated with loans originated from 2005 to 2007. Losses taken in the 6 quarters through the end of 2008 by these firms and firms they acquired are substantial, estimated at approximately $400 billion for the 19 BHCs participating in the SCAP. They include charge-offs, write-downs on securities held in the trading and in the investment accounts, and discounts on assets acquired in acquisitions of distressed or failed financial institutions.

II. B. General Description of the Exercise

The BHCs were asked to estimate their potential losses on loans, securities, and trading positions, as well as pre-provision net revenue (PPNR) and the resources available from the allowance for loan and lease losses (ALLL) under two alternative macroeconomic scenarios. Each participating firm was instructed to project potential losses on its loan, investment, and trading securities portfolios, including off-balance sheet commitments and contingent liabilities and exposures over the two-year horizon beginning with year-end 2008 financial statement data. Firms were provided with a common set of indicative loss rate ranges for specific loan categories under conditions of the baseline and the more adverse economic scenarios. Firms were allowed to diverge from the indicative loss rates where they could provide evidence that their estimated loss rates were appropriate. In addition, firms with trading assets of $100 billion or more were asked to estimate potential trading-related market and counter-party credit losses under a market stress scenario provided by the supervisors, based on market shocks that occurred in the second half of 2008.

The BHCs also were asked to project the resources they would have available to absorb losses over the two-year horizon under both scenarios. These resources consist of PPNR—net interest income, fees and other non-interest income, net of non-credit-related expenses—and reserves already established for probable incurred losses at December 31, 2008. PPNR and the ALLL, combined with existing capital above the amount sufficient to exceed minimum regulatory capital standards, are resources that the firm would have available to absorb some of their estimated losses under the scenarios.

Teams of supervisors and analysts composed of members from each of the agencies reviewed and assessed the firms' submissions. Some teams had special expertise in particular asset classes, or in revenues, reserves, and capital, and other teams had special expertise in the specific participating firms. At the outset of the process, teams dedicated to evaluating particular categories of assets, revenues, and reserves evaluated the firms' submissions and actively engaged with the firms for several weeks to obtain additional information necessary to support the firms' estimates. Some firms were asked to provide additional information on the risk characteristics of their portfolios to supplement their initial submission. Examiners also reviewed and evaluated the quantitative methods that firms used to project losses and resources, and support for key assumptions. The supervisory analyses of losses built on individual firm-specific information about the risk characteristics of the portfolio, underwriting practices, and risk management practices.

These teams applied across-firm, comparative analysis to support their assessments. To facilitate this horizontal comparison, supervisors applied independent quantitative methods using firm-specific data to estimate losses and loss absorption resources. The quantitative methods were applied to all the firms to provide consistency in evaluating firms' estimates. The results of these analyses were then evaluated in the context of previous examination work and in the context of the indicative loss rates and macroeconomic scenarios provided by the supervisors to the BHCs at the beginning of the exercise.

To conclude the process, projected losses, revenues, and changes in reserves were combined to evaluate the amount and quality of capital that each firm should have at the end of 2010. Calculations were done on a post-purchase accounting basis and considered taxes, including deferred tax assets, and dividends on preferred stock. Under the more adverse scenario, if any firm is found to have less capital than the need projected by the SCAP assessment, supervisors will request those firms to take deliberate actions to augment their capital so that they will remain in an appropriately strong financial position and be able to lend and support financial intermediation. Thus the capital needs determined by this supervisory exercise should be viewed as a capital buffer designed to be drawn down as losses materialize should the economy be weaker than expected, and still be substantial enough at the end of 2010 for firms to be considered sufficiently capitalized. If the economy recovers more quickly than specified in the more adverse scenario, firms could find their capital buffers at the end of 2010 more than sufficient to support their critical intermediation role and could take actions to reverse their capital build-up.

II. C. Initial Guidance on Macroeconomic Scenarios

For implementation of the SCAP, the supervisors provided assumptions for two alternative macroeconomic scenarios. BHCs were encouraged to consider the broader macroeconomic conditions and adapt the assumptions to reflect their specific business activities when projecting their own losses and resources over 2009 and 2010. For example, local residential house prices would be expected to be a significant determinant in projected loan loss rates given their prominent role in mortgage and consumer lending in recent years. Projections under two alternative scenarios also allow for analysis of the sensitivity of a firm's business to changes in economic conditions.

The baseline assumptions for real GDP growth and the unemployment rate for 2009 and 2010 were assumed to be equal to the average of the projections published by Consensus Forecasts, the Blue Chip survey, and the Survey of Professional Forecasters. The projections were based on forecasts available in February 2009 just before the commencement of the SCAP. The baseline scenario was intended to represent a consensus view about the depth and duration of the recession. The supervisors developed an alternative "more adverse" scenario to reflect the possibility that the economy could turn out to be appreciably weaker than expected under the baseline outlook. By design, the path of the U.S. economy in this alternative more adverse scenario reflects a deeper and longer recession than in the baseline. However, the more adverse alternative is not, and is not intended to be a "worst case" scenario. To be most useful, stress tests should reflect conditions that are severe but plausible.[3]

---

3. The "more adverse" scenario was constructed from the historical track record of private forecasters as well as their current assessments of uncertainty. In particular, based on the historical accuracy of Blue Chip forecasts made since the late 1970s, the likelihood that the average unemployment rate in 2010 could be at least as high as in the alternative more adverse scenario is roughly 10 percent. In addition, the subjective probability assessments provided by participants in the January Consensus Forecasts survey and the February Survey of Professional Forecasters imply a roughly 15 percent chance that real GDP growth could be at least as low, and unemployment at least as high, as assumed in the more adverse scenario.

The assumptions for house prices in the baseline economic outlook are consistent with the path that was implied by futures prices for the Case-Shiller 10-City Composite index in late February and the average response to a special question on house prices in the Blue Chip survey. For the more adverse scenario, house prices are assumed to be about 10 percent lower at the end of 2010 relative to their level in the baseline scenario.[4]

Since the announcement of the SCAP in late February, the economy has deteriorated somewhat and professional forecasters have revised their outlooks for GDP growth and the unemployment rate in 2009 and 2010. New information on house prices suggests that the market's expectation for house price declines is similar to what was anticipated in February. A large share of projected losses at banks are expected to be related to house prices, and the specified path for house prices in the more adverse scenario still represents a severe level of stress. Although the likelihood that unemployment could average 10.3 percent in 2010 is now higher than had been anticipated when the scenarios were specified, that outcome still exceeds a more recent consensus projection by professional forecasters for an average unemployment rate of 9.3 percent in 2010.

TABLE 1 ECONOMIC SCENARIOS: BASELINE AND MORE ADVERSE ALTERNATIVES
(Minus signs indicate negative values)

	2009	2010
Real GDP[1]		
Average Baseline[2]	−2.0	2.1
Consensus Forecasts	−2.1	2.0
Blue Chip	−1.9	2.1
Survey of Professional Forecasters	−2.0	2.2
Alternative More Adverse	−3.3	0.5
Civilian unemployment rate[3]		
Average Baseline[2]	8.4	8.8
Consensus Forecasts	8.4	9.0
Blue Chip	8.3	8.7
Survey of Professional Forecasters	8.4	8.8
Alternative More Adverse	8.9	10.3

4. Based on the year-to-year variability in house prices since 1900, and controlling for macroeconomic factors, there is roughly a 10 percent probability that house prices will be 10 percent lower than in the baseline by 2010.

	2009	2010
House prices[4]		
Baseline	−14	−4
Alternative More Adverse	−22	−7

[1]Percent change in annual average.
[2]Baseline forecasts for real GDP and the unemployment rate equal the average of projections released by Consensus Forecasts, Blue Chip, and Survey of Professional Forecasters in February.
[3]Annual average.
[4]Case-Shiller 10-City Composite, percent change, fourth quarter of the previous year to fourth quarter of the year indicated.

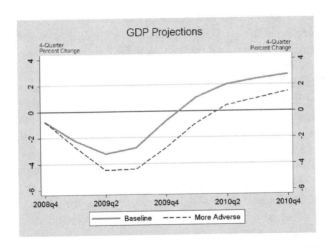

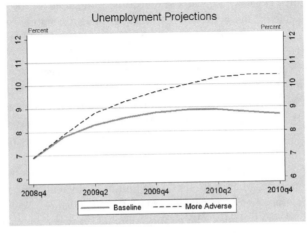

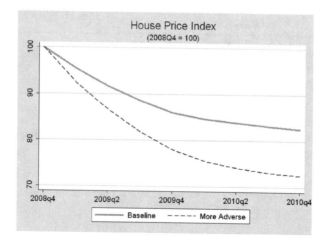

II. D. Initial Guidance on Loss and Resource Calculations

Loss Projections The participating BHCs were asked to project estimated losses on loans, securities, and trading-related exposures (for those firms with trading assets exceeding $100 billion), including potential losses stemming from off-balance sheet positions, for 2009 and 2010 that would be consistent with the economic outlooks in the baseline and more adverse scenarios. They were instructed to project losses for 12 separate categories of loans held in the accrual book, for loans and securities held in the available-for-sale and held-to-maturity (AFS/HTM) portfolios, and in some cases for positions held in the trading account. The BHCs were asked to make adjustments to reported balance sheet values of assets to reflect expectations of customer drawdowns on unused credit commitments, and other assets or exposures that might be taken back on the balance sheet in a stressed economic environment and due to pending accounting changes.

The specific categories of loans and securities included in the exercise are listed in the attached template. For the most part, these categories are based on regulatory report classifications to facilitate comparison across BHCs and with information reported by the BHCs in their regulatory filings. However, the BHCs were encouraged to provide more granular loss projections—that is, loss projections for sub-categories of the loan types specified in the template—to the extent that their internal calculations were built up from such information. In addition, the BHCs were instructed to report projections of losses that would be material deriving from other positions, businesses, or risk exposures that were not included in the template.

For loans, the BHCs were instructed to estimate forward-looking, undiscounted credit losses, that is, losses due to failure to pay obligations ("cash flow losses") rather than discounts related to mark-to-market values. To guide estimation, the BHCs were provided with a range of indicative two-year cumulative loss

rates for each of the 12 loan categories for the baseline and more adverse scenarios. BHCs were permitted to submit loss rates outside of the ranges, but were
required to provide strong supporting evidence, especially if they fell below the
range minimum. The indicative loss rate ranges were derived using a variety of
methods for predicting loan losses, including analysis of historical loss experience at large BHCs and quantitative models relating the performance of individual loans and groups of loans to macroeconomic variables. These loan-level
models were particularly important for residential mortgages, since historical
loss experience at BHCs may not be a reliable guide to future performance under
the baseline or more adverse scenario, given the path of home prices in recent
years.

The BHCs were asked to provide loss estimates based on outstanding balances of loans and securities on a global consolidated basis as of December 31,
2008 as reported in their FR Y-9C reports, adjusted to reflect any significant
mergers, acquisitions, or divestitures that an institution completed after that
date.[5] The BHCs also were asked to project losses on loans that could be drawn
down from unused credit commitments in place as of year-end 2008 and on
securitized assets that could be brought back onto the balance sheet under
stressed market conditions.

For securities held in the available-for-sale and held-to-maturity portfolios,
institutions were instructed to estimate possible impairment relative to net unrealized losses at year-end 2008 (as reported in the Q4 2008 FR Y-9C). Firms were
asked to address potential other-than-temporary-impairment charges that may
be required under both scenarios.

As noted above, BHCs with trading account assets exceeding $100 billion as
of December 31, 2008 were asked to provide projections of trading-related losses
for the more adverse scenario, including losses from counterparty credit risk
exposures, including potential counterparty defaults, and credit valuation adjustments taken against exposures to counterparties whose probability of default
would be expected to increase in the adverse scenario.[6] To calculate these losses,
the firms conducted a stress test of their trading book positions and counterparty
exposures as of market close on February 20, 2009, based on an instantaneous
re-pricing of trading positions equal to the changes in market pricing variables
that occurred over the period of June 30, 2008 to December 31, 2008. Aside
from the dollar loss estimates, BHCs were asked to disclose the positions that
were included in this analysis as well as the risk factors that were stressed and the
changes in variables employed (for example, changes in rates and spreads, and
percentage changes in equities, foreign exchange, and commodities). Firms were

---

5. The FR Y-9C reports contain balance sheet and income statement information for
bank holding companies.

6. Under the baseline scenario, BHCs were instructed to assume no further losses
beyond current marks.

also asked to provide the results of the stress tests conducted in the usual course of business from January 2009 or the most recent dates available.

Resources to Absorb Losses Institutions were also instructed to provide projections of resources available to absorb losses under the two scenarios, including pre-provision net revenue, and the allowance for loan losses, over the two-year horizon.

For purposes of this exercise, PPNR is defined as net interest income plus non-interest income minus non-interest expense. It is therefore the income after non-credit-related expenses that would flow into the firms before they take provisions or other write-downs or losses. The participating BHCs were instructed to project the main components of PPNR under each of the macroeconomic scenarios. The firms were instructed to explain clearly the assumptions underlying these projections, especially those regarding business or market share growth. Especially in the more adverse scenario, pre-provision net revenue projections materially exceeding their 2008 values would require strong supporting evidence in the absence of documentation of nonrecurring events that negatively affected 2008 net revenue.

Institutions were also instructed to estimate the portion of the year-end 2008 allowance for loan and lease losses available to absorb credit losses on the loan portfolio under each scenario, while maintaining an adequate allowance at the end of the scenario horizon. This calculation could either result in a drawdown of the year-end 2008 ALLL or indicate a need to build reserves over the scenario horizon. The adequacy of loan loss reserves was assessed against the likely size, composition, and risk characteristics of the loan portfolio at the end of the scenario in 4Q 2010.

Assessing Capital Needs in an Uncertain World

Projecting estimated losses and revenues for BHCs is an inherently uncertain exercise, and this difficulty has been amplified in the current period of increased macroeconomic uncertainty. The future path of GDP growth, unemployment, and home prices, for example, are unknown, with a wide range of plausible outcomes. Indeed, this increased uncertainty was a key motivation for the SCAP, as policymakers are interested in restoring confidence that BHCs have sufficient resources to continue to lend to creditworthy borrowers across a wide range of macroeconomic outcomes.

Forward-looking assessments across a range of possible outcomes including more adverse environments, commonly referred to as "stress tests," are regularly used by both institutions and supervisors and are regularly integrated in traditional risk-management practices. This approach provides additional information to firms and supervisors about the vulnerability of a BHC by examining how it might fare under different economic scenarios. This type of analysis, however, is itself subject to considerable uncertainty, including uncertainty about the range of potential macroeconomic outcomes to consider, the relationship between BHC results and macroeconomic scenarios, the degree to which historical relationships will continue to be relevant in a more stressed environment, and the potential changes to consumer behavior in response to both macroeconomic and institutional changes.

Nevertheless, this type of exercise can be extremely useful in helping supervisors and analysts broadly understand a BHC's risk, especially in periods of high uncertainty. Moreover, a stress test provides a systematic, disciplined framework for gauging the magnitude of capital buffers that might be needed by different firms to absorb losses under plausible "what if" scenarios.

III. SUPERVISORY REVIEWS AND ASSESSMENTS

III. A. Supervisory Review of the BHC Submissions and Benchmark Assessments

The supervisory review and assessment of the loss and resource estimates submitted by the participating BHCs were critical parts of the SCAP exercise. This review involved the work of more than 150 people from the supervisory agencies, including senior examiners, economists, and financial analysts. Staff was organized into teams, each of which focused on examining a distinct aspect of the loss and resource projections across all 19 participating BHCs. In particular, there were teams charged with examining loss projections for consumer portfolios, commercial and industrial (C&I) and commercial real estate loan (CRE) portfolios, AFS and HTM securities portfolios, trading account assets, and counterparty credit risk, and teams examining projections of PPNR and ALLL coverage. There were also advisory groups composed of specialists in accounting, regulatory capital, and financial and macroeconomic modeling.

These teams were charged with evaluating the quality of the firm submissions so that each submission had sufficient information on data, methods, and assumptions to be analyzed. The teams were responsible for analyzing the loss and resources projections from a cross-firm perspective, using supporting information supplied by the firms as part of the SCAP exercise. This work was informed by supervisory information and knowledge of the on-site examination teams at each of the participating BHCs. The objective was to evaluate the projections submitted by the firms and the approaches used to generate those numbers. A key aspect of this analysis was to understand the particular parameters and assumptions employed and their consistency with the macroeconomic scenarios provided, as well as the models and methodologies used to generate the loss and resource estimates.

Aside from a direct review of the assumptions and models used in loss and resource projections submitted by the participating BHCs, the agencies developed independent benchmarks against which to evaluate the submissions. One set of benchmarks was the indicative loan loss rate ranges provided to firms prior to their preparing assessments of potential losses in their accrual loan portfolios under each macroeconomic scenario for the categories of loans on the SCAP template. The ranges are based on loss rate estimates calculated by the different supervisory agencies participating in the SCAP, using methodologies both currently in use by the agencies and some especially designed for this assessment. All the ranges are estimates, reflecting the uncertainty inherent in the likely loss experience of large banking companies in stressful economic environments.

The agencies used a variety of approaches to calculate indicative loss rates across the different types of loans. These approaches for residential mortgages included "micro" models of default and loss-given-default built on information about individual loans, models based on the performance of regional mortgage loan portfolios, and analysis of mortgages held by failing banks. For other consumer loans and for commercial lending (including various types of commercial real estate lending), the agencies estimated loss rates using techniques such as regressions of historical charge-off or default data against macroeconomic variables such as home price appreciation and the unemployment rate and analysis of loan-level data derived from supervisory sources. A variety of other statistical analyses were applied to the historical experience at large BHCs to estimate loss rates and resource availability.

These indicative loss rate ranges, although useful as general guides to aggregate banking sector losses, do not reflect important differences across firms that could affect performance and losses in significant ways. Thus, the agencies also developed more detailed benchmarks for losses and resources incorporating granular, firm-specific information on factors such as past performance, portfolio composition, origination vintage, borrower characteristics, geographic distribution, international operations, and business mix. These benchmarks were intended to provide a common background in discussions with the firms about their analysis and as additional information to help supervisors determine where results should be adjusted.

As with the indicative loss rate ranges, these benchmarks also made use of models and approaches already in use to monitor risk and firm condition as part of the on-going supervisory oversight process, as well as methods developed specifically for the SCAP exercise. These estimates drew on much of the same data provided by the participating BHCs as part of their SCAP submissions and were provided in response to specific requests from the supervisory teams.

These supervisory benchmarks provided important information to the teams evaluating the BHC submissions, since the benchmarks were calculated using consistent methodologies across firms, while still incorporating detailed firm-specific information about the BHCs.

The intent of the overall process was to bring together as much information as possible about the specific firm and empirical evidence on loss rates and resource availability in order to provide the best judgment on potential losses and revenues in economic conditions that are weaker than expected. Loss and revenue projections submitted by the firms were adjusted to ensure consistency across institutions and consistency with the macroeconomic scenarios defined for the exercise. These adjustments reflect a combination of the analysis of the supervisory teams, benchmarks developed by the teams and by economists and analysts working at the agencies, and supervisory judgment and knowledge of the individual firms in the exercise. A synopsis of the assessment process by category is described below.

III. B. Supervisory Review and Benchmark Assessments by Category

First and Second Lien Mortgages Supervisory teams for the residential mortgage portfolios evaluated the firms' submissions, which described the portfolios, methods used to project losses, and important assumptions in those methods. As part of a special request for this exercise, the participating BHCs provided detailed and uniform descriptions of their residential mortgage portfolio risk characteristics. In particular, firms provided information on type of product, loan-to-value (LTV) ratio, FICO score, geography, level of documentation, year of origination, and other features. First mortgages, home equity lines of credit (HELOCs), and closed-end second-mortgage products were each evaluated separately. Each firm's models, assumptions, and circumstances were evaluated independently and relative to those of peer firms to determine adjustments to the firm's submission. Assumptions about prepayments and new originations were normalized to be generally consistent across firms. Portfolios were then analyzed using firm-specific portfolio attributes and common loss estimation methodologies calibrated to industry-wide data. Certain attributes, in particular FICO, LTV bands, vintage, product type, and geography, were found to be strongly predictive of default. These attributes were used to further evaluate submissions by the firms, and where necessary, loss estimates were adjusted to better reflect portfolio characteristics in a consistent way across firms.

Credit Cards and Other Consumer Loans For credit cards, the supervisory teams evaluated methods used to project losses and benchmarked each firm's results against historical trends in these portfolios (for example, loss, paydown/runoff, roll rates, utilization) in the context of the two macroeconomic scenarios. Firms submitted detailed information on their credit card portfolios. Data included FICO scores, payment rates, utilization rates, and geographic concentrations. The teams developed specific portfolio risk profiles in order to make cross-firm comparisons to gauge the reasonableness of the loss estimates submitted by the firms. Once normalized for assumptions, adjustments to loss rates were made where necessary, but in general the supervisory results were relatively close to the BHCs' estimates.

For other consumer loans, which are composed mainly of auto loans, personal loans, and student loans, firms provided information on FICO scores, LTV, term, vehicle age, and geographic concentration. This detailed data were evaluated along with the analysis of the underlying components of each firm's portfolio, including historical loss experience. Supervisors also examined various performance measures to assess the relative riskiness of the portfolios across firms to arrive at projected loss rates.

Commercial and Industrial Loans Analysis of C&I loan loss projections was based on the distribution of exposures by industry and by internal rating provided by the firms. In many cases, these ratings were mapped to default probabilities by the firm; in other cases, this association was established by supervisory analysts. This information was confirmed and supplemented by external measures of risk, such as expected default frequencies from third party vendors. Supervisors evaluated firm loss estimates using a Monte Carlo simulation that projected a distribution of losses by examining potential dispersion around central probabilities of default. The approach produced a consistently-prepared set of loss estimations across all the BHCs by combining firm-specific exposure and rating information with standardized assumptions of the performance of similar exposures. The results of this analysis were compared to the firms' submissions and adjustments made to ensure consistency across BHCs.

Commercial Real Estate Loans For commercial real estate (CRE) loans, firms were asked to submit detailed portfolio information on property type, loan to value (LTV) ratios, debt service coverage ratios (DSCR), geography, and loan maturities. The supervisors analyzed loans for construction and land development, multi-family property, and non-farm non-residential projects separately. The supervisors employed common industry vendor models, and developed proprietary models, to generate independent loss estimates for each portfolio. Specifically, for loans maturing in 2009 to 2010, the supervisors constructed a model that compared current LTV ratios to benchmark LTVs in order to assess the probability that borrowers would be able to refinance their exposure. For loans maturing beyond 2010, the team used vendor models that incorporate factors such as property type, LTV, DSCR, and geographic market factors. For construction loans, the geography and nature of the project received special attention. The resulting loss estimates were compared with the firms' submissions.

Other Loans This category is highly heterogeneous, including farmland lending, loans to depository institutions, loans to governments, and other categories. For most categories of other loans, a firm's loss record over the past five years was used to provide a relative ranking, and to assess the firm's submission.

Securities in AFS and HTM Portfolios The majority of securities in the AFS and HTM portfolios are Treasury securities, government agency securities, sovereign debt, and high-grade municipal securities. Private-sector securities include corporate bonds, equities, asset-backed securities, commercial mortgage-backed securities (CMBS), and non-agency residential mortgage backed securities (RMBS). About 15 percent of the portfolio is non-agency RMBS or CMBS. Supervisors focused their efforts on evaluating the private-sector securities portfolio for possible impairment, obtaining details of each security, such as collateral type, vintage, metropolitan area, and property type, as well as elements of each security's structure, such as credit ratings, current credit support, and carrying and market values. Each security was tested to determine if the security would become impaired during its lifetime. Loss estimates were based on an examination of more than 100,000 securities identified by the Committee on Uniform Security Identification Procedures, or CUSIP. For each securitized asset, credit loss rates on underlying collateral, consistent with those loss rates used for unsecuritized accrual loan portfolios, were weighed against current credit support levels for the securities. If the current level of credit support was considered insufficient to cover projected losses, the security was written down to fair value with a corresponding "other than temporary impairment" charge, in accordance with accounting guidelines, equal to the difference between book and market value. Each corporate and municipal bond was evaluated for future OTTI potential based on indicators of downgrade likelihood, including information from market credit spreads. For each equity security, OTTI was determined when the stressed market value was below the carrying value. Supervisors evaluated the position marks based on portfolio characteristics and ratings to identify anomalies and to identify conservative or aggressive practices and methodological outliers among the BHCs. Special attention was paid to institutions that had greater concentrations of accumulated other comprehensive income (AOCI) relative to tangible common equity, as AOCI forms the basis of potential recognizable losses in earnings, and hence core capital, in a given period.[7]

New FASB guidance on fair value measurements and impairments was issued on April 9, 2009, after the commencement of the SCAP. For the baseline scenario supervisors considered firms' resubmissions that incorporated the new guidance. However, for the more adverse scenario, in order to reflect greater uncertainty about realizable losses in stressful conditions, supervisors did not incorporate the new FASB guidance.

Trading Portfolio Losses Losses in the trading portfolio were evaluated by applying market stress factors to the trading exposures for the five firms with trading assets exceeding $100 billion, based on the actual market movements

---

7. AOCI is a measure of accumulated unrealized gains and losses on AFS securities, based on current carrying and market values.

that occurred over the stress horizon (June 30 to December 31, 2008). The supervisors used information on trading book positions from the firms' internal risk-management reports to project loss amounts under the defined scenario. Supervisors then compared each firm's submission to its own scenario and investigated areas where the loss estimates or gains were significantly different from the supervisors' estimates. Supervisors reviewed all of the firm's assumptions, such as the shocks to prices and spreads, the methodology used by the firm to value the assets, and whether material exposures and assets were included in the stress test. Areas where the BHCs' and supervisors' estimates diverged were identified and investigated, and final loss estimates were revised accordingly. In addition, the SCAP included an incremental default risk (IDR) estimate for firms' trading book positions.

Counterparty Credit Risk Analysis focused on assessing the reasonableness of counterparty credit risk (CCR) loss estimates stemming from exposure growth and credit valuation adjustments associated with the market shocks applied to the assets in the trading books. Specifically, the supervisors reviewed the firms' loss estimates for mark-to-market losses stemming from credit valuation adjustments (CVA) consistent with the trading shock scenario.[8] During the assessment process, supervisors developed a view of the quality of each firm's loss estimate, and made adjustments to the firm's loss estimates where appropriate to reflect factors such as consistency in the application of the trading asset shock; the comprehensiveness of coverage of counterparties and products; the prudent treatments of legal netting, collateral and margin; and soundness in the stress methodology employed.

Supervisors also requested that firms calculate an IDR loss estimate reflecting counterparty credit losses from default. The methodologies and the quality of firm submission varied. In some cases, supervisors developed independent estimates of the potential losses from counterparty defaults under the more adverse scenario.

Pre-Provision Net Revenue Analysis of firm submissions for PPNR started with a critical assessment of the business projections that were included in the BHCs' submissions. In particular, the submissions and their underlying assumptions were assessed for consistency with the overall macroeconomic scenarios. To help in its work, the supervisors also reviewed copies of the firms' internal management and financial reports. For example, "ALCO packages," including information about the yield curve assumptions, net interest income projections, and economic value of equity assessments made by the firms as part of their business planning processes, were reviewed and compared with the assumptions

---

8. A credit valuation adjustment taken against a given trading counterparty reflects the decline in the value of the obligation owed by that counterparty due to deterioration in the counterparty's creditworthiness, and directly impacts a firm's earnings and the value of the its assets.

used in firms' SCAP projections.[9] The supervisors also examined historical trends in the main components of PPNR—net interest income, noninterest income, and noninterest expense—for each firm using data from regulatory reports and from public financial statements. This evaluation involved a critical assessment of the firms' estimates based on supervisory knowledge of each firm's revenue drivers and the risks to those drivers. This analysis was then used to modify key assumptions in firms' forecasts (for example, projected growth rates and stock price indexes) to make them more consistent with the scenarios provided in the stress test. Peer analysis was also developed during the process and used to identify trends and outliers.

Supervisors also examined the historical relationship between PPNR and its main components to measures of macroeconomic activity, and examined firm-specific differences in the composition of PPNR, assessing which components have been more volatile in the past, and thus less likely to be sustainable in strained economic conditions.

Supervisors weighted the estimates arrived at through these techniques and compared them with firm submissions. Where supervisors' analysis produced lower estimates of PPNR than those provided by the firm, the supervisory estimate was applied.

Allowance for Loan and Lease Losses The supervisors developed benchmarks based on projections of the required level of reserves at the end of the scenario. The goal was to determine the level of reserves needed at year-end 2010 for two distinct portfolios, the "vintage" loans remaining from year-end 2008 and the newly extended credits over the scenario horizon. To arrive at the vintage loan total, supervisors began with the year-end 2008 loan book balance, by loan segment, and reduced these balances based on the estimated losses calculated for this exercise. New loans were estimated based on information provided by the firms as part of this exercise or, if no loan growth information was provided, by assuming that any new loan growth represented the replacement of estimated loan losses between 2009 and 2010. Reserve needs for the vintage and new loan portfolios were determined by assessing potential losses on these portfolios in 2011 and assuming reserves sufficient to cover these losses. Loss rates for vintage loans were calculated as each firm's 2010 loss rate by loan category, reduced by the anticipated average percentage reduction in loan losses in 2011 as calculated from firms that reported this information. For newly extended credits, which would likely be underwritten under more prudent lending standards, loss rates by loan category from 2007 were used to represent the expected losses in 2011.

---

9. The ALCO package is information generated by a bank holding company's "Asset-Liability Committee," containing historical information, analysis, and projections of the evolution of the firm's assets and liabilities, associated funding costs, and liquidity risk exposure and management.

III. C. Accounting Adjustments

The supervisory team assessing consumer credit losses worked closely with accounting specialists in the agencies to ensure that the firms' projections were consistent with accounting standards. Additionally, supervisors evaluated the potential impact of the proposed changes to FAS 140 which are expected to be implemented in January 2010. Based on information provided by the BHCs, implementation of the proposed changes to FAS 140 could result in approximately $900 billion in assets being brought onto the balance sheets of these institutions. Risk-weighted assets were increased by about $700 billion to reflect this projected consolidation. The on-boarding of assets also factored into our assessment of ALLL needs, and those assets were treated as new loans.

A second critical set of adjustments were made to recognize the impact of discounts taken by institutions on purchased impaired loan portfolios acquired during mergers, as governed by SOP 03-03. Several of the participating BHCs acquired loans at significant discounts as part of mergers. Based on the information provided by the BHCs, these discounts totaled more than $90 billion.[10] These discounts were considered in assessing possible future losses for these firms under the two scenarios, since such discounts make up a large portion, and possibly all, of projected future losses on impaired acquired loans in the two scenarios. The approach used in the SCAP was to project losses on the original balances of the impaired acquired loans (that is, balances with the discounts added back to bring the impaired loan balances back to their contractual principal at the date of acquisition) and then to net these losses against the discount that the BHCs took at the time they acquired the loans.

III. D. Determination of Capital Needs

As part of the submission process, each BHC reported projections of Tier 1 capital and common stockholders' equity for the end of 2009 and 2010. The BHCs' projected evolution of capital over the scenarios reflects a combination of credit losses, PPNR to absorb losses, and the need to generate appropriate ALLL at the end of the assessment horizon. These estimates served as a useful benchmark for the SCAP, but were not necessarily consistent with the final projections of losses and revenue the supervisors made for the BHC.

---

10. The reduction in projected losses relating to purchase accounting adjustment for the two scenarios is less than this amount. Some portion of the credit losses reflected in this discount may take place after the end of the scenario or may reflect market loss assumptions at the time of acquisition that are more severe than those assumed by the BHCs and supervisors in the supervisory loss projections. Some of the discount not related to credit losses is captured by the BHC in "accretable yield", which is part of pre-provision net revenue (such amounts are amortized into income over the estimated life of the loan in accordance with GAAP).

As a result, supervisors projected pro forma capital for 2010 for each BHC using the revised estimates of credit losses and revenue. The basic algorithm began with 2008 Q4 measures of equity capital and regulatory capital from Y-9C reports. Pro forma equity capital was estimated by rolling tax-adjusted net income (PPNR less credit losses less reserve builds reflected on a net of tax basis) for the two-year horizon through equity capital. The estimated losses were on a post-purchase accounting basis.[11] This effectively treats losses and provisions as an instantaneous event that is offset by revenue earned over the period. Projected reserve increases over the assessment horizon imply a net need to provision for future losses, which reduced resources available to absorb legacy losses and increased capital needs. Finally, supervisors estimated the impact of payments of preferred dividends and incorporated the impact of regulatory capital rules such as limits on the inclusion of deferred tax assets in Tier 1 Capital. This generated projections of pro forma capital levels absent any further changes in capital participation by private investors or the U.S. Treasury.

To determine the necessary capital buffer, supervisors did not rely on a single indicator of capital, but examined a range of indicators of capital adequacy including but not limited to pro forma equity capital and Tier 1 capital, including the composition of capital. Tier 1 capital, as defined in the Board's Risk-Based Capital Adequacy Guidelines, is composed of common and non-common equity elements, some of which are subject to limits on their inclusion in Tier 1 capital.[12] These elements include common stockholders' equity, qualifying perpetual preferred stock, certain minority interests, and trust preferred securities. Certain intangible assets, including goodwill and deferred tax assets, are deducted from Tier 1 capital or are included subject to limits.[13]

Supervisors have long indicated that common equity should be the dominant component of Tier 1 capital, so a measure of voting common stockholders' equity (essentially Tier 1 capital less preferred stock, less qualifying trust preferred securities, and less minority interests in subsidiaries) was also examined. The Board's capital adequacy guidelines currently state that voting common stockholders' equity generally should be the dominant element within Tier 1 capital, so the approach is consistent with existing capital guidelines and does not imply a new capital standard. This analytical work provided an initial estimate of capital needs for each BHC to remain appropriately capitalized even if the more adverse scenario materializes.

---

11. For purchased impaired loans, the projected Tier 1 Capital and Common Stockholder's Equity incorporated credit losses and provisions that reflect consideration of the discounts on purchased impaired loans and any adjustments made by the SCAP if the estimated credit losses exceeded the credit loss portion of the discounts on the purchased impaired loans as of the acquisition date.

12. *See* 12 CFR part 225, Appendix A, § II.A.1.

13. *See* 12 CFR part 225, Appendix A, § II.B.

The initial assessment of the capital need was conveyed to the BHCs in late April. The final capital assessment will include actual results year-to-date, including 2009 Q1 operating performance and corporate activities, such as sales of specific assets or business or capital events, such as a new issuance of equity securities. Supervisors evaluated this information considering the safety and soundness of individual BHCs and the stability of the broader financial system.

Appendix:
The SCAP Templates

Loan and Security Categories to be included in the Loss Estimates*
(Loss Amounts in Billions of Dollars)

	Outstanding Balance Q4 2008	Loss Estimates		
		2009	2010	TOTAL
LOANS				
First Lien Mortgages				
Prime				
Alt-A				
Subprime				
Second/Junior Lien Mortgages				
Closed-end Junior Liens				
HELOCs				
C&I Loans				
CRE Loans				
Construction				
Multifamily				
Nonfarm, Non-residential				
Credit Cards				
Other Consumer				
Other Loans				
COMMITMENTS AND CONTINGENT OBLIGATIONS				
List by type the amount and assumed losses related to commitment draw-downs and other contingent obligations				
SECURITIES				
Available for Sale				
Held to Maturity				
TRADING ACCOUNT (including traded loans)				
	For the more adverse scenario only: report total dollar loss amount, table identifying positions captured and those not captured in the stress tests, risk factors stressed, and size of risk factor changes assumed.			

* Form to be completed once for the baseline scenario and once for the more adverse scenario. If there are positions, businesses or risk exposures not captured on this template that would materially affect losses under the baseline or more adverse scenario, please include estimates of those losses in addition to the losses associated with the positions included on this template.

Resources to Absorb Losses*
(Amounts in Billions of Dollars)

	2009	2010	TOTAL
PRE-PROVISION NET REVENUE			
Net Interest Income			
Non-interest Income			
Non-interest Expense			
ALLOWANCE FOR LOAN LOSSES			
(1) ALLL at end of previous year			
(2) ALLL at end of year			
ALLL Resources: (1) – (2)			

* Form to be completed once for the baseline scenario and once for the more adverse scenario.

Post-Scenario Tier 1 Capital*
(Amounts in Billions of Dollars, end of period)

	Q4 2008	2009	2010
Tier 1 Capital			
Sum of Tier 1 Elements			
Common Stockholders' Equity			
Risk-Weighted Assets			

* Form to be completed once for the baseline scenario and once for the more adverse scenario.

INDEX